This volume for our friends
Gill & Pete Ford, and
Norm & Fran Dymond

READ THIS

It's frightening how some people, though adept at walking and scrambling, have none of the mountain sense usually learned through decades of mountain wandering, problem solving and familiarity with mountains in all weathers.

Learn to read topo maps and be able to find a grid reference. Turn back if it looks too hard for you, if you can't handle loose rock, if the river is too high, if you can't hack a 10-hour day, or if the routefinding is out of your league. Turn back from a summit or ridge if a thunderstorm is approaching or if conditions are made dangerous by rain, snow and ice. At *all times use your own judgement.* The author and publisher are not responsible if you have a horrible day or you get yourself into a fix.

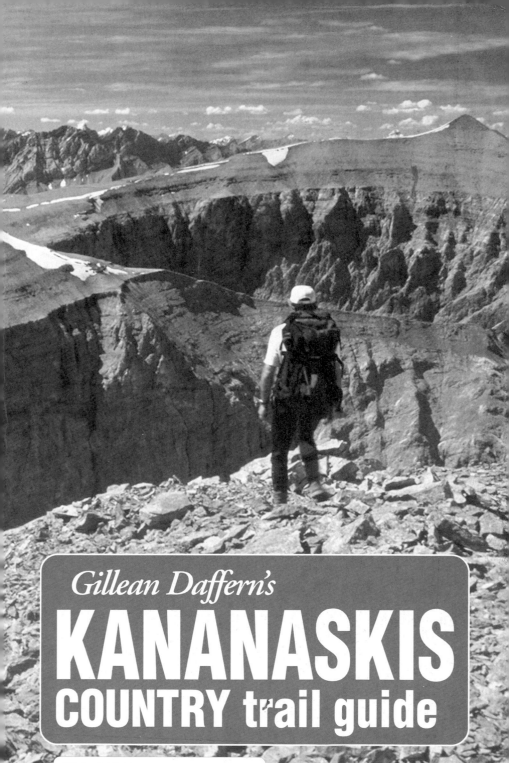

Gillean Daffern's

KANANASKIS
COUNTRY trail guide

Third Edition   Volume 2

Canadian Cataloguing in Publication Data

Daffern, Gillean, 1938-
Kananaskis Country trail guide

Previous ed. has title: Kananaskis Country: a guide to
hiking, skiing, equestrian & bike trails.
Includes index.
ISBN 0-921102-31-3 (v.1) -- ISBN 0-921102-48-8 (v. 2)

1. Hiking--Alberta--Kananaskis Country--Guidebooks. 2.
Trails--Alberta--Kananaskis Country--Guidebooks. 3. Kananaskis
Country (Alta.)--Guidebooks. I.Title. II. Title: Kananaskis
Country: a guide to hiking.
GV199.44.C22K36 1997   917.123'32043   C95-910504-2

ISBN 0-921102-48-8

The publisher gratefully acknowledges the
assistance provided by the Alberta
Foundation for the Arts and by the federal
Department of Canadian Heritage.

The Alberta
Foundation
for the Arts

Alberta
COMMUNITY DEVELOPMENT

COMMITTED TO THE DEVELOPMENT OF CULTURE AND THE ARTS

Copyright © 1997 Gillean Daffern

Printed in Canada by
Kromar Printing Ltd., Winnipeg.

 **Published by
Rocky Mountain Books
#4 Spruce Centre SW
RMB Calgary, Alberta T3C 3B3**

CONTENTS

ACKNOWLEDGEMENTS

The following people have been extremely helpful in the search for information: Don Cockerton, Pat Ronald, Avril Derbyshire, Roger Myer, Terry Beck, Ken Powell, Richard and Louise Guy, Ken Orich, Gord Lehn, Dave Cox, Dale Jackson, Joyce and Jim Marshall, Dave Higgins, Donald Smith, Merrily Aubrey and Jon Rollins.

All photos are by the author unless from the collection of Alf Skrastins. Thanks again, Alf!

Visit our web site at:
www.rmbooks.com

Rocky Mountain Books
www.rmbooks.com

K Country Web Site
http://www.gov.ab.ca/~env/nrs/
kananaskis/index.html

PHOTO CAPTIONS
Front cover: #255, Cat Creek Hills. Ascending the southwest ridge on a beautiful fall day. Across the Highwood River valley are Mts. Strachan, Muir and McPhail.

Title page: #319, Banded Peak. View from near the summit of: Outlaw/Banded col, Outlaw (showing ascent route from the col) and Mt. Cornwall (far right).

Contents page: #260, Grass Pass to Trap Creek. The view from Fir Creek Point of Grass Pass and Mt. Head. Raymond Patterson's Boundary Pine has changed little in 60 years.

Opposite: #283, Gorge Creek trail. The cascades of the north fork below the trail.

Page 15: #322, Little Elbow trail. Beautiful Lower Tombstone Lake.

Page 303: #273, Windy Point trail in Death Valley. A typical foothills landscape of aspen meadows.

Back cover: #275, Foran Grade Ridge. Looking down on Windy Point trail and across to Windy Point Ridge.

PREFACE TO THIRD EDITION

Two big changes. First, all ski trails are out and in a book of their own *Kananaskis Country Ski Trails*. If you want to walk the ski trails I suggest you use the maps from that book. Likewise, all interpretive trails and very short walks can be found in *Short Walks for Inquiring Minds #1, Canmore and Kananaskis Country*. This is to make way for a spate of new hikes, including a further sampling of ridge walks and easy ascents available to hikers.

Second, this guide has been split into two volumes. Volume 2 covers the Highwood, the upper Oldman and Livingstone areas, and the Sheep, Elbow and Jumpingpound river drainages. Volume 1 covers the rest: Canmore and the Bow Valley, Kananaskis Valley, Spray/Smith-Dorrien, Peter Lougheed Provincial Park and adjoining areas of The Ghost and Elk Lakes Provincial Park in B.C.

Between editions, highways have been rebuilt and new parking lots put in. Many trails have been refined, even completely realigned in some cases. Trails in this area are constantly affected by ongoing logging and the search for oil and gas, all of which makes life for a guidebook writer frustrating. Special mention should be made of the 100-year flood in the spring of 1995 which ripped out bridges, caused road washouts and rearranged riverbeds.

We have a new Wildland Provincial Park at the headwaters of the Elbow-Sheep which gives the area greater environmental protection. There's no change in regulations for hikers.

In these days of severe cutbacks, Kananaskis Country is asking for the public's help in maintaining trails. For more information contact the Trails Task Force Group, c/o Friends of Kananaskis Country, Suite 201, 800 Railway Avenue, Canmore, T1W 1P1. 403-678-5508, FAX 403-678-5505.

KANANASKIS COUNTRY

It's kind of fun listening to Japanese tourists pronounce the name Kananaskis. The strange name dates back to 1858 when explorer John Palliser named the pass he was about to cross "Kananaskis Pass, after the name of an Indian, of whom there is a legend, giving an account of his most wonderful recovery from the blow of an axe which had stunned but had failed to kill him, and the river which flows through this gorge also bears his name". Possibly the Indian in question was the great Cree Koominakoos who lost an eye and part of his scalp in a battle with the Blackfoot in the Willow Creek area, but made a miraculous recovery and showed up at Fort Edmonton some weeks later "ready to take to the warpath again".

THE CONCEPT

Today the Kananaskis passes, Kananaskis Lakes and the Kananaskis River form the heart of Kananaskis Country (or K Country as it is more commonly called), a provincial recreation area established October 7th, 1977 to "alleviate congestion in National Parks, and to provide greater recreation opportunities for Albertans".

Although former Alberta premier Peter Lougheed certainly deserves credit, it was actually Clarence Copithorne, rancher and MLA for Banff-Cochrane and Minister of Highways, who got the ball rolling with the reconstruction of Highway 40—the future Kananaskis Trail. Copithorne's vision for the Kananaskis Valley was one of strenuous physical outdoor activity accessible from a good road but with minimal services. As we all know, that simple idea turned into grand plan called Kananaskis Country encompassing a lot more country (over 4000 square hectares) and a lot more development. Namely: interpretive centres, picnic areas, campgrounds, one alpine village, two Olympic venues, riverbeds refashioned for competition and trails built for every conceivable sport.

LOCATION

K Country is located on the eastern slopes of the Canadian Rockies, west and south of the Olympic city of Calgary, Alberta. From the city outskirts the eastern boundary is only a 20-minute drive away.

The west boundary adjoins Banff National Park, then runs down the Continental Divide. The northern boundary is delineated by the Trans-Canada Highway and the fringe communities of Exshaw, Dead Man Flat and Canmore. The eastern boundary coincides neatly with the Bow-Crow Forest reserve boundary, while the southern boundary is marked by Highway 532 (Johnson Creek Trail).

GETTING THERE

Calgary is served by major airlines and several bus companies. Greyhound buses run west along the Trans-Canada Highway to Canmore, but stops are infrequent. That's it as far as public transportation goes. You need a car.

The core area described in Volume 1 is usually accessed from the Trans-Canada Highway via Highway 40. The areas covered in this volume are generally reached from the east via the border towns of Bragg Creek, Turner Valley and Longview.

WINTER ROAD CLOSURES FOR VOL. 2

December 1 to June 14th: Kananaskis Trail (Hwy. 40) between Kananaskis Lakes Trail and Highwood Junction.
December 1 to April 30th: Hwy. 940 between Cataract Creek campground and Wilkinson Summit.
December 1 to May 14: Elbow Falls Trail (Hwy. 66) at Elbow Falls, Powderface Trail south of Dawson trailhead, Sheep River Trail (Hwy. 546) at Sandy McNabb Recreation Area, Gorge Creek Trail, McLean Creek Trail between McLean Creek campground and Fisher Creek day-use area.
*** Hwy. 532 (Johnson Creek Trail) while not closed is not maintained.

KANANASKIS COUNTRY

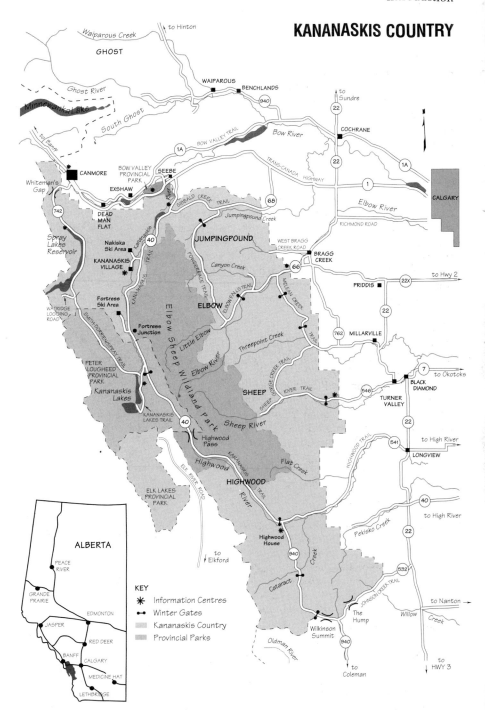

KEY

✳ Information Centres
•─• Winter Gates
Kananaskis Country
Provincial Parks

WHAT TO EXPECT

The country covered by Volume 2 is quite different from that of Volume 1, even along the Continental Divide. Peaks are lower, much less spectacular, lacking glaciers, but still possessing cirques and lakes and a number of high passes leading over into B.C. This is the country beloved by Raymond Patterson, a wild place with no official trails but plenty of logging roads that can be put to use. Heavy winter snowfall keeps some trails closed until July.

In the east there are friendly foothills covered in Lodgepole pine and aspen, the south and west-facing meadows increasing proportionally the farther south you go. While the quality of routes can't compare with those farther west, this is grand walking country, a place to get fit. Wear runners and black socks for equestrian trails.

In between are the Front Ranges comprising the spectacular Opal, Fisher, Misty, Highwood and Livingstone ranges which offer the hiker many glorious days, exploring a canyon perhaps, or discovering a lake or waterfall. It's here where you'll find lots of easy peaks to scramble up and grassy ridges to wander over, Mist Ridge being a prime example.

WEATHER TRENDS

Hiking season generally starts in April in the far eastern part of K Country and ends by November. In some lean snow years you can hike right through the winter in places like the Jumpingpound. Conversely, trails along the Great Divide may not be clear of snow until mid July.

Snow can fall in any month of the year. Just as likely, temperatures can rise to the mid 30s Celsius, leaving me and others who suffer from heat as limp as a dish rag. Generally, low cloud is not the problem it is in other mountain ranges of the world. Rain is often associated with late afternoon thunderstorms that have accounted for a number of fatalities in K Country. So if climbing a big peak start early and aim to be off high ground before the afternoon clouds start rolling in. Should it occur, the Indian summer can be glorious through September and October. Warm days, cold nights, no thunderstorms, no flies, no mosquitoes and no flowers, but then you can't have everything.

NATURAL HISTORY IN A NUTSHELL

I urge you to buy the appropriate field guides or Ben Gadd's all-in-one *Handbook of the Canadian Rockies*.

Mammals Most commonly seen in this area: elk, moose, Mule and Whitetail deer, Bighorn sheep, coyotes. Less common: wolves, goats, lynx, bobcats, cougars and wolverines. Black bears are found everywhere, while grizzlies are more prevalent in the Highwood and Oldman areas west of Hwys. 40 and 940. Having said that, the odd grizz goes walkabout in the foothills, forcing regular trail closures. In June of 1996, for example, Bike City's mountain bike race was cut short when a grizzly pulled down a moose on Elbow Valley trail of all places. At such times, rangers very properly rush out to close all trails in the immediate area with tape and notices.

Then there's the usual bevy of beavers in every foothills valley, porcupines in spruce forest more to the west, ground squirrels, tree squirrels, chipmunks, picas, marmots, muskrats, fishers, martens, ermines and mink.

For this volume add feral horses and cattle let loose for the summer. Other animals you might see are pack horses, pack llamas and pack goats.

Birds Most common: Whiskey Jacks (the ones that gather around when you stop to eat), Clark's nutcracker, hummingbirds (wear red), ravens, crows, chickadees, kinglets, woodpeckers, Northern flickers, mallards, cowbirds, Great Grey owls and particularly birds of prey like Golden eagles, Peregrine falcons and assorted hawks that inhabit the grassy eastern slopes of the front ranges.

Fish Trout (Cutthroat, Rainbow, Brown, Bull), Grayling. Some lakes are stocked.

Vegetation Trees range through fire-succession Lodgepole pine and aspen forests in the east to spruce, fir and larch combos at treeline in the west. Douglas Fir is spasmodic. Whitebark pine and my favourite Limber pine pose picturesquely on windy, rocky ridges in the southern part of the area such as the Bull Creek Hills.

Between the Great Divide and the eastern boundary is a tremendous variety of flowers. You'll need two field guides: one for the mountains and one for the prairies. Buffalo bean and Sticky red geraniums are predominant in the meadows of the foothills. In high windy places look for Alpine poppies, fuzzy Woolly fleabanes and a Polemonium at its northernmost range. Lupines (blue and white) grow south of Highwood Pass.

Obvious edibles: saskatoons , choke and pin cherry, strawberries, raspberries, blackcurrants, gooseberries and blueberries along the Divide.

POSSIBLE HAZARDS & NUISANCES

River crossings Larger rivers like the Highwood, Sheep and Elbow are impassable during spring runoff and after prolonged rain. Schedule river crossing trips for summer on. Official equestrian trails and unofficial trails/routes have no bridges. Caribbean water it is not: the water is often numbing even if it's only knee deep. If cold makes you feel sick to your stomach, wear neoprene socks.

Bears and other beasts At all times be aware of bears, but particularly in early spring and late fall. A fall coupled with bad weather and a scanty berry crop drives grizzlies to the valley bottoms in search of easier pickings. Should a bear hibernate hungry be extremely wary the next spring. Often K Country will close a trail until a bear has moved through the area. Contact the visitor centres for information on sightings. If bears are a worry to you carry a bear repellent, which costs a lot less than Troy Hurtubise's hundred thousand dollar grizzly suit. In the paranoia over bears we often forget that elk and moose should be given a wide berth, especially in spring when with young and in fall during the mating season when males get very ornery.

Hunters and bears In the area covered by Volume 2 hunting is allowed everywhere except within the Sheep River Valley Sanctuary and within 375 m of Hwy. 541 and Hwy. 40 between Highwood House and Highwood Pass. September to November is the time to dress in psychedelic shades of orange and pink. Supposedly Sunday is a safe day, but I wouldn't bet on it. Some hunters shoot at anything that rustles, including their own party (cautionary tale of a friend at West Bragg who was forced to raise a white hanky on a stick). The other danger occurs when hunters shoot an animal late in the day and after dressing it out, leave it lying overnight with the intention of coming back the next day for the meat. Often a grizzly gets there first and woe betide any innocent hiker happening along. K Country grizzlies, apparently, have learned to associate a rifle shot with an easy meal.

Although you may not agree with hunting, it's sometimes useful to chat with hunters who can tell you, for instance, that three grizzlies have been doing a five-day circuit through the hunter's camp and that they left that morning headed up Bishop Creek which is where you were going.

Ticks, etc. Between about March and mid June ticks are abroad and are found mainly in areas where there is lots of sheep, such as Mt. Ware and Gunnery Mountain. In such places wear light colours and long pants tucked into socks so you can spot them running up the *outside* of your clothing.

While mosquitoes and horse flies can be a darn nuisance they don't give you quite the same horror.

Cattle In all the foothills valleys and as far west as Little Elbow recreation area, Highwood Junction and Lost Creek you'll run into herds of cattle. I would like to reassure visitors from Europe that bulls are quite placid; you can walk right past them without them budging an inch. Sometimes cows get panicky and run, often in the direction you are going. It requires strategy on your part to outmanoeuvre them.

Loose rock In Calgary an insurance company's ad on a billboard once read "as firm as the Rockies" which made me laugh aloud. The Rotten Rockies aren't called that for nothing, the sedimentary limestone being subject to extremes of heat and cold. Of course there *is* firm limestone but it's safer to expect the worse. On scrambling pitches develop the technique for pushing back handholds. Be extra careful of rockfall in gullies. On routes you'll run into scree— lots of it. Use sheep trails where the scree is more stabilized.

Logging and logging trucks Logging can delete trails without notice. Ongoing changes and additions to logging roads, i.e. Lost, Cataract and Etherington creeks and Oldman River area, keeps a guidebook writer on her toes and tearing her hair out. Bridges over rivers appear, then disappear the next year. Logging trucks are presently a hazard in Etherington and Oyster creeks and on Jumpingpound Trail, McLean Creek Trail and in the West Bragg area.

Fire When necessary, please respect the ban on open fires. Should you wish to report a fire telephone numbers are listed on trailhead signboards.
Interestingly, in 1911 thousands of fire notices were posted all around the forest reserve boundary in English, German, Icelandic, Gallician, Cree, Chipewyan, Norwegian, Russian, Hungarian, Hindu, Japanese and Chinese!

PRACTICALITIES

BUYING MAPS
The perfect map does not exist. Government 1:50000 topo maps of the area are still in imperial, which makes things extremely difficult to figure out when passes, peaks and distances are all in metric. Here and there contour lines are way out, features like lakes, glaciers, streams and meadows are sometimes missing or marked incorrectly. Often trails are marked wrongly, a mistake from 20 years back not corrected over several editions.

Road and official trail alignments are much improved in the good-looking 1:50000 recreation maps by Gem Trek Publishing. Unfortunately, contour lines are at 200 ft intervals, and cutlines, logging and exploration roads have been omitted, which means these maps are not adequate for the serious hiker.

Provincial Resource Base Maps from Alberta Energy and Natural Resources, updated fairly regularly, show cutlines and exploration roads, logging roads and trails. It's disappointing that they can't be relied upon and very often reality is nothing like what is shown on the map.

A FEW RULES TO KNOW ABOUT
*No registration is necessary for overnight trips. However, registration boxes at information centres and at some trailheads act as a safeguard as long as you remember to register back in after the trip.
* Respect trail closures.
* Dogs must be on leash so they don't run after wildlife.
* Mountain bikes are allowed on most trails in Volume 2 excepting all interpretive trails, Nihahi Ridge, Fullerton and Little Elbow Tombstone Lakes section. Read individual trail descriptions or, better, buy Doug Eastcott's book *Backcountry Biking in the Canadian Rockies*.
* If fishing you require an Alberta licence.

CAMPING

Official campgrounds by the highways fill up quickly in the summer. It's galling to find every campsite full of campers whose idea of exercise is the walk to the biffy, so book ahead if you can. After Labour Day the situation eases.

Camping in the backcountry

Official backcountry campsites with picnic tables, portable biffies and bear bars are scattered throughout the Elbow and Sheep areas. Camping is allowed almost anywhere with one exception: No camping at Tombstone Lakes.

SUMMER FACILITIES

The Highwood

Use Longview on the eastern fringe for gas, groceries, motels, campground and eateries. Laurie Powell's Highwood House convenience store has groceries, books, ice cream, homemade snacks, gas, diesel and resident hummingbirds and is open May 15-October 31. Adjoining is the Visitor Information Centre open May 15-Labour Day. Campgrounds at Etherington Creek (closes Nov. 30th) and Cataract Creek on Hwy. 940; Green Ford 10 km east of the K Country boundary on Hwy. 541. Strawberry campground is open September 1-November 30th for hunters. Group campgrounds at Etherington Creek and Highwood River.

Livingstone and Oldman

Campground at Indian Graves (Hwy 532). Just south of K Country on Hwy. 940 is Livingstone Falls. Campground and unofficial sites up Oldman River Road.

Sheep

Sheep River Visitor Information Centre at Long Prairie Creek. Campgrounds at Sandy McNabb (closes November 30th) and Bluerock—Hwy. 546; Fisher Creek, North Fork—McLean Creek Trail (hwy.). Group campground at Sandy McNabb. Gas, groceries, restaurants at the entrance town of Turner Valley.

The Elbow

The Elbow Valley Visitor Information Centre adjoins Gooseberry campground. Other campgrounds: McLean Creek (McLean Creek Trail), Paddy's Flat, Beaver Flat, Little Elbow (closed November 30th)—all on Hwy. 66. Group campgrounds at Gooseberry, River Cove and Paddy's Flat. Elbow Ranger Station is located opposite Allen Bill Pond day-use area. Gas, groceries, restaurants at the entrance hamlet of Bragg Creek.

Jumpingpound

Jumpingpound Ranger Station west of Pinetop day-use area. Campgrounds at Sibbald Lake and Dawson (latter closes November 30th). Group campgrounds at Sibbald Lake and Pine Grove.

TELEPHONE NUMBERS

NOTE: for government establishments use the toll-free line 310-0000
Kananaskis Country Head Office in Canmore 403-678-5508

Information centres
Highwood House 403-558-2151
Sheep River Valley 403-933-7172
Elbow Valley (weekends) 403-949-4261
Elbow Valley Ranger Station (weekdays) 403-949-3754
Chain Lakes Provincial Park 403-646-5587 (for information on Hwy. 532)
Barrier Lake 403-673-3985 (for information on Jumpingpound, all of K Country)

Campground reservations
Bow Valley Park Campgrounds (for Jumpingpound) 403-673-2163
Elbow Valley Campgrounds (all other areas) 403-949-3132

Group campground reservations
Head Office, Canmore 403-678-5508

Facilities
Highwood House 403-558-2144

Emergency 591-7767

USING THE BOOK

TYPES OF TRAILS

Official trails maintained by Kananaskis Country and Forest Services are a mix of new and old trails, logging and exploration roads, fire roads and cutlines. Expect parking lots at trailheads, biffies and the occasional picnic table. Junctions are marked with signposts of the "You are here" variety. En route most trails have directional arrows or red markers located on trees or posts. If the trail is shared by equestrians, bridges will be lacking.

The Great Divide Trail built by the Great Divide Trail Association, is a narrow trail marked by red rectangles on trees. Two rectangles indicate a junction or sudden change of direction. Some approach routes to the GDT are marked with pale blue rectangles. This applies to only a few routes in the Highwood/Oldman areas.

Unofficial trails sometimes have no obvious trailhead, are neither signposted nor marked in any way, except, perhaps, for the occasional piece of flagging or cairn. They follow well-established pack trails, game trails, logging and exploration roads and cutlines. Creek crossings are the norm.

Routes Carrying on from the second edition, the third edition introduces more easy climbs and ridge walks ranging from hands in pocket strolls along grassy hogbacks to gruelling uphill flogs in excess of 1000 m to the top of a mountain. In the upper end of the range you can be sure of scree and possibly a pitch or two of easy scrambling and mild exposure. Hard hats are not necessary and, unless otherwise recommended, neither are ropes *in optimum conditions when the mountain is devoid of snow and the weather is good.* There may be remnant people trails or game trails, but mostly there's no trail at all. Most routes include some bushwhacking.

DIRECTIONS

"Left" and "right" always apply to the direction of travel.

RATING DIFFICULTY

No attempt has been made to classify trails. What's difficult for one person is easy for another. It's all relative. Read the description carefully. If you're having a horrible time, turn back and try something easier.

RATING TIMES

Times are dependent on too many variables — everybody chugs along at a different rate. Some will be carrying heavy packs, others, like me, make frequent flower stops. And then there are the underfoot conditions to consider, the weather and so on.

Half day means up to 3 hours
Day, up to 6 hours
Long day, up to 10 hours *plus*
Backpack, overnight camping.

Some trails, particularly those in the west Highwood, are suitable for "bike 'n' hike" trips which cuts down the time considerably.

MAPS

Maps in the back of this book should not be used in place of topo maps. They do, however, attempt to redress a few problems. For instance, they have been redrawn in metric from topo maps, with contours at 100-m intervals and shading starting at 2500 m (8,200 ft.). We have done our best to mark the following accurately: roads, trails, cutlines, logging and exploration roads. Please write the publisher if you find any discrepancies so we can make corrections.

GRID REFERENCES

Government topo maps have blue grid lines running east-west and north-south. Each line is numbered. The first two numbers indicate the grid line forming the west boundary of the kilometre square in which your point is located, and the third number the estimated number of tenths of a kilometre your point is east of that line. The fourth and fifth numbers indicate the grid line forming the south boundary of the square and the last number the estimated number of tenths of a kilometre your point is north of that line.

THE TRAILS

201 ARETHUSA CIRQUE — map 17

Half-day, day hikes, backpack
Unofficial trail & route, scramble to
Burns Lake, creek crossing
Distance 1.5 km to trail end
Height gain to trail end 122 m
High point 2286 m at trail end
Map 82 J/10 Mount Rae

The meadows at the head of the cirque. Photo shows Little Arethusa (left), Mt. Arethusa and the slope to col GR447071.

Opposite: option Little Arethusa, the final ridge to the summit.

Access: Kananaskis Trail (Hwy. 40). One km south of Highwood Pass, park on the shoulder of the highway. From the east side of the highway, a good trail starts in the trees just south of the creek crossing. NOTE: This section of Highway 40 is closed between December 1st and June 15th.

An easy trail into the cirque immediately south of the better-known Ptarmigan. Apart from the attractions of flowery meadows, this is the quick and dirty route over to Burns Creek in the Sheep River drainage that was always rumoured to exist! Watch for collared grizzly #24 doing the rounds.

The main creek is deeply incised all the way up to treeline. Don't go near it. Instead, follow a good trail that climbs gradually up the right (southeast) bank through spruce-fir forest into the larch zone with its moist draws and glades chockful of Glacier lilies and asters. At about GR442063 the trail peters out on the bank of the right (east) fork in a large flat meadow. A wide open view of valley heads and surrounding mountains helps you decide where to go next.

Most people head up the grassy slope between the two forks to treeline at about GR443068 (which means crossing the east fork and an extra height gain of about 152 m). From here, ongoing options include a stroll into the cirque between the Arethusas and an easy climb up Little Arethusa. You're also in perfect position for the grunt over to Burns Lake, or at least to the ridge from where Mt. Arethusa is a difficult scramble, totally out of the scope of this book (see Kane's *Scrambles in the Canadian Rockies*). The unnamed summit at GR452069 is a much more feasible objective for walkers.

201A Little Arethusa

Distance from hwy. 2.7 km, height gain from hwy. 576 m, high point 2740 m (GR433075). This is the summit 800 m southwest of Mt. Arethusa, a superb viewpoint for Highwood Pass and attained with not a lot of effort.

From GR443068 traverse northwest across the mouth of the cirque between both Arethusas, then gain a convenient grassy terrace at a slightly higher level and traverse west from where you get a splendid view of Storm Mountain with its left-curving strata. On attaining the "corner" you're standing at the base of your objective's south ridge which is a very moderate scree slope. A choice of sheep trails coalesce higher up onto a sort of rising bench (big clumps of Woolly Fleabane and Roseroot) that steers you to the edge of the eastern precipice with its vertigo-inducing view of the cirque.

The ridge above is tapering dramatically. The route, however, takes a comfortable line on large scree on the left side of the ridge between buttresses sweeping down into Highwood Pass and the huge drop on the right. The first cairn isn't the top but it does at least allow a group to sit and eat lunch together. The real summit is a bit farther on and has standing room for two. Careful you don't kill yourself trying to get photos of the knife-edge ridge connecting with Mt. Arethusa, the sight of which is

enough to give walkers jelly legs. Climbers of course are used to such sights. Here is a chance for advanced scramblers to peruse Mt. Arethusa and Mt. Rae, neither of which turn me on. I think it's something to do with all those black screes. For me the view west is the main attraction: an end to end view of Highwood Pass complete with toy cars in the parking lot.

201B To Burns Lake

Distance from hwy. 4.6 km, height gain from hwy. 518 m, height loss 442 m to Burns Lake, high point 2682 m. Allow about 3.5 hours going in, 2.5 hours coming out from the tarn. This is a demanding route for experienced masochists, weighed down with camping gear, who haven't got time to hike in the sensible way via the Sheep River. If you're doing a loop, plan to come out this way. It's a lot easier. Expect steep slopes, lots of scree and loose rock, and an intermittent game trail used by grizzlies doing the crossing.

Ascent of southwest slope 244 m Start from GR443068. Vertical rock ribs preclude a direct approach to the col at GR447071. You have to use the slope farther to the left.

The slope's lower third is distinguished by broken-up horizontal rock bands. Gain the *top* of the top layer from either the left or the right, then climb a short way to intersect a horizontal sheep trail. Traverse right to a vertical streak of fine yellowish-coloured scree that appears to extend to the ridge.

1. Drag yourself up the scree until, quite high up, another good sheep trail presents itself, this one heading diagonally right. An awkward step up one of those vertical white rock ribbons (cairn) precedes the crossing of a broken rib and a brief finish on black scree. This is the best descent route.

2. Continue traversing on sheep trail, crossing a thin spine of white rock to the above mentioned rock rib much lower down. Step up a white rock ribbon to a cairn. Either zig briefly uphill, then grope up the left side of the broken rib, searching out bits of bedrock, or traverse farther to

another cairn on black scree to the right of the rib. From here I found the uphill climb with occasional cairn unpleasantly steep and eventually cut back left. But it's up to you. Both join route No.1's traverse line on either side of the rib. Personally, I would rather grovel up route No.1 where I know I'm not going to get bonked on the head with a rock.

The sheep trail tops out at a cairn on the broad southeast ridge of Mt. Arethusa about 55 vertical m above the col. For those of you going in reverse direction this is the second (higher) cairn with a grand view of Storm Mountain. Stroll down to the low point. If you feel up to it, the mountain to the east is easily collectable.

Descent of northeast slope, 289 m to tarn At the col turn left down a shallow draw. Without warning the ground drops away and you're gaping at this vertigo-inducing view of Burns cirque which seems a million miles down. If you look carefully you'll discern trails weaving down the easy rocks on the right-hand side of the gully to the scree below. Someone's even drawn a red arrow on a slab. There's certainly nothing to be frightened of here except loose rock. Though the 'trails' continue down the screes and slabs of the right bank, at first opportunity I advise cutting left on another trail into the gully bed below a dripping red wall. Quite apart from shelter from exposure, the gully bed offers the easiest and quickest route up or down. Pass a cliff on the right with a cave. Much lower down at a rocky outcrop a trail heads left across the scree slope. Ignore it and scrabble down farther to a small drop-off that is almost level with a grassy bench starting a little distance to the left. Here go left on an obvious trail leading to easy ground on the bench. For the upper tarn continue along the bench. For Burns Lake, descend slopes of mixed grass, scree and rock to the left of the gully. See #277 for further details.

*Below, left: southwest slope.
Right: northeast slope.*

to tarn

202 MOUNT LIPSETT — map 17

Day hike
Unofficial trail
Distance 6 km to summit,
6.8 to lower summit
Height gain 718 m
High point 2580 m
Map 82 J/10 Mount Rae

*Summit rocks. Looking east to
Storm Mountain.*

Access: Kananaskis Trail (Hwy. 40). Park on the shoulder 13.2 km south of Highwood Pass and 3.7 km north of Mist Creek crossing. NOTE: This section of Highway 40 is closed between December 1st and June 15th.

Once and for all, the real Mt. Lipsett as shown on Wheeler's boundary survey map sheet 8 of 1916 is this two-headed summit to the east of Highway 40! Unaccountably, starting with the Bow River Forest tourist map of 1927 and over successive editions of the topo map and provincial resources map the name has migrated across Highway 40 to the southeast summit of Highwood Ridge (GR443031). It finally landed in the middle of Grizzly Ridge at GR427032, an error compounded by the enigmatic entry in Alberta Culture and Multiculturism's *Place Names of Alberta Volume 1* published in 1991.

Now that that's off my chest, let me say there are some terrific grunt routes up west-facing grassy slopes. However, the only trail follows the long southeast ridge. Read on:

Head up the grassy cut on the north side of the highway to a survey marker that fortuitously marks the entrance to Mt. Lipsett's exploration road. Follow into trees, keeping left just before you reach the former highway (grassy track).

Cross and climb over a berm, continuing on the exploration road as it climbs the left bank of the creek between Lipsett and Mist Mountain. Shortly it turns left. The cloying smell of clover is your lot for the next little while as the reclaimed road doodles about the forest at the foot of the southeast ridge, gaining altitude at an exasperatingly slow rate. Keep right at the first questionable junction you come to and after that take every uphill option that presents itself. Road cuts disclose coal seams at many points. On gaining the southeast ridge proper, the road wanders along the west side. Again keep right. At treeline it makes a big zig onto west slope meadows, then crosses to the east slope for a stint before recrossing the ridge for a final run-out. Leave it at the crossover point and carry on up the broad ridge to a subsidiary top and from there to the summit, stacked with splintered rocks. Look across at Mist Mountain exhibiting colourful bands of rock strata and back down the southeast ridge to Odlum Ridge across Storm Creek.

To lower summit Drop 122 vertical m to the broad saddle between the two summits. Regaining most of the height lost, climb grass, then shale to the lower summit at GR462019. Now you get a grandstand view of Highwood Pass which can only properly be appreciated from the heights.

Optional descent If two vehicles are available, consider descending the lower summit's delectable south ridge to the highway at GR458999. A bit of deadfall low down is a small penalty to pay for a route nearly all on grass.

 # 202, Mt. Lipsett. Looking across the saddle to the lower peak of Mt. Lipsett. Highwood Pass and Highwood Ridge in right background.

#203, Nameless Valley. View from the head of the valley of the nameless ridge which offers an optional return route. In the background is the east peak of Odlum Ridge (#213).

203 NAMELESS VALLEY — map 17

Day hike
Unofficial trail
Distance 3 km to col from access 1,
5 km from access 2
Height gain 433 m to col
High point 2301 m
Map 82 J/10 Mount Rae

Access: Kananaskis Trail (Hwy. 40).
1. Park on the shoulder 13.2 km south of Highwood Pass/3.7 km north of Mist Creek crossing.
2. Park on the shoulder 16.1 km south of Highwood Pass/ 800 m north of Mist Creek crossing.
NOTE: This section of Highway 40 is closed between December 1st and June 15th.

When creeks, cols, passes and ridges have no name it puts the guidebook writer in a bind, meaning me. I notice other countries solve this problem by calling the feature *Innominate* Tarn or Col de l'*Innominata*. Anyway, this is a fairly easy hike up a nameless valley clothed in bright green grass, real high waving stuff through which generations of elk have flattened a trail to the nameless col below a nameless ridge.

From access 1 (usual) Head up the grassy cut on the north side of the highway to a survey marker that fortuitously marks the entrance to Mt. Lipsett's exploration road. Follow through trees, keeping right just before you reach the former highway (grassy track). Turn right, heading east and parallel to the highway. Cross the unnamed creek flowing between Mt. Lipsett and Mist Mountain. Exactly 300 paces *before* the next nameless creek crossing (our valley creek) look for a cairn and flagging tied around a rock on the uphill bank.

 From access 2 pick up the former highway on the north bank and follow it westwards, keeping left, to the valley creek. Turn right in 300 paces.

 The elk trail is initially faint but improves after a trail from a wallow joins in from the left. Very quickly the angle eases and you reach the meadows. Unseen as yet,

Mist Mountain makes its presence felt by casting shade over the valley by late afternoon. The trail edges closer to the valley creek the higher you climb, ultimately climbing the last few metres up a dusty draw to the col at GR498010. Bunch grass makes a comfortable seat from which to study the foreshortened view of Mist Mountain. You can trace the route taken by #204 up the drainage.

Optional return via nameless ridge 2482 m
Loop distance 6 km from access 1, add 190 m height gain. The broad grassy ridge to the east of the valley makes a lovely circuit using the former highway as the connector. No trail.

 From the col head east up 183 vertical m of moderately-angled grass and shale to the ridge's high point at GR503010. From the higher vantage point Mist Mountain sticks up like a thumb, though you *still* can't see the summit. Turn your back on the mountain and walk southeast over two minor bumps with orange-weathered sandstone outcrops that make a cheery combination with the green turf. Soft hollows out of the wind invite you to linger and appraise the neighbouring ridges of Mist and Odlum should they be on your hit list of ridge walks.

 When the summit ridge comes to an abrupt end at GR513997, slip down a steep slope of long grass requiring little wind to set the whole hillside in rippling motion. Aim for 2 o'clock and with luck you'll hit the end of an exploration road, a short offshoot of the former highway. On the other hand, should you miss it, you'll undoubtedly intersect the former highway somewhere along its length.

204 MIST MOUNTAIN, east ridge route — map 17

Long day scramble
Unofficial trails, route
Distance 5 km from hwy.
Height gain 1331 m from hwy.
High point 3138 m
Map 82 J/10 Mount Rae

Access: Via route #203 at the col.

It's always satisfying to climb a high mountain, particularly Mist Mountain which certainly grabs your attention as you drive up the Highwood River valley. Amazingly, this southern aspect offers an easy route for walkers (moderate scree, some easy scrambling, no exposure), and is particularly interesting if you take the route touted by Nanton's Dave Birrell who to date has climbed the mountain seven times in emulation of High River's Don King who with the Blayney brothers made the first ascent back in 1946. If we hadn't bumped into Dave during his sixth ascent, we would still be grinding our way up the descent route. Thanks Dave!

Mist was named by Dominion geologist George Dawson during a rainstorm on the same day he named Storm Mountain and Storm Creek. It attracts bad weather all right and as the memorial plaque on the summit testifies, this is no place to be in a thunderstorm. Start at dawn or camp part way and be down by early afternoon. Water is available en route.

To the lip of the cirque The col at GR498010 is a good place for second breakfast and for scrutinizing the first part of the route. First you have to get into the drainage to the north, preferably without losing too much height. Traverse left and downwards across rubble, where every klutzy move sends rocks skittering down the steep hillside. Aim for the bottom of the big scree slope and you should hit the creek where it's enclosed in a gully. If the traverse doesn't appeal (in my estimation the worst part of the whole trip), drop straight down grassy slopes to the valley bottom (camping spots) and work your way up from there.

Climb toward the cirque, either via grass to the right of the scree or via the fun rock rib between the grass and the gully enclosing the stream. At a temporary levelling cross the creek at the one place where water is available without resorting to gymnastics.

South face Climb the easy slope of Dryas and some scree. At the top, peruse the foreshortened south face, all scree with a maze of little white slabs set at a moderate angle, the whole bounded on the right by a perpendicular rock rib. There are two ways to go initially:

1. Climb steeper scree above to below the ascending rock rib, then traverse diagonally up left below the solid rock until you hit a narrow rocky gully. Clamber up scree ledges to its right and return to the gully above the rock step at a bend.

2. Utilizing the descent route, traverse left and cross a rock rib back toward the creek. On your right is the narrow rocky gully. Pick a line up its *left* side and join route No.1 above the rock step where it bends left.

The gully shallowing to groove is the key to the south face. While, admittedly, you can drag yourself up the slope almost anywhere, why do so when you've got an interesting (and easy) staircase of alternat-

Above: Starting up the east ridge.
Opposite: Mist Mountain showing ascent route.

ing scree and slab steps? Not having thighs like Dan Jensen, I like to stop now and then to look at the view behind which is growing in magnificence, mountains heaped upon mountains appearing over the rim of the southeast ridge.

The angle falls back just before you reach the east ridge at about GR487018.

East ridge Anyone who arrives here tired will find no satisfaction in the prospect ahead: the east ridge rearing up like the bow of a battleship. In such cases it helps to compare the left-hand slopes with the beetling precipice on the right. In close-up the ridge is neither narrow nor steep and you'll find yourself searching out little scrambly slabs in preference to scree. Above the step, continue along a broad horizontal scree ridge to its end, then turn right and cross a neck to the summit. Suitably narrow, it supports a couple of untidy cairns, a wooden cross and the memorial plaque to Stash Minasiewicz who was killed by light-

ning—a salutary reminder. Look down between your feet at Highwood Pass and Mt. Lipsett which is seen as a mere foothill. A scrambler's route comes up from Lipsett and joins another following the northwest ridge from Storm Mountain.

Descent route Backtrack a few metres to the east ridge. Descend the south ridge a short way, then veer left, wild leaping down runnels of fine scree to the cirque below; all your laboriously amassed steps squandered in minutes. The cirque bottom is a huge ash tray, a resting spot for rocks rolled down from all sides. This makes tedious the next section, a narrow draw. Pick your way between rotten rocks and fossil beds to the left of the fledgling stream. The draw opens out momentarily. Where the creek turns right, steepening and deepening, stay left and walk below the ascent gully, cross a small rock rib and join your ascent route at the top of the easy Dryas slope. Drop down to the stream, cross, etc. and return the way you came up.

23

205 MIST CREEK — map 17
(via Rickert's Pass to Sheep trail)

Long day hike, backpack
Official trail with signposts, red markers
Distance 11.8 km, 8.8 km to pass
Height gain 555 m, height loss 548 m
High point 2332 m at pass
Map 82 J/10 Mount Rae

Below: View from Storm Ridge, looking down Mist Creek (left). To right are the four cirques bounded by Mist Mountain, Misty Basin being the closest. The route up Mist Mountain follows the upper part of the left-hand skyline ridge to the summit.

Access: Kananaskis Trail (Hwy. 40) at Mist Creek day-use area. NOTE: This section of Highway 40 is closed between December 1st and June 15th.
Also accessible from Sheep trail (#276) at Burns Mine junction.

Guess who? Doctor George (Dawson) made this very trip in July of 1884. En route he visited Misty Basin, then climbed over the pass to Sheep Creek where he found good quality anthracite coal and in longhand wrote "a more complete examination might lead to the discovery of workable deposits", so preceding the infamous Julius Rickert by 12 years. Dawson named Mist Creek and Mist Mountain, though some think the name derives not from the tendency of the mountain to attract bad weather, but from clouds of steam arising from the hot spring whenever the temperature falls below freezing.

Since the old days, the Indian trail up Mist Creek has not remained inviolate. It's been overlaid by exploration roads at both ends and in mid section by a pack trail that during K Country years has been realigned to dryer ground. Overall, a fairly easy route but steep on the north side of the pass. Unofficial options are available from the valley head.

The trail leads out to Highway 40. Cross, then turn right onto the former highway. Shortly turn left onto the Mist Ridge exploration road that heads up Mist Creek valley. After about a kilometre's uphill you come to an unmarked junction where routes #206 and 207 turn right up a side valley.

Transfer to a trail and drop into the side valley. Such is the dip I would wish for a suspension bridge, especially if lugging a bike along. After this it's fast, easy stepping through pine forest, burned over several times, later changing to spruce. Give thanks to ranger Freddie Nash who in the 1936 holocaust held the fire "at the edge of the old green timber". From occasional meadows, you can measure your progress by the juxtaposition of four cirques to the west. When level with the fourth cirque under Storm Mountain (Misty Basin) an unofficial trail turns off to the left (see option).

To Rickert's Pass The official trail turns right here and starts the winding climb to Rickert's Pass. Catch glimpses to the left of a blackened forest, a 1990 controlled blaze gone horribly wrong (all the little tree critters caught unawares by a sticky gel called napalm pumped from a heli torch onto the spruce from helicopters). Personally, I'm mystified why the Forest Service would even choose this area to open up more grassland for wildlife when there seems to be plenty around already. A final zig up a grassy slope offering a perfect view up Misty Basin to Storm Mountain gains you the pass, a rocky defile separating Mist Ridge to right and Storm Ridge to left.

Julius Rickert, sporting a trademark handlebar moustache, was a self-styled mining engineer from the eastern U.S. but let it be understood he was of French nationality, no less than the Count de Braban. Later, it

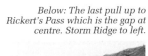

Burns Mine

Above: Burns Mine near Sharp's Creek.

Below: The last pull up to Rickert's Pass which is the gap at centre. Storm Ridge to left.

was discovered the title belonged to the Crown Prince of Belgium after Pat Burn's lawyer Paddy Nolan found a 1932 photo of the real count and countess in *L'Illustration Journal Paris*, but that's another interesting story with no room for it here. Regardless of his doubtful credentials, it was Rickert who in 1896 with ex-cop Arthur Brown was sent to prospect for coal up the Sheep River and having no doubt read Dawson's account headed straight up Rickert's Creek to Rickert's Pass. Note the black-streaked hillsides falling away from Mist Ridge that on closer inspection reveal hundreds of little coal heaps below ground squirrel holes.

To the Sheep River The descent to the Sheep River is a "practical though steep and rough descent" wrote Dawson. It certainly is a steep drop, a sustained climb in the opposite direction that the caretaker at the Burns mine in the 1920s, Bill Sumners, reckoned he could run up in 45 minutes. Incredibly, he was in his early 70s at the time! Following the old trail, you zig down the steep, north slope into the fir forest of Rickert's Creek with blazes dating back to the beginning of the century.

The trail emerges above a bank and descends the far side of it onto a heap of coal spoil in the heart of Pat Burn's Coal Mine. Below, a tram line disappears into rubble covering an adit. Here, turn left onto a road that plunges to the Sheep River valley bottom. At the bottom of the hill cross Rickert's Creek to the T-junction with Sheep trail near the corral.

Because the official way misses out everything interesting, I recommend history buffs follow the gentle windings of the grassy road instead (see sketchmap). At the first bend take a side trip to another mine located halfway to Sharp's Creek where you'll discover coal spoil and an incredible amount of historic junk including frame buildings in ruins, drill bits, hundreds of pipes made in Okotoks and iron bins. As a final treat it takes you past the foundations of the townsite in townsite meadow.

OPTIONS

Misty Basin

Distance 3 km from trail, height loss 30 m. The fourth cirque, the head of Mist Creek proper, was described by Dawson as having "green alpine meadows and slopes, with scattered clumps of Lyall's larch". And great campsites.

As indicated previously, you turn left off Mist Creek trail onto a narrower trail (no sign). Traverse spruce forest, then drop briefly through meadow to a vague four-way intersection where you turn right (blazes) and travel through patchy forest and meadow, crossing four side streams. Another short descent brings you into the big flowery meadow at valley bottom (hunters campsite to left) where returnees should note a piece of plastic tied to a tree meaning "this is where you climb up into the forest". Still the trail continues into the upper basin, a heavenly spot of flat meadows, smelly onion beds, larches and a sparkling stream. Ahead is Storm Mountain, grassy Storm Ridge to right and to the left a ridge where Dawson pointed out the folding and faulting of lower Mesozoic strata.

Misty Basin. Photo Alf Skrastins.

Storm Ridge

Distance 7.5 km circuit from Misty Basin, height gain/loss 655 m, high point 2615 m. The ridge projecting northeast from Storm Mountain to Rickert's Pass makes a splendid trip incorporated with Misty Basin where you might think about camping for the night. Tacking it on to Mist Ridge is another possibility. Just make sure you pack headlamps and an extra pair of legs. While there are no technical difficulties, there are a lot more ups and downs between tops than is apparent from the topo map.

West to east At the head of Misty Basin follow the trail up the right-hand fork a way, then climb 229 vertical m up a grassy rib to the right of a draw, aiming for the col at GR473063. You'll be spellbound by the view of Mt. Rae and the cirque at the head of Burns Creek which is certainly enticing if you haven't already been there. To its right are the Rae Creek Hills where you can sort out the various routes.

Set off northeast along the ridge. Rather surprisingly, the ridge to the first top is composed of large blocks and is relatively narrow, lined on the left by rotten red cliffs with out-jutting pinnacles. A bit of steep scree (sheep trail available) gains you the summit.

Descend a two-tier drop to a col where we found a summer snowbank. A second top capped by orange scree is followed by a longer descent to a third col. All the way along, the left side is hung with those rotten red cliffs, now interspersed with massive conglomerate ribs, while the right side rolls grassily away into Misty Basin. It's tempting to miss out the third top by a traverse, but that would be cheating, so press on up the hogback to GR485071. This summit has a quite magnificent ridge winging out to the north above the cirque enclosing Sharp's Creek.

Continue down the grassy east ridge to a fourth col. The fourth top (large cairn) requires more effort up steep grass crossed by little rock bands. Looking down on the black forest of Mist Creek is depressing, much better to feast your eyes on Mist Ridge and the Sheep River where a large portion of Sheep trail is revealed. From down there this top appears sharp, meaning you're in for a steep descent to Rickert's Pass. And so it proves: two undercut rock bands require substantial detours to the right. You literally drop into the defile crossed by Mist Creek trail at the very last moment.

Storm Ridge. The view from fourth top of the ridge extending from Storm Mountain (left). In the foreground is third top rising above Sharp's Creek. Mt. Rae at far right.

206 MIST RIDGE — map 17

En route to the highest summit (farthest right) from the saddle between the south and north summits.

Long day hike
Unofficial trail & route
Distance 12 km to Rickert's Pass,
circuit with Mist Creek 23 km
Height gain 1020 m
High point 2515 m
Map 82 J/10 Mount Rae

Access: Via Mist Creek trail (#205) at two places: the 2 km point at about GR525997, and at Rickert's Pass.

Another great ridge walk brought to everyone's attention by Alf Skrastins in the *Foothills Wilderness Journal*. It lies in a rain shadow area and is often bathed in sunlight when mere kilometres away across the valley the Misty Range is shrouded in rain clouds. Though easy, it is long. Hiking the ridge in its entirety to Rickert's Pass and returning down Mist Creek trail takes, at

minimum, eight hours. Luckily, if time is getting short or as a thunderstorm is brewing, you can escape into Mist Creek from almost any point along the ridge. Wait until July.

Start off along the Mist Creek exploration road. At about GR525997 where the route up Mist Creek becomes trail, turn right with the road up a side valley to the northeast. Keep straight where a side road takes off to the right (see #207).

Unexpectedly, the road drops in two zigs to valley bottom, clearly a design fault

29

on the part of the road engineer. After a side creek crossing (last water, camping spot) start the climb all over again. Long zigzags take you out of the trees into the meadows to a col at GR535017 where you're treated to a view of Gibraltar Mountain. Continue to another col at GR530020 where the road ends. Ahead, through the V is a picturesque hillock with a crown of trees. Farther to the left is a fabulous view of Mist Mountain showing route #204 in profile. While a game trail carries on, don't follow it unless you'd rather traverse than follow the tops to the ridge's low point. So you turn right here and walk up the easy slope to the south end of the south summit at GR531023 (2432 m).

The ridge between the south and north summits is ruler-straight, comfortably broad throughout with rocky outcroppings here and there poking up through short-cropped grass scattered with sheep pellets, but is by no means flat. A third of the way along, it dips sharply to the low point, then after a respite, rises over a series of endless false tops to the highest summit GR513059 (2523 m). Interestingly, not too far below the ridge to the right, there is a small stream that used to flow through a gap to Mist Creek, but which I learned has been pirated by Cliff Creek cutting back. Incidentally, anyone thinking of escaping down Cliff Creek is in for a nasty surprise.

From the high point, gaining the northernmost summit—the best viewpoint—entails an easy scramble up a rock band. Now you can look across to Rickert's Pass and view Mist Creek trail dropping steeply to the Sheep River. From here, turn west, dropping steeply to a col and meeting up with another traversing sheep trail that missed out the highest summits. The final top at GR506061, guarded from this direction by a difficult rock band, is not often visited and should be bypassed by the sheep trail low down on the left side. Instead of regaining the ridge most people just keep following the trail that joins Mist Creek trail just left of the defile which is Rickert's Pass.

View from near Rickert's Pass of the highest summit (centre), and the rocky top that is bypassed on the right side. Photo Alf Skrastins.

207 RIDGE BETWEEN MIST & PICKLEJAR CREEKS — maps 17 & 18

Day hike
Unofficial trail, then route
Distance 5 km from trailhead
Height gain 625 m
High point 2392 m
Map 82 J/10 Mount Rae

A bird's-eye view of the Highwood River valley and Hwy. 40. The flat-topped mountain covered in snow at top left is Plateau Mountain.

Access: Via Mist Creek trail (#205).

A shorter, easier alternative to Mist Ridge, but one netting an even better view! A couple of loops can be made with Picklejar Creek trail (#208) to Picklejar Creek day-use area, which, by happy chance, is only 500 m south of Mist Ridge trailhead.

Start off along the Mist Creek exploration road. At about GR525997 where the route up Mist Creek becomes trail, turn right with the road up a side valley to the northeast. A long rising traverse beneath the east flank of your ridge brings you to a road junction. Turn right. Your new road makes four uphill zigs, then heads straight to the col at GR544000, a barren spot sporting a few larches between two grassy ridges.

The road resumes the other side of the col, makes one big jog onto the ridge to the west, then ends, leaving you to wade up bunch grass to the summit (GR542999). Tombstone-like rocks make wonderful backrests as you count beetle cars conveying tourists up and down the Kananaskis Trail from Highwood Junction to Highwood Pass. The view is amazingly extensive for such a low ridge, taking in Mist Mountain to Plateau Mountain, all of the Elk and High Rock ranges to the west and the Highwood Range to the east.

OPTIONAL RETURNS via Picklejar Creek trail (#208)
1. Valley From the col descend the southeast slope and intersect Picklejar Creek trail on the southwest bank of a developing creek.
2. Ridge Walking down the lovely southeast ridge prolongs the great view. Steps are staggered, each succeeding step starting a little more to the right. Because of trees on the flats, the possibility of being lured off track is great, so think "right". A longer, steeper step down grass with ankle-breaking aspen stalks (and remnant trails) leads to a shoulder. Push through a few trees to gain Picklejar Creek trail. Turn right.

The grassy north fork of Picklejar Creek. Behind is Mt. GR558012.

208 PICKLEJAR CREEK — maps 17 & 18

Day hike
Unofficial trail
Distance 5 km
Height gain 488 m
High point 2240 m
Map 82 J/10 Mount Rae

Access: Kananaskis Trail (Hwy. 40) at Picklejar Creek day-use area. NOTE: This section of Highway 40 is closed between December 1st and June 15th.

Contrary to what you might expect, the main trail up Picklejar Creek does not lead to Picklejar Lakes, but makes for the scenic pass between Picklejar and Cliff creeks where you're in position to connect with Mist Ridge (#206) below its south summit, climb ridge GR547003 or knock off a few summits of the Highwood Range. A secondary trail to Picklejar Lakes is described under # 209.

The trail starts beyond the hitching rail. There is opportunity within the first few minutes to go astray. After the first short rise be sure to TURN RIGHT off the "main" trail and cross a streamlet (mud, rocks). The valley trail continues above Picklejar Creek, at the narrows climbing onto the open shoulder of the ridge to the

north. Thereafter, the trail settles into a lovely traverse through pine woods.

Around the forks all tributaries are deeply incised which is why Picklejar Creek has never been a feasible route to Picklejar Lakes. Nearing the first tributary from the northwest, the trail is forced upstream. Near treeline, cross the creek and traverse the lower slope of ridge GR547003 towards Picklejar's north fork. Still too deep. More traversing is necessary before you can contour into its shallowed-out creek bed and cross it.

En route, at about GR553997, a cairn and a blaze downhill indicates the **trail to Picklejar Lakes**, the Picklejar Connector.

The upper valley is relatively flat and open, filled with bunch grass that grows higher than in any other valley I've been to. In this sort of vegetation the trail along the east bank tends to disappear. Look for it on shale as you enter the pass at GR549008. This is a larch place, sited below the bouldery skirts of the Highwood Range.

209 PICKLEJAR LAKES — map 18

Day hike
Unofficial trail, creek crossings
Distance 4.2 km to first lake
Height gain 450 m to pass
High point 2179 m
Maps 82 J/10 Mount Rae,
82 J/7 Mount Head

Access: Kananaskis Trail (Hwy. 40) at Lantern Creek day-use area. NOTE: This section of Highway 40 is closed between December 1st and June 15th.
Also accessible via (#279C) Waterfall Valley.

"The fishing is so good it's like catching fish in a picklejar". This popular trail is not quite the doddle you might suppose. It's actually quite a trudge over a pass and it always amazes me when I see anglers setting off from the parking lot just as everyone else is returning to their cars. I assume they carry lanterns in their tackle boxes. Fishing interest apart, the lakes are located in a gorgeous alpine basin.

Oddly enough, you don't follow Picklejar Creek to get to Picklejar Lakes(usually). The valley you are about to start up is Lantern Creek, one valley to the south. A good trail starts from the east side of the highway a little north of the day-use area and heads up the left bank.

After a preliminary section through trees, gaining height, the trail undulates across steep grassy hillsides, finally dropping to valley level at the forks. Cross the north fork. Shortly, the trail turns due north and you drag yourself up hot, dry, shaley hillside to the pass at GR567982.
Low route Slither down 30 m of mud to gushing Picklejar Creek. On a stinking hot day the cool spruce forest is heaven. (Across Picklejar Creek you can pick up the Picklejar Connector headed for #208. See options.) For the lakes, turn right and follow the south bank up to first lake.

High line Another trail climbs a short way up the grassy ridge to the right (east), then makes a downward traverse across shale and scree to first lake.

Campsites are located across the outlet in the trees of the north shore.

You can have a good time exploring the basin. Picklejar Lakes are paternoster lakes, each one set a little higher in its own saucer of rock and connected one to the

Third Picklejar Lake.

33

other by trails. At first lake you can watch trout darting about making shadows on soft brown sand. Second lake is surrounded by drowned trees, the fourth is supplied with fresh water from a spring on its north shore. The third and largest lake is blue and very deep. Circumnavigating the shoreline as one is wont to do with lakes, gives you an uneasy feeling—so clear is the water—of traversing above some precipitous boulder slope.

Just as interesting is the wildlife which includes beavers (their handiwork evident at second lake) and grizzlies in Lantern Creek. At first lake I've had a good laugh watching picas scampering about between my feet, snipping flowers for winter supplies while Golden eagles soared overhead in frustration, "Oh no, here's some more people coming". Another animal to look for is Jon Jorgensen's goats. After decimation through over hunting, about 20 were transported here in August of 1993 from the Lilloett area of B.C. I'm only surprised they survived at all after being captured by nets thrown from helicopters, flown via Dash 8 to High River, trucked to K Country, then slung in nets under helicopters to this spot. Despite the biologist's best-laid plans, many have wandered off elsewhere.

The Picklejar Connector. Looking northwest from the meadow towards ridges GR542999 (#207) and GR547003.

OPTIONS

To Junction Creek

Distance 500 m, height gain 213 m. For scramblers. From between third and fourth lakes head for the col at GR579992, the left hand of two low points and grovel up a yellow streak of steep scree. See #279C.

To Picklejar Creek (#208) via the Picklejar Connector

Distance 2.5 km, height loss S-N 137 m, height gain S-N 46 m. A generally clear trail that works well either way, opening up the possibility of a point to point. It starts from across the outlet of first lake near campsites and follows the north bank of Picklejar Creek to an H-junction with the "low route".

Keep right. Shortly, the trail climbs the bank, then heads gently downhill through forest into willows lining a side creek. Cross the side creek and continue downhill into open forest below a boulder fan. In a meadow the trail starts rising to intersect a grassy side creek at about GR559996. For anyone scree bashing up peak GR571003, this is where you would start from.

Descending, round an open hill. Cross a stony side creek (cairn), then traverse the lower slope of a second hill en route to the north fork of Picklejar Creek (cairn in creekbed). A faint trail climbs the bank to #208 (cairn, blaze), gained at about GR553997.

210 LINEHAM CREEK TRAILS — maps 18 & 21

Day hikes
Unofficial trails & routes, creek
crossings
Distance to trail junction 1.5 km
Height gain to trail junction 122 m
Maps 82 J/7 Mount Head,
82 J/10 Mount Rae

Access: Kananaskis Trail (Hwy. 40) at Lineham Creek day-use area. NOTE: This section of Highway 40 is closed between December 1st and June 15th.

Lineham Creek is just one of three creeks in Alberta named after John Lineham, the founder of Okotoks. The idea of going into this particular creek had never turned me on, possibly because the topo map had it totally covered in a green wash. But one day by merest chance we dropped into the valley from the ridge tops and were much taken by its sense of wildness.

Game/hunter trails can be baffling at times, so routefinding skills are needed.

To the trail junction The trail leaves the far end of the parking lot and climbs along the left bank of Lineham Creek, its narrow V-shaped entrance well concealed by the western outliers of the Highwood Range. Beyond the canyon overlook (note detached pinnacle), the trail passes between the outliers, climbing up and down lush meadows with lupines and paintbrushes.

Back at valley bottom, the main trail crosses the creek and recrosses above the north fork. At the base of Lineham Ridge there is a trail junction at GR597926 on 82 J/7. (At high water omit both crossings by following a fainter trail along the left bank. Just before the mouth of the north fork, a smaller creek that materializes on your right [the north fork tributary] should be crossed at the first opportunity. Head across to join the main trail after its second crossing.)

210A Lineham Creek

4.5 km from junction to head of cirque, height gain 685 m, high point 2438 m. This is the route up the main fork.

At the junction keep right, staying on the left bank of Lineham Creek. Shortly, you're puzzling over the trail in long grasses and willow brush as it multiplies into numerous strands. Don't worry; at the bend they all come together to make one good trail. You're now heading north under the left bank which has beginner hoodoos. Across the valley is a round hill with a steep open slope facing the creek, and to its left a side creek from the east. Just above the confluence with this side creek the trail crosses the main creek, climbs steeply up the east bank, then runs along the north bank of this east fork, seeming to end in a flat, fairly open area near hitching rails.

The trail turns left (north) up a dry side valley, losing itself in a mishmash of vegetation. Watch for it climbing the left bank. Shortly, it makes a diagonal traverse back down to valley bottom where another confusing section, mainly because of the multiplicity of trails, ends in a large meadow. Opposite a protruding right bank, the trail, once again clear, climbs the left bank and heads to a forested ridge enclosing the valley head. At about GR602950 there is a four-way intersection.

I'm taking you into the first cirque to the east. So at the four-way intersection turn right (east) and follow the trail as best you can down to another west-flowing side creek. Cross and head upstream into meadow country where this particular trail disappears for good. A little farther on you discover the creek's source: a perfectly round pool, three metres deep, icy cold and clear fed by underground springs. From here you head up and left into the cirque entrance and meet the cirque creek. Follow it up past waterfalls and through a wee canyon into the cirque head below one of the most spectacular of the Dogtooth Mountains that, sadly, from this direction looks more like an old dog's molar.

On each side of the mountain there is a col reached by straightforward scree. The right-hand col at GR618963 (2545 m) looks along the north face of the Highwood Range. Unfortunately, you can't quite see the tarn at the head of Trap Creek though you do have a grandstand view of "Patterson's Peak" where Raymond Patterson nearly came to grief 60 years ago. Go for the one at GR615967 (2515 m), a more satisfactory vantage point offering a vertiginous view into the cirque at the end of Junction Creek trail and all down Junction Creek to the interpretive signs on the other side of the Sheep River. (If doing hike #279A, pointing out the col will impress your friends.)

OTHER OPTIONS
Start from the four-way trail junction at GR602950. I've never followed the trail heading north, but odds on it leads to the upper valley, following the terrace where you can pop in and out of another three cirques. The col GR586978 at the head of Lineham Creek is an easy scree trudge with a view into Picklejar cirque. From here it appears peak GR583979 is a surer bet than from Lineham Ridge.

210B Lineham Ridge 2515 m

Distance 5 km to point GR582972 from trail junction, height gain 875 m from parking lot. This has become one of my favourite places despite that first foray in a fall blizzard. For the most part, there's an amazingly good trail to treeline, after which you're tramping up an easy-angled grassy ridge. Real grass, not just Dryas. A fine vantage point from which to study all the eastern cirques of Lineham Creek.

At the junction in Lineham Creek keep left and climb the bank onto the flat south end of the ridge. Continue through open pine forest, watching for blazes, particularly where the trail wends left to a steepening all across the ridge. Be alert for an intersecting game trail (you'll know if you've passed it because the trail peters out). Climb up right on game trail to patchy meadows on the east side of the ridge. Turn left uphill. In long grasses the trail is hard to find, but you should be able to pick it up where it returns to the pines. It's good after that.

Gradually the forest opens up and cliffs appear on the east flank. The trail ends below the first meadow section, the ridge broadening at this point, a little mane of rocks running up the ridge line. This is followed by the rock ridge. Anyone unhappy with the considerable drop on the right can piece together snippets of trail on the more gently-inclined left slope.

Arrive at a saddle, then continue up the ridge, which is once again narrowing and steepening above a drop-off. Pass a cairn, descend slightly, then climb up to a post stuck in a cairn at GR582972 (82 J/10). This is a wonderful spot to end the walk. Apart from the view, which takes in everything between Plateau Mountain and the Opal Range, the Elite Plus Ultra quality grass is endorsed by the Canadian Chiropractic Association. (Scramblers! The connecting ridge to peak GR583979 is moderately difficult with one exposed traverse.)

Optional return via Lantern Creek
From the post descend the occasionally steep ridge to the left of the gully into Lantern's southeast fork. This valley is a lot more complex than it appears from above, where it seems you can navigate from one "flat" meadow to another. Even under the trees long grasses conceal ankle-breaking rocks and rotted logs. Strangely, there are no game trails that we could find. Aim for the confluence of the southeast and east forks. Cross the east fork and join Picklejar Lakes trail (#209) just east of the north fork crossing. Not particularly recommended.

Lineham Creek, at the entrance to the first cirque to the east.

Grassy Lineham Ridge, looking back down from the post. To the left is the main fork of Lineham Creek.

211 RUNNING RAIN LAKE — map 17

Day hike
Unofficial trail, metal tags on trees,
blazes, creek crossings
Distance 2.7 km to lake
Height gain 153 m
High point 2057 m
Map 82 J/10 Mount Rae

Access: Kananaskis Trail (Hwy. 40). Park 3.9 km south of Lipsett day-use area in a parking area on the west side of the highway, or 4.3 km south of Lipsett day-use area where the guard rail ends. NOTE: This section of Highway 40 is closed between December 1st and June 15th.

This is a well-used anglers' trail to a fishing pond. Notwithstanding three river crossings, it's a rather nice walk to a larch cirque below the Elk Range.

From the end of the guard rail a trail descends the bank and crosses a broad beaver dam between ponds to Storm Creek. Wade. The trail continues downstream to the creek issuing from Running Rain Lake, then turns right and climbs a steep bank of running mud, which is not, I assure you, representative of the rest of the hike. Now that you've gained the bench, it's easy going through forest with blazes of all ages. At km 1.8 you cross the creek.

On the southeast bank the trail climbs a little more steeply into boggy meadows. Cross a mud wallow on a log, head uphill a bit to a tag, then traverse right for some metres to red flagging on a tree where the trail once again becomes distinct (all of which should be memorized for the return). Follow tags #29 through 27 back to the creek and cross. Tags continue across juicy meadows to #24 at the lake, the numbering system as puzzling to me as a book on Java programming.

Running Rain Lake is magnificently located at the dead end of the valley, its olive green waters backdropped by the precipitous wall of the Elk Range. A beaver dam spans the outlet making a circuit of the lake easy. On the northwest shore White bog orchids grow rampant below spruce forest, while the drier southeast shore is a yellow and white kaleidoscope of arnicas, ragwort, valerian and snowy white paintbrushes.

Running Rain Lake and Mist Mountain.

212 ODLUM CREEK TRAILS — maps 17, 18, 20 & 21

Long day hike
Unofficial trails, major creek crossings
High point 1966 m at pond
Map 82 J/7 Mount Head,
82 J/10 Mount Rae

Access: Kananaskis Trail (Hwy. 40).
A Lantern Creek day-use area.
B Lineham Creek day-use area. However, most people park on the shoulder of the highway 1.3 km north of the day-use area (usual start). NOTE: This section of Highway 40 is closed between December 1st and June 15th.

Compared to neighbouring valleys Odlum Creek hasn't a lot to offer: lots of lodgepole pines, some rather dreary ponds, the highest exquisitely placed below some falls. Unfortunately, the falls are at their best when the Highwood River is impassable early on in the season. There are two routes, neither qualifying for favourite trail in the Canadian Rockies. Personally, I would make this a bike' n' hike trip via route B.

212A From Lantern Creek day-use area via the cutline. Distance 8 km to pond, height gain 334 m.

Walk north along Highway 40 to a cutline access road on the left, the entrance partially blocked by a huge boulder painted with a red letter "M". Follow the access road, keeping left, down to the Highwood River. Wade across to the west bank and continue along the road that swings around to the right to join an E-W cutline. Turn left and follow the cutline-road up two very steep hills paved with river pebbles onto a flat bench above Odlum Creek. A gushing side creek below open slopes marks the departure point for Odlum Ridge (see #213).

Soon after, the cutline-road descends to Odlum Creek and crosses it twice, but why bother to go through all the hassle of removing boots when there's a passable game trail along the north bank? Next up is a 3.5 km-long straight, a gradual uphill culminating at a junction with a very overgrown road to

right that is the return route from Odlum Ridge. As you descend, disregard minor roads to left and right and cross the north fork, noting a hunters' campsite on the left. Join the main Odlum Creek logging road in a large meadow, site of Pete Schweindt's 1960s sawmill. Head left to the bridge over Odlum Creek where you join route B.

212B From Lineham Creek day-use area via the logging road. Distance 11 km to pond from usual start, height gain 314 m.

From Lineham Creek day-use area walk north up Highway 40 for 200 m to the road sign. Turn left onto the Odlum Creek logging road and follow it to the Highwood River ford at 1.2 km. From the usual start you can just hop down the bank direct to the river crossing. Even in fall the water is knee deep.

The road climbs a hill, then is virtually flat to Loomis Creek crossing. On the right is a rundown biffy tenanted by a family of pack rats with a remarkable collection of plants and mushrooms.

Splash across Loomis Creek, staying on the road that bends to the right (to left is the shortcut trail used by anyone going up Loomis and Bishop creeks). In 800 m the Loomis Creek logging road heads left. The following straight below the forested ridge is pleasant enough going, but makes you wish for a bike. At the big bend where the road—FINALLY—turns west into Odlum Creek, the road splits. Left is shorter.

The even longer stretch along the south bank of Odlum Creek is broken halfway by a very large meadow (sawmill site) scattered with gear wheels and other artifacts and backdropped by Mt. Odlum. During the slight descent to the bridge over Odlum Creek the main logging road is obvious, so

39

unless you're a complete dumdum you shouldn't be wandering off on vegetating side roads either down to the right or up to the left. Of course, you may be looking for a way over to Loomis Creek, in which case it appears the side road *east* of the side creek crossing before Odlum Creek bridge, the one headed towards the gap at GR498929, may get you started in the right direction.

To Odlum Pond

Either way, you're standing on the bridge over Odlum Creek which is the only easy reference point I can think of. Heading west, walk along the south bank for a few metres, and pick up a cutline that improves quickly, soon joining a logging road coming in from the left. When the road crosses the creek, stay on the south bank trail. Pass a small brown pond amid waterlogged meadows and drowned spruce, then come to the drier and more cheerful environs of Odlum Pond itself. The avalanche slope to the south has littered the shallow pond and surrounding meadow with amputated

branches, while trees along the north edge of the pond have had their crowns snapped off. The backdrop is the best part, two waterfalls slopping down the headwall, and as one stream racing for the pond.

GOING FARTHER
212C North Fork wanderings
Distance from bridge to moraine 2.6 km, to Hwy. 40, 7 km. Odlum's north fork has a little more to offer: larches for one thing, and a route over to the nameless valley to the north.

The hard part is finding the start. From the bridge over Odlum Creek head north on the main Odlum Creek logging road past Pete Schweindt's sawmill site. Which, in a mess of radiating roads, is the right one? The first road to right is route A. The next *obvious* inverted Y-shaped road is the wrong one but good to know about if you're a climber lusting after peak GR467937 because it climbs the ridge between the two forks, and when it ends at some flagging a game trail takes over. How far it goes I don't know. We followed it until we could see the

Looking south from Knoll GR473950 into the north fork of Odlum Creek. Mountains on left-hand page include Bishop Ridge and to its right, Mt. Bishop. On the right-hand page are Mt. Loomis (above figure) and Mt. GR467937.

glint of open slopes between trees, then took off right down another trail into the north fork at scree line.

Anyway, in between these two obvious roads are more roads starting from the far edge of the sawmill site. The one you want is directly left of the north fork and distinguished by an exceptionally tall dead tree on its left side. Climb gently uphill past a couple of side roads on the left to the north fork where you share the stony creekbed a way. Avoid by following a horse trail on the left bank, crossing over when you see the road transfer to the north bank. This occurs where the creek bends left.

Continue along the road, keeping left twice, and follow a line of metal posts leading to a fenced-off Snow Survey Station, that, sources say, is a remnant of "Mt. Odlum ski hill", a candidate for the 1988 Olympic Winter games. Continue past a side road to right and when the road ends, continue on the trail to some meadows. Easy uphill going through larches ends in a terminal moraine (route to Mt. Odlum).

To valley to north When the road ends make a beeline for the pass at GR471948 (cairn), a truly delightful walk through open forest with multiplying larches

---

DETOUR knoll to east at GR473950
Climb 122 vertical m to a rocky little summit with cairn, the absolute west end of Odlum Ridge and a fabulous viewpoint gained with little extra effort (see photo below).

Using an elk trail, descend the steep north slope into the head of the unnamed valley to the north, at this point a huge flat meadow with meandering stream. Head downstream on the right bank. A good trail starts up in patchy trees, a third of the way down the valley crossing to the northwest bank for a long, easy stint taking you out to Storm Creek where it fragments in patchy meadows with deadfall around a wallow. Wade Storm Creek and climb the bank to Highway 40, gained about GR482982 to the right of the guard rail.

#212. Odlum Ponds from the base of the headwall. In
the background is Odlum Ridge.

#213. Odlum Ridge. View of east peak from the
black pinnacles at east/centre col.

213 ODLUM RIDGE — maps 20 & ~~19~~ 17

Long day hike
Route, creek crossing
Short circuit 17 km from trailhead
Height gain 990 m from trailhead
High point 2496 m
Maps 82 J/7 Mount Head,
82 J/10 Mount Rae

Access: Via Odlum Creek trails (#212, route A).

The ridge between Odlum and Storm creeks rises out of the trees to three high summits first climbed in 1916 by the Boundary Commission who established camera stations on the east and west peaks. Despite help from intermittent game trails, a circuit of the tops is a strenuous, though technically easy undertaking.

Leave Odlum Creek trail as mentioned, below open slopes left (west) of the gushing side creek. Crisscrossing game trails facilitate the initial climb onto east peak's grassy south ridge that lies farther to your left. On the ridge proper, the trails consolidate into fewer strands that all head in an up and down direction and eventually meld into one good trail leading to a flat shoulder. (Even A.B. would be hard pressed to keep smiling up *this* slope!) Continue climbing past a large distinctively-shaped cairn plainly seen from the highway which marks the point where the ridge turns west, becoming narrower and gravelly as it approaches the summit of east peak, at 2496 m the highest point on the ridge walk.

Descend 100 m of steep grass to east/centre col. Either contour below the gap on the left side or, much more fun, traverse the black pinnacles, a loose arrangement of big blocks and slabs covered in curly black lichen. Here and there, urine from resident packrats has built up thick encrustations of a white calcareous material.

The ridge rising to centre peak is at first an untidy mix of black-lichened slabs, gravel and krumholz. When the angle eases, it becomes grassy, a green highway leading to the summit and carrying on over and down the north ridge like a bright ribbon into Storm Creek.

From the summit cairn, head southwest into the gap between centre and west peaks (100 metre drop). An easy-angled slope sandwiched between cliffs and spruce trees crouched low to the ground leads to west peak (which boasts an even more tantalizing northwest ridge descending to Storm Creek). Continue southwest to a subsidiary top—the site of "Storm Creek No. 2" camera station.

Return via Odlum Creek The descent to Odlum Creek requires careful navigation and tracking skills. Head south through forest and glades stinking of elk to a creek at GR499956 on 82 J/7. Intermittent game trails on the right bank cross to the left bank at the bend and converge on the dead end of an overgrown logging road starting only a few metres above the stream. This road, marginally better than the forest, leads in due course to the cutline you started out on. Turn left and follow it back to your starting point.

All the ridge
From west peak it's easy going to the pass at GR471948 where there is the option of returning via Odlum Creek's north fork (20 km loop) or via the valley to the north, which requires two vehicles or stashed bikes (15 km one way).

The broad undulating ridge has lost all seriousness and is overrun by spruce and many larches. Initially, you follow strips of meadow along the ridge line. Farther west, little rock bands are encountered, one final steep pull gaining you the rocky knob directly above the pass. See #212C.

Loomis Lake glitters in the afternoon sun.

Opposite: Little Loomis Lake, backdropped by Mt. Loomis.

214 LOOMIS LAKE — map 20

Long day hike, backpack
Unofficial trails, creek crossings
Distance 12 km to lake from Hwy. 40
Height gain 679 m from Hwy. 40
High point 2301 m
Map 82 J/7 Mount Head

Access: Via Odlum Creek trails (#212) route B.

Hikers who stick to official trails are missing one of the finest mountain tarns in all of the Canadian Rockies; only Lake McArthur in Yoho shares the same incredible colour.

The logging road is bikeable to just past the second sawmill site at km 8. After this expect steep sections and some scree. Because of river crossings, notably the wading of the Highwood River, reserve for later in the season. Be alert for grizzlies.

Leave Odlum Creek logging road at Loomis Creek crossing. On the opposite bank take the left-hand trail, a steep shortcut to Loomis Creek logging road. Here, turn left

(west) and thread the narrows which requires another four river crossings. At km 4 Bishop Creek coal exploration road (#215) turns left across the creek in the vicinity of hunters' camps. Ahead, the distinctive grouping of mountains about the head of Loomis Creek comes into view.

The next 4 km is a boring stretch along the north bank through one sawmill site to a second larger one at about GR507924. Early on you pass a road to the left leading to another site on the south bank which I record as having a cabin back in the 1970s. If your eyes are glazing over from logging road stupor, seeing grizzly tracks in the mud is a sure cure to do the trick. Only a couple of years back, while sipping coffee at the hunters' camp and saying politely "no, we haven't seen any game", we chatted to a wildlife biologist and this is how we learned that every year in the fall a sow and her cubs do a five-day walkabout, up Bishop Creek, over to Loomis Creek and back down through the hunters' camps. This cycle is repeated over and over until hibernation, which is very worrying if you don't know where you are in the cycle and have only a bicycle pump for protection. Fortunately, the bears appear well behaved and there have never been any incidents.

Enter sawmill site number two (meadow) which is bisected by a small stream. Beyond the meadow the road crosses the creek from Little Loomis Lake and descends to valley bottom. As you go, note fingers of overgrown logging roads on the right. From the low point the road climbs steeply through Englemann spruce, traverses a slide path and ends.

A good trail carries on and crosses intervening forest to a draw confining the Loomis Lake creek. Turn upstream, cross the creek four times and enter an idyllic flat meadow through which the stream murmurs over flat brown rocks. To your left rises an incredible 40 storey-high terminal moraine that holds back the lake. The creek has a unique start. About halfway down the wall it blasts out of a hole in the scree as a waterfall, sees daylight for a few seconds, then sinks back into the scree and resurges much lower down in the trees.

From the end of the meadow the trail climbs very steeply into all-out larch forest, then continues up scree, wending left to the top of the moraine wall. You'll be thrilled by the glorious colour of the lake: ultramarine stirred with cobalt and turquoise, glittering at midday under the sawtooth ridge of an unnamed mountain on the Great Divide. Though the setting is undeniably austere, all along the moraine top manicured meadows sweep down to the lake at sunbathing angle and the only thing that intrudes on the beauty of the scene is one of those darn creel survey boxes.

OPTION
Little Loomis Lake (GR493920)

Beautifully sited, this little lake is tinted jade and rimmed by quickmud covered by a deceitful scattering of brown rocks.

From Loomis Creek Distance 1.3 km, height gain 243 m. Not pleasant, a long pants job. After crossing the creek issuing from this lake, take the third overgrown logging road to the right. Push between spiky Christmas trees. At road's end, identified by the lack of Christmas trees, clamber over deadfall on your way up a gully shallowing out to a draw. This brings you to a scree slope. Go right, following the bottom edge of the rocks through a belt of trees onto another scree slope where a clearer trail materializes and transports you to the south bank of the creek. Follow the creek past a little bit of karst to the lake.

From Loomis Lake trail Distance 1.5 km, height gain 79 m, height loss 183 m. This route crosses the high ridge jutting northeast from Mt. GR482911. Just below the scree line head right along a bench. When you cross a tongue of talus use the lowest, best sheep trail, the one that continues up a tongue of grass and spruce to the right-hand col at GR492916.

The north slope is shale where even the sheep have resorted to zigging. On gaining the hanging valley below Mt. Loomis, follow down the stream, lined with arnicas and ragworts, to the lake at the lip.

215 BISHOP CREEK — map 20

Long day hike
Unofficial trail, route, creek crossings
8.5 km to col from trailhead
Height gain to col 588 m from trailhead
High point at col 2240 m
Map 82 J/7 Mount Head

Access: Via Odlum Creek trails (#212) route B, then Loomis Lake trail (#214).

The Bishop Creek trail and the ridge above reveal unexpected delights that certainly thrilled me the first time I walked this way. Wolf and grizzly sightings are an extra bonus. It's always seemed to me the ideal trail for clubs with A and B groups, B doing the easy walk to the col and A group striding manfully over the ridge tops (easy scrambling and steepish slopes). Biking to the junction of Loomis and Bishop creeks shortens the day considerably.

At the 4 km mark, turn left off Loomis Lake trail onto the grassy Bishop Creek coal exploration road which straightaway

Mt. Bishop and Bishop Ridge from the old road.

crosses Loomis Creek (for the sixth time). After a stint along the bank top, the old road settles into a gradually ascending traverse along the northwest flank of Bishop Creek, aiming for an island of coal bearing Kootenay Formation sandstones. The best part is the meadow below the grassy hill at GR524911, a good viewpoint for The Hill of the Flowers crosshatched with dead white trees. Sadly, 60 years after the holocaust there's still not much sign of regeneration. As you turn the corner Mts. McPhail and Bishop come into sight, as well as Bishop Ridge. At the following indent the road passes about 120 vertical m below the col at GR521909. To the right of the dry creek, between a stump and a cairn, a trail climbs to the col. Leave it for the descent and continue along the road as it crosses avalanche slopes to a junction.

To the col GR521909 Turn right and zig back across avalanche slopes to the col. The road ends shortly after on the grassy hillside of hill GR524911.

If you're like me, while everyone else has a sensible sit down to conserve energy, you'll be stuffing your cheeks with trail mix and roaming around looking at interesting things. Here you can do two things, either stagger up 90 vertical m of grass to the hill top (2330 m). Or stroll northwesterly into the basin at the head of a Loomis Creek tributary that is chock-full of larches and overlooked by the intriguing northeast face of Bishop Ridge.

OPTION

Bishop Ridge 2554 m

Add on 1.5-2 km to the trip, height gain from junction 427 m. If yearning for the ridge tops keep left at the junction. You will have observed that the road is entering a side valley, the hillside above becoming grassy and striped with freestanding rock wafers. In the shadow of Mt. Bishop the road almost touches the little creek, then swings right and soon ends. Leave it just beyond the zig and transfer to a game trail climbing the draw of the creek to the high col at GR512899. Judging by the proliferation of tracks—sheep, wolf, grizzly—the 100 vertical m of shale is a superhighway over to Loomis Creek. You can see the trail continuing down the north slope, opening up for humans another possibility: a loop with Loomis Creek.

Turn right up the broad rough ridge and scramble over a succession of rocky humps to a top. A grassy ridge connects to the high point at GR516906. Though you are a little too close in to get a really clear perception of the Elk Range, this is still a marvellous viewpoint, one of my favourites. Some of the new features you can see include Mts. Aosta and Joffre, Mist Mountain, Odlum Ridge, Mts. Glasgow and Banded Peak, Mt. Burke and Plateau Mountain, the whole of the Highwood Range and a corner of Loomis Lake.

There are two ways down to the col at GR521909 where B party awaits. Both are fairly steep and require the odd detour. The north ridge route leads to a col at GR514911 from where it's an easy walk into the larch basin and out below the northeast face to the col and exploration road.

The direct route is the east ridge which overlooks the northeast precipice and some pretty fantastic rock scenery including twin blades of rock 30 m high and a few centimetres thick. Seemingly!

Return From the col take the shortcut trail to the left of the draw to the road lower down and turn left.

The twin blades on the northeast face of Bishop Ridge. The view from the east ridge.

216 MCPHAIL CREEK — map 20

Long day hike, backpack
Unofficial trails, creek crossings
Distance 10 km to campsite
Height gain 289 m to campsite
High point 1813 m to campsite
Map 82 J/7 Mount Head

Access: Kananaskis Trail (Hwy. 40) at Cat Creek day-use area. Use the far end parking lot. NOTE: This section of Highway 40 is closed between December 1st and June 15th.

Mt. McPhail (Pyramid), the mountain dominating McPhail Creek.

The old "Elk Trail" from the Elk River over Weary Creek Gap and down McPhail Creek was used by generations of Kootenay Indians hunting elk. Today, large numbers of elk still graze the slopes around McPhail Creek, crossing the Highwood River in late fall to their wintering grounds on the western outliers of the Highwood Range. Which is why the highway closes on December 1st.

For a period of its history, the valley was known locally as Bunk Creek after bunks of logging sleighs were found stacked up against the forge of Mr. Wilson's abandoned logging camp. The Wilson Lumber Company took over leases from Lineham about 1920 and for a few years cut lodgepoles for telephone poles, mine props and fence posts. In *The Buffalo Head* Raymond Patterson describes zigzagging back and forth across McPhail Creek (the bridges had all collapsed) as he followed the old logging road to the camp which was sited "on a little flat on the right bank of the creek, tucked up against a low cliff". Even in 1936 the buildings were in bad shape—the logs rotting, the roofs falling in. In Patterson's day, this logging road was the key to the inner sanctum. When you reached the camp you found a way up the bank to the "Elk Trail" on the bench.

The subsequent bulldozing of cutlines and new logging roads has changed the line of approach. The present route is along the valley's major logging road which follows the route of the old Indian trail to within half a kilometre of the headwall. It makes sense to take a bike, though I urge you to spend more than one day at the valley head. Three is about right. And watch out for covered wagons!

To Muir Creek turnoff Starting from the far end of the parking lot, the old road travels north through buttercup meadows alongside the Highwood River. Keep left at the first junction and right at the second one. 2.3 km from the trailhead, the road fords the Highwood River upstream of McPhail Creek confluence (knee deep at the best of times).

Climb uphill. Either stay on the old road as it rounds the bend (keeping right at Carnarvon Lake trail junction at the 2.6 km mark), or take the shortcut. That's the trail turning right at the top of the hill. On rejoining the road above the junction, turn right.

Heading north, the road winds above McPhail Creek on the bank top. Two shortcuts are available on the left side. At a third, everyone should turn left onto a meadow trail that cuts off the corner. Keep left twice and reach an E-W cutline. Turn left and shortly rejoin the road that comes in from the right. Finally, you're turning your face to the mountains.

A sharp dip precedes a junction in a large meadow where Muir Creek logging road turns off to the left at the 6 km mark. (See #217, Muir Creek to Strachan Ridge.)

To campsite At the following split, shortcut left on a corduroy road which eliminates one hill. Rejoin the main road, keep left and start the descent to McPhail Creek. Shortly after recrossing the cutline, the road levels off by riverside meadows with beaver ponds and again divides at a lumber campsite, a logical lunch spot or interim camping area 8 km in from the trailhead.

Follow the right-hand road uphill to an intersection with the cutline. Turn left. For the next 2.5 km, the road/cutline roller coasters through the narrows into the inner basin. Between the first and second rises, it bridges a copious stream with a log shack on its southeast bank. The third, final and highest rise climbs over the shoulder of The Hill of the Flowers but unless you're bound for its summit, detour around the bottom of the hill to the left.

The inner basin, devastated by the 1936 holocaust, "Literally not a living thing—not even a willow", has been extremely slow to rejuvenate. Charred stumps litter the valley floor and surrounding ridges; only small patches of spruce forest remain below the Lake of the Horns and on The Hill of the Flowers. The first trees to have come back are the willows and the aspens, poor stunted specimens that in fall spread their own blaze of orange across the valley.

Cross two side creeks (the first one is bridged), then watch for a small clearing on your right which is the unobtrusive entrance to Lake of the Horns trail. Located 50 m in from the road is the usual camping area for people wanting to do A, B and C.

216A Weary Creek Gap

Distance 4 km from campsite, height gain 433 m, high point 2246 m. Generations of ungulates moving between the Elk Valley and the Highwood River have gouged a staircase up the headwall of McPhail Creek. From below it's not easy to pick out. In 1936, after one failure to climb the headwall by its left-hand side, Raymond Patterson was only alerted to the trail's presence by the movement of sheep.

Continue along the road. Wade the more copious stream issuing from Lake of the Horns, then in another kilometre, wade McPhail Creek and climb to road's end, about half a kilometre distant from the headwall. Carry on in the same direction along faint game trails that veer right toward McPhail Creek below the waterfall.

The elk trail starts on grassy slopes to the right of the waterfall and climbs diagonally from right to left, utilizing comfortably wide ledges between crags. The going is unexpectedly easy. Twenty minutes walking should see you at the top where you discover the source of the waterfall is a tarn rimmed with a few live spruce and many dead ones lying on the lakebed. The whole of the uplands between Mts. Muir and McPhail is in far worse shape than the inner basin; after 60 years, it's still a graveyard of hollow tree trunks bleached white by the sun of many summers.

The elk trail dissipates hereabouts, but picks up again about 100 m beyond the tarn and can be followed without too much trou-

#216A. View from the top of the headwall of McPhail Creek valley and The Hill of the Flowers.

ble up the right-hand side of the valley to the top of the first step. Cross the meadow to the left-hand side of the valley where the trail, becoming clearer with every metre gained, climbs above a second step and veers left into Weary Creek Gap—a long, narrow pass contained by walls of spruce. A cairn marks the actual watershed at GR524842. The Weary Creek exploration road starts up a half kilometre down the south flank.

A slightly higher pass to the north at GR517846 offers the view lacking at Weary Creek Gap itself. It's best gained by a direct march from the top of the second step; this way you're sure to pass Patterson's spring, a short-lived stream that feeds tiny islands of firm green meadow, each one big enough to hold one tent. Just over the brow of the hill lies the Great Divide, at this point a wide, windy plain distinguished by a long line of lichen-covered cairns built by the Boundary Survey in 1915. Now you get the view. Far off to the northwest rises Mt. Joffre and the stiletto-like peaks of the Italian Group, that tantalizing area at the headwaters of Cadorna Creek which George Pocaterra always referred to by its Stoney name, *Nyahe'-ya-Nibi*, meaning "Go-up-into-the mountains country". The big, solitary mountain to the southwest that sorely puzzled Raymond Patterson some 60 years ago and too far away to be marked on your topo map is Mt. Harrison, the last of the 11,000 footers to be climbed. Mt. McPhail, an unattractive heap of boulders from this direction, was climbed (almost) by Patterson on October 1st, 1936, to report on fire damage. He had a lot of bad things to say about the forestry departments of Alberta and B.C. of the time who "waited until the thing had become unmanageable before acting. Between the two, in the interests of economy, they have burnt off the watershed of a continent".

216B Lake of the Horns

Distance 1.5 km from campsite, height gain 396 m, high point 2210 m. A lake of unusual depth cradled between Mt. McPhail and Horned Mountain had its first recorded visit by Patterson in 1935. He described the headwall below the lake as, "a nasty-looking proposition; it was high, smooth and

#216A. Weary Creek Gap, looking into B.C.

#216 B, Lake of the Horns under Mt. McPhail.

slabs up which you zig on ledges—left, right, left—to gain the top. The lake is only a couple of steps away, the grand austerity of the scene softened by fragile strips of meadow along the north and east shores. The lake, by the way, is not named after the horned peak to the north but after horn coral fossils.

216C The Hill of the Flowers

Distance 1.6 km from logging road, height gain 549 m, high point 2400 m. Shaped like a beached green whale, The Hill of the Flowers stands aloof from the backbone of the Elk Range, its solitary position making it an excellent viewpoint. In fact, it was while hunting sheep on its upper slopes, that Patterson and Adolf Baumgart discovered the Lake of the Horns glinting in the low October sun of 60 years ago.

The normal route up the south ridge starts from the high point of the McPhail Creek logging road as indicated. A good trail leads through aspens into a sheltered meadow of gaillardias, asters and bluebells. The trail ends here, so using whatever game trails you can find, push your way through aspen thickets and clamber over huge deadfall to open hillsides beyond.

Drifts of lupines cover lee slopes like a blue haze. In sunny hollows where the grass grows tall you'll recognize Sticky purple geraniums, Slender beardtongues, flax and many other flowers more commonly associated with the prairies. The forest is never more than 100 m below the ridge on the east face of the hill, and it's here at timberline among the lingering snowbanks of early summer that you'll find your acres of golden Glacier lilies. Halfway up the hill, larches grow in the shelter of impenetrable spruce hedgerows that cushion the force of battering west winds. On the highest slopes, with no protection for either hiker or plant, the delicate flowers of lower altitudes are replaced by hardy alpines lying close to the gravelly ground: forgetmenots, cinquefoils, smelowskias, stonecrops and rose-roots, fleabanes, Moss campions, Umbrella plants and everlastings.

very steep, and there was nothing to hang on to—a couple of small trees widely separated, a patch of grass, a bit of wild rose and a bit of buckbrush, that was all". Which way did he go? Obviously not on the line of today's trail which is an easy scramble rarely requiring the use of hands. Don't plan on camping at the lake.

The trail continues beyond the campsite area, climbing along the north bank of the creek issuing from the Lake of the Horns. The going is steep, your progress punctuated by frequent stops to clamber over huge deadfall. By the time the bank levels off, you are too high above the creek and must traverse downhill to the base of the headwall. To your left the creek rushes headlong between gleaming walls of white limestone. Keeping to less vertiginous right-hand slopes, the trail makes its way up steep grass into a clump of spruce (rest, shade), then continues up scree to a finale of white

#216D. The summit of The Hill of the Flowers, looking into McPhail Creek valley and across to Mt. Muir (right).

#217. On Strachan Ridge, looking towards Mts. Strachan and Muir.

217 MUIR CREEK TO STRACHAN RIDGE — map 20

Long day hike
Unofficial trails, creek crossings
Distance 13 km from Hwy. 40
Height gain c. 533+ m from Hwy. 40
High point c. 2103+ m
Map 82 J/7 Mount Head

Access: Via McPhail Creek trail (#216). Turn left at km 6 onto the Muir Creek logging road.

This route takes you to the open ridge northeast of Mt. Strachan for a spot of ridge wandering. Routefinding skills are needed on the trail section which has a few steep hills. I recommend biking the McPhail Creek bit, and if you're willing to push for the sake of a freewheeling downhill at the end of the day, carry on to the end of the Muir Creek logging road.

Muir Creek The Muir Creek logging road crosses McPhail Creek (log upstream). Keep right. Pass below a cutline resembling the 60 m ski jump at Canada Olympic Park, then turn left and switchback to the cutline above the jump. Turn right and plod up three rather less vertiginous hills. Keep an eye out for where the road turns off to the left. Descending slightly, it swings left to cross Muir Creek via a collapsed bridge (last water). From here, Mt. McPhail is a dead ringer for the great pyramid of Khufu. The local name *was*, in fact, Pyramid. No slur intended on N. R. McPhail of the Surveyor's General staff, but as many people point out, K Country has the ugliest place names of any mountain area thanks to A. O. Wheeler who had a fixation on World War I. But back to the road. It continues steadily uphill on the left bank of Muir Creek past old log loaders and at km 11 ends quite suddenly at about GR575868.

Onto Strachan Ridge You might think that to reach the ridge you just carry straight on up the hill. Take it from me, those Menziesia bushes are murder. Why not use the trail? Just before the road ends a good trail takes off to the right, reaching the ridge top much farther to the southwest around treeline. Start off by ducking under a tree leaning over the trail, then at a junction go left uphill and step over deadfall. The trail levels momentarily, then heads downhill (not quite reaching Muir Creek) into rough ground that looks like it's been grabbed by a front end loader then thrown back down in lumpy clods of grass, spruce, mud and deadfall. For some reason I always envisage this area with bears lurking behind spruce trees and deadfall, but in reality they probably hate it as much as I do. Use the detour trail (blazed) that circles around to the left.

A short, steep climb on original trail precedes a long pleasant stretch. At a split go left to avoid a fallen tree. After crossing a dry creek the trail turns left, wriggling steeply up a shallow draw to the right of an open rib with deadfall. At the top wend right to attain Strachan's northeast ridge. Where the angle eases off the trail is vague and requires special attention for the descent. (The trail appears to cross over the ridge, heading southwest into Carnarvon Creek.)

Turn right and head southwest along the ridge. Treeline, meaning the demarcation between living and dead trees, offers the first really good views of Mts. Strachan and Muir. Trees downed in the 1936 fire smother all the ridges hereabouts, making travel unpleasant. For instance, Mt. Muir has an enticing north ridge but do you really want to flog all around the head of Muir Creek at the pace of a disgruntled turtle? On Strachan's northeast ridge you eventually run out of deadfall, but ultimately run up against the bulwark of the northeast buttress.

218 CARNARVON LAKE — maps 20 & 21

Long day
Unofficial trail & scramble, creek
crossing
Distance 10 km from Hwy. 40
Height gain 595 m from Hwy. 40
High point 2149 m
Map 82 J/7 Mount Head

Opposite: The headwall in the days
before a chain was fixed.
Inset: Beautiful Carnarvon Lake.

Access: Via McPhail Creek (#216).
Also accessible from Strawberry Hills (#220A).

This exceptionally beautiful blue lake, on a par with Loomis, demands a price in the form of an exposed scramble. Nevertheless, on any summer weekend you'll see anglers lumbered with tackle box and rod struggling up the "bad step", their lives literally hanging by a thread. Despite a chain, nervous walkers will appreciate the security of a safety rope; 30 m of 7 mm perlon should be sufficient.

Although the headwall is clearly exciting, the rest of the route along logging road is tedious, best tackled by bike.

Leave McPhail Creek trail at the junction at 2.6 km. Turn left onto the Carnarvon Creek logging road which is rough for bikers in the vicinity of McPhail Creek crossing, but improves as it winds higher up the hillside onto a bench above Carnarvon Creek. Pass two overgrown roads and one good road to the right at a slight bend (option). The next junction comes a few metres after a side stream crossing on a downhill and is the important one for route #220A at the 5.5 km mark.

Turn right and ignoring a grassy shortcut to the left, climb a hill. Pass two overgrown roads to the right, and then a third that makes a loop with the option road. After this junction the road descends slightly, then climbs in earnest to the bare shoulder of Mt. Strachan which gives you a good look at the headwall. Don't descend all the way to valley bottom. About halfway down, a cairn and branches laid across the road guide you onto the Carnarvon Lake trail.

The Headwall The trail climbs a bit, then traverses fans of steep scree between cliff bands to the comfort of a vegetated gully down which flows the infant Carnarvon Creek. From the base of the upper fall, scramble diagonally right up a groove to a ledge. When the ledge merges with the rock face, climb the 10 m slab above with the aid of a chain hanging down between the slab and a corner. Remain vigilant on easier ground above where one careless step could send you over the edge. A short scree traverse to finish with and suddenly, shockingly, the ground tips back into the horizontal plane. You've reached the lake.

From the outlet a scrambly trail follows the north shore around to good camping spots below the meadows of the Divide. Looking back toward the lake's outlet you can see why the gap is known as Gunsight Pass.

OPTION
To Muir Creek
Distance to Muir Creek logging road 2.6 km, height gain 265 m, height loss 143 m, high point 1957 m. A steep climb on logging roads, then bushwhack. Strictly a utility route not to be done for pleasure.

Head up the third side road to the right as indicated. At a split go either way. We went left, then turned right at the cabins. Keep straight. Shortly after the alternate road comes in from the right, the road becomes hopelessly overgrown. Transfer to a trail that leads onto the ridge. So far so good.

Unfortunately, game trails down the north flank peter out in Menziesia jungle and locating the end of the Muir Creek road at GR575868 is like finding the proverbial needle in a haystack. Good luck!

219 FITZSIMMONS CREEK TO BARIL CREEK — map 21

Day hikes
Unofficial trails, creek crossings
Distance 10 km via usual access
Height gain 329 m
Height loss 110 m
High point 1859 m
Map 82 J/7 Mount Head

Usual access: Kananaskis Trail (Hwy. 40) at Fitzsimmons Creek day-use area. NOTE: This section of Highway 40 is closed between December 1st and June 15th.
High water access: Forestry Trunk Road (Hwy. 940.) About 600 m south of Highwood Junction a wide track starts from the west side of the highway.
Also accessible from Baril Creek to GDT (#221) and from the Strawberry Hills (#220A).

In 1915, the old trail up Fitzsimmons Creek provided the Boundary Commission surveyors with access to Baril Creek and Fording River Pass. Since then, it's not only been overlaid by a logging road but the whole area has been crosshatched by cutlines and logging roads the extent of which can only be appreciated from the air. The logging road is quite pleasant and provides hikers with access to the Strawberry and Coyote hills.

Usual access Wade the Highwood River. Follow the grassy road downstream a way, then across the flats to the north bank of Fitzsimmons Creek where you pick up the trail from Highway 940. Turn right.

From Highway 940 add on 2.5 km one way! "Beaver Dams trail" takes a meandering line through forest, gradually descending to beaver ponds in the Highwood River valley bottom. Cross Fitzsimmons Creek to the Fitzsimmons Creek logging road on the north bank and turn left.

The bench below the Strawberry Hills. Mt. Armstrong is the backdrop.

To Strawberry Hills west leg logging road
The logging road zigs uphill to a bench, then travels along it below the open slopes of the Strawberry Hills. At 4 km from the trailhead, it dips to the north fork. Downstream is a campsite. To your right a trail (#220B) shortcuts to Strawberry Hills east leg logging road.

Cross the creek. At the following right-hand bend, note a trail doubling back left to a super deluxe camping area with (in 1992) picnic table, bench, open-air biffy with toilet seat and the customary moose horns tacked to a tree. As the road rises keep left twice and come to an important T-junction with route #220A at the 5 km mark.

To pass Turn left (south) into a darker forest. From now on, unless significant, I won't even mention the mishmash of secondary roads the major road ploughs through. Straight off, the road rises ruler straight through spruce forest. A slight descent precedes a bend to the left (cutline ahead) where the road bridges Fitzsimmons Creek. Straightaway, Coyote Hills road turns off to the left at the 6 km mark. Climbing again, the road describes two semicircles. Note the steep, useful-in-descent shortcut bridging the second semicircle. Just before the top end of the shortcut a well-used trail to the left offers an alternative meadow route to the pass area. Otherwise, stay on the major road as it heads south through a zillion fire succession lodgepole pines. The alternative trail comes in at a kink to the left, and is difficult to spot. Resuming its southward direction, the road heads down the middle of a wide grassy right-of-way "the avenue", signifying the pass between Mt. Armstrong and Coyote Hill.

To Baril Creek Keep left. At the next division which way you go depends upon your destination. If making for Fording River Pass or Etherington Creek via the Great Divide Trail, turn right on a switchbacking road that drops onto Baril Creek trail west of the sawmill site. If Baril Creek, Highway 940 or Etherington Creek via route #221 is your objective, keep left and descend to Baril Creek trail at the junction immediately west of the first Baril Creek crossing.

OPTION
Coyote Hills logging road
Distance to end of road 4.7 km, height gain 265 m, high point 1905 m. An easy forest trail along the north flank of the Coyote Hills to viewpoints.

Your willowy road leaves the left side of Fitzsimmons Creek logging road just after the bridge crossing at 6 km. Initially, it heads wrong-way-downstream so as to round the north end of Coyote Hill (in 1915 a camera station for the Boundary Survey). Now trending southeast on the opposite flank of the hill, it starts rising through a multiplicity of side roads turning off to left and right. A short descent precedes a bend where the road heads off in a new north-easterly direction to a viewpoint for Mts. Armstrong and Bishop, Mist Mountain and the Strawberry Hills. A few metres on, at GR638807, pass a side road to left (see descent shortcut).

Ahead is the highest hill with a wavy grass top. Alas, this is not the road's objective. Shortly, it turns southeast and climbs up a draw to the col at GR645801 between two small hills. Climb the hill to the east for a fabulous view up Baril Creek to Fording River Pass.

Descent shortcut If you're willing to forsake trails the distance can be cut in half. Some guesswork is needed and you may get your feet wet.

Return to GR638807 and turn right on the dead-end road heading out along a side ridge. When both end, drop about 50 m into the valley to the north which is flat and relatively open. Slosh to beaver ponds marked on the topo map, then follow the left side of the creek to where it's intersected by a trail. Turn left. Shortly after the trail becomes road, find a trail heading right to Fitzsimmons Creek just downstream of the north fork confluence. Cross and walk up to Fitzsimmons Creek trail.

220 STRAWBERRY HILLS — map 21

Day hikes
Unofficial trails, creek crossings
Map 82 J/7 Mount Head

South access: Via Fitzsimmons Creek trail (#219) at two locations.
North access: Via Carnarvon Lake trail (#218). At km 6, turn left at the logging road junction.

In between Fitzsimmons and Carnarvon creeks rise the Strawberry Hills, a group of sprawling hills with three distinct summits and alluring southwest slopes of grass, limber pines and *Fragaria virginiana*. Along the west side a logging road offers fast access between routes #218 and #219, should you want to connect. Mostly, you'll meet bikers and the odd covered wagon.

A wintry scene on the southeast hill.

220A Fitzsimmons Creek to Carnarvon Creek

Distance 10 km, height gain 183 m, height loss 235 m, high point 1905 m. A scenic route over a pass between the west hill and the long grey bulwark of Mt. Armstrong.

At the 5 km T-junction on Fitzsimmons Creek trail, turn right (north) onto west leg logging road. (Alternatively, after crossing the north fork, keep right twice and gain the west leg a little north of the T-junction. Turn right.)

Cross the north fork to a junction with east leg road, and turn left. The road climbs gradually below grassy slopes, high up bending left past a log loading ramp. Turn next right on a shortcut that delivers you back to the main road just below west pass at GR597827.

Descend the north flank past skid trail stripes to right, then left. At one point a break in the trees offers a view of Carnarvon Creek and its headwall. At a cutline shortcut, it's nicer to keep left on the road. Wend right at a junction, winding down (keeping left) to the obvious T-junction with the east leg.

Turn left. Descend to Carnarvon Creek, cross and climb to Carnarvon Lake trail on the bench top.

220B Southeast hill

Return loop 10 km from south access, height gain 305 m, high point 1966 m. The best top for grass and views.

Follow Fitzsimmons Creek logging road to the north fork crossing at the 4 km mark. Turn right. A shortcut trail heads along the north bank, splits temporarily, then climbs to east leg logging road at about GR619823. Turn right. About half a kilometre before south pass, leave the road and climb open slopes to the summit of the southeast hill. Look down on a complexity of logging roads through which you can trace the routes to Baril Creek and Coyote Hills.

All on grass, cross to the lower summit at GR624833, then descend the lovely south ridge to Fitzsimmons Creek trail.

NOTE: Continuing along the east leg logging road to Carnarvon Creek is not too interesting unless you're doing a survey of log loading ramps. See *Kananaskis Country Ski Trails* for a detailed sketchmap.

221 BARIL CREEK TO GREAT DIVIDE TRAIL — map 21

Day hike, backpack
Unofficial trail, pale blue rectangles
painted on trees
Distance 9 km to GDT
Height gain 290 m
High point 1818 m
Map 82 J/7 Mount Head

Access: Forestry Trunk Road (Hwy. 940). 3.3 km south of Highwood Junction turn into a parking area on the west side with trail sign.
Also accessible from Fitzsimmons Creek to Baril Creek (#219).

The old Indian trail up Baril Creek has been overlaid by logging roads and cutlines, and the route is now a tedious one. But because it's relatively short, this is the usual way in to the wonderful country about Fording River Pass.

A trail leads to a logging road. Turn left and follow the road as it bends right, crosses a cutline and descends to Baril Creek valley bottom at a junction. Stay left and recross the cutline. In meadow, again cross the cutline and wind along the bank top. Cross the cutline, passing a log loading platform on your right. Keep straight twice and recross the cutline at an angle. It was here while gingerly walking around a bull standing immobile in the middle of the trail that we were treated to some coyote music, from, appropriately enough, the Coyote Hills across the valley. We watched and listened fascinated as a pack howling somewhere in the trees was answered by a lone animal on a hilltop, who slowly made his way down the ridge toward the group. A few minutes after disappearing into the aspens there was a great welcoming chorus of excited yips. Who says this trail is boring!

You're now into the long stretch through pine forest where the road twining about the cutline is obvious. At GR633786 join a major logging road that has come over the ridge from Etherington Creek (see option). Turn right and follow this new road downhill to Baril Creek. Cross via two logs.

On the far bank top turn left onto a cutline (road ahead leads to Fitzsimmons Creek). A short way on take the second road to the left and descend past side roads to right and left to Baril Creek. Wend right, walking alongside the creek to mill site meadow with its line of stakes painted pale blue at the tips. Cross and continue along the road, keeping straight at a second junction with Fitzsimmons Creek trail.

Cross Baril Creek on two logs and climb a hill. Before the top detour right on a trail that rejoins the road on the other side of the hill at a left-hand bend. Drop to Baril Creek. DON'T CROSS. Instead, turn left on a grassy side road. Shortly, turn right on a trail that crosses the creek farther upstream and in about another 500 m intersects the Great Divide Trail at signs and registration book. Turn right for James Lake (campsites) and Fording River Pass.

OPTION
To Etherington Creek
Distance 4 km, height gain 107 m, height loss 177 m, high point 1875 m. Not to be hiked for its own sake, this logging road has value as a connector between the two valleys.

At GR633786 turn south and on good road zig to the route's high point. A little farther on, come to a signed T-junction with Baril Loop snowmobile trail on the point of looping back to Etherington Creek.

On snowmobile trail/logging road turn left down the hill. Turn sharp right at a T-junction and climb to a ridge (side trail to left) where you get a view of sorts through the trees. A long gradual descent passing four side roads to the right brings you to Etherington Creek at signpost GR663766.

#221. Baril Creek cutline west of the
first creek crossing.

James Lake, 100 m beyond the Baril Creek/GDT
junction. A popular camping spot.

#222. Etherington Creek trail during bridge construction prior to logging.

222 ETHERINGTON CREEK TO GREAT DIVIDE TRAIL — map 21

Day hike, backpack
Official snowmobile trail with sign-
posts, creek crossings
Distance 7.5 km to GDT
Height gain 200 m
High point 1834 m
Map 82 J/7 Mount Head

Access: Forestry Trunk Road (Hwy. 940) at Etherington Creek campground. Drive past the campground access road to the winter camping /equestrian staging area parking lot on the left with biffy, picnic tables and notice board. Park well away from the ramps. Can be accessed by trails from the far end of C loop.
Also accessible from Baril Creek (#221) by the option.

The Etherington Creek logging road provides the easiest of all accesses to the Great Divide Trail. Consider a bike 'n' hike day trip with either Rye Ridge or the Lunch Stop Meadow sections of the GDT.

At the time of publication the valley is being logged, specifically the section shared with Loggers snowmobile trail. I'm assured this will not affect the route in any way.

Continue up the road. Keep right at the group camp access road, walking between equestrian campsites. At a widening, keep right on the road and go around a gate.

The dirt road winds along and crosses Etherington Creek on a good bridge. Pass through the narrows between Raspberry Ridge and a rocky ridge to the north into meadows. At 2.6 km there is a junction. Keep right. (The better road, alias the Raspberry Pass snowmobile trail to upper Cataract Creek, heads left and crosses Etherington Creek on a bridge to Raspberry Pass. Not recommended for hikers, bikers and horses who loathe bogs.) In a few metres a signpost indicates Baril Loop snowmobile trail to right which is also the hikers' route to Baril Creek. See option #221.

Stay left in the valley bottom, passing a grassy road climbing the hillside to join the option. Shortly, cross Etherington Creek on a bridge assembled on October 14th, 1996 at 4 pm—the last of the bridges as far as I know. A stony stretch alongside the river opens out into a sawmill site, truly a lovely big meadow with a view of Baril Peak. The road (grassy in 1996) curves back into pines, passing two side roads to left and a campsite. Wade Etherington Creek. On the northwest bank once more, pass a couple of steep side roads to right before coming to a signed junction with Baril Loop snowmobile trail on the east bank of a side creek.

Cross the side creek. Keep left, then cross Etherington Creek twice in quick succession. Climb to a signed T-junction at about GR716632. (The left-hand road which crosses Etherington Creek is the continuation of Etherington snowmobile trail, the one that dabbles with the Great Divide Trail on Rye Ridge.)

The road ahead (now Loggers snowmobile trail) climbs to a bench. Keep straight, in 900 m curving right into the narrower, densely forested north fork lusted after by loggers.

The Great Divide Trail comes in from the left before the road enters small meadows. At one time the Rye Ridge section was hard to locate from this direction; red trail markers all faced the other way. Someone has since tied some blue, yellow and red flagging around a tree.

223 RASPBERRY RIDGE LOOKOUT — map 24

Day hike
Unofficial trails
Distance 4.5 km
Height gain 649 m
High point 2356 m
Map 82 J/7 Mount Head

Above: The eastern escarpment of Raspberry Ridge showing the zigs of the fire road. The new trail climbs the second ridge from the right.

Access: Forestry Trunk Road (Hwy. 940). Six km south of Etherington Creek campground and 1.5 km north of Cataract Creek bridge, turn west onto the Cataract Creek logging road and park, making sure the gate is unobstructed.

Since the second edition, most of the fire road to Raspberry Ridge Lookout has been rehabilitated, including the crucial zigs up the east face. And this is the part with the raspberries *and* saskatoons! As a result a new trail has developed, built on the premise that the shortest distance between the bottom and the top is a straight line. It certainly requires a lot more effort than the fire road! It does, however, cut an hour off the fire road on descent.

Round the gate, then turn right onto the narrower Raspberry Ridge fire road (alias Valley Bottom snowmobile trail) which is also gated. After the right-hand bend there is a junction. The wider snowmobile trail turns left and descends to Cataract Creek. You keep straight on the fire road rehabilitated to trail.

Wind uphill through pine forest, the climb interrupted by a dip to cross a side creek. On the far bank, miss out two zigs by the shortcut trail straight ahead. Turn left and resume the winding climb. Raspberry's eastern escarpment is coming into view, eight parallel grassy buttresses separated by bushy draws. The new trail climbs the buttress to the left of the lookout!

Shortly after entering meadow at the base of the escarpment you reach an important junction at GR689736 where the fire road starts long-sweeping zigs onto the south ridge. Unless you enjoy walking on the slant, don't go.

Instead, turn right on the trail that corkscrews relentlessly up the grassy buttress for well over 330 vertical m. At the top it sneaks between crags onto the summit ridge and joins the fire road. Turn right. Alpine rock gardeners will delight in herbaceous borders of Jacob's ladder, Alpine forgetmenots and purple Alpine rock cress. Around the lookout building grows Artemisia with leaves redolent of lavender.

The full grandeur of the view is at last revealed, its extensiveness requiring binoculars and the 1:250,000 Kananaskis Lakes map. Look up and down the Great Divide where the eye is drawn by a spate of new cutblocks cunningly hidden from the highway. Far to the south is Crowsnest Mountain (off the map) while Mist Mountain is preeminent to the north. To the east rise the full length of the Highwood and Livingstone ranges. Of particular interest here is Mt. Burke's Cameron Lookout which was replaced by this one in 1954.

#223. Near the summit of Raspberry Ridge. Photo shows the steepness of the eastern escarpment.

#224. Upper Cataract Creek meadows just east of the mill site. Mountains left to right:
Farquhar, unnamed and unclimbed, Holcroft, unnamed and Scrimger.

224 UPPER CATARACT CREEK TO GREAT DIVIDE TRAIL — map 23

Half-day, day hikes, backpack
Unofficial trails with pale blue rectan-
gles painted on trees
Distance 10 km to GDT
Height gain 213 m
High point 1844
Map 82 J/7 Mount Head

Access: Forestry Trunk Road (Hwy. 940.) Six km south of Etherington Creek campground and 1.5 km north of Cataract Creek bridge, turn west onto the Cataract Creek logging road and park before the gate.

The logging road leading to the Great Divide Trail and beyond to the very foot of the High Rock Range is unexpectedly pleasing, largely due to the type of country it travels through: the wall-to-wall meadows of the valley, the winding trout stream, the ever-present backcloth of the mountains. Know that beyond Lost Creek turnoff, a newer road supercedes the one described in the second edition.

Perkinson's Cabin.

SMALL WHISKEY PICNIC AREA
showing grave and rustler's cabin

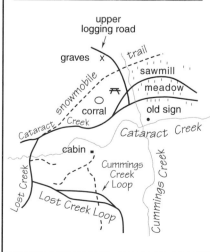

To Small Whiskey picnic area and Lost Creek junction (an easy bike). Beyond the gate keep left on the road that descends, sweeping right, into Cataract Creek valley. In 1956 the beautiful meadows between Highway 940 and Lost Creek were earmarked for a reservoir which luckily came to naught. Cross a snowmobile trail, then cross Cataract Creek twice, a slight hill preceding the long straight to mill site meadow at GR672708. Keep left here. West of the small side creek the road heading right is the upper logging road that winds across the southeast flank of Rye Ridge to the head of Cataract Creek. Shortly after, the snowmobile trail comes in from the right (red marker) and Lost Creek logging road turns left across Cataract Creek.

Back to that upper logging road. A short way up the left side is Small Whiskey picnic area, a fine base for amateur historians who can check out the area's fascinating history. See sketchmap.

Calling Owen Beattie! The cross does *not* mark the long-lost grave but a meat cache dug in 1993 by loggers. The grave lies beyond the intersecting snowmobile trail on a little knoll, refound after a prolonged search by readers Jim and Joyce Marshall. Their story—one of disappointment, frustration (changing landscape, oldtimers dying before the location could be revealed) and finally jubilation—is an amazing saga far too long to be told here. But now there is an urgency to mark the grave before the upper logging road is reclaimed. Alarmingly, trucks have driven right across the grave all unknowingly. As a temporary measure all four corners are staked and flagged.

Over 50 years ago the grave was dug up and revealed *two* bodies, one an unknown white man, the other a Stoney Indian (Enoch Ear?) clad in bibbed overalls with brass buttons, both bodies remarkably well preserved in coffins made from poles. It's thought the men were connected with the cabin across Cataract Creek which is remarkably well hidden in deep timber. It had to be. It was used in the mid 1800s by horse rustlers and whiskey runners travelling a secret trail near the Great Divide to avoid detection. In 1930 ranger Gordon Davis rediscovered what he called the Diamond Trail after following diamond-shaped blazes cut by a knife. Even then the trail was covered by 10 m-high trees. The cabin, Davis noted, was built of logs without nails, had a fireplace in one corner, no windows and a heavy door below the usual set of moose horns. Its unique waterproof roof was constructed from two layers of carved-out poles laid trough up and trough down. Nearby were old rain slickers (Fish Brand of a century before), remains of riding boots and a square four-gallon oil can reading "Prairie City Oil, Kansas City". Empty .44 shells littered the floor. Well, Davis did it up a bit, like cutting a window in the west wall, and for nine years used it as a trapper's cabin. Nowadays, the cabin is a ruin mashed by fallen trees. Joyce theorizes the burls on nearby trees are the result of gun shot.

To Perkinson's Cabin At Lost Creek junction keep straight. The road climbs around a bend to a junction at a viewpoint. Turn left and drop to valley bottom. Cross the river and turn right (Faller's snowmobile trail to left). Recross to the north bank. Ignore two side roads with red markers to right, then keep right at a split. Shortly, the main road turns left down a hill. At the edge of a huge cutblock a snowmobile trail (red marker) turns right (Cataract loop, which follows a cutline to the upper logging road and the GDT). At the next junction there is a choice of route. Either stay on the latest logging road (easiest), or as per snowmobilers (red marker) turn left onto the old road which drops to a dip. On the climb out of it DON'T turn left at GDT approach markers. From the top follow a long straight. Old road and new road meet in front of the cabin at a side creek.

Built and fitted out by range riders (table, shelves, chimney), it nowadays sees use as an emergency shelter by chilled snowmobilers, sodden backpackers, weary trail crews working on the Great Divide Trail, the lone individual out searching for the Lost Lemon Mine, a party of sheep hunters who after a frustrating day on the hills felt impelled to write a poem about it beginning with "We climbed the mountain high and steep". The registration books and graffiti reveal some fascinating stories. Plan on camping in the meadow.

To GDT Continuing west, cross another side creek on bridge. At the junction go straight up the hill on old road (newer logging road crosses Cataract Creek). Near the end of a straight, GDT markers and flagging indicate a left turn onto a trail that heads toward Cataract Creek. On the bank top, a flurry of red rectangles marks the T-junction with the Great Divide Trail. Go left for Cataract Plateau, right for Rye Ridge.

OPTION
Superdirect route to Rye Ridge used by bikers and snowmobilers Continue on the old road. Half-way up the second horrendous hill keep straight. Cross the upper logging road, then a cutline. Now you're set.

225 LOST CREEK TO GREAT DIVIDE TRAIL — map 23

Day hike, backpack
Official snowmobile trails, unofficial trails
Distance 11.5 km to GDT heading north
Height gain 146 m
High point 1859 m
Maps 82 J/7 Mount Head,
82 J/2 Fording River

Below: The beautiful meadow upstream of the bridge.

Access: Via Upper Cataract Creek (#224). **Also** accessible from Oyster Creek to Lost Creek (#228).

The logging road up Lost Creek is far from being an aesthetic hiking trail, particularly the first four kilometres of it, which sees regular use by logging trucks from Spray Lakes Sawmills. I recommend a bike, particularly if heading for the alpine on a day trip. Logging goes back to the first decade of the 20th Century when Lineham's No. 2 camp was sited in the valley. It's reported that some firs were so big around that six foot saws were unable to cut the full depth.

Start off along the Upper Cataract Creek logging road. At the 5 km mark bear left onto the Lost Creek logging road which bridges Cataract Creek. Keep right (Cummings snowmobile trail to left) and climb onto a bench high above Lost Creek. Pass a secondary road to the left. (Another snowmobile route leading to Cummings Creek and ultimately over a forested ridge to Wilkinson Creek.) After 3.2 km the road bridges Lost Creek to a former mill site on the west bank and a junction with Faller's snowmobile trail.

Turn left at the mill site. Gone is the grassy track. In its stead a gravel road (Oyster Excursion snowmobile trail) bisects a beautiful meadow backdropped by the nameless peaks of the High Rock Range, thankfully missing the picturesque pine shown at left. You arrive at a junction.

To GDT, heading north Turn right on a logging road heading straight for the mountains (west). Watch for where the Great Divide Trail joins in from the left.

To GDT, heading south Keep straight. Shortly, bridge Lost Creek alongside the Boy Scout bridge tied together in 1980 by 10 boys from the 153rd Scout group in Calgary. Keep straight and cross the south fork. Note a cutline to left as you enter trees. At the next junction leave the snowmobile trail (also route #228 to Oyster Creek) and turn right up a grassy logging road. Intersect the Great Divide Trail on the brow of the hill.

226 OLDMAN RIVER TO GREAT DIVIDE TRAIL — map 23

Day hike, backpack
Unofficial trails, creek crossings
Distance 6 km
Height gain 198 m
High point 1990 m
Map 82 J/2 Fording River

Access: Forestry Trunk Road (Hwy. 940). 28.8 km south of the junction with Johnson Creek Trail (Hwy. 532), turn west onto the Oldman River Road signed "Oldman Recreation Area". Drive up the road, passing a camping area at 2.1 km, the group camp and horse corrals at 3.2 km, Hidden Creek at 7 km, Shale Creek (for Cabin Ridge) at 8.2 km, Cache Creek and Oldman River Falls at 19.3 km, Slacker Ck/Soda Creek (for Windy Pass & Beehive Mountain) at 22 km and Pasque Creek at 24 km. At about 27 km turn left at a split in the road and park/camp down in the meadows by the Oldman River. If you miss the turnoff you soon hit a gate on the logging road.
Also accessible from Oyster Creek to Lost Creek (#228).

Together with a cutline, the Galena Miracle Mine access road (the road to Bearspaw's claims) make a very fast, if not too interesting approach to the Great Divide Trail. LOGGING IS IN PROGRESS but should not significantly affect the route. There may even be a bridge over Straight Creek.

In fall, the whole area is besieged by hunters, some of whom don't seem too particular about leaving carcasses lying around for the grizzlies to sniff at. This is not a scenario you wish to stumble across unless testing one of Troy Hurtubise's grizzly suits.

Return to the junction and turn left on the logging road. Pass an active chain of beaver ponds in the valley bottom. At a bend, the logging road turns right up a hill (gate). Stay left on the older Galena Miracle Mine road and wade knee-deep Straight Creek. Nothing too exciting behind the name Straight Creek. However, as you plod along the valley road consider the names Slacker Creek and Pasque Creek which you crossed on the drive in.

Looking down on the Oldman River valley from near Oyster Creek. Beehive Mountain to left.

Slacker Creek first. During World War I when young men slow in volunteering for the army were being rounded up, a group of young cowboys went into hiding in the hills. Late in fall with snow lying on the ground, they headed up Savanna Creek with a string of pack horses. At some point along the trail to Oyster Creek they headed south down a sufficiently remote creek and there built a log cabin (now in ruins) without knowing their hideaway was only 1.5 km from the trail up the Oldman River (though this has no bearing on the outcome). It was the long boring winter that did them in. All but one decided the excitement of the army was preferable and headed home the next spring. The remaining slacker made his way into the U.S. and, as it turned out, was the lone survivor of the war!

Pasque Creek, on the other hand, has suffered a name change. *After* World War I, demobbed fighter pilots, requisitioned by the Forest Service to fly single engine biplanes over forest areas to look for fires, were first required to patrol the country on horse. One party, taking the same route as the "slackers", headed up Savannah Creek onto the ridge south of Pasque Mountain, intending to follow the trail to Oyster Creek and return back down the Oldman. Saddle sore, they decided to shortcut down the first creek heading south. Bad choice. Quite apart from the nightmare of dense bush, requiring much work with the axe, they found themselves in the bottom of a canyon, cut off by falls. There was nothing for it but to backtrack. Caught out by dark, they spent a night out with no blankets, food or mosquito repellent, swearing and cussing. And that's how the creek and the ridge behind was called "Profanity".

Interestingly, at the mouth of Profanity in 1884, geologist George Dawson found a small volcanic outcrop, a remnant of the gold bearing Crowsnest volcanics. Before you can say "Lost Lemon Mine found", know that the Crowsnest gold rush of 1983 fizzled out. The traces of gold were so minute they could be seen only by electron microscope and X-ray equipment. Clearly, grinding up the whole mountain was not economically viable, though the instigator wrote a book about it and recouped some of his losses.

So these are things to look for on the drive back. As well as a fabulous view of The Elevators at the head of Cache Creek.

But back to the valley road. Turning off to the right is a logging road west of Straight Creek, then the Oyster Creek cutline (#228) just as you enter the meadows about Oyster Creek—another knee-high paddle (hunters' campsite on the right). The flat section of road ends after paddle number three (another campsite to right). Starting here, you climb into the old forest on reclaimed road.

At a side creek another churned-up road heads right to join a NE-SW cutline. Don't be tempted. This is the most miserable of routes heading west, a combination of deep black bogs separated by hills shaped like anticlines. Instead, cross the creek. Leave the mine road, its pleasing angle replaced by a grunt of a trail to its right which climbs a steep hill. Horses must hate the mud and its not too grand slithering down it in the rain either, especially if you're clinging to a bike. It runs along the bank top for 300 m to the bottom of a circular bog. Round the bottom of the bog (being careful not to turn left on a road that connects to the mine road), then a little way up the other side take off into the forest again at red flagging. Touch the NE-SW cutline briefly, then swing left to avoid another bog. Cross a copious stream, then climb uphill to regain the cutline once and for all. Turn left.

After a hump, the cutline settles into a gradual uphill climb. The mine road comes in from the left and a few metres later takes off on the right. It's here where you take the middle prong of three forks. A mountain view and a few windings precede your arrival at a four-way intersection with the Great Divide Trail (red rectangles and a cairn). Turn left for Dutch Creek. Turn right for Memory Lake campsite, Galena Miracle Mine and Lost Creek.

227 GALENA MIRACLE MINE — map 23

Descending the trail to the adit (centre). This slope holds the snow until about mid July.

Day hike
Unofficial & official trails, creek crossings
Distance 8.5 km from Oldman River Road
Height gain 564 m from road
High point 2377 m
Map 82 J/2 Fording River

Access: Via Oldman River to Great Divide Trail, then via the Great Divide Trail (#229), Oldman River to Lost Creek section.

Opened in 1920, the mine closed in 1938 after only 50 dollars worth of lead, silver and zinc had been removed—not even enough to pay for the building of the road up the Oldman. The mine and its environs deserve more than a quick visit from the GDT! Bring a flashlight.

You're at the upper junction of the mine road with the Great Divide Trail. If still on bike at this point, follow the mine road which makes a big sweep out onto scree slopes before returning to the ridge. From road's end hike up the grass for 10 minutes.

On foot I recommend the shortcut. In larch forest, climb the ridge on a trail which peters out on grassy slopes rolling up against the bulwark of the Great Divide. Already there is a fabulous view of Mt. Lyall and Beehive Mountain (the spiritual home of the

Old Man in the eyes of the Blackfoot) that from this direction have a decided lean to the east as if pushed by the winds that blow with such ferocity in this part of the country.

The mine is much higher up than you think and situated 20 m down the precipice on the right. The first things you notice as you peer over the edge are iron stanchions poking up from the scree and a trail leading down to the mouth of an adit. Closer investigation reveals two tunnels 100 m long, one of which is shaped like the letter T with arms extending 50 m in either direction. An ore cart and section of rail still remain inside. Other carts have tumbled to the bottom of the slope and can be seen from the GDT.

This is the place where Banff celebrity Bruno Engler nearly got the chop in 1954. A misstep while taking a photo, and he was helplessly spread-eagled on the brink of a 60 m-drop off with a torn Achilles tendon. With the help of his friend Fritz Frei it took him two hours to reach the car on the mine road which could be driven in those days.

228 OYSTER CREEK TO LOST CREEK — map 23

Long day hike, backpack
Official snowmobile trail, creek
crossings
Distance 12 km to Lost Creek
Height gain 207 m
Height loss 146 m
High point 2027 m
Map 82 J/2 Fording River

South access: Via Oldman River to Great Divide Trail (#226).
North access: Via Lost Creek to Great Divide Trail (#225).

The cutline near the watershed.

The fastest and least interesting way between the Oldman River and Lost Creek, though not totally without interest at the south end. Basically, you follow a cutline and snowmobile route signed "Oyster Excursion". The trail as marked on the topo map is completely wrong.

If you have a yen for lost trails and a week to spare you can search for the old pack trail used by early travellers including Doctor George who discovered a massive bed of fossil oyster shells *Corbicula accidentalis* and *Ostrea glabra Wyomingensis* at the head of Oyster Creek. I have been unable to find any sign of the trail in the south fork of Lost Creek; no doubt it's been overlaid by the cutline and logging road. Which brings me to logging. ONGOING LOGGING by Cowley Forest Products is affecting the first part of the route.

SOUTH TO NORTH
To the watershed From the Galena Miracle Mine road in the Oldman River valley at GR677539 head right via cutline up a steep grassy bank to the best viewpoint on the whole route: a profile of "singularly bold" Beehive Mountain, (named by Dawson), and a panorama extending past shapely Mt. Lyall to Mt. Gass.

Follow the cutline into the forest. On the edge of a large boggy meadow leave it momentarily and follow the sensible blazed trail around to the left and across an offshoot

of meadow. Why return to the cutline when you can continue following this lovely old trail through the old forest? It delivers you back to the cutline at a cutline crossroads. NOTE: Last minute news is of two cutblocks across the route; supposedly, the cutline and trail are still obvious. Whatever, at the crossroads cross the NE-SW cutline and head straight down the bank to the first creek crossing which heralds the meadow section.

Actually you can cut out crossings No. 1 and No. 2 by a flog along the east bank. It makes sense to give them a miss because at crossing No. 3 you're above the forks and there's only half the water to slosh through. The boisterous west fork arises under the Great Divide, all its headwaters crossed by the GDT. Down here, you walk between two noisy creeks rigged with monitors measuring stream flow.

Shortly the cutline reverts to its northerly direction on the west bank of the north fork. The going is easy, mostly along flat willowy meadows with slight variations to ponder over like "Do I climb over the dry ridge in the trees or skirt around the bottom on boggy meadow?" About 800 m above the confluence you cross an active logging road come in from Straight Creek and headed up the west fork. Between the first and a second side creek crossings, a wide track (Pasque snowmobile trail) turns off to the right and crosses Oyster Creek, bound for Wilkinson Creek.

A campsite with horse rail lies level with the upper forks. Here, in quick succession, the cutline makes No. 4, 5, 6 and 7 crossings of the left fork. Strangely, a track crosses the left fork before No. 4, runs along the top of a little ridge and crosses back above No. 7. What this signifies, I have no idea. Having not found the huge bank of fossil oysters by this point my imagination was ready to suggest the whitish coloured rock on the ridge top was what I was looking for. In our haste to be back before dark there was no time to investigate. Always remember: if you don't look into something on the spot, you'll regret your lost chance when you get back home.

This is the end of the meadows with a last view back to Beehive Mountain and Mt. Lyall. The last lap to the pass is all through spruce forest, a straight, rising cutline to the watershed that is marked by a yellow snowmobile sign.

Oyster Creek valley between the logging roads and the cutline. In the background is Beehive Mountain (left) and Mt. Lyall.

To Lost Creek The cutline continues more steeply down the Lost Creek side between dark and impenetrable forest where you can collect a Safeway bag full of bits fallen off snowmobiles and all terrain vehicles like wing mirrors and pieces of reflectors. Scraped down to mineral soil for the benefit of snowmobilers, the cutline is perennially muddy, ideal for seeing what has used the cutline lately. It's always comforting to find grizzly prints going in the opposite direction and know you must have passed each other like ships in the night.

In 1.2 km turn left off the cutline onto a connector road leading to a logging road (snowmobile signs). Turn right at the T-junction. Some way along at a cutblock is a junction. The grassy road heading left bisects the Great Divide Trail on the brow of the hill.

After a belt of trees, the cutline comes in from the right. You cross a south fork, note a logging road coming in from the right and cross Lost Creek by the side of the Boy Scout bridge. Just a little farther on is a junction with a logging road. Turn left for the Cataract Plateau section of the Great Divide Trail, go straight for Cataract Creek.

229 THE GREAT DIVIDE TRAIL — maps 23 & 21 (Oldman River to Fording River Pass)

Long day hikes, backpack
Official trail
Total distance 37.5 km

From small beginnings in 1974 when a core group of six people undertook a feasibility study under the Federal Opportunities for Youth Program, the Great Divide Trail Association has grown to a number of individuals and supporting organizations "dedicated to the establishment of a protected corridor for the proposed Great Divide Trail and to the initiation of the Trail's construction and maintenance in all sectors outside the National and Provincial Parks".

Below: Oldman River to Lost Creek section. Looking south from the saddle between knobs No. 3 and 4 to unnamed mountains.

Trail building began in 1977 with the section described in this book.

The GDT resembles a good game trail which is one reason why I love it so much. Apart from the inevitable dips to cross major creeks, it also keeps high, wandering along at treeline, seeking out meadows and viewpoints. Marking the trail throughout are red rectangles painted on trees; two rectangles indicate a junction or sudden change of direction. Approach routes are marked with pale blue rectangles. On open ground look for small cairns. Sections can be hiked individually using approach routes and a bike.

Oldman River to Lost Creek

Distance 14 km
Height gain 557 m
Height loss 670 m
High point 2240 m
Map 82 J/2 Fording River

South access: Via terminus of Oldman River to Great Divide Trail (#226).
North access: Via terminus of Lost Creek to Great Divide Trail (#225).

The larch section. Overall, this is a fairly strenuous section, giving new meaning to the word 'undulating' as you wind in and out of cirques at the head of Oyster Creek's west forks below a succession of grey nameless summits. End with a steep drop into Lost Creek. Because you're tucked under the east wall of the Great Divide, expect snow until July.

To Galena Miracle Mine turnoff At the four-way junction at the terminus of #226 from the Oldman River, turn right (north). En route to the mine road you pass Memory Lake in a meadow, and then an official GDT campsite. Turn left on the old road which is no longer rehabilitated. After it curves right, ignore side roads to the left and cross a little creek. Zig left. Not too far along be alert for red rectangles on the uphill slope indicating a shortcut that delivers you to the road much higher up. (If you want an easier time of it, just follow the mine road.) Puffing up this shortcut which is developing its own even steeper shortcuts, you're hard pressed to appreciate the splendid views, and the fact that you've entered the larch zone. On topping out on the road, turn right and have a bit of a rest. The left-hand zig on a ridge is the jumping-off point for Galena Miracle Mine higher up the ridge. This is also where the GDT leaves the road at a flurry of red rectangles and heads north.

To Lost Creek The descent into the cirque is straightforward until you come to two gullies. We recently hiked this section in early summer, so desperate were we to avoid the fall hunters, and discovered snow lingers a long time in these north-facing gullies, and that new trails had come into being by people who'd come to the second snow-filled gully and gone "arghhh!" The theory is you cross one gully to a rib, cross the second gully, then traverse a slope of fine shale to a prominent post on level ground. Strangely, the traverse line is now quite faint as if people have gone off elsewhere (more about that in the next but one paragraph). At the post your attention is drawn to scree slopes above littered with paraphernalia tumbled down hundreds of metres of scree from Galena Miracle Mine above: a coal cart, wheelbarrow, indecipherable bits of metal which someone told me were pinion gears. It piques your interest in the mine which is best visited as a separate trip. Carry on to the low point of the cirque which features a meadow, a creek with water and a boulder pile.

Let's go back to that post a moment. If you're coming in reverse direction, the most prominent ongoing trail is not the official one but another that crosses the second gully higher up, traverses *above* the first gully, by which time you realize the official trail is down below, but you aren't about to lose height so you climb onto the ridge to meet the trail to Galena Miracle Mine. That's OK. Just turn left downhill and in moments reach the mine road a little above the official route.

Still dithering on the rib between snow gullies? The official trail seems to have been replaced by a well-used trail (possibly used by horses) that descends the near edge of the gully for 30 vertical m to where it bottoms out, then cuts left to the creek issuing from the heart of the cirque. It follows the left bank upstream between steep slopes to a fork. Here, wild animals cross the main creek and melt into the trees like the wolverine I once saw. You, however, follow the left fork through meadow to intersect the official trail at the low point in the cirque.

Having FINALLY arrived at the low point in the cirque by some means or other, it's time to move out and around to the next one. The trail crosses the right fork and in subalpine spruce climbs 150 vertical m over a ridge into the next cirque to the north. Halfway down is a camping area on the left followed by a much steeper drop to the cirque floor. This is a beautiful spot: flat meadow with buttercups and two tarns. Cross the tarn creek a little upstream of the trail. Descend farther to a low point at another creek crossing.

Gird yourself for a long uphill climb. At a split keep left. Enter flower meadows above a spring, then wander along the demarcation of larches with meadows and scree fields to a viewpoint above an unexpected drop-off. Below the true Mt. O'Rourke traverse the head of a tiny cirque—the day's high point.

The trail now sets northeast, following a knobbly ridge jutting out from O'Rourke. Turning your back on the mountains, head below No. 1 knob to the col at GR637596 where a view is disclosed to the north. Losing height slowly, wind around the south end of knobs No. 2 and 3 on mostly open slopes rejuvenating slowly after a burn, to the saddle west of knob No. 4 (marked on the topo map by a triangulation point of 7446 feet). If you've resisted temptation so far, No. 4 is worth a climb for a satisfying look at where you've been.

The trail gains the ridge north of No. 4 and heads north, taking in knob No. 5 (cairn). In front there is a view of the next section of the GDT over Cataract Plateau which is that long grassy ridge extending rightwards from Mt. Farquhar. To Farquhar's right, looking absolutely spectacular from this direction, is the unnamed, unclimbed Mt. GR604661.

The drop into Lost Creek is initially steep, muddy fir forest, the slope (and trees) easing in mid section before the final drop to a logging road which is one terminus of route #225. If you turn right you'll come to a junction, where a right turn returns you to the Oldman River via Oyster Creek.

The GDT crosses the road and winds downhill to Lost Creek. Cross via two logs. No trail was built across the meadow. Aim for a tree island (red rectangles), then for a postbox red registration box at the edge of the forest. In meadows again, note a side trail to right leading to woodsy campsites. The main trail crosses meadow harbouring my favourite pink paintbrushes, then bridges the west fork of Lost Creek to a logging road, another terminus of route #225 up Lost Creek. For the Cataract Plateau section of the GDT turn left. For Cataract Creek and Highway 940 turn right.

Lost Creek to Upper Cataract Creek via Cataract Plateau

Distance 6.5 km
Height gain 457 m
Height loss 433 m
High point 2271 m
Maps 82 J/2 Fording River,
82 J/7 Mount Head

South access: Via terminus of route Lost Creek to Great Divide Trail (#225).
North access: Via terminus of route Upper Cataract Creek to Great Divide Trail (#224).

Despite the substantial height gain, this is not a hard walk to a staggeringly beautiful bit of alpine country. Strangely, the cartographers have covered it all in green. With a 2 km hiatus in the trail at the apex *still*, after 10 years of ongoing negotiations with Fish & Wildlife, you'll need to do a little easy routefinding.

Follow the logging road toward the mountains. Shortly, keep left at a division (cutblock to right). A few metres on, before the creek crossing, turn right onto an old packers' trail (red rectangles). Cross another logging road.

Logging roads done with, though not cutblocks (the one on the right remaining visible for some way), you climb a moderately-inclined slope on twisting trail to a

Cataract Plateau section. Descending into the grassy coulee where the trail ends temporarily. leaving you to climb the hillside opposite. Mountains left to right: unnamed and unclimbed, Mts. Holcroft and Scrimger.

saddle. A couple of more zigs gain you the end of a southeast projecting ridge. A straight stretch (first views) brings you to a dip where the ridge curves around to the left and spreads, becoming Cataract Plateau, in reality the northeast ridge of Mt. Farquhar. With excitement building, you head into that wonderful country of larch meadows, catching glimpses of Mts. Farquhar, Holcroft and Scrimger up ahead. Now if you were to leave the trail and head west you'd find yourself walking on tundra amid lichens, mosses, krummholz and pools of standing water mirroring the sky, a place where Fish & Wildlife contrive to make you feel guilty for being there. The plateau is an elk hot spot, apparently, and raising the heartbeat of elk is a no-no until hunting season when they can be safely shot at.

At a sign telling you why the trail is ending shortly, you head down the right side of the ridge into a deep grassy coulee at GR625660. Now what? There is no trail,

markers, cairns or flagging for the next 2 km. Climb out of the coulee onto the ridge at GR623663 which is loosely connected to the plateau at the coulee head. From its gravelly top there are unrestricted views of the plateau proper, Mts. Farquhar, Holcroft, Scrimger, the unclimbed peak between the first two and a succession of summits marching north.

Descent Walk north along the open crest of the ridge, being careful not to scare the elk. Where the ridge dips below treeline watch for flagging and the reappearance of the GDT winding down right-hand (northeast) slopes to Cataract Creek. Cross the bridge and climb the bank to the junction with Upper Cataract Creek trail #224 (right) and the next section of the GDT over Rye Ridge (left).

Upper Cataract Creek to Etherington Creek via Rye Ridge

Distance 6.5 km
Height gain 259 m
Height loss 244 m
High point 2109 m
Map 82 J/7 Mount Head

South access: Via terminus of route Upper Cataract Creek to Great Divide Trail (#224).
North access: Via terminus of route Etherington Creek to Great Divide Trail (#222).

So what if you share it with a snowmobile trail and assorted logging roads! This is still a beautiful section following a wind-swept ridge.

The trail initially heads toward the mountains through cinquefoil bushes massed along the riverbank. Close to the north fork, it turns north and climbs quite steeply to a logging road. Turn left and follow the road uphill to a T-junction with a cutline opposite a cutblock. Turn right. Cross the upper logging road and continue to a four-way junction with signpost advising the turnaround point of Cataract Loop snowmobile trail and the start of Etherington snowmobile trail to Etherington Creek.

Rye Ridge section Shamefully, the trail has been steamrollered by the logging road cum snowmobile trail. So turn left up the road. Directly after the cutblock (fine view of Mt. Etherington and Mt. 601726 with its fabulous east ridge in profile) a snippet of trail to the right is worth taking if you value dry feet. Back on road, you gain height exceedingly slowly through fir forest where only the sighing of the wind through the treetops indicates you've reached the ridge. At a right-hand bend forwarned by a yellow sign go straight (flagging), climbing up grass onto wind-blasted meadows dotted with spruce and pine thickets, islands of calm if you can fight your way through to the hollow centres. The route follows cairns around the edge of the escarpment which curves like a boomerang above screes dribbling into the south fork of Etherington Creek.

Rejoin the road for a stretch which incorporates a little bit of open ridge—the snowmobilers' viewpoint—before heading back into trees where it crosses over to the east side of the ridge. Not so the GDT which

Baril Peak from Rye Ridge.

leaves at a cairn and climbs to the high point of Rye Ridge. Who would guess the other side is a patchwork of large cutblocks?

It's a wonderful walk down the north ridge at the demarcation of east side forest and meadows sweeping down to Etherington Creek. Look across to the great rock peak of Mt. Baril. Lower down in forest, the trail at one point zigs within a few metres of the road in a cutblock. (If heading down Etherington Creek, I would definitely transfer to the road at this point and follow it out to #222 at about GR642750.)

Wade Etherington Creek and cross the valley meadow (no trail) to a camping area in the trees. The trail, resuming, climbs over a low ridge between forks to the narrower valley of the north fork. Jump the creek and at a flurry of flagging join a logging road on the east bank. Turn left for the next section of GDT. Turn right on #222 for Highway 940 via Etherington Creek.

Mt. Bolton and Fording River Pass from Lunch Stop Meadow.

Etherington Creek to Baril Creek via Lunch Stop Meadow

Distance 5.5 km
Height gain 274 m
Height loss 320 m
High point 1950 m
Map 82 J/7 Mount Head

South access: Via terminus of Etherington Creek to Great Divide Trail (#222).
North access: Via terminus of route Baril Creek to Great Divide Trail (#221).

The shortest link has the steepest pull over a treed ridge with one viewpoint. In Etherington Creek, Cowley Forest Products is due to START LOGGING IN THE FALL OF '97. Right now it is uncertain exactly how the first part of the trail will be affected, so keep alert for red markers and flagging. OK?

For about 800 m the GDT will share the reopened logging road as it heads farther up the north fork of Etherington Creek and crosses it. After this it appears one road will branch left, the main road continuing on *beyond* the recrossing (single log bridge) before turning left en route to cutting areas on the northeast flank of Baril Peak. At this turn the GDT goes straight, gaining height exceedingly slowly through the old forest, at the last, changing direction and character by zigging up steep hillside toward Baril Peak. The reason for this deviation is Lunch Stop Meadow on the watershed—acknowledgedly a welcome viewpoint and the only one. Somewhere high up, the GDT will narrowly miss future cutblock 0231.

From here it's all downhill into Baril Creek—an awful flog in reverse direction. In an area of intersecting grassy logging roads low down, keep a close watch on the red rectangles; keep left of the first road you come to, turn right onto a second road but follow it for only a few metres before resuming your downward course on the trail. At valley bottom cross Baril Creek on a wide log to a logging road on the north bank, turn right and arrive within minutes at the junction with Baril Creek trail straight ahead and the Fording River Pass section of the Great Divide Trail to left.

Fording River Pass

Distance 5 km from James Lake
Height gain 555 m
High point 2368 m at pass
Map 82 J/7 Mount Head

East access: Via terminus of route Baril Creek to Great Divide Trail (#221).

Fording River Pass, renowned for the magnificence of its cirques, is currently the northern boundary of the Great Divide Trail. The initial problem is getting around the south slopes of Mt. Armstrong. Although there is a perfectly good exploration road along the north bank of Baril Creek, the GDT that twines about it is a lot more enjoyable and, a huge plus in my books, it adroitly avoids the road's grade 7 hill. But please yourself. Most people walk into the area via Baril Creek (#221) and spend several days doing side trips.

At the junction in Baril Creek, turn left. Climb the hill to a T- junction above James Lake, a shallow body of water filling a depression. The right-hand trail leads to campsites at the lake's outlet, then on to Baril Creek exploration road.

Turn left, traversing grassy banks to the exploration road. Cross. An uphill stint through trees north of the road brings you back to the road below the first grade 7 hill. Cross and traverse, in so doing, omitting the hill and a dogleg. Rejoin the road at a rock pile where Baril Creek valley turns north. The road makes a wide sweep around to the left. The cairned trail climbs over the top, a great place to view Mt. Armstrong, Baril Peak and Mt. Bolton (though not the pass).

Entering the spruce-filled valley head, the trail stays right of the road initially. Just after you bridge a lively side creek issuing from the Bolton/Armstrong col look for a cabin, sans roof, dating back to the turn of the century.

Below: Fording River Pass area from Armstrong viewpoint. The left-hand page shows the tarn at the pass and Cornwell Cirque.

Regain the road. You get no idea from looking at the topo map that the valley head is enclosed by a broken ring of cliffs forcing the road way over to the left. The trail climbs up the left side of the road, crosses, then climbs very much more steeply up the hillside to the north. On reaching a cliff band, traverse left (white flagging, paint splodges) and join the road at the top of the headwall. Turn right.

The final stretch on road crosses a rugged landscape of grass, krummholz, stunted larches and polished bedrock littered with rocks dropped by melting glaciers. Below Mt. Bolton a wooden tripod marks the watershed. Half a kilometre to the south a glint of water indicates the true pass at a tarn, the usual camping spot.

Beyond the tarn is Cornwell Cirque, well known for its horizontal strata. John Travers Cornwell, age 16, was a member of the gun crew aboard the H.M.S. Ches-

The right-hand page features Mt. Bolton, the ridge facing being the usual route of ascent. A trail crosses the col below into Aldridge Creek (right).

ter. His job as sightsetter of the forecastle gun was severely tested during the Battle of Jutland in 1916, when everyone around him was lying dead or injured. Though mortally wounded himself, he stayed quietly at his post until the action was over, thereby earning the Victoria Cross for Bravery. It was thrilling to learn from Donald Smith that Scouts Canada has the Jack Cromwell Decoration which recognizes "suffering undergone in a heroic manner or perseverance in the face of disability".

Imagine a constant flow of cars and semis grinding over the summit on the highest paved highway in Canada; busses pulling into the summit parking lot to let tourists read a slate of interpretive signs about cirques and glaciers. It could happen. Every so often East Kootenay municipalities endorse building a highway over the pass from Elkford to Highway 40, citing it would be great for the B.C. tourist industry and that mining operations in B.C. could save millions of dollars each

Fording River Pass at the exploration road. In the background is Armstrong viewpoint (the dark triangle) and Mt. Armstrong.

The head of Aldridge Creek. The tarn in the cirque between Mts. Armstrong and MacLaren.

year by the reduction in transportation costs for fuel, supplies and commodities. The latest threat was in 1987 when the Economic Planning Group in association with Willis Cunliffe Tait and Company and Novacorp Consulting Inc. actually prepared a report for Highway 43 Association, costing out the 70 km of new road.

Into B.C. The road carries on, winding down the west slope past a tarn to a road junction with Fording River road. Ongoing backpackers looking to extend the GDT should keep straight, then turn left down the Aldridge Creek road, though what you do when you reach the Elk Valley is uncertain because, right now, there is no ongoing trail.

OPTIONS

All three options start from the col between Mts. Bolton and Armstrong at GR574783. If camped at the tarn this means a height gain of about 46 m over a distance of 2 km. Getting there is not quite as simple as you might expect. Use the 7,500 foot contour on the topo map to avoid running into boulder fans below Mt. Bolton.

If camped below the headwall, follow a rough trail up the left bank of the lively stream issuing from the col (unmarked on topo map). Distance 1.5 km, height gain 254 m.

A Aldridge Creek tarns

A 5.5 km circuit from the col, height gain and loss 192 m, high point 2327 m. An easy walk, partly off trail, to three tarns.

In summer you don't need to go all around the boonies to reach the celebrated cirques at the head of Aldridge Creek. From the Bolton/Armstrong col, a trail descends the northwest slope, trending right across scree into Aldridge Creek valley bottom. Cut across to Aldridge Creek exploration road, turn right and follow it up to a pale blue tarn tucked between Mts. Armstrong and MacLaren at GR582800. The going is everywhere flat and open below Armstrong's long line of crags.

Next, contour around the grassy south flank of Mt. MacLaren into the cirque between MacLaren and Mt. Shankland at GR565800. Here you'll discover another two tarns which cartographers are remiss in not marking on the topo map.

When returning, do not make a beeline for the col (unsuspected, the creek is deeply entrenched). Aim farther to the left and pick up the road.

B Mt. Bolton 2691 m

Distance 1 km from the col, height gain 479 m. A straightforward walk up scree and boulders.

Though Bolton can be clambered up from any direction (we took the direct route from the pass), I recommend the northeast ridge which is easier angled. From the Bolton/Armstrong col simply follow the broad ridge of reasonably stable scree and rocks coated in black lichen to the top. You'll appreciate a couple of wind shelters.

Because the mountain is solitary, it's an excellent viewpoint taking in the pass area and Aldridge Creek, and an entire western panorama, a complex vista for which you'll need help from the 1:250,000 Kananaskis Lakes map. Some of the more obvious peaks are Mt. Harrison, Mt. Abruzzi (with glacier) and Mt. Joffre.

C Armstrong viewpoint GR584790

Distance 1 km from the col, height gain 479 m, high point 2691 m. An easy scramble to the pointy end of Mt. Armstrong's southwest ridge.

From the Bolton/Armstrong col head northeast along a broad grassy ridge turning to rubble at the final pyramid. Keep to the ridge where the footing is firmer.

In my opinion, this is the classic viewpoint for Fording River Pass (see panorama on the previous page).

To the summit? It's tempting to carry on along the ridge to the summit of Mt. Armstrong. Unfortunately, not far before the demarcation of grey and orange rocks there's an impasse: a step down—a slanting ledge dangerously covered in rubble sandwiched between two stretches of downclimbing. Only scramblers need continue.

Optional descent route Consider the lovely southeast ridge if returning to the trail below the headwall.

The Bolton/Armstrong col, showing the trail leading into Aldridge Creek at left. Ahead rises Armstrong's southwest ridge to Armstrong viewpoint.

230 PASQUE MOUNTAIN — map 24

Day hike
Unofficial trails, route, creek crossings
Distance 6.5 km to summit
Height gain 735 m
High point 2543 m
Map 82 J/2 Fording River

Access: Forestry Trunk Road (Hwy. 940). 8.5 km
south of Cataract Creek bridge, park on the west
side of the road at the entrance to a logging road
at a gate. NOTE: This section of Highway 940 is
closed between December 1st and April 30th.
Also accessible from Upper Wilkinson Creek
(#231).

Pasque Mountain in the southwest corner of
K Country has a lot to offer the connoisseur
of ridge walks, including larches. Incredibly,
it was first climbed by the Boundary Survey
crew in 1915 who set up camera stations on
both summits. But more thrilling for me than
the ridge or the views is the fact that Pasque
is the northernmost limit for that gorgeous
Sky pilot *Poleminium viscosum.*

Access to open slopes is made easy by a
progression of logging roads, cutblocks and
exploration road. After this expect rough
walking and some easy scrambling. Bridges
are currently in.

Start off by walking along the logging road
(old highway). Just after crossing Wilkinson Creek by bridge, turn right at a junction
and cross a smaller creek issuing from the
north side of Pasque Mountain. In a large
cutblock, made even larger since the second edition, the road splits, the left-hand
one being Cummings Creek snowmobile
trail offering boring old routes to Lost and
Oyster creeks.

Just before the 'Y' turn left (southwest)
and walk through to another cutblock. No
logging road now. About level with a few
token trees left standing in the middle of the
block, search the left edge of the trees for a
snippet of coal exploration road that
crosses the creek into another cutblock.
Walk the left edge for a few metres to the

resumption of the road that heads left (east)
and downhill to a tributary.

Cross the tributary and wind steeply
onto the end of a ridge at GR716632. It's a
long haul up the ridge above grassy slopes
sweeping down to the tributary and on
gaining the main body of the mountain
you'll appreciate a layabout meadow with
a view back to the cutblocks.

Continue along the road, climbing into
lovely spruce-larch forest extending all
around Wilkinson Creek at treeline. The
windings sharpen into three zigs during the
final climb up grassy slopes onto the extreme north end of the north ridge at
GR710613. If you want to shortcut, a trail
heads left at the beginning of the first zig.

To north summit Head south along the
broad ridge and up a gradual slope to a
minor top covered in cheery clumps of
purple Bladder locoweed. Between here
and the north summit follow either the
rocky crest or the meadow trail to its left,
or do a combo. Any trail peters out on flat
ground below the north summit at
GR713594, a rocky knob in topped by a
magnificent cairn built in 1915. Naturally, the mountains of the Great Divide
draw the eye to the west. Particularly eye
catching are twin towers to the left of
Beehive Mountain known to Nanton area
residents as the Cache Creek Elevators, or
The Elevators for short. To this day the
left-hand tower remains unclimbed despite numerous attempts.

To summit Set off along a ridge of big
black blocks showing disturbing evidence
of frequent lightening strikes. Shortly it
turns left, descending to a low point, and is
crossed by two rockbands. The first step
requires a few metres of scrambling. The

Top: View south from the minor top to the north summit (left).
Middle: Looking south along the ridge connecting the north summit to the high point (left).

Bottom: The horseshoe. Looking south from about GR738608. The high point is out of sight to the right.

second can be turned to left or right. All around here on rocky ground you'll find Sky pilots thrashing madly in the wind. While the blue flowers are beautiful, the ladder leaves if rubbed give off an amazing imitation of a skunk that's just been cornered by cats. Look for more clumps as you walk up the easy final slope to the summit. Usually it's found growing much farther south on the high ridges of Waterton National Park where it thrives in high altitude sun and constant wind.

From the collapsed cairn (Boundary Survey's No. 1 camera station), the view to the south makes you yearn to carry on walking along a chain of high grassy ridges between the Oldman and the Livingstone rivers. With help from exploration roads crisscrossing the area, the ridges could be joined up to make a high-level walk lasting several days.

GOING FARTHER
The Horseshoe

Distance round trip 16.5 km, total height gain 1061 m. If you tack on the ridge to the east, the 2490 m summit at GR745597, and the ridge heading north to make a horseshoe, the sun will have travelled halfway around the sky and be setting in the west as you stagger down to your vehicle. You emerge on Highway 940 at Wilkinson Summit, the trailhead for upper Wilkinson Creek trail (#231). So this means either a westward plod down the highway to your starting point (add 3.5 km) or a second car.

The east ridge of Pasque gives new meaning to the word "undulating". Four tops, counting in Pasque's summit, are separated by three cols. All descents feature a small rock band that in every case requires a detour to the left. The tops are all round and shaley. I was in seventh heaven at the third top, running from one clump of Sky pilot to the next. Then again, the first col has marvellous larches, which make you think you should be here in the fall and not in the flower season. The last col has concentric circles of scattered brown rocks. From here you look north into the meadows of upper Wilkinson Creek. If your knees are on the blink, this is the escape place. Otherwise, make another climb up the usual shale and grass to the summit at GR745597 (2490 m) which was also visited by the Boundary Survey. The actual top is a cockscomb of rocks farther to the right.

Head north along the wide north ridge, flat grass giving way to crunchy rocks. From Pasque Mountain I'd looked across with some alarm at this section of ridge. It looked narrow. In reality it's nothing of the kind and although it's fun to scrabble along the crest of blocky black-lichened rocks, it's faster to take the game trail on the left side. Again the ridge widens, rising slightly and becoming grassy. STOP. The first time we did this ridge we carried on to the bitter end and dropped off the north end, literally swinging from tree to tree to gain trail #231 which, in our ignorance, we crossed and bushwhacked out to Highway 940.

When sitting above col No. 3 we were alerted to a better route by two trail bikers who roared out of the trees in the valley below, revved up to the col, took a turn or two around the concentric circles, then zoomed back the way they'd come—all this in the time it takes to wolf down a Mars bar.

So I recommend leaving the ridge at about GR738608 and heading west down the side ridge (grass, pines, some shale) to intersect Upper Wilkinson Creek trail. Turn right and follow it out to Highway 940 at Wilkinson Summit. Everything is made clear in the sketchmap for route #231. Another advantage of this route is lots of icy cold water at the first side creek crossing.

If you're walking the highway to your starting point, keep left just before the parking area on the pass, using the former grassy road to shortcut the big bend.

231 UPPER WILKINSON CREEK — map 24

Day hike
Unofficial trails with flagging & blazes
Distance 5 km the long way, 4 km the short way
Height gain 192 m
High point at meadow c. 2194 m
Map 82 J/2 Fording River

Access: Forestry Trunk Road (Hwy. 940) at Wilkinson Summit, 12 km south of Cataract Creek campground access road and a few metres west of Plateau Mountain Road. Park on the south side of the highway at the entrance to the old road which is identified by three strategically placed boulders. NOTE: Between Cataract Creek and Wilkinson Summit, this section of Highway 940 is closed between December 1st and April 30th.

The problem of getting into upper Wilkinson Creek nagged away at me for years. It took a few visits of thrashing up and down the bush between Wilkinson Creek and the west fork of the Livingstone River before everything became clear: how various trails connected or didn't connect. At a low point in morale I was convinced the trail bikers I had seen on Pasque Mountain had come in from Savanna Creek!

So here it is: a very pleasant forest walk into the beautiful meadow of the east fork, where you have the option of joining Pasque Mountain horseshoe. Unless in a hurry, use the long (trail bikers') way.

The east fork meadow under the north ridge of GR745597 which is part of Pasque Mountain horseshoe.

Long way
Follow the old road, keeping left at a junction into a snake-like meadow running parallel to the highway. The road hugs the left edge of the trees, passing a row of snow stakes, a rain gauge and sign 'Snow Course', then a corral on the left side. Just after the corral, cross the meadow into a short draw. At its head a good trail starts in the trees (flagging).

Follow the trail uphill and across an intersecting NE-SW cutline into open forest. Shortly after crossing some rocks you descend to a junction (flagging, blazes) where the left-hand trail sets out toward Savanna Creek but, sadly, doesn't get too far. Turn right and descending slightly, re-intersect the cutline.

Cutline shortcut To cut out half a kilometre, turn right at the cutline. A short downhill, two tiny creek crossings and an easy climb is all it takes to regain the trail. Turn right. Just below the junction on the right side is a red tree tag where the short way comes in.

Short way
Right now, this route is for the acutely observant who don't get alarmed when they lose the trail and can continue to stride uphill confident of hitting either the cutline (leftish) or the trail (rightish). If you haven't been up this way you'll have a harder time finding your way down because the flagging at the upper end is so far apart it requires a search party to navigate between flagged trees.

Livingstone

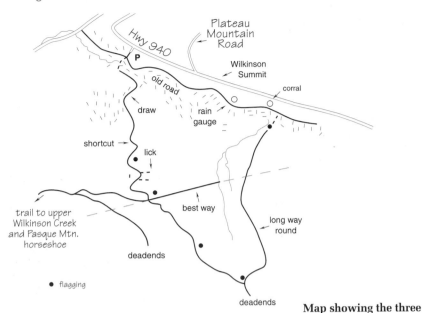

Map showing the three accesses from Highway 940

If you're willing to give it a go, follow the old road, keeping left, into the longitudinal meadow. Almost straightaway, cross the meadow at the rock where it's the least boggy. Turn left and follow a game trail near the right edge of the forest past the line of stakes to a draw heading right. The trail continues through the draw to a big meadow. Just before the meadow turn left up another trail and follow topo directions. Know that shortly after the bench the better trails all make a beeline for the salt lick farther to the left so you have to resist and navigate from flagging to flagging on a more nebulous trail if you want to emerge near the top of the cutline at red tree tag 'Permit 338 WGC PTY 36'. Turn right, then right when you hit the long way trail.

If you're coming off Pasque horseshoe, this is by far the fastest route.

To the cirque From the cutline the trail meanders along, climbing slightly to a junction with flagging. Turn right (the left-hand trail, strewn with branches, peters out). You drop slightly below the steep gable end of a ridge, then round the ridge into upper Wilkinson Creek valley. Coming up is a lovely stretch through forest and glades. If in any doubt at game trail junctions, follow the flagging (which is not mine). The only side trail worth following is the first one to the right marked by a Labatt Wildcat Beer can and that I assume leads to the creek. Farther on you climb across a side ridge with a view of Pasque Mountain. Shortly after this the trail appears to end at a grassy side slope falling to the east fork (last flagging).

Cross the grass and pick up the trail in the trees *slightly lower down*. Near valley bottom it again disappears in some grass. Look for it rising below a large rock back into trees on a rocky rib, after which it's easily followed to the large meadow filling the flat cirque floor. This is a heavenly spot, sheltered on three sides by grassy ridges, with clumps of spruce and larch, and sprinklings of buttercups and onions.

To col No. 3, Pasque Mountain horseshoe From the end of the meadow walk up the right-hand gully (trail) to the bottom of the headwall. Climb grass, wending right, then back left to the col.

232 UNNAMED RIDGE GR735660 — map 24

Day hike
Unofficial trails and route
Distance end to end 11 km
Height gain 713 m
Height loss 896 m
High point 2405 m
Maps 82 J/2 Fording River,
82 J/7 Mount Head

Access: Forestry Trunk Road (Hwy. 940).
South end Ten km south of Cataract Creek bridge and 1.2 km west of Wilkinson Summit pull into a small parking area on the southwest side of the highway at GR733630. NOTE: This section of Highway 940 is closed between December 1st and April 30th.
North end Cataract Creek day-use area.

When I first suggested walking the ridge between Highway 940 and Plateau Mountain my friends looked at me in disbelief. From the highway it certainly looks to be boring forest and as if to emphasize the point, the topo map has it covered in a green wash. The reality is something quite different, a splendid ridge of grass and rock, not in the least dull, though the trees spill over the crest here and there. Just walking to the top and back is the least exciting option. I recommend an end to end ridge walk using two vehicles.

To top Start up steep grassy hillside opposite the parking area. Keep right of the bluffs as you climb onto the south end of the ridge.

As you head north, follow one of several game trails through flat open forest to the right of soggy fens. An open slope with a couple of stakes, signifying who knows what, marks a steeper climb up a definable ridge. Near the top the angle eases and you enjoy a very pleasant walk to the cairn.

North ridge None of the above takes too long. It's the ridge to the north that eats up the hours and this is going downhill! Beyond the summit cairn it undergoes a dramatic change, becoming relatively narrow

and undulating with alternating grass and blocky crags covered in black lichen. If you want to be back before dark give the rocky crests a miss by traversing game trails to one side or the other. The crests can be entertaining, though. I remember hanging grimly onto the security of a Whitebark pine above a 7 m drop. Don't laugh. A slip from 7 m can still bash your head in.

All this leads into a brief treed section within which the rocky ridge is still evident. Again, go either left or right where necessary. Suddenly, out of the trees rise grassy bluffs with cliffs down the west side and evidence of Homo sapiens in the shape of a fire circle, and a large cairn with pole. A little farther on is another cairn perched on the final rocky knob, a superb viewpoint for Cataract Creek, Hell's Ridge and all views north.

To Cataract Creek A game trail leads down to the gap at GR723718. Beyond is a forested knob that is missed out.

So you go left at the gap, descending in a northwesterly direction sandy hillsides crammed with matchstick pines grown to adolescence, which means there are lots of dead standing trees to topple as you push through. Childish I know, but good fun. Run into a band of matures just before you hit Highway 940.

Turn right and walk down the highway to Cataract Creek picnic shelter and parking lot. If you're lucky enough to hit the road at the right place, you can use a snippet of old road to the left. Much nicer walking. Now for that beer you stashed away in Cataract Creek!

#232, Unnamed Ridge GR735660. Looking back at the summit from farther north along the ridge.

#233. Polygons on Plateau Mountain.

233 PLATEAU MOUNTAIN normal route — map 24

Day hikes
Unofficial trails, routes
Distance 6.7 km to south end,
7.5 km to north end
Height gain 344 m to south end,
305 m to north end
High point 2524 m
Maps 82 J/2 Fording River,
82 J/7 Mount Head

Access: Forestry Trunk Road (Hwy. 940) at Wilkinson Summit. Turn north onto Plateau Mountain Road (which accesses several sour gas wells on the plateau), and drive for 3.7 km to a parking area on the big bend at GR743663. A gate precludes further travel. NOTE: Between Cataract Creek and Wilkinson Summit, this section of highway is closed between December 1st and April 30th.

Plateau Mountain is unique in the Canadian Rockies. Once a nunatuk rising above the glaciers of the last ice age, a refuge for animals and plants of that period, it is today a steep-sided mesa with over 14 sq. km rising above the 2300 m level.

Back in 1937, geologist Joe Irwin reckoned Plateau was the most perfect oil dome he had ever seen. It's true. Below the summit sandstones lurks an anticline of Rundle Group limestones harbouring oil and gas retained in traps. After the area's gold rush fizzled out in 1931, the search for oil was on in Savanna Creek, Dry Creek and on Flattop or Table Mountain as Plateau was then called. A road was built from Skeen's Mine over The Hump to Dry Creek where Anglo-Canadian Oil began drilling for oil. Things didn't really get going, though, until the 1950s when gas was discovered and roads were extended from one end of the plateau to the other. Today, Husky Oil continues to operate two gas wells on the summit, even though a large part is now an ecological reserve. This means no motorized vehicles, no hunting sheep, no collecting of rare plants and butterflies.

There are no trails to the top, only company roads leading to lonely gas wells. Use a bike, wind willing. Once up there, it pays to get off the beaten track by either walking around the edges or just plain wandering about, field guides to hand, searching for uncommon alpines such as Pygmy bitter root *(Lewisia pygmaea)*, the Flame-coloured lousewort *(Pedicularis flammea)*, Yellow fleabane *(Erigeron ochroleucus)* and *Primula egaliksensis,* a smaller edition of the Bird's-eye primrose.

Continue along Plateau Mountain Road which makes two zigs out of the trees to a saddle, then winds up the western escarpment at a break in the cliffs to the top. En route you get your first introduction to Plateau's famous "patterned ground". What happened is that continual freezing and thawing during a colder, wetter era forced the larger rocks upwards and outwards from areas of finer material into an amazing self-perpetuating pattern of circles and polygons. On steeper ground the stones are aligned in stripes.

At GR767654 arrive at a road junction.

233A South End Road
Turn right on a dead straight road. To your right the peaks of the Great Divide, nearly all pyramidical in form, are strung out along the horizon like a paper cutout. On your left the ground rises ever so slightly to Plateau's high point which is determined solely by a cairn. Just before well 5-32 a grassy road forks left (#234).

Above: Looking south along the east edge of Plateau Mountain near the waist. Peaks of the Great Divide poke up above the horizon.

Keep straight to a spate of warning signs preceding well 6-29, an RCMP radio tower and a Canadian & Western Natural Gas weather station. Continue on trail to the cairn at the edge of the southern escarpment overlooking Highway 940, where a new view is disclosed of the Savanna Creek anticline, Pasque and Crowsnest mountains, and Cabin Ridge which is one long highly recommended ridge walk.

Optional return via Dry Creek From well 5-32 head west above the buried pipeline to the escarpment where an access trail, shaped like the letter M on its side, descends the hillside into Dry Creek, so named after drilling results were disappointing back in the 1930s. Pick up the valley road at valves and follow it out to Highway 940 at GR753625.

233B North End Road
Turn left at junction GR767654 onto the forever road. For a few weeks each summer the whole tundra to the left will be plastered with yellow buttercups. It was here I once saw grown men lurching around with butterfly nets, stuffing unlucky captives into the killing bottle. I was horrified to learn selling our butterflies to Japan is a lucrative business. (This is one occasion when I would have welcomed a few stewards around for a ticking off.) So that's how I learned Plateau is also a butterfly hotspot—watch that caterpillar crossing the road!

A few scraggly spruce growing in the lee of the raised track precedes road's end at the site of an abandoned well where you'll find a plaque in the shape of Siamese-twinned hexagonals telling you about Plateau Mountain ice cave, which is not visible and is closed to the public. In fact, I'm only surprised it was found in the first place. Maybe someone with binoculars spotted it from the summit of Sentinel Peak.

So you can trog off to the ice cave and back, or walk around the eastern escarpment to GR771675 where, at Plateau's narrow waist, you're only a few steps away from the road.

GOING FARTHER
To the Ice Cave (c. GR775700)
Add on 3 km return. An easy scramble.

From the plaque descend and head northeast along a broad grass-topped ridge jutting out into Salter Creek. Just over top GR773702, in a bit of a dip, look for a small spruce growing in the lee of a white rock. Walk right (southeast) down the steepening side slope. Grass turns to orange scree with evidence of footprints. Above a gully, traverse *right* above the low cliff. Where the cliff ends, descend alongside the rock to the top of another low cliff. Shuffle left between the two cliffs on a firm, narrow ledge—a more thrilling approach to the cave can hardly be imagined!

Where the ledge widens out to grass are two caves, the first a pack rat metropolis, to its right the much larger ice cave entrance, gated in 1972 by the Alberta Forest Service. This closure came about after the publicized visit by the McMaster University cavers in 1967. More visitors led not only to smashed ceiling pendants but also to a rise in cave temperature, causing many of the ice plates to melt and develop small icicles.

Inside it's a glittering fairyland of hexagonal, plate-like ice crystals, extruded fingers of ice, rare and delicate ice flowers and corkscrew stalactites. Apparently, the entrance leads to a large room partially floored with ice. Two decorated passages leave the room, one with a floor of ice and walls and roof covered by ice crystals. The ceiling gradually lowers until it's necessary to crawl under pendent ice crystals into a small ice-filled grotto.

Ice cave entrance.

234 PLATEAU MOUNTAIN, EAST RIDGE LOOP — map 24

Day hike
Unofficial trails, scramble & route
Distance 16 km return
Height gain 680 m
High point 2524 m
Maps 82 J/1 Langford Creek,
82 J/2 Fording River

Access: Forestry Trunk Road (Hwy. 940). A few metres west of the junction with Johnson Creek Trail (Hwy. 532) turn north up a Husky Oil exploration road. Park at the locked gate.

There's no better way up Plateau Mountain than by this east ridge, the narrowest ridge available to scramblers who will enjoy a pleasant amble up broken rock with no exposure. The rest of the loop is easy walking, but given the terrain, slightly tricky from the routefinding point of view, especially if the cloud's down. I recommend biking the first 6 km along exploration roads to well 08-32.

To cirque Follow the road beyond the gate, eventually dropping to meadows alongside a bubbling Livingstone Creek. At km 3 (post) wend left on a shabbier road up a hill (the right-hand road leads to well 07-5, Hailstone Butte and Sentinel Pass).

The new road winds about a lot. You intersect an old road and the pipeline right-of-way from well 07-5, after which the road is both winding and relentlessly uphill. If you've taken my advice you'll likely be pushing the bike. Think descent! After crossing the cirque creek you turn right (another underground pipeline plummets down the hillside to the left), making a beeline for well 08-32 at 2187 m located in the cirque floor . As you face west your ascent ridge is the one on the right. Bounding the cirque to the left is a broad boulder field, scene of many descents with bike.

To summit First you have to climb onto the gable end of the ridge. Cross the cirque creek, then find a truly excellent game trail that tackles the steep grass slope in a rising

traverse from left to right, passing between rock bands en route to the top. The ridge end is flat and broad, mostly grass with stringers of bushy spruce. To your right the ground sweeps so shallowly down to another cirque it tempts you to hop off the ridge and explore its green meadows.

Walk to the base of the rocks. Ahead, the ridge narrows and steepens dramatically. Two steps can be avoided by going around to the right. The first has a rocking stone on the top, the second a crack up the front that can be scrambled up. Smaller steps lead to the plateau at GR774648.

Head southwest to the high point of Plateau Mountain (a scarcely recognizable cairn), located at about GR77264 in the middle of patterned ground.

Return loop Still heading southwest, pick your way across patterned ground to intersect a grassy old road that has forked off the south end road. Turn left. Careful! It's here where bikers go wrong and end up shouldering their bikes down the boulder field above well 08-32. What happens is that you come to a bit of a hollow (well site) beyond which the road carries on in a more easterly direction. Don't follow it. Transfer to a line of upraised rocks to its right, a reclaimed road that leads down to the saddle at GR 782635. En route is a glorious view framed by the steep walls of the southern cirque.

Continue following the line of rocks down the grassy slope to the east. Shortly it turns left (north), becoming a recognizable trail as it traverses flowery hillsides below boulder slopes. In trees it widens to grassy road leading straight to well 08-32.

FOOTNOTE: If you've brought a bike, a 15 minute rush is all it takes to get back to your car. You can be sipping coffee at Laurie's while those poor souls on foot are still flogging it out.

Bottom: Looking along the broad part of the east ridge towards the plateau.

Top: a closer view of the upper ridge showing the two steps.

235 SENTINEL PASS & PEAK from the south — map 24

Day hike
Unofficial trails, route
Distance 7 km to pass
Height gain to pass 305 m
High point 2118 m
Maps 82 J/1 Langford Creek,
82 J/8 Stimson Creek

Above: Sentinel Pass below
Plateau Mountain.

Access: Forestry Trunk Road (Hwy. 940). A few metres west of the junction with Johnson Creek Trail (Hwy. 532) turn north up a Husky Oil exploration road. Park at the locked gate.
Also accessible from Pekisko Creek to Salter Pass (#249).

This is by far the quickest way to historic Sentinel Pass, especially if you've got a bike! Plan on including historic Sentinel Peak which was already named when George Dawson passed below the peak in 1884. The going is easy.

Follow the road beyond the gate, eventually dropping to meadows alongside a bubbling Livingstone River, named, I presume, by John Palliser after fellow member of the Royal Geographical Society Dr. (David) Livingstone. At km 3 keep right on the better road.

In another 1.1 km turn right onto the very much rougher Hailstone Butte fire road which follows the north fork through a scenic steep-sided valley. At GR803669 the north fork dribbles (if it moves at all) through a gap in the left-hand valley wall.

Follow a trail through this gap into a string of flat meadows where the valley opens out. Ahead is Sentinel Peak looking easy pickings from this direction. Note a cutline heading through the trees to the left. Though followable, it's not my choice of route to the pass. I much prefer the meadow route and its easy trail along which many well-known people have trod including would-be prospectors George Pocaterra, reporter Fred Kennedy and the Brewster boys, all in 1931 en route to the Twin Creek gold fields.

So you follow this trail of broken dreams, cutting off corners and crossing the dry creek three times before entering the biggest meadow of them all. Near the head of the meadow on the right is a low grassy gap in the ridge which lures, then disappoints when you find an impossible cliff on the side overlooking Corral Creek.

At meadow's end the creek turns left into a steep-sided draw. The trail crosses the creek at the entrance and climbs steeply up the bank into some trees, emerging a short distance later into the environs of the pass. The trail continues along the right bank top of a short-lived tributary before splintering into game trails unravelling all over flat featureless meadow with low willow bush and clumps of spruce. Plateau Mountain to the west looks impressive while Sentinel Peak to the east looks the place to go for views.

Sentinel Peak (2373 m)

Add 1.2 km from pass, height gain from pass 255 m. Anybody can walk up the gently-inclined backside of this mountain for a fabulous view.

Head north toward the shallow cirque at the head of Pekisko Creek that divides Sentinel's southwest face into two halves. Walk up the right half—trees, grass and finally orange-coloured scree—to the summit ridge and turn left.

If you aren't used to such places, stand well back of the eastern precipice for the rock is unusually friable. There used to be a bronze memorial plaque wedged in the summit cairn but I couldn't find it on the last occasion I was up there. A more fitting memorial for loved ones would be hard to imagine, for this mountain which is such a landmark from the east, is conversely a magnificent viewpoint for these same foothills and prairies (on a clear day you can see Calgary). You can see why it was once touted for a lookout which went to Hailstone instead. For anyone carrying on into Pekisko Creek, this is a wonderful opportunity to sort out the intricacies of the northern half of Sentinel Pass trail where it joins #249 near Salter Pass.

OPTION RETURN
Just as easily, anybody can return to Sentinel Pass trail via the broad south ridge. After a slight rise, the scree is replaced by grass. What a view to the south! The eastern escarpment can be seen in context, running all along a series of ridges with gently-sloping west sides. At the col GR802684 drop 30 m into the big meadow to the right where you can pick up your outgoing trail.

Sentinel Peak from Plateau Mountain. Route from Sentinel Pass (just out of sight at lower right) follows the gently-inclined slope.

236 HAILSTONE BUTTE LOOKOUT — map 24 & 25

Day hikes
Unofficial trails, route & scramble
High point 2363 m
Map 82 J/1 Langford Creek

Access A: Forestry Trunk Road (Hwy. 940). A few metres west of the junction with Johnson Creek Trail (Hwy. 532) turn north up a Husky Oil exploration road. Park at the locked gate.
Access B: Johnson Creek Trail (Hwy. 532) at The Hump parking lot west of the fence.
Also accessible from Pekisko Creek to Salter Pass (#249), and from the western terminus of Iron Creek Pass (#246).

Hailstone Butte is a high grassy ridge, more often than not raked by west winds moving at Mach 2. Quite apart from the two hugely different routes presented here, there are other ways up sans trails. Such as the south ridge route which can be added to A to make a loop. Personally, I'm rather fond of the rocky east ridge from Johnson Creek, which offers glimpses into Johnson Creek's colourful canyon.

Above: The 1952 lookout on the edge of the cliff.

Below: The summit from the south. Route B comes up from the right, taking a line just left of the cliff in profile.

236A Via the Fire Road

Distance 9 km, height gain 543 m. The fire road is the longest, easiest route to the summit. Over half of it has been incorporated into the Husky Oil road system and is best tackled by bike.

Follow the road beyond the gate, eventually dropping to Livingstone River meadows. At km 3 keep right on the better road. In another 1.1 km turn right onto the very much rougher Hailstone Butte fire road.

Enter a steep-sided valley curving around the north end of the butte, the road slowly rising out of the valley onto Iron Creek Pass, a flat, featureless expanse below Hailstone's eastern escarpment. The climb starts here, four easy zigs up grass to the summit ridge. Turn left and make a beeline for the summit.

The lookout is the second one on Hailstone Butte. In 1979 it replaced a one-room box erected in 1952 that was removed in the summer of 1982 after it appeared to be in danger of falling over the eroding cliff edge.

Optional descent via the south ridge is for people who can do without a trail. Prolong the enjoyment by walking south along the broad ridge to a summit of equal height. Plateau Mountain stays in view all the way, blocking distant vistas, while to the south increasingly closer views of the Windy Peak Hills enables you to sort out the various options with future trips in mind. A substantial drop to a saddle is followed by an easy rise to top GR818626. Descend the moderate southwest ridge mostly on grass to Highway 532 from where it's a half kilometre walk back to your vehicle.

236B From The Hump

Distance 1.5 km, height gain 336 m. The quick and dirty route for hikers who can handle a little easy scrambling. Incredibly, the graduating grade 4 class from Nanton Elementary came up this way for 10 years, bearing poems and drawings for the lookout, the teacher being none other than "panorama" Dave Birrell.

Descending route B below the lookout.

Cross the highway onto a grassy ridge. A trail starts up and leads into a valley that sees regular visits by Olga Droppo's class in flower identification. Follow the occasionally faint trail to somewhere around the valley head at GR818645. (There is the option here of traversing the unpleasant scree slope poised above Johnson Creek canyon to the fire road route.)

Turn left and flog up ever steepening grass rolling up to the rock band, either on a rib or via a shallow gully, perhaps weaving around a few crags. Starting a little way left of the high cliff immediately below the lookout (traces of a trail), scramble up the bottom tier of rock. A trail above leads up easier ground to a weakness in the upper band. You should top out a little south of the helipad. Watch that wind!

237 WINDY PEAK HILLS, MIX & MATCH IDEAS — map 25

Half-day, day hikes
Unofficial trails & routes, creek crossings
High point 2249 m at Windy Peak
Map 82 J/1 Langford Creek

Top No. 1 above The Hump. In the background is Hailstone Butte showing the upper part of route B.

Access:
1. Johnson Creek Trail (Hwy.532) at The Hump. Use a parking area on the south side of the Texas gate and pond.
2. Johnson Creek Trail (Hwy. 532) 1.5 km southwest of The Hump. Via trail #238 to Timber Creek Pass.
3. Forestry Trunk Road (Hwy. 940) at South Twin Creek. One km or 0.9 km south of the junction with Johnson Creek Trail park just south of the Texas gate. The exploration road starts between the gate and the creek.

We're talking here about a compact group of grassy ridges of which Windy Peak is the highest summit, lying in the angle between Johnson Creek Trail at The Hump and Forestry Trunk Road. Their greenness and gentle slopes are in keeping with the old name for the northern half of the Livingstone Range: the Comagh Mountains as shown on Arrowsmith's map of 1862. Owing to some configuration of the mountains to the west, the Windy Peak Hills are incredibly windy. Lenticular clouds are a familiar formation above the ridge tops; south- and west-facing slopes are bare, dotted with sprawling mats of krummholz.

It's these open slopes that make the hills so attractive. By using the two trails up the Twin Creeks and by following in-between ridges you can concoct circuit walks varying in length from a few hours to a full day. A few ideas follow.

In 1931 the area around North and South Twin creeks, the Livingstone River and Dry Creek was the site of much hullabaloo when gold was purportedly discovered. The year before, King Bearspaw (grandson of Jacob Bearspaw of Lost Lemon Mine fame) had been prospecting in the area and was being followed around by two prospectors, Billy Windiate and Jack Hagerman, who thought Bearspaw was onto something big. (Well, he did discover the Galena Mine up the Oldman.) When he gave them the slip for two weeks and later turned up at the King George Hotel in High River with gold in his hand, Windiate immediately staked a claim. Fuelled by *The Albertan's* headline "may be lost El Dorado!", everyone immediately thought "Lost Lemon Mine" and before you knew it the stampede was on.

In those days this spot could only be reached on foot or by horse. Some drove to Willow Creek, some to Skeen's Mine, then walked over The Hump or Timber Creek Pass. Others came in over Iron Creek Pass, Sentinel Pass and Beaver Creek. One hopeful walked all the way from Blairmore clad in light clothes and Oxfords carrying a stick over his shoulder from which dangled a large jug of wine at one end and a small sac of grub at the other. For 10 frantic days the locality of the Twin Creeks became Twin City, a camp of 400 odd gold prospectors.

Access 1

The most popular access. Who can resist open slopes rising above the parking lot? A trail develops and takes you to ridge top No. 1 at GR832635 (2179 m). From the summit a lovely open ridge sweeps down to Johnson Creek trail (#239) with which you can make a point to point or a strenuous loop. Or continue over top No. 2 at GR840632 (2149 m) to Timber Creek Pass from where you can again drop into Johnson Creek via #238, or, using the same trail, head west to Highway 532.

Access 2

Using #238 to Timber Creek Pass via North Twin Creek puts you between tops No. 2 and 3. By heading over Nos. 2 and 1 to The Hump you can return alongside Highway 532 on a meadow trail. Alternatively, climb up top No. 3 at GR844626 (2155 m). From the summit, a ridge edged with sandstone crags runs east to Lake-at-the-end-of-the-ridge, a tantalizing eye of blue. Or drop onto the 3/4 col and return down South Twin Creek, crossing the cutblock to North Twin Creek and access 2.

Access 3 via South Twin Creek

Interestingly, Carl Rickert of Rickert's Pass fame had a cabin and trapline up this valley. A little way up you cross to the northwest bank into a huge cutblock that extends north into North Twin Creek. Continue along the old road, climbing gradually now to the col at GR848618.

Either head north to Timber Creek Pass over top No. 3, or climb over top No. 4 and on up steeper slopes to Windy Peak. Return via the northwest ridge (exceptional views of Mt. Livingstone and Hailstone Butte) to South Twin Creek.

The best walk with maximum ridge is to start from access 1, following tops Nos. 1,2,3, and 4 to Windy Peak. Descend the northwest ridge into South Twin Creek, then cut across the cutblock into North Twin Creek (access 2). Return alongside Highway 532 to The Hump. Total distance 9 km, total height gain 683 m.

View from top No. 3 of top No. 4 and Windy Peak.

99

238 NORTH TWIN CREEK TO JOHNSON CREEK — map 25

Day hike
Unofficial trails, flagging and blazes,
minor creek crossings
Distance 6.5 km
Height gain 137 m
Height loss 433m
High point at pass 2057 m
Map 82 J/1 Langford Creek

South access: Johnson Creek Trail (Hwy. 532). Park 1.5 km southwest of The Hump.
North access: Via Johnson Creek trail (#239) at GR847656.

A scenic two-parter using the Timber Creek exploration road through a pass in the Livingstone Range, then a flagged, blazed, occasionally faint trail into Johnson Creek. Use the south half to make designer loops with ridges south of The Hump and with Windy Peak.

View from near Timber Creek Pass of Timber Creek.

To Timber Creek Pass The Timber Creek track starts from the east side of the highway and straightaway crosses the north fork of North Twin Creek. Zig left, then right into North Twin Creek valley with its remnants of spruce forest. Two km from Highway 532 reach Timber Creek Pass at GR842628.

To trail junction On the north side of the pass, where the road traverses steep grassy slopes, you're treated to a colourful view of Timber Creek spread out below in a chequerboard of pines and aspens. The bits of distant blue are Chain Lakes Reservoir. Back in trees, the road winds down to the saddle at GR852640 offering a new view of Hailstone Butte. (The road carrying on into Timber Creek valley is described in the second edition.)

To Johnson Creek At the saddle's right-hand bend, amid piles of orangy-coloured rocks, a narrow trail leaves the left side of the road to a gate in a drift fence. Wend right at easy descent angle through pines growing on shaley ground. A steeper drop precedes a long thin glade, then it's back to the trees again. The trail becomes faint where it emerges on a grassy rib between two creeks (no flagging.) Make a beeline for the left-hand creek—the southeast fork of the south fork of Johnson Creek—and cross at flagging.

In the meadow steer for a flagged tree, then pass to the right of a huge boulder to intersect a trail heading up the south fork. Turn right downstream back into bush. Recross the southeast fork using the second crossing (the first leads to a salt lick), then keep left. Cross a large meadow, veering right and downhill to Johnson Creek trail in the valley bottom.

239 JOHNSON CREEK — map 25

Half-day, day hikes
Unofficial trails, creek crossings
Distance Indian Graves to The Hump 8 km
Height gain 1800 m east to west
High point 2026 m at The Hump
Map 82J/1 Langford Creek

Below: Looking up valley to Hailstone Butte.

Access: Johnson Creek Trail (Hwy. 532).
East Indian Graves campground access road.
West The Hump, summit of Hwy. 532. Use small parking area north of the pond.
In between highway accesses
1. Grassy track on the south side, approx. 6.2 km west of K Country boundary, 100 m west of the intersecting cutline GR869677.
2. Johnson Creek random camping area, approx. 8.3 km west of K Country boundary.
Also accessible from North Twin Creek to Johnson Creek (#238).

This is a complex route using trails, old roads, and a pipeline right-of-way through a beautiful pastoral valley. Walking from end to end seems a bit pointless when the highway is only a few minutes walk away at any given point, unless, of course, you want to emulate Frank DuRocher. Use sections for short strolls or with other trails to make loops, i.e. starting at access 2, head west up Johnson Creek, take #238 to Timber Creek Pass, climb over the ridges to The Hump, then return down Johnson Creek or the

delectable ridge to the east. Also from access 2, head up Johnson Creek to Bear Pond (#241) and return down the north fork (#240). Or, casting an even larger circle, incorporate Hailstone Butte, Iron Creek and Willow Creek (or shortcut via Iron Lake to the north fork).

The creek was known as Johnson's Creek. I don't know why it should be named after Link Johnson, an American steam engineer who worked for DuRocherville Mining, because it was his employer, Frank DuRocher, who discovered five coal outcrops while walking down the valley after the usual trip to look for the Lost Lemon Mine. He built his eight-room DuRocherville on the flats at Willow Creek accessed by a rough corduroy track, the forerunner of today's Highway 532. The DuRocherville mine, however, is not seen on this hike. By all accounts it was a very successful operation, between the years 1918 and 1923 sending coal over the Muirhead trail to Nanton.

EAST TO WEST

Cross the highway into meadows alongside Johnson Creek. A trail appears and takes you upstream. It crosses the creek to the southwest bank and meets a NW-SE cutline. Jog left on the cutline, then right on an old road. On your left a cutline access road climbs to the ridge top. A few metres on cross another old road that takes you out to **access 1** across the river (keep right on the far bank). (For the curious, the road to left delves into a side valley, then climbs up the right-hand hillside and ends abruptly. A game trail carries on, splintering below the northeast face of summit GR865653.)

The valley trail next enters a large meadow occupied in fall by "Animal Shack", a hunter's canvas tent decorated with drawings of dinosaurs and game wardens. Recross Johnson Creek. Keep left and cross the north fork of Johnson Creek into the random camping area which is **access 2**.

Keep left and on old road recross Johnson Creek for a long stint on meadows below coal prospects. Go either way to cross a side creek. The next *good* trail to left is route #238 to North Twin Creek. Shortly after, you cross the south fork below waterfall steps and come to a fork.

South bank trail Go straight, crossing grassy hillside to a ford over Johnson Creek. Keep left as you climb a steep hill that curves around to the left and becomes a pipeline right-of-way. Near the apex of the hill, the north bank trail joins in from the right. Keep straight.

North bank trail The more scenic meadow and aspen route turns right and crosses Johnson Creek straight away. On narrow trail, contour between the creek and the highway, at one point coming within a few metres of the road sign announcing Bear Pond parking lot. On joining the pipeline right-of-way, turn right.

A few steps on, the first (overgrown) trail to Skeen Mine turns right. Keep straight, descend and cross the canyon fork. Climb uphill. At a post a side trail to right offers much the better route to Skeen Mine. The right-of-way continues climbing to a relief section, then ends with stiff pull up meadow to The Hump.

Detour to Skeen Coal Mine
Ernie Skeen (former employee of DuRocher) and Laone (daughter of Ed Mason) later operated their own mine between 1922-26, sending coal down Willow Creek to Rice Creek oil well.

Floods have demolished the upper part of the access "road" and some of the cabin and barn site. On the hillside look for coal spoil and some logs marking the entrance to an adit. Shifting scree has completely hidden a second entrance higher up the slope to the right.

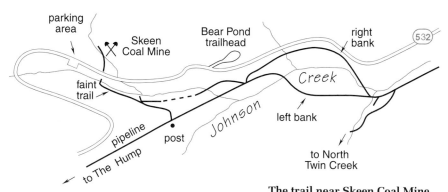

The trail near Skeen Coal Mine

240 NORTH FORK OF JOHNSON CREEK — map 25

Half-day, day hike
Unofficial trails
Distance 2.8 km to meadow end
Height gain 128 m to meadow end
High point 1707 m at meadow end
Map 82 J/1 Langford Creek

Above: Heading up the long
meadow towards the lower slopes
of Hailstone Butte.

Access: Johnson Creek Trail (Hwy. 532). Approx. 8.3 km west of K Country boundary and 5.5 km east of The Hump, park at the random camping area on the east side of the highway just west of the bridge over the north fork.
Also accessible from Bear Pond to Iron Creek (#241).

This short, easy trail leads to the long meadow below the eastern escarpment of Hailstone Butte—a delightful spot where you can idle for hours.

Cross the highway. Follow a trail along the left (south) side of the north fork, in places recognizable as the old logging road dozed by Ed Mason who logged the north fork of Johnson Creek after it was burned over in the 1910 fire. Initially, the trail stays close to the stream, then, narrowing to single cow width, moves away to cross a side creek near a two-log cabin ruin. After crossing a small luxuriant meadow, it returns to the north fork, following a forested bench high above the deeply entrenched stream. In this way, both trail and stream turn west and enter the long meadow backdropped by the eastern buttresses of Hailstone Butte.

Wade another kilometre to meadow's end at the foot of the mountains. At the height of summer the grass grows thigh-high and is resplendent with red and white sticky geraniums and yellow buttercups. En route you intersect the trail between Bear Pond and Iron Creek (#241).

GOING FARTHER

At the far left-hand corner of the meadow at about GR832664 cross a muddy streamlet and still on trail head up a small side valley to the south of the main creek which is now closeted in a bit of a gorge. Be sure to stay on the north bank; don't cross the creek or follow what appears to be a better-used trail branching right near the beginning. When the ground levels, the trail turns right onto a bench below a steep, grassy escarpment carpeted with thousands of blue lupines. A dead tree propped in an upright position marks the end of the trail. Walk a little farther until you can look across at the north fork falling in cascades down a rocky gully. Both the gully and the escarpment are vulnerable to a determined attack by anyone aiming for Hailstone Butte.

241 BEAR POND TO IRON CREEK — map 25

Day hike, backpack
Unofficial trails, creek crossings
Distance to Bear Pond 0.5 km, Big Iron Pond 2.5 km, Iron Creek 3.5 km
Height gain 159 m to Iron Creek
High point 1783 m
Map 82 J/1 Langford Creek

Access: Johnson Creek Trail (Hwy. 532). 10.5 km west of K Country boundary turn right (north) into a parking lot.
Also accessible from Iron Creek Pass (#246), and from the North Fork of Johnson Creek (#240).

Even if you do spend most of your day walking, this is a useful trail for anglers moving on from one fishing lake to another, the only two lakes in K Country to be stocked with Grayling. The country is lovely, a rolling mix of lush meadows, aspen copses and pine forest backdropped by Front Range peaks.

To Bear Pond From the parking lot trudge up a well-used trail likely in the company of anglers laden down with tackle boxes, rods and six packs. Straight off look for some unusual albino Lupines in the first meadow. Just beyond a tiny brown pond the trail splits, going all around Bear Pond. I prefer the right-hand trail for views. So cross the dam built to enlarge and deepen the lake for overwintering trout, then head up the east shore.

At the pond's north end, keep right where a trail shortcuts across to the west bank trail via the lakeshore. At a small round clearing with fire circle leave the lake trail and turn right (north).

To the north fork of Johnson Creek Immediately after a stump on the left side, turn right, climbing gently to the watershed. Keep straight where a trail joins in from the left and drop steeply down the north slope. The trail levels then fades away in a grassy avenue. Make for a clump of three trees at the entrance to the big meadow at the head of Johnson Creek's north fork. A little farther out you'll undoubtedly hit the meadow trail (#240) at about GR835665.

To Iron Lakes Turn left. In a few metres turn right on a fainter trail that crosses the meadow. Jump the north fork and aim for a large cairn where the trail becomes clear. Cross another fork and on a much improved trail veer diagonally right, then up left to a pass on the watershed ridge at GR834673. The pine forest, hereabouts, is cluttered with deadfall.

Don't turn left along the ridge line. Drop down the very steep north slope to Big Iron Lake at a creel surveybox. I recommend a sortie along the south shore for the view of Sentinel Peak across the water. Back at the box, follow the trail around the west shore to the north shore where a strip of "grass" turns out to be tightly packed flowers. From this direction Big Iron is the colour of Big Rock Traditional. Such is the fantasy of hot and sweaty hikers.

To Iron Creek The trail carries on, heading east to Little Iron Lake, then turns north again between little brown pond eyes. Jump a tributary of Iron Creek, then cross a large meadow dotted with willows on loan from a Stephen King movie. A slight uphill precedes a steady downhill to the right bank of another Iron Creek tributary that is followed to a T-junction in Iron Creek valley at GR832683.

If heading east turn right and after about 500 m cross Iron Creek to the main valley trail (#246). If aiming for Hailstone Butte fire road, turn left. Cross the side creek, then Iron Creek via a beaver dam to the main valley trail.

#241. *Looking across Big Iron Lake to Sentinel Peak.*

#242. *A typical scene in Willow Creek.*

242 WILLOW CREEK TO PEKISKO CREEK — maps 25 & 22

Day hike, backpack
Official snowmobile trail with markers,
creek crossings
Distance 11 km
Height gain 192 m
High point 1640 m
Maps 82 J/1 Langford Creek,
82 J/8 Stimson Creek

Access: Johnson Creek Trail (Hwy. 532) at Willow Creek. 3.7 km west of K Country boundary, park at the mouth of a dead-end road on the southeast side of the highway. This is the road nearest Willow Creek bridge.
Also accessible from Pekisko Creek trail (#249), the eastern terminus of Iron Creek Pass (#246) and the western terminus of Stimson & Hay Creeks trail (#245).

This former OHV road is a useful link between Highway 532 and Pekisko Creek trail where you can pick up ongoing connections to Highways 940 and 541. It also serves as an artery for trails peeling off to east and west: Indian Graves Ridge (#243), Willow Creek Hills (#244), Stimson & Hay Creeks trail (#245), Iron Creek Pass (#246) and Corral Creek (#247), all of which can be utilized in a variety of loops incorporating the mother trail. Biking recommended.

Known to Indians as *Stiapiskan*, meaning "Ghost Hound", Willow Creek exhibits none of its sinister connotations. On the contrary, the valley is pastoral, replete with grazing horses and cattle, and bounded by low, friendly hills to the east and the familiar profiles of Hailstone Butte and Sentinel Peak to the west.

Now for the essentials. Start from the opposite (northwest) side of the highway at a gate. At 2 km, just past a side creek, a reclaimed road (#244, Willow Creek Hills) turns off to the right. A few metres on, pass a cutline access road on the right, then intersect an E-W cutline. The first side road to the left—very much grassed over—

is Iron Creek Pass trail (#246). Intersect a N-S cutline. The next side road to right, (followed in quick succession by two cutlines), is another route onto the Willow Creek Hills.

Cross a larger side creek, then ford Willow Creek. Corral Creek trail turns left in the big meadow just before the road recrosses to the north bank (bypass trail available). In 1 km ford Willow Creek for the third time. Straight off, at GR845716, a trail heads upstream along the west bank, offering an alternate route to the GR837726 mark, as well as access to route #245 over the hills to Hay Creek.

The road follows a side creek, then crosses into the valley of the west fork that arises under Sentinel Peak. Descend meadow to the west fork and cross at GR837726 where the alternate trail comes in from the right. Veering left, the road threads a gap in the hills to the north, leaving the Willow Creek drainage for that of Pekisko Creek.

Enter a long meadow holding two dark ponds. 1.5 km downstream of the ponds, keep left and cross the pond creek to the west bank. Arrive shortly afterwards at the four-way road junction with Pekisko Creek trail (straight, left with snowmobile sign) and the road to Devil's Bite (right) which crosses into Sheppard Creek and so passes out of K Country.

Following the fence along the ridge top.

243 INDIAN GRAVES RIDGE — map 25

Half-day, day hike
Unofficial trail & route
Distance 2.9 km, 4 km to well site
Height gain 198 m
High point 1661 m
Maps 82 J/1 Langford Creek,
82 J/8 Stimson Creek

Access: Johnson Creek Trail (Hwy. 532) at Willow Creek. 3.7 km west of K Country boundary, park at the mouth of a dead-end road on the southeast side of the highway. This is the road nearest Willow Creek bridge.

The shapely ridge on the north side of the highway above Willow Creek bridge is a huge attraction to campers from nearby Indian Graves who on any given weekend can be spotted crawling up the craggy west face. A much easier route exists. Read on....

Start from the opposite (northwest) side of the highway at a gate. Almost as soon as you set foot on Willow Creek OHV road, turn right up the buried pipeline right-of-way. Cut left through a belt of aspens to open slopes above. As the slope steepens

head right for the barbed-wire fence and its trail which follows the grassy southeast ridge to the top. The steeply dipping rocks of the west face have been eroded into tight arches called flatirons.

You can easily extend the walk by following the fence trail north along the undulating ridge line to GR883711. The views are unexpectedly fine for so modest an altitude.

GOING FARTHER

At ridge end the trail drops to a gap, then, still following the fence, climbs to Dome Petroleum's well site at about GR873718. If you've got this far you may as well utilize either the ascent or descent trails for route #244—depending on how far you want to walk, 7.5 km or 10 km—and make a loop back to your starting point.

244 WILLOW CREEK HILLS — map 25

Day hike
Unofficial trails
Distance 4.5 km, total loop 10 km from
Willow Creek trailhead
Height gain 265 m
High point 1743 m
Maps 82 J/1 Langford Creek,
82 J/8 Stimson Creek

Below: Looking out to Hailstone Butte and its foothills from the west side of the ridge.

Access: Via Willow Creek (#242), 1.5 km and 3.5 km from the trailhead.

An easy walk to a viewpoint on the Willow Creek Hills. If you do the loop, route finding is easier in the clockwise direction.

Two kilometres from the trailhead at GR876693, turn right onto a rehabilitated exploration road signed "No Motorized Vehicles". It's easy to confuse the road with a better defined cutline access road a few metres farther on. Look for a bright green swath that sweeps north, then west of a small creek dividing the Willow Creek Hills from Indian Graves Ridge. The "road" ends at a gap in the hills near a fenced-in meadow at GR873718, a Dome Petroleum well site during the 1970s.

Pick up a trail that climbs half a kilometre up the ridge to the south. This is a heavenly spot. Spring comes early to these hills and although the snow lingers on Hailstone Butte and Sentinel Peak to the west, here on the open hilltop, the silky shimmer of new grass is already resplendent with magenta shooting stars.

Loop This requires a little more expertise in routefinding. Retrace your steps a few metres and look for a steep trail descending the west side of the ridge, a rather nebulous trail between widely-spaced pines for the first little while. It soon develops into a good trail and then into a road. Intersect a minor NE-SW cutline. In a short distance, re-intersect the cutline, disregard a cutline access road heading right, then keep straight at a four-way junction with a major NW-SE cutline, carrying on down the road. Intersect a minor cutline near the bottom of the hill just before exiting onto Willow Creek trail at GR860707.

If you walk the route in reverse direction, this road can be identified from neighbouring cutlines by its easier angle and by bands of red and blue paint encircling the occasional tree on the uphill slope.

245 STIMSON & HAY CREEKS TRAIL — map 25

Day hike
Unofficial trails, creek crossings
Distance 11 km to Willow Creek, loop
19.5 km
Height gain 421 m
High point 1734 m
Map 82 J/8 Stimson Creek

Access: Johnson Creek Trail (Hwy. 532). Park at Stimson Creek 1.5 km west of K Country boundary and 2.3 km east of Willow Creek bridge. The trail is signed "No Motorized Vehicles" at the trailhead.
Also accessible from Willow Creek (#242) at the 6 km mark.

Limber pine.

Using old roads, this route takes in the headwaters of Stimson and Hay creeks, then crosses the Willow Creek Hills to Willow Creek. Make a loop with #242 if you can hack 2.5 km of road bashing to get back to your starting point. Alternatively, this is a perfect trail for a Thanksgiving Day stroll!

Gaining little height, the grassy road follows the east bank of Stimson Creek through meadows rutted by cow trails. To your left beaver ponds alternate with dams of varying ages making lines across the valley floor. At the forks, the track follows the right-hand (north) branch through a wooded defile into a south fork of Hay Creek. Be alert for turkeys scratching around in the undergrowth. Experts think they're an offshoot of turkeys released as an experiment on the Porcupine Hills in 1973.

Nearing Hay Creek valley, the road crosses in quick succession the south fork, then Hay Creek itself upstream of the confluence. From down below, Limber pines crowning the long ridge bounding the valley to the east resemble an unrestrained bonsai garden.

In a large meadow you turn left, following a new road that heads west along the north bank of Hay Creek toward the Willow Creek Hills. Cross a N-S cutline and wade through waist-high grasses to a high point on a side slope—a satisfying viewpoint where contented cows have flattened out deep depressions. At the height of the colour change the hiker who has got this far is rewarded by the dazzling tapestry of aspen forests blending orange, yellow and rich green-gold colours depending on clones.

Shortly after the road descends to creek level it turns south and makes a beeline across the willowy mouth of the west fork to a big meadow where it peters out. It picks up again at the point where it turns west into the spruce forest of the upper south fork. After passing a large beaver pond and dodging precariously balanced aspens, zig right, then left up open slopes onto the backbone of the Willow Creek Hills. To view Hailstone Butte and Sentinel Peak you have to make a detour to the south.

Continue through a gate in the drift fence, then descend forested west slopes to Willow Creek, which is reached just north of the tiny side creek you have followed down the hill. At GR845722 you intersect a trail running alongside the creek.

For Highway 532 turn left. Shortly after crossing to the west bank, you join Willow Creek OHV road at GR845716. (For Pekisko Creek turn right and join the road at GR837726.)

#245. The trail in Stimson Creek before it turns up the right fork.

#246. Starting the descent into grassy upper Iron Creek from Iron Pass.

246 IRON CREEK PASS — map 25

Day hike
Unofficial trail, creek crossings
Distance 8.5 km to pass
Height gain 570 m
High point 2057 m
Map 82 J/1 Langford Creek

Access: Via Willow Creek (#242), 2.8 km from the trailhead.
Also accessible from Hailstone Butte fire road (#236A) and from Bear Pond to Iron Creek (241).

Incredibly, this trail was once part of a well-used route to the Livingstone River from Nanton, dating back to at least 1913. The trail is good and clear to Iron Lakes turnoff. After that, the final stretch out of the valley to the pass is confusing.

At GR869696 turn left onto a grassy old road. Ford Willow Creek, then swing left to join a NW-SE cutline. Turn left and a few minutes later, on the north bank of Iron Creek, turn right onto a continuation of the road that shortly refashions itself into two diverging cutlines. The left-hand NE-SW cutline is the one you want, but because the start is overgrown, follow a cow trail along riverside meadows until a trail returns you to the cutline. About a kilometre farther on, turn left at a four-way intersection onto the old pack trail.

The trail leads back to the creek for a brief sortie on the south bank. Back on the north bank, you cross the (same) NE-SW cutline, and begin a steady climb through pine forest to salt licks and the sunny aspen woodlands of mid valley. In a large meadow where the trail is lost, the general line of travel is obvious and you should have no trouble getting back on track. Two trails crossing the creek access the trail to Iron Lakes.

About 6 km from Willow Creek the valley narrows dramatically, with steep rocky slopes pressing in from both sides. The trail is much less distinct, especially in the area of a drift fence stretched across the valley floor. After the fence watch carefully for where the trail crosses to the south bank and back. At the big bend to the south, avoid rock steps laced with falls dried up in the heat of summer by a sharp climb up scree to the bank top.

Soon after the trail flattens veer left above the falls and follow bits of trail between dense spruce thickets back into the creekbed above all difficulties. Pick up a trail on the east bank. Higher up, the trail switches to the west bank and is plainly seen climbing out of the grassy valley head onto the pass below Hailstone Butte. You can picture the scene back in 1931 during the Twin Creeks gold rush: weary prospectors leading their pack-horses around those spruce thickets, maybe adjusting a pack or two before the final push. Two women who were along had the right idea. Why take a chance on their being gold when they could set up a stopping house and get money from board and food? So they staked a claim on the spring right at the head of the creek which is not a place I would have chosen myself.

The pass is a spongy expanse of sedges and spruce thicket, dotted with tiny beer-coloured ponds. Rather than squelch through the middle of it, contour under the white rock ridge to the right until you can pick up the trail again on drier ground. Hailstone Butte fire road is reached at the point where threads of water trickling out of the fen are gathered into a culvert under the road and emerge on the far side as the infant Livingstone River. If making for Hailstone Butte lookout, turn left. For Sentinel Pass, walk down the fire road for 1.2 km to where another branch of the Livingstone River comes in from the north, then follow route #235.

247 CORRAL CREEK — map 25

Day hike
Unofficial trail, creek crossings
Distance 5 km
Height gain 290 m
High point 1798 m
Maps 82 J/8 Stimson Creek,
82 J/1 Langford Creek

Access: Via Willow Creek trail (#242). 4.2 km from the trailhead turn left at GR857712.

Although the Corral Creek exploration road doesn't go anywhere—it dead-ends below the unassailable face of Sentinel Peak's eastern escarpment—it does open up some really fine foothills country for people wanting to get off the beaten track.

Right at the start don't be misled by a white sign luring you across the creek into cutblocks on the north bank. The Corral Creek exploration road heads up south bank meadows for half a kilometre before crossing to the north bank. Shortly, recross to the south bank for a long stretch before crossing No. 3 below the forks. So far the valley has been flat and open; the tinkle of water spilling over beaver dams a constant background noise.

With a crossing of the north fork the scenery changes drastically. Begin a steep climb through dry pine forest, stopping often to admire the bristly hill behind you at GR830707 (likely a more worthy objective). At the top of the hill intersect a NW-SE cutline offering a route of sorts into the more pastoral headwaters of the north fork and onward to the six-way junction on Pekisko Creek trail.

Descend and for the fourth time cross the main fork of Corral Creek and a much smaller stream arising from the little cirque at the valley head. The road dead-ends in another kilometre, deadfall in every direction discouraging further progress. In any case, cliffs are blocking the way ahead. (The low point in the cirque rim is easily reached via route #235.)

Looking towards the valley head. The low point is easily reached via route #235.

248 BEAR CREEK — map 22

Day hike
Unofficial trail, creek crossings
Distance 9 km to pass
Height gain 564 m
High point 1966 m
Maps 82 J/8 Stimson Creek,
82 J/7 Mount Head

Access: Drive Highway 22 south of Longview to the Bar U Historic Site. Turn west onto Pekisko Creek Road (Hwy. 540) and drive past St. Aidan's church to a junction with the historic E. P. Ranch, owned for 43 years by Edward, Prince of Wales. Keep right, entering the Cartwright Ranch. The Cartwrights are agreeable to visitors passing through their land en route to Kananaskis Country as long as you ask permission. On occasion the gate across the road at the ranch buildings is kept locked during times of high fire hazard or when the road is too poor for driving. About 2 km past the ranch buildings you arrive at Miller Creek Road junction. Park here. The trail starts between two posts in the angle between the two roads.
Also accessible from the southern terminus of Zephyr Creek (#258).

The pack trail up Bear Creek connects with Zephyr Creek trail at Zephyr/Bear Pass and up to now has been used mainly by hunters after sheep and bear. Providing you take precautions and remembering that no hunting is permitted on Sundays, don't let this fact deter you from visiting Bear Creek in the fall when the valley is at its most beautiful.

Initially, the route is an old road that makes a beeline for the gate in the K Country boundary fence. Keep left, and still on the road head southwesterly across the skirts of the hills toward Bear Creek. Shortly after the second side creek crossing intersect a NW-SE cutline on the oblique and then a major NE-SW cutline at a right angle. The road descends to Bear Creek and turns up valley, en route crossing another side creek and a second NW-SE cutline.

The open hillsides of the north slope.

Where the valley pinches in, the road reverts to pack trail. Apart from one five minute section along the south bank halfway to the col, the trail winds in and out of the folds of the hills high on the north bank, traversing dry, open hillsides luxuriating in the warmth from the midday sun, even in late fall when ice is curdling on the stream below you and there is a dusting of snow on the shaded facets of Grassy Mountain to the left.

As you climb higher, the number of cattle dwindles to twos and threes, the hillsides become stonier and patches of dark spruce appear—survivors of the Phillip's fire. At the valley head the trail climbs to the right of a round, forested hill, aiming for the lowest gap between Bear and Zephyr creeks at GR747785.

The view from the col is cut off by hillsides and ridges in all directions so I suggest you either climb up the grassy slope to the north, or, if you have an hour to spare, get onto the north ridge of Mt. Burke which is vulnerable to a determined party from several locations near the pass.

113

249 PEKISKO CREEK TO SALTER PASS — maps 22, 25 & 24

Day hike, backpack
Unofficial trail, creek crossing
Distance 13.5 km from Miller
Road junction, 8.5 km from K Country
boundary
Height gain from boundary 396 m
High point 1935 m
Maps 82 J/8 Stimson Creek,
82 J/7 Mount Head,
82 J/1 Langford Creek

Above: the view from the bench of Sentinel Peak (left) and Plateau Mountain. The route follows the defile between Sentinel Peak and the forested hill to the right.

Access: Drive Highway 22 south of Longview to the Bar U Historic Site. Turn west onto Pekisko Creek Road (Hwy. 540) and drive past St. Aidan's church to a junction with the historic E. P. Ranch, owned for 43 years by Edward, Prince of Wales. Keep right, entering the Cartwright Ranch. The Cartwrights are agreeable to visitors passing through their land en route to Kananaskis Country as long as you ask permission. On occasion the gate across the road at the ranch buildings is kept locked during times of high fire hazard or when the road is too poor for driving. About 2 km past the ranch buildings, you arrive at the Miller Creek Road junction, a possible parking spot if Pekisko

Creek Road to left is in too bad shape. In order to drive a further 5 km to the K Country boundary, you need dry conditions and a vehicle with good clearance.

Keep left, then. Ford Pekisko Creek at a picnic area and bump along to McConnell Flats named after resident Gordon McConnell who was lost in a snowstorm and perished. It was also the site of Alberta's first weather station, set up in 1890 by Duncan Cameron (of Cameron's Lookout and former bookkeeper at the Bar U). To your right a side road descends to a picnic area above McConnell Falls.

Pass through a second gate level with Major Burke's house. Ford Pekisko Creek a second time and pass through a third gate. The road re-crosses the creek near its confluence with Greenfeed Creek at a picnic area, then climbs uphill to a parking area at the Kananaskis Country boundary fence.

Also accessible from the northern terminus of Willow Creek (#242), the northern terminus of Sentinel Pass (#235) and the eastern terminus of Salter Creek (#250).

The old Indian trail up Pekisko Creek (George Dawson used it in 1884), later turned cattle trail to Cataract Creek, since augmented by cutlines and exploration roads and formerly the domain of the explorer, range rider and hunter, is finally a mountain bike trail, a section of something called "the Willow Creek Wanderer". This is not what you wanted to hear, but don't cross it off your list of hiking trails. It's still a good trail for people on foot who want to explore the lovely meadow country at the back of Mt. Burke. Backpackers should use it in conjunction with other trails to make loops, such as Sentinel Pass, Iron Creek and Willow Creek, or Salter Creek, Lower Cataract Creek, Zephyr Creek and Bear Creek.

It's really an extension of the Pekisko Creek Road that carries on from the boundary fence across the long meadow to the site of Pekisko Ranger station, built by Freddy Nash and removed to the Cartwright Ranch in the 1950s. 1.2 km farther on there is an important four-way road junction. Willow Creek (#242) is straight ahead (snowmobile sign). You turn right (west), following a vegetating road also marked by snowmobile signs. Descend to riverside meadows. A feature of this route is the number of side roads and cutlines heading west into the foothills below Mt. Burke, something that people yearning to get off the beaten track can take advantage of. (The first of these is the Salt Creek cutline which leaves the right-hand side of the road a few metres above the confluence and gets you in position to climb foothill GR786757.)

Keep left and climb onto an open bench with a grand view of Sentinel Peak and Mt.

Burke, the valley between backstopped by Plateau Mountain. In another 2 km the road ploughs through a five-way, star-like intersection with cutlines. Opposite the third side valley to the west the road fords Pekisko Creek.

Entering the enclosed upper valley, the road faded to track rises gradually along the grassy northwest flank. From close-under, Sentinel Peak is an arresting sight; it's hard to realize this mountain's an easy walk-up from the back. On your right, a cutline zooming up the hillside is one you can safely ignore! Level with the forks, the easterly approach to Sentinel Pass trail—a cutline—plummets equally steeply to the west fork from the left-hand side of the track (see option).

This signals an overall steepening for the next half kilometre, beginning with two zigs. Keep right and come to a three-way junction in a clump of spruce where the westerly approach to Sentinel Pass turns left (see option).

The main track continues on the same line, traversing a steep grass slope above snow fences to the track's high point which is in the trees and viewless. Descend, keeping right, into a large meadow—Salter Pass more or less—where a beautiful view is revealed of Mt. Burke's southeast outlier and Salter Meadows. See Salter Creek (#250) for the ongoing route to Cataract Creek campground.

OPTION
Sentinel Pass
Distance 6 km, height gain 350 m, high point 2118 m. Long before there were roads, a trail between the plains and the Oldman River ascended Pekisko Creek to the pass between Plateau Mountain and Sentinel Peak, then descended to the Livingstone River. After being used during the Twin Creeks gold rush of 1931 the trail was neglected for decades, no doubt owing to the intrusion of exploration roads and cutlines overlying everything and locked gates discouraging access. Too bad we can't preserve some of these historic routes.

Nowadays, not too many people reach the pass from this direction even though it can be achieved in one very long day from Salter Creek. The usual route is from the south via #235. With two vehicles and interchangeable bikes consider a point to point between the two trailheads....

From Pekisko Creek trail you must first descend into the west fork of Pekisko Creek. There are two ways of doing this:

1. From the east via cutline 1.4 km east of Salter Pass descend a steep shaley cutline into the west fork close to the forks. Ascend an equally steep hill out of the valley onto a bench above the south fork. At a T-junction with the west route road (overgrown to the right) turn left.

2. From the west via old roads About 750 m east of Salter Pass watch for a three-way junction in the clump of trees immediately following the grassy side slope with snow fence. Turn right down a grassy road into meadows just above the west fork. Where the better road swings left stay right on another road that crosses the dry boulder bed of the creek and, better defined, climbs gently onto a bench above the south fork. Push through a scrap of dense overgrowth to a T-junction with the cutline. Keep straight.

Walk south along the grassy road which shortly reduces to trail. Here is a chance to examine the upcoming headwall and the old trail seen zigging up scree to the left of the rock band. In half a kilometre you cross the creek, then follow the east bank to a tangled meadow watered by a muddy side creek where the trail is lost. Follow a game trail up the left bank of the side creek until above the mess of downed trees, then cross and wade meadow to the trees on the far side where you should pick up the old trail. It's quite obvious.

As you climb, the trail's pleasant windings change into tight well-constructed zigs up a scree slope to the left of the encircling rock band. A long traverse to the right leads to a grassy bench above the cliff. At the cairn, descend slightly, aiming to cross the south fork on flat ground between two gorges. More zigs through trees gets you to the top of a second bench. Gradually the trail fades in low brush, not that it really matters, for the final stretch to the pass is an easy walk up open slopes. However, in reverse direction you could well have problems locating the trail.

Likewise, finding the trail heading south is just as difficult. The pass is wide, flat and featureless. Basically, keep left and pick it up on the north bank of the infant Livingstone Creek.

Option, Sentinel Pass. On the long traverse up the headwall below the cliffs of Sentinel Peak.

250 SALTER CREEK — map 24

Day hike
Unofficial trail, creek crossings
Distance 7 km to pass
Height gain 283 m
High point 1935 m
Map 82 J/7 Mount Head

Sentinel Peak peeking over Salter Pass. This is the meadow where the trail divides. The major trail to Pekisko Creek veers left into the trees.

Access: Forestry Trunk Road (Hwy. 940) at Cataract Creek campground access road. A few metres before the campground gate turn right into a small parking lot. Backtrack to an old road marked by a snowmobile sign which starts near Salter Creek bridge.
Also accessible from the western terminus of Pekisko Creek trail (#249).

Salter's Brook—with an apostrophe—was named by George Dawson in 1884 after his packer. He moaned, just as you will, about the stony creekbed that is continually crossed and recrossed. Nonetheless, this is flat easy walking between Plateau Mountain and Mt. Burke to the pass between Salter and Pekisko creeks.

Almost straightaway the old road crosses Salter Creek to the south bank, then winds pleasantly for the next 1.8 km or so through meadows and aspen groves to Plateau Creek which carries the water. Cross. Up to now the valley has been wide and pastoral, but now the walls close in and are clothed in spruce forest. The road is forced back and forth across the dry stony creekbed 14 times. The flash floods of 1995 have done a thorough wrecking job in rearranging the creekbed so you'll just have to go with the mess. 2.5 km from the trailhead, the two starts to Mt. Burke trail turn off to the left at cairns marking the spots.

After this junction carry on in much the same sort of way, or follow a higher trail along the left bank—the original pack trail up Burke. After a side creek crossing, the valley floor widens and the slopes on both sides break out in slabs, scree patches and thrusting buttresses pockmarked with intriguing caves. Shortly after crossing side creek GR768715, avoid a section of stony track by transferring to a bypass trail on the left side. Keep right at a junction; the left-hand trail, overlain by branches, leads to Salter Meadows. Back on track, enter a long meadow extending to the pass, en route crossing Salter Creek for the last time at a fire ring and horse rails. Up ahead, the top half of Sentinel Peak is poking up above the gap. In the vicinity of the pass the better track to Pekisko Creek veers left into the trees. A few metres along, a side trail leads to a campsite with running water.

EXPLORING FARTHER

At the indistinct junction in the vicinity of the pass follow the meadow track to the true pass at the demarcation of meadow and forest, as you go noting a trail returning to the Pekisko Road. The track descends and ends shortly, but a trail continues, curving around to the right into a meadow with a magnificent view of Sentinel Peak. The question is, does this trail continue into the valley below Plateau Mountain ice cave? Here's scope for further exploration!

OPTION
Salter Meadows

On the bypass pack trail keep left instead of returning to the main valley track. Step over the branches. The trail crosses a side creek, follows the right bank a way, then climbs dry sandy meadows to a rib from where it heads at a much easier angle to the col at GR784718 on the southeast ridge of Burke.

I'm pleased the meadows have become part of Plateau Mountain Ecological Reserve. As if to prove the point, Audrey, Harry and Jackie of CRAGS discovered growing here the Pygmy bitterroot (*Lewisia pygmaea*) which the authority firmly states is found only in Waterton.

Now from the col you can either wander up the grassy ridge to the left or onto the bouldery top to the right for a fresh perspective of Plateau Mountain and Sentinel Peak and the pass in between. It was while sitting on the boulder top stuffing ourselves with fruitcake that we became aware of a Wolf spider staring up at us with eight big black eyes. Then we noticed another one, then dozens more rushing toward us from every direction, rappelling down vertical faces as fast as they could go. Muttering "aargh" we were off of there in two seconds flat. So eat your lunch anywhere else!

View from Spider Rocks of the meadows and the south peak of Mt. Burke.

251 MOUNT BURKE — map 24

Day hike
Unofficial trail
Distance 8 km to summit
Height gain 845 m
High point 2450 m
Map 82 J/7 Mount Head

Access: Via Salter Creek (#250).

Mt. Burke certainly looks intimidating to non-scramblers. That this mountain was chosen for a lookout is amazing. Even more amazing is the pack trail that was built to the summit along the southwest ridge, an exciting route on a par with Black Rock in the Ghost. Bring water and a 1:250,000 Kananaskis Lakes map for identification of major peaks.

Cameron Lookout.

Set off up Salter Creek. At 2.5 km an old wood sign tacked to a tree "To Cameron Lookout 3 miles", possibly totally consumed by porcupines, points to the start of the trail to your left. There are actually two starts: a shortcut followed 50 metres farther on by the more gradually-inclined lookout trail. Both were marked by cairns, and tin cans on sticks in the creekbed until the 1995 flash flood washed it all away. I'm told someone has rebuilt the cairns.

The soft forest trail corkscrews back and forth up the tapering ridge to treeline. A short, grass slope is prelude to an unimaginably wild landscape of yellow scree slopes and cliff bands that could frighten the fainthearted beginner hiker.

Cross the crest of a short rocky ridge badly exposed to gusting crosswinds. This was a traumatic place for pack horses who were often led one at a time across this narrow section to more comfortable slopes beyond. On the final approach to the summit, you can either stick to the trail that traverses scree slopes above a rock band or scrabble up the ridge direct, being careful not to trip over the old telephone wire protruding here and there from the rocks.

Cameron Lookout's standard 12 x 16 ft. floor space occupies the entire summit. Built in 1929 (see cornerstone), it was superseded in 1953 by Raspberry across the valley to the west. Although it lacks a door and is generally in a dilapidated condition, it serves well enough as a refuge from wind. The original cooking stove complete with kettle is still in the corner, but the old-fashioned oil heater was removed when the lookout was abandoned and now resides in the Forest Technology School museum in Hinton. You are probably wondering where the lookouts got their water from in the days before helicopters. It seems it was a chancy, even risky business that involved suspending a bucket over the northern precipice to catch drips percolating down through the summit boulder field.

The lookout trail originally started from Pekisko Creek. By coincidence Duncan Cameron ran Alberta's first weather station in 1890 at McConnell Flats, while Major Burke, sheriff for High River, lived nearby in a house that can be seen during the drive up Pekisko Creek.

#251, Mt. Burke. On the rock ridge, looking west to the Great Divide.

#252, Lower Cataract Creek. Upper Falls from the viewpoint.

252 LOWER CATARACT CREEK — maps 24 & 22

Half-day, day hike
Unofficial trails, creek crossings
Distance 14.5 km, to upper falls 4.2 km
Height loss S-N 198 m
High point 1652 m
Map 82 J/7 Mount Head

South access: Forestry Trunk Road (Hwy. 940) at Cataract Creek campground. The route (old road) starts behind campsite #27. Alternatively, a trail leads onto the flats from between sites #72 and #73.
North access: Highwood Trail (Hwy. 541) at Sentinel day-use area. Follow the access road toward the picnic area. The route (logging road) starts from the south bank of the Highwood River opposite the parking area with interpretive sign "Trails through time".

True to its name, lower Cataract Creek is an attractive blend of waterfalls, deep green pools, riffles and quiet stretches where the water moves lazily over shallow pebble beds.

Most campers head for the upper falls. Adventurous hikers should consider going right through, utilizing the old pack trail that crosses the creek three times. Bear in mind the Highwood River at the north end is impassable during runoff and over knee-deep the rest of the year.

SOUTH TO NORTH, DOWNSTREAM
From campsite #27 a grassy road heads down the flats for 2.7 km to the side creek at GR733756, en route picking up the trail from campsite #72. Since the second edition the river has shifted east, engulfing two chunks of road. In both cases transfer to a trail along the bank.

Cross the side creek and turn left on a rough trail running along the east bank of Cataract Creek. At questionable places look for yellow flagging. For instance, at the first junction turn left downhill. Cross a dry, stony gully. Less than 100 m on is an important flagged junction offering a choice of route. If just going to upper falls viewpoint, keep straight.

Via upper falls Keep straight. Shortly the trail climbs the bank to a junction. Go either way; both trails join at a superb vantage point for upper falls above a rocky bluff. Likely this is where Doctor George came to a shuddering halt in 1884. He and his party tried to get down Cataract Creek to the Highwood but "two miles below Salter's Brook" came abruptly to the edge of a gorge into which the river plunged "making a picturesque fall". Finding no vestige of a trail beyond and thinking it would be difficult if not impossible to take animals farther, they turned back and went up Salter Creek instead.

To the pack trail Just beyond trails's end walk up the hillside for about 70 vertical m. The drop-off on the left peters out just before you intersect the trail (flagging and blazes). Turn left down the hill.

Via the flagged, blazed horse trail The trail turns right up the grassy bank onto a bench, then corkscrews up the slope to a higher bench. Head left, ultimately intersecting the route from the falls at the point where the trail, better defined, *starts to drop*. Descend, initially on stony ground (cairns), then above cliffs to a cairned junction. (The left-hand trail leads to the river slightly upsteam of the ruddy-hued weeping wall featured in a K Country poster.)

Go straight, climbing over a side ridge to grassy headlands overlooking middle falls. Descend more gradually to river level, following the odd cairn around the first half of an S-bend to an easy ford marked by blazes on the east bank and a large cairn on the west bank. Luckily, the water is subdued for the next 1.5 km, because it's crossed twice more before the trail settles on the west bank for good.

A long canyon of chutes and pools forces the trail high on a bench where it joins a logging road just after the side creek crossing at GR715814. The next side creek is the turnoff to Mt. Mann. At canyon's end the road enters lovely riverside meadows where you're tempted to linger. Likely you'll miss the turnoff to Zephyr Creek.

Lower falls drops into the last canyon. Here, the road climbs around the east ridge of Mt. Mann, then moves away from the creek and descends to flats bordering the Highwood River. Wade the river to the parking lot on the north bank.

To Zephyr Creek

Turn right at GR715832, your new "road" positively identified a little way in by a large square rock. In 200 m it fords Cataract Creek and, much improved, rises slowly through pine forest into that large meadow north of Mt. Burke. Head right and intersect the Zephyr Creek exploration road (#258) near the edge of the trees.

View from Mt. Mann of lower Cataract Creek and the long north ridge of Mt. Burke. Over the ridge is Zephyr Creek and the deep gash of Painted Canyon.

OPTION
Mt. Mann 1905 m, GR708841
4.5 km return from trail, height gain 396 m.
This is the hill looming over Sentinel day-use area. The name "Mann" was in common use before the 1920s, perhaps commemorating Mackenzie and *Mann* who had a tie camp on Cataract Creek in the early 1890s. It's also known as The Battleship.

This is by far the best way up (says me, who's twice been up from the soggy east side for some stupid reason). The south ridge route uses game trails; in fact, the problem here is *too many* game trails. Plan on a separate day from Sentinel day-use area.

At side creek GR714819 follow a game trail along the right bank (ignoring side trails crossing the creek and others heading right) until level with a draw on the right (north) side. Climb either the draw or the grassy ridge to its right (for the view). Using game trails, continue in the same direction and intersect the broad summit ridge.

Starting just right of the crest, follow the ridge trail through alternating trees and meadow. It's more undulating than you think, and ends with a steep pull to the summit. The meadow on the east side is a lovely viewpoint.

253 LOWER ETHERINGTON CREEK & HELL'S RIDGE — map 21

Half-day, day hikes
Unofficial trail, creek crossing
Distance 6.5 km between accesses
Height loss S-N 152 m
High point 1646 m
Map 82 J/7 Mount Head

Access: Forestry Trunk Road (Hwy. 940).
South end Just north of the entrance to Etherington Creek campground, park in a small parking area on the east side of the highway just north of Etherington Creek crossing.
North end Just south of the bridge over the Highwood River there is a small parking area for one vehicle on the west side of the highway at the sign "Logging Trucks". Alternatively, park at Highwood Junction where you're in position to call in at Laurie's after the hike.

Some might consider the original highway along the east bank of Etherington Creek as "wasting your time in the Canadian Rockies". Personally, after the stress of being in a city all week, I find this easy forest trail just the tonic. One late fall we kicked aspen leaves about and laughed at the antics of five Blue grouse.

Ideally, walk south to north in the downhill direction and have a vehicle at both ends. One problem to doing the whole trail is that you have to wade Etherington Creek at the north end. Still, on a hot day this may be just what you're yearning for. Alternatively, traverse Hell's Ridge which encloses the valley to the east, and return to your starting point via the old road (or vice versa). Or use it as a side trip to a grassy hilltop with a great view.

Looking south along Hell's Ridge.

South to north
Cross the highway bridge, then turn left. The old road starts between two boulders meant to deter OHVs. The trend is downhill, though undulating, and you can get a good stride going on the smooth grassy-earthy surface of the old road which displays its age by occasional outbreaks of corduroy. Though views are few, the forest of aspen, spruce and pine is very open, so there isn't a closed-in feeling. Twice you draw close to Etherington Creek which lies at the bottom of a canyon. Who would have thought it!

Pass through the drift fence near a pancaked shack. A little farther on you descend more steeply a shallow draw between a mini ridge on the left and the north end of Hell's Ridge. The road flattens, winding right, then left to the Highwood River flats. It comes within a stone's throw of the river, then turns left, running parallel to it into a meadow, a dumping ground for carcasses. Watch for where it turns sharp left into the trees, then resumes its parallel course to the river, passing to the left of a private trapper's cabin built in 1978. Keep

123

left and arrive at Etherington Creek. Wade the shallow end of a pool with flat shingle bottom. On a stinking hot day this is the place to be: sitting on an underwater ledge at the deep end with an ice cold can of pop from Laurie's close to hand. OK, so she doesn't sell beer. You'll have to bring your own.

On the west bank it's easier to follow the creek upstream a very short way before climbing up the bank via the cow trail that reaches Highway 940 opposite the north end parking area.

Incidentally, for those of you doing the route in reverse, there are some superior bathing pools in Etherington Creek just across from the south end parking lot.

Hell's Ridge

9 km loop from south end, height gain N-S 573 m, height loss N-S 427 m, high point 2057 m at GR702791. Two-thirds of the ridge dividing Etherington and lower Cataract creeks is covered in pines. Not too much there for the walker you would think. Ah, but have you noticed the northern third that is grass? It turns out to be a truly terrific flower garden, worth a paddle across Etherington Creek. And what's more, a good game trail runs all along the ridge top to GR702791 and beyond. There are no good trails onto the ridge but getting there is not too strenuous.

To the ridge The ridge is most easily accessed from the drift fence on Lower Etherington Creek trail. Either climb hillside to its left or follow a game trail up the draw a little distance to the right. The forest is open everywhere. Basically, you follow one side or the other of the fence, lying in trip position, up a side ridge to the ridge top at GR688824. The upper slope is all grass, and ends with 2 m of scrambling.

A fantastic view has opened up of the High Rock Range and the Highwood River valley. Maybe you'll be lucky like us and watch entranced as an Antique Automobile Club pays a visit to Highwood House for gas and coffee.

Walking north A trail runs south along the ridge top out of the trees into meadows sweeping down the west slope into Etherington Creek. And what meadows they are, the grasses long and rippling in the west wind, punctuated here and there by picturesque Limber pines. This leads into the roller coaster section which features three grassy humps, more humpy-looking from the south side. It's mainly here where you'll find flowers growing in the damper hollows: masses of Silky lupines and... well, I'll let you make your own list. Views are even more extensive and now include Junction Hill through Holy Cross Mountain to the Bull Creek Hills where you can pick out a half dozen routes. Return the same way or....

Continue to GR702791 Shortly the trail enters pine forest spilling over onto the west side of the ridge. Except on rocky ground the trail is generally clear. At low point GR701794 the trail disappears in grass. Pick it up again at a steepening of the ridge where the trail climbs from right to left to regain the ridge top. Note some flagging on a tree. Shortly after the second flagged tree the ridge walk ends on top GR702791. If uncertain where you are, a meadow on the south side enables you to use your GPS. (The trail seems to continue southwards, but I've never followed it.)

Turn west and descend a moderately steep pine ridge with a couple of relief sections. Keep right of a creek all the way down, threading together bits of game trail and ground disturbed by hooves. Gain Lower Etherington Creek trail just north of the side creek, which, for anyone doing the ridge in reverse, is the first side creek you come to when walking the valley trail from south to north.

The name of the ridge is not mine. The drift fence gives you a clue. It was named long ago by rancher Carson Rogers who in his own words "had a hell of a time rounding up the cattle".

254 CAT CREEK TRAILS — map 21

Half-day, day hikes
Unofficial trails, creek crossings
Map 82 J/7 Mount Head

Access: Kananaskis Trail (Hwy. 40). NOTE: This section of Highway 40 is closed between December 1st and June 15th.
1. Park at the side of the highway 3.3 km north of Highwood Junction or 2.3 km south of Cat Creek bridge.
2. Cat Creek day-use area. Use the first parking area on the left opposite the picnic shelter.
3. 300 m south of Cat Creek bridge, park on the north side of the highway at the entrance to a logging road.

The elk corral in Deer Head Meadows.

Although George Dawson reported coal in the Highwood as early as 1882, it wasn't until 1910 that Harry Ford leased 11,637 acres of government land at one dollar per acre per year and developed what came to be known as the Ford Mines at Cat Creek. In winter it was a perpetual struggle to keep the wagons moving along the Lineham Company Road which, of course, was the forerunner of Highways 541 and 40.

As you see from the sketchmap, by using the Mine Haulage Road, the camp road, a recent logging road and shortcut trails, you can have a fine time devising your own routes varying from easy half-day wanderings to a full-day trip around Cat Creek loop.

To the Mine

From access 1: The Mine Haulage Road

Distance 4 km to the forks, height gain 143 m. Deer Head Meadows offers the longest and most beautiful approach, but know the bears love it too, so don't go alone.

The old road leaves the north side of the highway and circles into the southeast end of Deer Head Meadows, a long, erstwhile channel of Cat Creek winding sinuously between the Cat Creek Hills and a low forested ridge to the southwest. Despite what is shown on the topo map, no river runs down it. You travel at the foot of the southeast ridge of the Cat Creek Hills, bend

right, then swing back left past the elk corral where elk were tagged some 15 years ago. Ahead, the draw dead ends at a seasonal pond, blocked by gravel deposits now covered in trees.

The road climbs onto the forest ridge to the left. At a junction with the better camp road keep right and wind around the head of the draw past a road descending to the pond. After the left turn, note a grassy road (#255) heading right onto the west ridge of the Cat Creek Hills, then a road to left shortcutting across a bog to the camp road. Bear left (grassier road ahead) and watch for where the trail from accesses 2 and 3 joins in from the left at blazes.

Descend to the forks, en route passing an adit and, low down, a side road to the right at GR632877 (cairn) which is route #255A up the Cat Creek Hills.

Cross the side creek to a road junction in the meadow at GR631878—a perfect camping spot close to Cat Creek. There used to be a corral in the angle between the two roads.

Turn right. The road climbs along the north bank of the side valley to a division. A right turn leads to the mine site where there's little to see other than coal spoil, filled in adits and the remains of a bridge in the creekbed below.

From access 2: The camp road

The shortest route to the forks using shortcut trails between zigs. Distance 2 km, height gain 113 m.

Walk back to the highway and turn right. As soon as you've crossed the bridge over Cat Creek turn left onto a grassy strip cutting across to the previous highway—a wider grassy strip. Follow it to the left through aspen meadows with cattle. Just before Cat Creek (bridge out), step right onto the camp road connecting Ford's camp and the Haulage Road. (The camp was located across Cat Creek in the big meadow crossed by the interpretive trail.) Unless you want to make a wide sweep to the right via road, look for a red fleur-de-lis (dating back to the World Scout Jamboree in 1983) marking a well-used shortcut climbing the bank. On regaining the camp road turn left and round the bend (another fleur-de-lis). Not too far along, turn left on shortcut trail number two which climbs well back from the canyon rim and joins the Haulage Road (blazes) shortly before its descent to Cat Creek. Turn left.

DETOUR to falls viewpoint
Just before the bend on the camp road, step left on a narrow trail. In two ticks you're looking between your toes at lower Cat Creek Falls and tourists.

The surefooted can continue on a somewhat dicey trail to a viewpoint for the upper falls, then climb to shortcut number two.

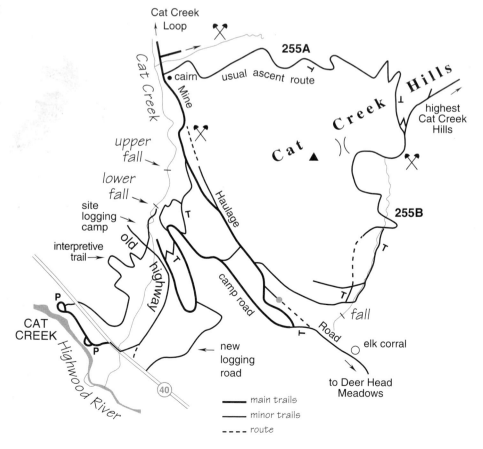

Cat Creek Loop. The pass at GR644890.

From access 3: Logging road

A variation on access 2. Follow the logging road uphill through pines into a Post and Rail cutting area. After the road turns left and ends in a small meadow transfer to a narrow cutline-like trail that emerges between two trees daubed with orange paint onto a bit of grass adjoining the camp road. Turn right and join access 2 near the bend.

Cat Creek Loop

Loop 5.5 km from the forks at junction GR631878, height gain 283 m, high point 1954 m. A more strenuous trip taking in two forks of Cat Creek and the pass between at GR644890. At high water creek crossings can be tricky.

Anticlockwise Turn right (east). The road climbs along the north bank of the side valley to a division. Go left. The road ends shortly. A blazed trail carries on, undulating across grassy banks, at one point dipping to the creek. Even before you reach a circular meadow for orientation the trail is already turning north to climb a draw (pines and alders) to the pass at GR644890. Actually, the trail forgoes the gap and climbs onto the ridge to the east where lopped trees reveal a view of the Highwood Range.

Why not take a side trip higher up the ridge into meadows? With two vehicles, consider crossing ridge GR660878 to the pass GR663867 at the head of route #257, a route which surprises you with its marvellously open aspect.

But back to the trail which continues down the north slope on a rib. Low down another trail joins in from the left. In valley bottom go either way at a split to the bank of another east fork of Cat Creek.

Cross and head downstream on a trail hard to spot in long grasses until after it crosses a north fork. At a blowdown in a meadow detour left and enter the narrows, a lovely kilometre-long stretch lined with cliffs, the creek, embowered by tall firs, rushing through chutes and over little steps. Shortly after crossing the mouth of a dry gully, the trail crosses to the south bank and makes a beeline for the end of a road.

Follow this road all the way to the start of the loop. Where it crosses the creek and back, stay on the left bank. Next up is a difficult crossing of Cat Creek at high water. That safely accomplished, head south on Cat Creek's west bank, in less than a kilometre recrossing to the east bank. (Omitting both crossings is very trying.) The final pleasant stretch is punctuated by having to cross a corner of the creek under an outjutting outcrop of coal.

255 CAT CREEK HILLS, MIX & MATCH — map 21

Day hikes
Unofficial trails, routes
High point 2149 m
Map 82 J/7 Mount Head

The summit. Behind is Junction Hill.
Route #256 follows the right-hand ridge.

Access: Via Cat Creek Trails (#254). See sketchmap.

These smooth grassy hills with outcrops of sandstone conglomerate rise enticingly to the east of Highway 40 at Cat Creek. They're especially delightful in fall when snow blankets the mountains to the west. As you can see by the sketchmap for #254, numerous variations can be made using the following three routes and the Cat Creek trails.

255A From the Mine Haulage Road at GR632877

2.3 km to summit, 4.2 km from Cat Creek trailhead via access 2, height gain 478 m, 591 m from access 2. The longest, easiest approach.

To the west ridge At GR632877 (cairn) turn right on a side road that climbs gradually across the south slope of the side creek through spruce forest, with glimpses now

and then of the mine site across the creek. The road disintegrates where it climbs a filthy draw between coal banks, but at the top resumes its form and easy windings. One long zig with alder infiltration gains you the west ridge. Below the exit the road splits. The best option goes left in two short zigs. Going straight requires tunnelling through alders, but strangely, as shown by the fleur-de-lis symbol at the exit, this was the route used by World Scouts in 1983. Route #255B comes in from the right.

To the summit Turn left past prospects. The road soon ends, but a good trail carries on along the west ridge above a sandstone escarpment allowing views of Cat Creek loop. A steep finale up meadow ends at the apex of west and southwest ridges. Actually, the true summit lies a little higher in trees but there's little point in going because this is much the better viewpoint for the Great Divide.

255B From the Mine Haulage Road at GR635868

The direct route onto the west ridge which also happens to be the steeper and more scenic route, uses two exploration roads and a trail bridging the gap.

The turnoff from the Mine Haulage Road is a little hard to spot, the road being grass at this point. It improves as it traverses grassy hillside above the seasonal pond. Go either way at a split. Within spitting distance of a V-shaped draw where this particular road ends above a small crag with seasonal waterfall there is a junction. What you do next depends on how much water is running down the draw.

If water is running, and this is also the nicest route in reverse, head left up a connecting road to a T-junction with a parallel road also ending in the draw. There is a gap of about 100 vertical m between here and the upper exploration road. Walk left a short way, then climb grassy hillside to the left of the draw. Higher up, where the angle steepens, a trail heads diagonally right below outcrops, then crosses a steep grassy slope on the side of the V to a coal prospect. This marks the bottom of the upper exploration road which is really an extension of the road used by #255A. Follow the road back to the draw.

If the draw is dry simply walk up it and intersect the upper road.

The upper road winds beautifully, recrossing the draw and climbing gradually up the left side of it into pine forest covering the west ridge. Note a fleur-de-lis marker on the left. In meadow keep left, unless you wish to take in the fabulous view from the prospect at the end of the side road to the right. Back in trees, the ground levels and route #255A come in from the left side of the ridge at a fleur-de-lis marker. Keep straight for the summit, following directions for #255A.

Descent via the southwest ridge

A beautiful route to Deer Head Meadows on partial trail.

From the summit head down the grassy southwest ridge. A trail, which develops as you climb through some trees, takes you through a small rock band toward the rocky knob GR648868. Unless you want a scramble, use the trail that traverses left and slips over the shoulder of the knob and down the other side to a col. Climb in trees, but, again, before reaching the top GR645864, traverse left to gain its south ridge. Descend a short distance to a flagged dead tree where you're treated to an uninterrupted view of the Highwood River valley. Here descend the west flank, a simple grass slope funnelling into a shallow draw filled with aspens. In Deer Head Meadows turn left for access 1, or right for access 2.

Descending the southwest ridge. View through the flagged dead tree of Mist Mountain and the Highwood River valley.

#256. One of many beautiful Limber pines on Junction Hill's south ridge.

256 JUNCTION HILL — map 21

Half-day, day hike
Unofficial trails & route
Distance to col 1.5 km, to summit 3 km
Height gain 678 m
High point 2233 m
Map 82 J/7 Mount Head

Access: Kananaskis Trail (Hwy. 40). 1.3 km northwest of Highwood Junction, or 4.3 km southeast of Cat Creek bridge, park on the west side of the highway at a viewpoint parking lot. Your trail (coal exploration road) leaves the east side of the highway a few metres to the south. NOTE: This section of Highway 40 is closed between December 1st and June 15th.

The high predominantly grassy hill overlooking Highwood Junction to the north and called Junction Hill by rangers is mightily attractive to cattle, grizzlies and humans. While you can wander up the south slopes *almost* anywhere, the suggested route starts you off on a good trail that in itself makes a good half-day trip to a col. The rest is mainly route, a moderately steep pull up the south ridge to the summit, one of the Highwood's great viewpoints. With two vehicles, consider combining this route with #257.

To the col The grassed-over coal exploration road heads across lovely meadows with Limber pine sentinels. Numerous offshoots head left to prospects. Below on the right, Highwood House comes into view as well as a fenced-off experimental plot and birdhouses for bluebirds so old, according to Laurie, no one can remember who put them up. Later, the road winds in and out of copses and crosses two tiny creeks, after the second turning left and climbing straight for the col at GR658848. Through the gap is the distinctive shape of Mt. McPhail and the other peaks of the High Rock Range.

This last straight I forever acquaint with a hazard facing every hiker—the cattle drive. We had just left the col in the down-ward direction when we ran into some of X's cows. Some cattle just ignore you, but not this bunch. After the initial stampede, we managed through subterfuge to give most of them the slip, except for this one obstinate critter with a will of her own who outmanoeuvred us at every turn, we all ending up—she included—on the highway under the southeast ridge, 300 m lower down and nowhere near where we had started from. I've felt guilty about it ever since and hoped the X ranch wouldn't sue for harassment. So never mind the grizzlies; watch out for cows.

To the summit If going for the top turn right (north) and find the good game trail that traverses the two-headed knoll on its left side to another col at GR659852. Strike up the south ridge, a broad grass slope at this point dotted with Limber pines that will send you into raptures (see one example in photo opposite). Above the grass the angle eases and you crunch overlapping rock tiles among pines, keeping left all the while. At a flattening the summit comes into view, revealing a clear passage between shaley cliffs and last gasp trees on the right. An unexpected narrow finale brings you to the summit cairn perched above the precipitous east face which is quite a revelation if you haven't done #257.

For such a small hill the view is panoramic and includes the Highwood Range, all of the High Rock Range, the flat skyline of Plateau Mountain, Mt. Burke, Hell's Ridge, The Elevators and Beehive Mountain and Raspberry Ridge. With a geological map at hand it's kind of fun to trace the Kootenay strata northwards over the Cat Creek Hills to Mist Ridge.

257 FORD HIGHWOOD COLLIERIES ROADS — map 21

Day hikes
Unofficial trails
High point 1990 m at pass
Map 82 J/7 Mount Head

Access: Highwood Trail (Hwy. 541). 1.9 km east of Highwood Junction and 9.2 km west of K Country boundary park at the entrance to a gated road on the north side of the highway.

These two routes head up a tributary of Stony Creek not shown on the topo map to the unnamed pass at GR663867 just northeast of Junction Hill.

The two routes come courtesy of Ford Highwood Collieries who built the roads in 1944-5 while prospecting for coal on the east flank of Junction Hill. So while the title is accurate, it conjures up visions of the mines at Sparwood, which it is not. Meadows are the lure as you can see in the photo above, and the chance of picking off Junction Hill by the southeast ridge. I

should warn you the old roads are obliterated in spots, replaced by trails or infiltrated by alders, so some routefinding skill is needed.

Follow the road to the site of Ford Highwood Collieries camp, later a Minimum Security Camp, and most recently a camp for Young Offenders. Walk up steps to a playing field. Aim for the far left-hand corner to the right of a small creek and bench. In the forest, the road continues uphill to a junction.

Above: View from the valley road of Junction Hill (left) and pass GR663867.

257A Valley Road

Distance 3.5 km to pass, height gain 488 m. Keep straight, following the flagging. The road climbs gradually past a sawmill site to right and seemingly ends in the bog of a Stony Creek tributary. A trail carries on in a dead straight line across the waterlogged ground. Step over two rotting trees, balance precariously over rocks and corduroy, finally jumping the tiny creek. So what if your feet are wet from getting off route to look at Round-leaved orchids? On the far bank in aspen forest a trail heads upstream above the creek, now incised between grassy banks. Watch for where it turns right in road mode paved in long grass. Reaching meadows, it zigs left, right, left again, then apparently ends in some trees at a T-junction with a trail. Turn right, following the trail into more meadow. To your right, across a grassy draw is a grassy ridge at GR670860, a mere five minutes away and a fabulous viewpoint for your objective and Junction Hill which looks amazingly steep from this side. Farther to the right you look down into Stony Creek and across at the grey sides of Mt. Head and Holy Cross Mountain. End the trip here, if you like, lolling around squashing Silky lupines and geraniums.

But back to the trail. It enters trees to the left of the grassy draw and is narrow and faint in spots. Just after a similar trail joins in from the left, it reverts to road and meets the ridge road in an area of alder infiltration. You'll have to take my word for it!

So you keep right here and in the shadow of Junction Hill, traverse meadow and shale to the pass. (It's fruitless to follow the road higher up the hillside to cut No. 9.) This is a surprisingly dramatic spot, pinched between the verticality of Junction Hill and a lower ridge to the northeast whose dribbling pink screes make a nice contrast to the bright green grass. As you can tell by lopsided specimens of spruce and Limber pines, the west wind blows strongly through the gap.

257B Ridge Road

Distance 5 km to pass, height gain 520 m. Turn left. At the end of a long straight, five long zigs through a varied forest with openings back to Mt. Mann puts the road in a position to traverse the eastern escarpment of Junction Hill. Pass prospect No. 11 on the left and do a little pushing through encroaching alders. Coming up is the place where you transfer from one road to another. This occurs at a bend where the road starts to rise (soon ending, miles below the ridge top). At a cairn on the right side turn right onto a narrow trail and take 20 steps *in the downward direction* to a road end. I'm not sure whether it was intentional these two roads should never meet.

Follow the new road that continues following the line of the Holt coal seam past further prospects. Enter meadows. The high point is marked by prospect No. 6 not far below the southeast ridge of Junction Hill (see option). The road descends from this point, gradually infilling with alders so jam-packed it requires an off-road detour to reach the valley road junction. Keep straight and head for the pass.

OPTION FROM RIDGE ROAD
Junction Hill (2233 m) via the southeast ridge 1.2 km one way, add 304 m height gain. Trail, then route.

If you have a couple of hours to spare, who can resist a summit? Start from the high point of the ridge road at prospect No. 6. To its left a sheep trail makes a beeline for the ridge up steep grass. Near the top take the right-hand fork above small crags.

Junction's southeast ridge is a messy hodgepodge of rocks, trees and grassy hummocks. In some places you may be more comfortable traversing below a surprisingly sharp slabby crest. Some scree precedes the final grassy runout to the summit cairn. (See also Junction Hill #256 in case you want to do a two-car traverse.)

---

258 ZEPHYR CREEK — map 22

Day hikes
Unofficial trails, creek crossings
Distance 4.5 km to pictographs,
7.5 km to Zephyr/Bear pass
Height gain to col 520 m
High point 1966 m at col
Map 82 J/7 Mount Head

Access: Highwood Trail (Hwy. 541) at Sentinel day-use area. Turn first left into a parking lot. **Also** accessible from the western terminus of Bear Creek (#248).

Nine times out of 10 the archaeologically inclined will head up Painted Creek to the pictographs. Other options are Zephyr/Bear pass at GR747785, and for the keen ridge walker who's packed a spare pair of legs, the north ridge of Mt. Burke. The whole trip hinges on the crossing of the Highwood River.

From the far end of the parking lot head east on trail to the riverbank. Wade the Highwood River. On the south bank pick up an old road wending left to a T-junction on the west bank of Zephyr Creek with an E-W road. Turn right and follow this new road, keeping left, into the large meadow below the north ridge of Mt. Burke. On beaten-down grass follow the perimeter of aspens around to the left, through a few trees and into another arm of the meadow where the Cataract Creek connector comes in from the right. Turn left into the confines of Zephyr Creek valley. All is now simple. The road heads south on flat valley floor, crossing Zephyr Creek twice. Opposite the first side valley to the left, a cairn marks Painted Creek junction at GR731818.

To Zephyr/Bear pass Continue on the valley road, climbing through pine forest rapidly thinning to meadow. The road downgrades to trail, then crosses the creek and rises gradually to a sentinel rock where it cuts left up a steeper slope to the pass.

Looking back down Zephyr Creek to Holy Cross Mountain, Gunnery Creek and Pack Trail Coulee.

OPTION
Painted Creek

At Painted Creek junction turn left and cross Zephyr Creek. The trail heads into Painted Creek valley (which is heavily into white rock), crossing the creek six times, just easy steps across. At the narrows where two ridges meet look for rock paintings on a yellow, slightly overhanging wall on the left side, about 1 m up from the ground. In 1975 part of the wall collapsed, taking with it six of the eight paintings which lie in fragments beneath your feet—a jigsaw that can never be reassembled. What remains is a stick figure of a running man closely pursued by a large animal with erect ears and a long tail (buffalo?), and half of a bird trailing feathers which lies half a metre to the right. Higher up, tally marks presumably have some significance, though to me it looks like the artist, work done, was merely wiping his fingers on the rock to get rid of the red ochre. The artists, it seems, were Kootenai Indians who lived in the foothills some 300 years ago pre Stoneys, the paintings being the successful conclusion of a Vision Quest ceremony.

Let's get this clear! Pictographs are rock paintings and petroglyphs are rock carvings. Painted Canyon has both in at least two different locations which accounts for the awful confusion of visitors, even Stoneys who brought offerings of cloth and tobacco. Daniel Wildman Jr., of Morley, wrote in October 1923, "in the Spring you see on the rock pictures of tipis, pictures of people hunting the buffalo with their war bonnets on. The next time you will visit the spot the pictures are all changed, all different. It is a house with a ball on top, or a man walking followed by many dogs, or again the full moon. Next time, all the paint is changed, somebody is shown going up the mountains to hunt animals, to hunt bear, goat, sheep and jumping deer. Next time it will be the picture of a moose. At other times it is the moon with seven horizontal lines under the moon". I'm sure the recipient of the letter ethnographer Marius Barbeau said, "thank you very much"! But

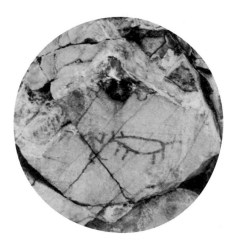

Rock painting at the narrows.

wait. There was a new development. Councillor James Rider of the Bearspaw Band added, "the pictures I had seen before had moved up higher. That is the third time they had moved up to my knowledge".

The upper pictographs/petroglyphs are much higher up the ridge. Climb a steep scree gully, then head left up a ramp of broken rock to gain the crest. Have fun looking for an entire bird, dancing figures and spirals.

OPTION RETURN
North ridge of Mount Burke 2292 m

Distance to ridge from col 1.8 km, round trip from trailhead 19 km, height gain to ridge from col 341 m, height gain from trailhead 1012 m. The hikeable half of Burke's north ridge is 8 km long, almost dead straight and undulates like the Loch Ness Monster. Scrambling can be avoided.

Starting from the sentinel rock at GR746784, head south up the left-hand headwater of Zephyr Creek. A narrow trail climbs the right bank, then when the angle moderates crosses to the left bank and climbs gradually to the wooded gap at GR748780. The trail continues, traversing a headwater of Bear Creek to the grassy saddle at GR752774. Now turn west and slog up steep grass to the north ridge, gained at about GR748773 (cairn). The view along both halves of the ridge is spectacular.

The ridge walk Heading north, drop easily to a col. Next up is an alarming looking rock step about 60 m high. The difficulty can be bypassed by a trail that cuts across the screes of the east face to the ridge beyond. If taken direct, traverse left and down below a cliff, then zig back right via a scree ramp, steeper and more horrible than it looks. From the top, be sure to look back at the celebrated Mt. Burke fault as shown in Geological Survey of Canada Memoir 291 (1958).

An easy section ends with a pinnacle signalling a steeper descent on slabby crest where you can take to the stony west flank. Cross an easy top to a col where a sheep trail joins in from the right.

This is where the ridge changes character, broadening and softening, though still undulating, a mix of rocks, Dryas, Juniper, Kininkinnick and trees. Opposite Painted

Creek you enter the meadow section and climb over two tops. Make a long gradual descent into trees where a trail materializes and takes you down to where the ridge divides into two arms. Veer left past a Vision Quest site, then swing right and down the draw between the arms. Emerge in the big meadow and pick up the trail from lower Cataract Creek that takes you out to Zephyr Creek trail.

Right: the pinnacle which is easily bypassed.

Below: The 8 km-long ridge from GR748773, showing the col and the scrambler's route up the rock step.

259 GUNNERY CREEK — maps 22 & 21

Looking back down the creek from near Gunnery Pass. Gunnery Mountain at top right.

Day hike
Unofficial trails & route
Distance 3.5 km to pass, 4.6 km to #260
Height gain 396 m to pass
Height loss 91 m to #260
High point 1875 m at pass
Map 82 J/7 Mount Head

Access: Highwood Trail (Hwy. 541) at Eyrie day-use area.
Also accessible from Wileman Creek (#260) in the big meadow at GR707888.

This is the creek distinguished by O'Shaughnessy Falls No. 2. Locals refer to it as "the creek at Gunnery Grade". Let me explain. A little farther west, above the present highway, you can make out the line of the pre-1920 road blasted out of rock by Billy Gunnery and called "Gunnery Grade under Billy Gunnery's Mountain". Back then there was a steep drop from the road to the Highwood River which has since migrated across the valley bottom. Continually undermined by the river and blocked by scree slides, it saw frequent accidents and closures. One scene from the 1926 Hollywood western "His Destiny" was filmed on this spot with ranger Freddy Nash, dressed in drag, doubling as leading lady Barbara Kent. Unfortunately, the movie's not available on video.

Use this lovely valley trail as an alternate route into Wileman Creek, as a quick approach to Holy Cross Mountain, or with Grass Pass (see #260 for details) to make an easy circuit *nearly all on grass* which is sure to become a classic. Alternatively, if used to steeper slopes with scree, and are capable of routefinding, climb to the notch or Gunnery Mountain for the view. From the latter two you can make loops using the highway—a chance to examine Gunnery Grade at firsthand.

To the pass The trail starts to the right of the falls at the top of the bank. After the initial climb, you traverse steep hillside above a mini canyon which gradually shallows out into meadows and aspen copses. Cross the creek nines times (usually dry), No. 9 crossing being level with the notch between Gunnery Mountain and Holy Cross. End up on the west bank. Go either way at a split, then cross a side creek in a draw (route to the notch).

Ahead is the final rise to the pass, a basin of easy-angled grass dotted with bushes, spruce and Limber pines. En route, join a better trail coming in from the left (remember this junction on the descent). It too fades, then reappears to take you through a draw to the pass at the demarcation of meadow and forest. The open ridge to the right can be followed to Grass Pass.

To Wileman Creek The trail heads downhill in spruce forest. Keep left (uphill trail likely connects with Grass Pass), go either way at a split, then keep left. Below steep meadow (route to Holy Cross Mountain), the trail curves right and down, becoming vague in an area of poplars. Just keep on the same line and pick it up again for the final stretch into Wileman Creek's big meadow. Cross to the east side of the meadow and join the very obvious old road that is route #260.

OPTION FROM GUNNERY CREEK
The Notch between Gunnery Mountain and Holy Cross Mountain at GR701864. Distance from Gunnery Creek 1.4 km, height gain 170 m, high point 1969 m. A terrific viewpoint reached by a game trail.

The trail is hard to pick up from the valley end. After hours of walking back and forth the best I can come up with is this: Leave the main trail at the side creek in the draw and follow a trail up its left bank to intersect another good trail. (Should you go right you'd end up at Gunnery pass.) Either turn left and where the trail starts to descend turn right up a fainter trail that climbs below a spring to intersect the traversing notch trail. Or, turn right across the draw, then on faint trail climb aspen hillside to gain the notch trail on the draw's right bank. (Unfortunately, the notch trail to right peters out in foraging meadows.)

In both cases turn left, gaining height slowly through forest, the trail improving markedly where it climbs across a scree slope into the spruce-filled notch between Gunnery and Holy Cross mountains. Follow it through the notch (lined with crags) to the meadows of the west exit with its surprise view of Highwood Junction and the Great Divide.

Return via creek to west The trail continues down and across the stony west slope. After crossing a V-shaped draw, it turns left down a ridge between the draw and a creek falling off Holy Cross Mountain. Where the ground levels, the animals head off towards Stony Creek on an unravelling trail. Follow the left (east) bank, staying high on terraces, sooner or later hitting a trail that takes you out to the highway.

OPTION FROM THE NOTCH
Gunnery Mountain GR702861 2088 m, add 122 m height gain. From the notch's west exit it's a simple plod through open pine forest to the summit cairn. The view is very much more extensive and now includes Mt. Burke, Plateau Mountain, Beehive Mountain and Junction Hill.

Return via the southwest ridge Head south along the summit ridge to the cairn where the southwest and southeast ridges fork. Descend the rocky right-hand ridge at the edge of cliffs. At one point it's easier to take to the trees of the west flank before returning to the grassy ridge of lower down. Intersect the east bank trail of the creek that takes you out to the highway.

View from the notch between Gunnery Mountain and Holy Cross of Baril Peak.

260 GRASS PASS TO TRAP CREEK — map 22

Day hike, backpack
Unofficial trails
Distance 3.2 km to pass, 9.5 km to
Trap Creek
Height gain 427 m
Height loss 305 m
High point 1875 m
Map 82 J/7 Mount Head

Access: Highwood Trail (Hwy. 541) at Sentinel day-use area. Turn first left into a parking lot.
Also accessible from Trap Creek (#262), and from Gunnery Creek (#259).

If you love meadows and Limber pines, this is the walk for you. Raked by warm Chinook winds, grassy Grass Pass is a popular choice for the short days of early spring and late fall. In summer with longer daylight hours I would extend the walk, either onto the Bull Creek Hills or connect up with Gunnery Creek to make a loop.

Following the road closure through crown land, this old exploration road is now the preferred route into Trap Creek with its own host of ongoing options. The lovely south fork of Trap Creek was named after Harry Wileman, a Montgomery type as described by Patterson, who was ranger at the Sentinel Ranger Station during the fires of 1936. Tragically, he died on the job in 1943 after an accident with a runaway team of horses. Although the fires devastated most of the Highwood Valley, Trap Creek and adjoining Sullivan Creek, somehow this valley remained largely unscathed. The spruce trees still grow tall here.

To Grass Pass Return to the highway and walk right (east) for a short distance. Just after a road sign announcing Sentinel day-use area, turn left onto the trail heading up Pack Trail Coulee. At the top of the initial climb turn left onto the old road, a junction marked by a recumbent Douglas fir. The forest in the lower part of the valley is filled with these old giants. After the track flattens you're into gnarled wind-twisted aspens. Jump the val-

Upper Wileman Creek, looking north to "Trapezium".

ley creek and make the final climb to the pass through bunch grass meadows below ridges flaunting shapely Limber pines. According to the Calgary Field Naturalists Society, this is a recommended place to view hawks. Unlike flowers that keep still, hawks can be notoriously difficult to identify, usually because they're so high in the sky. To complicate matters further, there are 'Immatures' and 'dark phases' to consider. If you hear "Keeeer-r-r, keeer-r-r" it's the more common Red-tailed hawk, a sound I lump together with loon calls and wolf howls in evoking the Canadian wilderness. If you haven't already done so, look behind for a bird's-eye view of Zephyr Creek and Mt. Burke.

Just before the pass is a star-like junction where you can choose an ongoing option. I haven't yet looked into it but possibly a forest trail heading northwest joins route #259 in upper Wileman Creek below Gunnery pass.

Holy Cross Mountain in close-up. The easiest route follows the right side of the shaft, then above the top rock band veers left to gain the east ridge just below the summit.

To Trap Creek via Wileman Creek Head north, descending below the open slopes of the Bull Creek Hills, a view ahead of a trapezium-shaped hill used as a surveyor's camera station in 1911. Enter a large, flat meadow resplendent in spring with magenta shooting stars where route #259 comes in from Gunnery Creek. From this vantage point your eyes are drawn to the Highwood Range on the left where clouds tend to get hung up on Mt. Head and Holy Cross Mountain.

From this close in scramblers can take a good look at Holy Cross' central gully which together with a large horizontal ledge conform lingering spring snow into the shape of a cross. First ascensionist Raymond Patterson climbed up the shaft of the cross in August 1937, and called it very steep. Sixty years later we found the slope merely moderate but endless. On June 6th, 1992, Don Forest, the first person to climb all 11,000 footers in the Canadian Rockies, celebrated his 72nd birthday on its summit with wine, birthday cake and presents.

Here's some more information for scramblers that alone is worth the price of

Grass Pass from the trail to ridge GR712868. Photo shows the trail to the Bull Creek Hills (top left) and the trail to Fir Tree Point (right).

the narrows. The valley opens out again near the confluence with Trap Creek. At a junction turn left and head west to Trap Creek crossing. Climb the bank to the T-junction with Trap Creek trail (#262) at GR715934.

OPTIONS FROM GRASS PASS
Fir Creek Point
Distance 1.2 km one way, height gain 15 m, high point 1890 m. Little effort is required to gain a better viewpoint.

At Grass Pass turn right (east), then immediately right onto a five-star cow trail that takes you out to Fir Creek point past two springs where generations of cattle have congregated. The point is a levelling of a broad ridge falling south from the Bull Creek Hills that overlooks Fir Creek. I love being among Limber pines and here is one of the most famous: Raymond Patterson's Boundary Pine. Apart from missing a bare arm, it looks pretty much the same as it did 60 years. Refer to the photo on the title page.

Ridge GR712868 and Gunnery Creek
Distance to ridge 800 m, to Gunnery Creek 2 km, height gain/loss to Gunnery pass 90 m, high point on ridge 1965 m. A slightly more strenuous trip to another Limber pine hot spot. Why not make a loop with #259?

At Grass Pass turn left (west). A former OHV road climbs steeply up the grass, levelling off as it veers south. Keep left here. The road ends on the ridge top at two cairns, a satisfying vantage point for Grass Pass, a beautiful sight in fall when grassy hillsides fade to palest gold. In the opposite direction look into Gunnery Creek from where you can spot the trail climbing to the notch below Gunnery Mountain.

To Gunnery Creek Backtrack down the first hill. Leave the road and head northwest along the broad grassy ridge dotted with Limber pines. A game trail appears out of the trees from the right (possibly the shortcut mentioned previously), and takes you nearly all the way along the ridge top to Gunnery pass. Alternatively, drop sooner into Gunnery Creek via a west slope game trail.

this book and comes courtesy of Dave Birrell. If you've ever wondered how to get up Mt. Head without actually rock climbing, head up a west fork from GR707897 to gain the southeast ridge falling from GR677905, then finish along Head's spectacular northeast ridge (moderate scrambling, some exposure). Apparently, the Stampede Ranch uses this route to instill self discipline in troubled youths.

Continue down Wileman Creek, crossing the tiny creek three times. Pass a cutline heading into the cirque between Head and "Trapezium". Recross the creek, wend left and join a cutline for a long straight stretch. If you're puzzling over the small size of the valley creek and wondering where all the water is, it's over there on the left, congregated in a long chain of beaver ponds.

As the valley pinches in, you cross Wileman Creek for the last time. Look back for a satisfying view of Holy Cross Mountain and Mt. Head, probably seen to their best advantage from this more distant spot. Back in forest, you cross the drift fence at

261 BULL CREEK HILLS — map 22

Day hikes
Unofficial trails, routes
High point 2179 m
Map 82 J/7 Mount Head

The south ridge route reached from Fir Creek. The usual route from Grass Pass follows the left-hand skyline to the highest summit (right).

Access: Highwood Trail (Hwy. 541).
A Via Grass Pass (#260) at the pass.
B Fir Creek. Park east of the creek crossing.
C Marston Creek. An overgrown exploration road starts from the north side of the highway about 300 metres west of Kananaskis Country boundary.
Also accessible from Trap Creek (#262).

This large group of hills lying between the Highwood River and Trap Creek offer superb hiking, often from April through to November. Definitely, one of my favourite places, but then, I'm a sucker for meadows with Monardas and Limber pines. With two vehicles or stashed bikes suggested routes A to D can be combined to make loops. For off-trail hikers there are numerous ways up the enticing slopes above Highway 541.

The Bull Creek Hills were named after Bull Creek which runs (or rather, *ran*) into Trap Creek. Not only has the name been missed off the latest edition of the topo map but it's been changed to Cutthroat Creek on the provincial resource map, a more recent

name suggested by an Alberta Fisheries biologist and *officially approved* in 1984, the rationale behind the name Bull Creek Hills *at the head of Bull Creek* having been completely lost sight of! Write forthwith to the Alberta Historical Resources Foundation Board in Edmonton and complain.

Usual access 261A from Grass Pass
2.5 km from pass, height gain 366 m.

Gain Grass Pass via #260, then turn right (east) up a steeply climbing OHV road imprinted in grass. Keep straight. Before reaching the ridge top, a trail angles left and traverses to a saddle overlooking Fir Creek at GR719880. The trail continues through a band of pines, then climbs southwest slopes to the broad summit ridge at GR723886 from where there's a thrilling retrospective view of Mt. Head and Holy Cross Mountain rising above the dark valley of Wileman Creek. Continue over two minor tops to the high point at GR733887 where you can look down into Trap Creek and sort out its various options.

261B Fir Creek
3.2 km to summit, height gain 746 m.

A trail starts near the road sign east of the creek and climbs the road cut into the few Douglas firs left after reconstruction of the highway in 1982/83. A double-track trail carries on through aspen meadows to a junction where the second edition trail went left. This time keep straight and cross a lovely side slope of grass and Limber pines into the upper valley where arrows lead to a campsite used by Scouts during the World Jamboree in 1983. The valley head is all meadow and boxed in on three sides by the Bull Creek Hills.

Ongoing trail-less options include climbing to the saddle at GR719880 where you join access A. My preference is to climb onto the ridge to the east and finish up the interesting south ridge—scrambling optional—to top GR727885 immediately west of the high point.

261C Marston Creek
4.5 km to summit, height gain 777 m.

The old road follows a fold in the grassy hillside, winding past small clumps of aspens and Limber pines to the watershed ridge. Descend alongside the boundary fence into Marston Creek named after Ed Marston who homesteaded on the creek in 1902. He was a colourful character, remembered chiefly for his set of false teeth made from cowhide! His wife was equally famous for her homemade wine into which she put everything including leftover dessert. "Bloody awful", said Raymond Patterson who always drank it, rather interested to find out what kind of effect it was going to have on him this time.

Shortly after crossing the creek to the north bank you come to a junction. The right-hand road climbs about 100 m up the south ridge of top GR743886. The left-hand valley road soon degenerates to cow trail at the end of a meadow and descends to Marston Creek. At a small north-side tributary cross the creek to the south bank. Recross just after the next tributary from the north at GR740874. After a brief sortie through trees in the angle between the two forks, the trail enters open hillside and dissipates, putting you in a good position to attack the highest summit—a steepish climb broken up by steps where the bulls like to lie in long grasses. It's obvious a circuit can be made using both branches of the road. It's an interesting walk across the eastern tops past the pinnacle.

261D Optional descent to Trap Creek
Distance 7 km, height loss 762 m. A useful route, mostly on trail, down the less interesting back side of the hills to Trap Creek.

Start from the highest summit at GR733887. Either descend the stony north ridge or the valley to the west into Bull Creek where you can pick up a trail on the far bank. Follow it down valley for about 2 km (lovely meadows), then turn left and left again onto a NW-SE cutline that crosses the heavily forested east slope of the hill GR734917. A final steep drop lands you on an exploration road in Trap Creek valley. Turn right, cross Trap creek and follow the road out to Trap Creek Road, gained half a kilometre inside the K Country boundary.

The celebrated leaning Douglas Fir.

262 TRAP (FLAT) CREEK — maps 22, 21 & 18

Backpack
Unofficial trails, creek crossings
Distance 19.5 km to the forks from east access, 6.6 km from #260
Height gain 436 m to the forks from east access
High point 2118 m at west fork tarn
Maps 82 J/8 Stimson Creek,
82 J/7 Mount Head, 82 J/10 Mount Rae

East access: Highwood Trail (Hwy. 541). Park on the shoulder 21 km southwest of Longview, just north of Trap Creek bridge . On the west side of the highway is a road guarded by a locked steel gate. The road you used to drive to K Country boundary has been closed to motorized vehicles indefinitely. Only the first kilometre of it crosses private land, the rest runs through crown land leased to ranchers for cattle grazing. The ranchers got fed up with featherbrained hunters who leave gates open, target practise on signs, splatter beer bottles, drive over fields and hillsides and harass and shoot cattle. You can see their point of view. However, you're allowed to walk or bike along the road. Out of courtesy and preferably dressed in Louis Garneau cycling shorts, aerodynamic cycling helmet with eight vents and shock absorber cycling gloves to show you're harmless, get permission from either The Buffalo Head Ranch (before the bridge) or the Stampede Ranch (after the bridge).

South access: Via north terminus of Grass Pass to Trap Creek (#260).

Also accessible from the southern terminus of High Rock Ridge (#263), and the western terminus of Sullivan Pass to South Coal Creek (#265).

Since the second edition the creek's name has reverted officially to Flat from Trap, even though the name Trap first appeared on Palliser's map of 1863 and is still retained on present topo maps. Both names are in local use, so please yourself.

Trap or Flat is a truly lovely valley, fairly quiet these days owing to the road closure. Unless you've got a bike, use route #260. Backpackers should make time to delve into the valley's more secretive places. A

The first view of Mt. Head.

week should just about do it. Consideration: If coming in from Grass Pass or going farther into the upper valley or up Head Creek, wait until mid summer when the river has quietened down.

FROM EAST ACCESS

To Wileman Creek Bike or walk 8 km along the old well road to the K Country boundary at a fence. From what I remember bouncing along in a car, the going to this point is basically flat with lots of meadow and cattle. Beyond the boundary fence minor roads branch off to the left, right (South Sullivan Creek road) and left, the old parking spot. Ahead is the locked gate at 8.3 km and a Texas gate. Keep straight on deteriorating road. (The left-hand road leads to a well site on the south bank of Trap Creek. Begun in 1942 by the Sullivan Creek Oil Syndicate, their Sullivan Creek No. 1 well later [1957] became the Dalhousie Oil Syndicate and Canadian Delhi Oil Limited Flat Creek No. 1 well. This is where you drop in off the Bull Creek Hills—see #261D.)

Cross a deep side creek and another Texas gate. Ahead is a superb view of Mt. Head, the right-hand skyline, quite by chance, the profile of a head. I say "quite by chance" because the mountain was named by John Palliser after Sir Edmund Walker Head, Canada's governor-general 1854-1861 and later governor of the Hudson's Bay Company. What a pity this is not the original Mt. Head. Palliser's sketchy map of 1865 places the mountain much farther northwest on the Great Divide. However, owing to inaccurate placement of both the Great Divide and the Highwood River (the side by side Elk and Highwood River valleys seem to have flummoxed everyone in those days), the true Mt. Head will forever remain an enigma.

Mulling over the likelihood of Fox or Mist or Tyrwhitt (unlikely) being the enigmatic Mt. Head, you arrive at a high point on the bend overlooking the confluence with Wileman Creek. Noticeably, hillside aspens have been battered by winds blasting over Grass Pass and funnelling down Wileman Creek, finally expending their energy against this corner, one of hundreds of "windy points" in Alberta's foothills. Here the road turns northwest and descends to riverside meadows about the junction with route #260 to the left at the 12.9 km mark (GR715934).

To High Rock Ridge junction Cross a side stream. About 600 m west of the last junction and just before another side stream, the road for High Rock Ridge turns off to the right at GR710937. There are perfect camping spots between the two junctions, each with river frontage.

Unguessed at you've been walking in and out of coal-bearing Kootenay strata and if you search the riverbank and hillsides to the right you may detect coal spoil dating back to the first decade of this century when Wellington Phillips Walker of High River operated the Walker Mine. Coal went out via horse and cart past Jack Freeman's cabin.

To Head Creek junction At 14.8 km, upstream of Head Creek confluence, you ford Trap Creek for the first time. In a few metres Head Creek exploration road turns off to the left at GR696943.

To Sullivan Pass junction In another 1.5 km the road recrosses to the northeast bank. If not going up Head Creek valley, you can avoid both crossings by following a trail along the northeast bank.

At 17 km you arrive at Spruce Bluff cabin—the jumping-off point for Sullivan Pass at GR681956. Built in 10 days in 1932 by Bert Sheppard and Dave Diebel, the cabin narrowly escaped the 1936 fire. Surrounding trees on the bluff were chopped and the cabin kept soaking wet both inside and out. This was not the Phillips Holocaust that was burning up the Highwood Valley, but the separate Trap Creek fire that started by lightning strike and went unnoticed in the general murk. By the time it was spotted from Junction Lookout it had laid waste half of Trap Creek, Head Creek and upper Sullivan Creek, which accounts for all the lodgepole pine.

To the forks Keep left and ford the creek for the third time. Another 2 km of flat going along outwash gravel flats sees you at the forks under the Dogtooth Mountains. Here the road crosses the creek and the north fork, then ends.

GOING FARTHER
The north fork is a place for adventurers. Spectacular scenery under Pyriform and Junction mountains, extensive meadows and a secret tarn are the lures.

The west fork "trail" crosses and recrosses the boisterous stream innumerable times. Where the creek turns south, the trail is on the east bank and can be traced through a remnant of old spruce forest as it aims for Patterson's Peak. This is the side Raymond Patterson had a go at climbing in the 1930s. With horror we read of his meteoric glissade hanging onto a rock and marvelled at his lucky escape. Immediately below the scene of his folly is a green tarn. Shallow and inclined to dry up, it's not the lake that draws the eyes, but rather the flower meadows around it that are the last subalpine meadows left in Trap Creek until the forest grows old again.

#262. Trap Creek just west of Spruce Bluff Cabin. Looking towards the Dogtooth Mountains.

#263, High Rock Ridge. A detour from the trail onto the ridge yields this fabulous view of Mt. Head.

263 HIGH ROCK RIDGE — maps 22 &19

Backpack, day hike from Trap Creek
Unofficial trail
Distance 12 km
Height gain 485 m
Height loss 347 m
High point 2085 m
Maps 82 J/7 Mount Head,
82 J/10 Mount Rae

South access: Via Trap Creek (#262) at 13.5 km.
North access: Via Sullivan Pass to South Coal Creek (#265) in the headwaters of Sullivan Creek at 5.2 km.

Between Trap Creek and the prairies there is a long ridge some 6 km in length that Raymond Patterson referred to as the High Rock Ridge because of its stoniness, although there's also lots of meadow to delight in. An exploration road traverses its length, connecting Trap Creek to Sullivan Creek, an easy walk that takes you to within 100 vertical m of the highest summit. Can be combined with #265 and Trap Creek to make a loop.

SOUTH TO NORTH

About 600 m west of route #260 turn right (north) up an exploration road at GR710937. For the first 2 km it winds across grassy slopes with Limber pines, then steepening, zigs through a curiously chequered region of matchstick pines and boulders onto the main ridge. For a while you hug the eastern escarpment (views of South Sullivan Creek beaver ponds), then turn west. The ridge is broad and flat at this point, a patchwork of forest, stones and arid meadow. Always ahead are the knobbly little summits that the road never quite attains. In fact the road descends slightly, then on the right side of the ridge, climbs diagonally across grass to its high point at about GR705965. (See detour.)

The road, descending slightly, begins a long traverse of the east face, crossing the two heads of South Sullivan Creek and hopping over two side ridges at cols. Just over the first col keep left at a junction. From the second col a cutline-like straight descends very much more steeply to a Phillips Petroleum Sullivan Creek gas well site where you pick up a more recent exploration road taking you out to route #265 in Sullivan Creek. Turn left for Sullivan Pass (trail), right for South Coal Creek (good road).

DETOUR
The ridge tops 2170 m
Distance to second top 1.5 km, height gain to first top 122 m. From the high point of the road you'd be a dull old codger to resist the high points of High Rock Ridge.

From near the road's high point a convenient trail heads up grass to the ridge. Turn right and tackle the first summit, gained at the last by a sporting 7 m scramble. I have resisted extolling the view from the road because I wanted you to come to the tops and enjoy an even more expansive view of the Highwood Range. On my first trip I was spellbound by the panorama of Holy Cross Mountain, Mt. Head, Patterson's Peak and farther to the right, the Dogtooth Mountains and Pyriform, all low mountains magnified by snow into Himalayan giants. Just to the left of Patterson's Peak is the little summit gained by route #264.

A second high point to the northwest involves picking your way down boulders and another scramble. Continuing all along the ridge to Sullivan Pass is not as easy as you might think once you leave the ridge top. Other options include dropping in on the road from GR695982, and descending easy west slopes into Trap Creek.

264 HEAD CREEK — map 21

Backpack, day hike from Trap Creek
Unofficial trails, creek crossings
Distance 8.5 km from Trap Creek
Height gain 885 m
High point 2515 m
Map 82 J/7 Mount Head

Access: Via Trap Creek (#262).

The incredible zigzagging exploration road up Head Creek dates back to the early 1960s when gypsum was discovered on a mountain top southeast of Patterson's Peak at GR 655936. Found and staked by V. Hume and S. Mason of Turner Valley, the gypsum's generally poor quality made economic development unlikely. Left with the legacy of a road, today's hikers will find this a surprisingly easy hike to a summit.

River crossing.

The route leaves Trap Creek road from its first stint along the southwest bank. After wading Trap Creek, you hardly have time to feel sick to your stomach before turning left up Head Creek valley. Keep your Tevas on for the first part of the route; the first six stream crossings are unavoidable and why waste time searching for crossing places? Splash through, I say.

In the narrows, slow regrowth after the 1936 fire allows thrilling views of hillsides bristling with white spires of wafer-thin rock. My favourite place in the stream occurs in this section at a confluence with a side creek coming in from the north face of Mt. Head. Bathtubs, showers, slides and jacuzzis are lots of fun even if the water does turn your skin blue. Pass between rock pillars into the upper valley which opens out with patches of meadow and spruce amid the general devastation.

The south fork, which carries most of the water, comes in at GR659921. It appears the scree ridge east of the south fork offers a reasonable scrambler's route to the west summit of Mt. Head. However, getting to the true summit looks a much more difficult proposition.

After another four creek crossings you end up below the stony southwest face of your objective. In quick succession, pass two side roads heading up the slope, cross a side stream, pass a side road, cross another side stream. Only then does the road start heading uphill in zigzags. Can you believe 29 zigs up a 300 m-high scree slope! If you want, the first six and a half can be avoided by the shortcut road between the two streams.

Gain the col between your little summit and Patterson's Peak to left which looks impregnable from this direction. Here the road turns right and makes a long traverse below gypsum outcroppings to a small summit at the apex of three ridges.

On the return, those inclined can romp down the scree immediately below the summit and pick up that first side road.

Opposite: Patterson's Peak from near the mine site.

265 SULLIVAN PASS TO SOUTH COAL CREEK — maps 21, 18 & 19

Backpack, day hike from Trap Creek
Unofficial trails
Distance 2.8 km to pass, 5.2 km to
#263, 11 km to South Coal Creek
Height gain 305 m to pass, 381 m to
South Coal Creek
Height loss to South Coal Creek 457 m
High point 1996 m at pass
Maps 82 J/7 Mount Head,
82 J/10 Mount Rae

Highwood access: Via Trap Creek (#262) at Spruce Bluff cabin.
Sheep access: Via Junction Mountain trail (#271) at two points in South Coal Creek.
Also accessible via the northern terminus of High Rock Ridge (#263).

Grassy Sullivan Pass is an excellent choice for a half-day walk from a campsite in Trap Creek. But it's not just a pretty viewpoint for Mt. Head. Let's say you're contemplating a south-north backpacking trip in the foothills taking in the Highwood, Sheep, Elbow and Jumpingpound. While there's a surfeit of connecting routes farther north, between the Highwood and the Sheep it boils down to this one pass.

Sullivan Pass, looking towards Mt. Head.

Trap Creek to Sullivan Pass
At Spruce Bluff cabin turn right off Trap Creek trail onto another exploration road. In 1 km keep left near Black Creek, true to its name a stinky morass of black soil oozing oil. (In case you're wondering, the right-hand road peters out a long way below the lowest gap in the ridge.) Leave Black Creek and the trees behind as you toil up steepening grass slopes to the pass, the second lowest gap in the ridge at GR678980.

Some locals call this pass "Grassy" which is not to be confused with Grass Pass. On a fine summer's afternoon when the usual westerly blast has softened to a light breeze, these south-facing meadows are perfect for idling away a few hours before starting back. On the other hand, anyone with itchy feet can wander the

meadows for several kilometres in any direction, even climbing far up the southeast ridge of Junction Mountain.

Sullivan Pass to Sullivan Creek
The barely-there exploration road drops into the cirque to the north, then down a headwater of Sullivan Creek to the junction with a newer exploration road at the northern terminus of High Rock Ridge (#263).

Keep straight and follow the new road down the valley, crossing a headwater and Sullivan Creek twice. High ridges on either side are clad in lodgepoles (the 1936 fire, remember), so view-wise it's not terribly interesting, as good a place as any to remember the pioneering Sullivan family.

Sadly, in the space of one month three of John Sullivan's kids died from the small-pox and are buried on the grass verge of Highway 541 near the Y Cross Ranch. Only a few years later John was dragged to death when his foot got caught in a stirrup. People were inured to tragedy in those days and with another five children to care for Mrs. Sullivan married a Mr. Hicks and lived to a ripe old age.

As you walk out of the hills there are several things to look for. At the left-hand bend at GR719023 the overgrown road from Trap Creek at the K Country boundary comes in from across the river. In the following dip, you cross a tiny side creek. The big flat meadow to the left is the watershed between Sullivan and South Coal creeks, so water-logged only moose go that way. I was aston-ished to learn that at one time this creek arose under Junction Mountain and was the major headwater of Sullivan Creek until South Coal Creek, cutting back, captured the head-waters in what's called stream piracy. Com-ing up next is an overgrown cutline on the left unaccountably marked by red flagging. A little farther on around a left-hand bend at GR721026 is a grassy road, indistinct at first, where you turn left. Hoofprints are a sure giveaway. (The exploration road continues past the K Country boundary, not to the old Sullivan place, Y Cross Ranch, but past the equally historic TL Ranch named after Tom Lynch, a pal of John Ware.)

Sullivan Creek to South Coal Creek

After the cutline joins in from the left a drift fence is crossed. The road/cutline then undulates across the forested east slope of the round hill to the east. Boring perhaps, unless you happen to meet the dive-bomb-ing goshawk. I remember it as the place we wore our packs on our heads.

On the South Coal Creek side the road parts company with the cutline.

For Junction Lookout turn left with the road which descends to an intersection with a NE-SW cutline in a bit of a meadow. In the semicircular meadow following, the road joins Junction Mountain trail (#271) at the forest edge, the official trail instantly identified by red markers on trees.

For Wolf Creek or Phone Line trails keep straight with the cutline as it descends through swamp (detour trail available) and intersects a NE-SW cutline. Cross another cutline and wind down to Junction Moun-tain trail (#271), at this point an old road close to South Coal Creek. Turn right. In less than half a kilometre to the east reach Wolf Creek/ Phone Line trail junction with signpost.

Spruce Bluff Cabin.

South Coal Creek gorge from the viewpoint.

266 WOLF CREEK — map 19

Day hike, backpack
Official trail with signposts & red
markers, major river crossing
Distance 11 km
Height gain 305 m
High point 1661 m
Map 82 J/10 Mount Rae

Access: Sheep River Trail (Hwy. 546) at Sandy McNabb Recreation Area. Drive all the way down the access road to the picnic area above the Sheep River.
Also accessible from the eastern terminus of Price Camp trail (#267), the southern terminus of Phone Line (#269), and the southern terminus of Junction Mountain trail (#271).

This trail follows exploration roads and cutlines through forest and meadows up Wolf Creek and over a low pass into South Coal Creek where Wolf Creek backcountry campground is located. Not too exciting one would think, but it does have one surprise in store as you'll discover. NOTE: During runoff dangerously high water levels in the Sheep River make this trail inaccessible from the normal access.

Just after the access road turns left at the bottom of the hill, a trail leads to the Sheep River. Wade across to a red marker downstream of Coal Creek. (The safer crossing place is upstream of Coal Creek in which case you have to cross Coal Creek as well.)

Turn left. The exploration road kicks off with a steep pull up the bank, then settles into a gentle climb, passing through a gate into a very large meadow above Wolf Creek. A view of Blue Ridge ahead—the pleated forest ridge—gives you some idea of how far you have to go to the pass which is located another 2 km beyond. In the meadow the road reverts to trail as it winds around the perimeter below a knoll. A little farther on at GR753083 there is potential for straying where a really good trail heads up the north bank of a copious tributary arising from the west flank of Mt. Dyson. This is NOT Wolf Creek. Keep left here, dipping to cross the tributary. Shortly you join a NE-SW cutline at a T-junction. If hiking in reverse direction, the route does NOT cross

Wolf Creek. Two Calgary women having successfully navigated from Trap Creek, *crossed Wolf Creek* as shown on an early edition of the K Country map and were lost in the cutlines for three days!

At the cutline, then, turn right and follow it into the inner fastness of Wolf Creek between Blue Ridge and Mt. Dyson. At the forks the cutline access road turns right up the north fork, then zooms up a steep slope to the watershed ridge. Rather than follow this impractical line, a trail swings farther west and follows the gently inclined valley to the pass. Open south-facing slopes allow a not too interesting view of forested headwaters. The best view is discovered by walking a few metres to your right. In this country of low relief, it comes as a huge shock when the ground suddenly opens up

into a savage, black shale gorge—the greatest moment of the day. Although short, the South Coal Creek version is just as impressive as its better-known counterparts, particularly if you can persuade a passing mountain biker to pose on the edge.

Descend an open draw, cross the cutline and pick up the cutline access road that takes you down the hill to South Coal Creek at the big bend. A lovely stretch through riverside meadows brings you to Wolf Creek backcountry campground where noises in the night are likely cows. Within the next kilometre the trail crosses to the north bank, intersects the cutline, then recrosses to the junction at GR717046 with Phone Line (right) and Junction Mountain trail (straight).

---

267 PRICE CAMP TRAIL — map 19

Day hike, backpack
Official trail with signposts & red markers, major river crossing
Distance 5 km
Height gain/loss E-W 61 m
High point 1509 m
Map 82 J/10 Mount Rae

Access: Sheep River Trail (Hwy. 546) at Sandy McNabb Recreation Area. Drive all the way down the access road to the picnic area above the Sheep River.
Also accessible from Sheep trail (#276), Wolf Creek (#266) and the northern terminus of Mount McNabb (#268).

An alterative start (or finish) to Sheep trail. SNAG: During runoff dangerously high water levels in the Sheep River make this trail inaccessible by the normal access.

Just after the access road turns left at the bottom of the hill, a trail leads to the Sheep River. Wade across to an old road *upstream* of Coal Creek. Head right, parallelling the Sheep River on a grassy terrace. Climb to a higher terrace and intersect a cutline and a

drift fence en route to Mount McNabb trail junction at the 2.2 km mark.

Here the trail moves away from the Sheep River into pine forest. Cross a NE-SW cutline and a little later on, March Creek whose north bank is followed upstream to a large meadow, the site of Mr. Price's Logging Camp of nearly 90 years ago. At two ruins the trail turns sharply right and drops to a major NE-SW cutline. Cross and arrive a few minutes later at the T-junction with Sheep trail.

268 MOUNT MCNABB TRAIL — map 19

Day hike, backpack
Official trail with signposts & red
markers, creek crossings
Distance 6 km
Height gain N-S 311 m
Height loss N-S 213 m
High point 1570 m
Map 82 J/10 Mount Rae

North access: Via Price Camp trail (#267).
South access: At the northern terminus of Phone Line (#269) and the eastern terminus of Green Mountain trail (#270) in North Coal Creek.

Despite one steep muddy hill at the north end, this is mostly an easy meadow walk. Most obviously make a day loop with Green Mountain trail (#270), Sheep trail (#276) and Price Camp (#267), or consider a backpack with Phone Line (#269) and Wolf Creek (#266) with a night spent at Wolf Creek backcountry campground.

NORTH TO SOUTH
Straight-off climb to a wooded pass a long way west of Mt. McNabb. Drop into a side valley of Coal Creek, cross a low ridge into another side valley—a velvety smooth trough of close-cropped grass—and follow it down *almost* to North Coal Creek, at the last moment turning right and crossing another two small ridges before finally reaching the banks of North Coal Creek. The south-facing meadows are beautiful and far off to the west, the pointy peaks of the Highwood Range are poking up above low, forested foothills.

Just before you reach the side creek at GR707096 under Green Mountain the trail crosses to the south bank. From this point on you can either follow the official trail which has too many creek crossings, or at first opportunity get onto the cheater's trail high on the northwest bank. Both join about 300 m east of the three-way junction with Phone Line and Green Mountain trails.

Left: Mount McNabb trail in lovely North Coal Creek. Green Mountain behind.

Opposite: #269. One of the tripods.

269 PHONE LINE — map 19

Backpack
Official trail with signposts & red
markers, creek crossings
Distance 7 km
Height gain S-N 180 m
Height loss S-N 228 m
High point 1673 m
Map 82 J/10 Mount Rae

South access: South Coal Creek at the junction of Wolf Creek (#266) and Junction Mountain trail (#271).
North access: North Coal Creek at the junction of Green Mountain trail (#270) and Mount McNabb trail (#268).

This undulating forest trail cuts across the grain of the country, more or less following the old telephone trail between Sentinel Ranger Station in the Highwood and Bighorn Ranger Station in the Sheep.

SOUTH TO NORTH

Straightway Phone Line crosses South Coal Creek to north bank meadows. Head upstream a little, then turn right up a side valley to a wooded pass at GR706053 where the trail teams up with a cutline access road coming in from your left. The road dips into a tributary of South Coal Creek (crossing at the same place as the N-S cutline), then swings away right and over a broad ridge of Lodgepole pines separating South Coal and North Coal Creek drainages. This is the first place to look for tripods. You can picture the scene in 1915. A string of pack horses, each carrying two rolls of #9 gauge wire, stopping every 60 m or so to drop off a coil. The construction crew coming along behind would stretch the wire, and with the aid of spurs, climb 5 m up a suitable tree, tie the porcelain insulators onto the wire, then attach the insulator to the tree with a large staple, so that if the tree toppled, the staple would pull out and allow the line to sag but not break. Insulator trees can be recognized by trimmed branches. When no trees could be found, tripods were built, from which

one gathers the ridges were bare of trees in those days.

Just over the height of land, a trail circumvents the road's foray into a bog, birthplace of a tiny stream, so when you see the road suddenly turning left into the meadow, keep straight, following red markers to a N-S cutline.

DETOUR to Hidden Lake

Hidden Lake is only five minutes walk away. Just walk right (north) along the cutline to the first drainage bump, then turn right onto a game trail leading through a few metres of forest to a grassy draw ending at the lakeshore.

Phone Line crosses the N-S cutline, then swings right along the bank of the bog stream, finally crossing it by bridge and doubling back to the road. Turn right and on road cross two low ridges well endowed with tripods into North Coal Creek. Walk downstream for about 400 m and ford the creek to a four-way junction with an E-W cutline on the north bank. Don't make the mistake of thinking the road opposite is Green Mountain trail. You must turn right and follow the cutline another 200 m downstream. Cross a side creek and climb to a three-way junction in a large, bright meadow under Green Mountain.

#270. Green Mountain trail in Dyson Creek. Dyson Falls in spate.

#271, Green Mountain. Looking back beyond the castle to the Sheep River valley. Some of the instantly recognizable mountains include Mist Mountain, Gibraltar, Mt. Burns and Bluerock Mountain.

270 GREEN MOUNTAIN TRAIL — maps 18 & 19

Day hike, backpack
Official trail with signposts & red
markers, creek crossing
Distance 3.5 km
Height gain W-E 107 m
Height loss W-E 137 m
High point 1646 m
Map 82 J/10 Mount Rae

West access: Via Sheep trail (#276) in Dyson Creek at two junctions.
East access: The junction of Mount McNabb (#268) and Phone Line (#269) in North Coal Creek.
Also accessible from the northern terminus of Junction Mountain trail (#271).

Although an important connector between Sheep trail in Dyson Creek and the Mount McNabb/Phone Line network in Coal Creeks, I use it to climb Green Mountain which is a feasible one day trip from Indian Oils trailhead via Sheep trail (#276)—even without a bike.

WEST TO EAST

From Sheep trail two accesses meet in a V at Dyson Creek crossing in the meadows. The official signposted trail is the one to take if coming from Indian Oils trailhead. Half a kilometre to the north another trail (Teskey Road) heads down the bank past the researcher's high chair used for counting ground squirrels. Just downstream of the crossing is little Dyson Falls where Collomia grows in the spray. Wade the creek above the falls and climb to the junction with Junction Mountain trail. Keep left.

Green Mountain trail descends slightly to cross a side creek, then climbs (keep right, then left) to a high point far above the low point in the watershed. The descent to North Coal Creek is a long drawn out affair, but the exquisite blending of meadows and aspen woodlands make this a very pleasant stretch to follow. Low down in a meadow a signpost marks the junction with Phone Line and Mount McNabb trails.

OPTION
Green Mountain 1844 m

Distance 1 km, 12 km return from Indian Oils trailhead, height gain from trail 198 m. Originally named Greenslope on Wheeler's map of 1895, this hill looks nothing from the highway, but concealed behind that facade of Lodgepole pines lies grassy slopes and fascinating sandstone escarpments facing west, definitely one of my favourite fun places. Make use of game trails.

There is no best way to start up the southwest ridge which is nebulous low down and tree covered. From the trail's high point descend the first hill, then climb up the slope to the left. Alternatively, head uphill from the high point to a supporting rib and turn right (some descent necessary to gain the proper ridge). Higher up, an up-down trail appears and leads to steep grass below the Castle. Aim right of the cliff, entering a secret valley between the Castle and the Cormorant. The castle is easy from this direction and its pinnacle a fun scramble. Tackle the escarpment above via the ridge to the right of the castle. Pass the mushrooms, then weave between Limber pines clinging to the rocks. At the top stop awhile to enjoy a superb panorama of familiar mountains, then continue through a few trees to a sheltered glade occupied by three survey markers. The actual summit, site of Wheeler's two camera stations, is the bare top farther to the left beyond the tree belt.

In line with the grassy southeast ridge is Mt. Dyson. "Why" Fran wanted to know " is the hill miles away from Dyson Creek?" That's because Coal Creek was called Dyson Creek on Wheeler's map of 1895.

271 JUNCTION MOUNTAIN TRAIL — maps 18 & 19

Long day hike to lookout, backpack
Official trail with signposts & red
markers, creek crossings
Total distance 16 km, 12 km to lookout
from Indian Oils trailhead
Height gain N-S 655 m
Height loss N-S 661 m
High point 2240 m
Map 82 J/10 Mount Rae

North access: Via Green Mountain trail (#270) 200 m east of Dyson Creek crossing. Day trippers to the lookout should start from Sheep River Trail (Hwy. 546) at Indian Oils parking lot and follow Sheep trail (#276) going east to Dyson Creek, then transfer to Green Mountain trail. NOTE: This section of Highway 546 is closed between December 1st and May 15th.

South access: Via the junction of Wolf Creek (#266) and Phone Line (#269) in South Coal Creek.

Also accessible from Sullivan Pass to South Coal Creek (#265) in two places.

Standing on a high grassy ridge below Junction Mountain, Junction Lookout is a big attraction, though not quite as popular as Moose Mountain on account of the longer approach. The north half of the route is fire road, boring for the most part; the other half is very pleasant trail despite umpteen creek crossings. Combine with other trails like Phone Line and Green Mountain to make a terrific weekend backpack.

NORTH TO SOUTH

To Junction Lookout From the junction with Green Mountain trail, Junction Mountain trail (the fire road) heads southwest, parallelling Dyson Creek. Pass a trail to left and a meadow with a pond.

At 2 km you toil up a ridge, the gradient easing as you wind in and out of all the headwaters of North Coal Creek on steep, heavily-forested east slopes. The spruce forest is hauntingly beautiful with a mossy understorey and running water in all the tributaries. At one point you touch a shaley

gap—momentary view of mountains to the west—then it's back to the forest grind. Eventually the fire road turns southwest (first view of the lookout) and arrives at col GR656046. Ahead are meadows!

The final stretch follows a broad, gently-inclined ridge, a bare-bones mix of grass, Dryas and stones, flagged on the east side by a line of wind-battered spruce with mis-shapen limbs. At GR658040 you reach the broad saddle separating Dyson Creek from South Coal Creek (see detour), then continue to two cairns and a horse rail marking the ongoing trail down the south flank.

It takes more than 100 m of remaining road to make you forgo the lookout and the chance of saying hello. The building is the third at this location, the first one being built in September 1929 when snow lay thick on the ground and pack horses plodded up a trail as yet unstumped. There's a wall overlooking the craggy south face where you can escape the wind and a seat made of rocks facing east because the principal view is of prairies and foothills, although you can look north and south along the edge of the Front Ranges between Moose Mountain and Mt. Burke. Disappointingly, the view west is obstructed by the high furrowed wall of Junction Mountain.

Detour to hill GR651038, 2301 m
From the saddle at GR658040 the grassy hill to the west is a popular diversion, the view much the same except it now includes the lookout.

The two cairns where the south flank trail leaves the fire road. In the background is hill GR651038 and Junction Mountain.

To South Coal Creek Backtrack to the two cairns and pass between them, following cairns across a grassy slope to the ridge falling south from the lookout. Here the trail resumes, descending the ridge to a red marker on a post, then dropping over the left edge. The trail tackles the steep east face with 12 zigs, crossing flowery meadows gradually yielding to pine forest, a wonderful section *going down*, but an arduous crawl in reverse. At the bottom you cross the creek emanating from the valley between the south and southeast ridges.

The next section to South Coal Creek is a gradual downhill. A bloodhound would be handy in three meadows where the trampled grass of the 'trail' is crisscrossed by other trails from cows and from hikers looking all round the edges for red markers. In all cases you walk the full length of the meadow. Between second and third meadows a junction with a game trail of equal quality requires a signpost. Look back one last time to the lookout.

Now in South Coal Creek valley and shortly to be *in* the creek, you head downstream through a beautiful valley of meadows alternating with mixed forest. It's flat, so good time can be made, splashing across the creek seven times. Even in late fall you'll be hard pressed to keep your feet dry so I hope you've brought your Tevas. After the second crossing the trail from the east ridge joins in from the left. After crossing No. 7, in a tiny meadow identified by two extra large spruce on the left edge with trimmed branches and a stump in between, the west route to Sullivan Creek turns right on a cutline access road (no sign).

Back in the trees you're transferred to the cutline access road. Cross a cutline. At a left-hand bend another cutline access road turning right is the boggy east route to Sullivan Creek.

A few metres on watch for a red marker where the route leaves the road (soon to cross the creek) and turns right on trail. Shortly come to a three-way junction with Phone Line (left) and Wolf Creek (right).

OPTIONAL DESCENT
The East Ridge

Anyone who loves ridge walks will be off like a shot along this grassy ridge with three separate tops. Amazingly, the whole route into South Coal Creek unravels beautifully. Expect no trail until the very end.

From the lookout head east past the word "Junction" spelled out in rocks painted white. The east ridge is rocky and unguessed at has two narrows if you decide to be sporting and keep to the crest. At the top GR672041 (cairn) the ridge turns southeast and you descend a long grass slope to a col. Climb the next top via a rising bench on the right side, then work your way up through rocky outcrops. The way down to the next col is not totally straightforward. Veer left and start down the rocky rib. Before the rib erupts in pinnacles, step off left into the trees and descend connecting openings. The third top features freestanding walls of cliffs on the west side. Go over the top or traverse right below the cliffs as we did (cheaters!) to the third col where luxurious grasses twist around your legs and contrive to trip you up. This is where you leave the ridge.

Below the col on the west side is a convenient grassy avenue between pines. Follow it down a long way, past springs, to a large meadow with amoeba-like fingers extending to left and right. Carry on down the left-hand finger to its end in a dip, likely the catchment area for a small creek starting farther left. Just above the dip turn left and follow an excellent cow trail along the creek's left bank all the way out to South Coal Creek. At the very end part company with the creek (unmarked on the topo map) and descend the bank farther to the left into a meadow where you join the official trail between creek crossings 2 and 3.

Looking along the east ridge from just below the lookout.

272 DEATH VALLEY — map 19

Day hike, backpack
Official trail with signposts & red
markers, creek crossings
Distance 12.5 km
Height gain S-N 222 m
Height loss S-N 274 m
High point 1539 m
Map 82 J/10 Mount Rae

Access: Sheep River Trail (Hwy. 546). Turn
left onto Sandy McNabb Recreation Area access road. Turn first left into the equestrian
parking lot.
Also accessible from the northern terminus of
Windy Point trail (#273), the eastern terminus of
Ware Creek trail (#292), and the southern terminus of 9999 trail (#294).

*The fence gate between Death
Valley and Ware Creeks.*

Although an important link between the
Sheep River and Threepoint Creek trail
systems, 90 per cent of people use it to make
loops with Windy Point, Sheep or Foran
Grade Ridge trails. Though the terrain
couldn't be easier, go when the ground is
bone dry. Anything less and you'll spend
more time figuring out how to dodge mud
than paying attention to your surroundings
which, though lacking the drama of crags
and steep slopes, have the friendly charm
of meadows and aspen woodlands.

The name, therefore, is intriguing, and
why this particular valley should be the site
of several deaths and disappearances *right
up to the present day* is a huge mystery.
Rumour has it a band of horses died in the
valley in the 1800s during a bad winter. It's
known the creek used to be called "Sinnot"
after Harry Sinnot who homesteaded near
the confluence with Ware Creek and that he
died mysteriously during a Christmas Eve
fire, not in Death Valley unfortunately for
our story, but in a little shack on Whiskey
Row north of Turner Valley. The most likely
explanation for the name arises from the
finding of a skeleton believed to be that of a
trapper who had gone into the valley some
years earlier and disappeared. The body
was respectfully buried where it was found

and the skull taken back to the Fisher Ranch
where it was placed on a fence post and
used as a football.

To Windy Point trail junction Start at the
signboard in the parking lot. Following
Sheep trail, turn right and cross Sandy
McNabb Recreation Area access road. In
less than 100 m turn right off Sheep trail
and cross Highway 546 onto what is also
Death Valley Link ski trail. The going is flat
and easy to the T-junction with Long Prairie
loop ski trail below an open ridge. Turn left.

At the next T-junction turn right. Lined
with aspens, the trail curves up grassy
hillside (mountain view) onto a wooded
side ridge. At the four-way junction with
Long Prairie Loop ski trail go straight (also
Death Valley loop ski trail), and descend
into Death Valley's drainage. In fact, the
stream you cross in the middle of a mud
bath is the infant Death Creek. On the far
bank turn right up the hill and leave the ski
trails far behind.

Over the next 2 km the trail gradually
descends to valley bottom where generations of beavers have constructed dams and
ponds up and down the creek. The mead-

ows are lovely and if it wasn't for the trail you'd thoroughly enjoy the walk to the T-junction with Windy Point trail at GR732181.

To Ware Creek Stay right, entering the narrows between high grassy banks where the trail is forced across the creek and back. High above the east bank is a grave marked by a small aluminum cross. Amid the flowers and with a wonderful vista of the valley lies Muriel Dixon, a Stoney from Eden Valley Reserve who was just 23 when she went to the Happy Hunting Grounds some 30 years ago.

Opposite the next side valley to the west, the trail recrosses Death Valley Creek and heads up the tributary. Navigating from post to post in meadow you cross the side creek twice before settling in for a long stretch along the left bank. Keep right twice where older trails went left.

Climb into aspen forest and pass through a gate in the fence. At the apex of the ridge turn right onto a descending NE-SW cutline. Near the bottom of the hill turn off to the left and cross a tributary of Ware Creek in a soggy meadow. Keep left on the far bank. Cross another aspen ridge, en route intersecting an E-W cutline. A gradual downhill through alternating meadow and aspen forest ends in a large meadow above Ware Creek. Jump a tiny tributary to a signpost on the west bank at GR717221. Ware Creek trail turns left, 9999 trail heads for Ware Creek.

Death Valley meadows at the junction withWindy Point trail. Note the bridge.

273 WINDY POINT TRAIL — map 19

Day hike
Official trail with signposts & red
markers
Distance 6.5 km
Height gain S-N 198 m
Height loss S-N 232 m
High point 1600 m at pass
Map 82 J/10 Mount Rae

Usual access: Sheep River Trail (Hwy. 546).
3.3 km west of the winter closure gate at Sandy
McNabb Recreation Area, turn left into a parking
lot. Walk 100 m farther west along Highway 546
to where Windy Point trail crosses the road.
NOTE: This section of Highway 546 is closed
between December 1st and May 15th.
South access: Sheep trail (#276) at the junc-
tion 200 m downslope and south of the usual
access.
North access: Death Valley trail (#272) at
GR732181.
Also accessible via the northern terminus of
Foran Grade Ridge (#275) at the pass.

A lovely part of the trail in Death Valley.

This is the alternate way into or out of
Death Valley. Use in conjunction with
Sheep trail and Foran Grade Ridge to make
a popular 7 km half-day loop. Or combine
with Death Valley trail and Sheep trail to
make a much longer 15 km loop from
Sandy McNabb Recreation Area.

The foothills country is beautiful; the
trail a mess in its middle section. I recommend wearing gaiters.

FROM SOUTH ACCESS
At the sign post (fallen in 1996) climb the
grassy bank below the **usual parking lot
access** to Highway 546. The trail crosses the
highway just right of Windy Point Creek and
climbs up Swamson's Draw to the pass between Windy Point and Foran Grade ridges.
Trail #275 turns off to the right.

Through the pass, the trail starts a long
gradual descent into the mixed forests of
Death Valley, initially following the east
bank of a tributary. After crossing the creek
and a fence signifying the boundary of

Sheep River Wildlife Sanctuary, you start
running into mud the width of the Trans-
Canada Highway—dual carriageway,
where every tentative movement either for-
wards or sideways is a squelch. Where to go
when the horses who hate it as much as we
do are making increasingly wider detours?
With considerable relief you enter a
meadow. Make for a raised island of aspens
(red marker) where the trail turns left and
crosses a tributary. On the far bank keep left.
(The trail to right is a shortcut to Death
Valley Creek at the beaver ponds.)

The Windy Point trail heads north, following a forested rib of high ground above
Death Valley Creek. Drop to another tributary and turn right. In a few metres the trail
fords Death Valley Creek at GR732181. Use
the bridge a few metres downstream. (The
discernable trail that comes in across the
tributary to the bridge is the old Death
Valley trail which is no longer in use.)

On the east bank of Death Valley Creek
join Death Valley trail at a T-junction.

274 WINDY POINT RIDGE — map 19

Half-day hike
Unofficial trail & route
Distance 1.5 km to summit
Height gain 275 m
High point 1752 m
Map 82 J/10 Mount Rae

Access: Sheep River Trail (Hwy. 546). 4.5 km west of the winter closure gate at Sandy McNabb Recreation Area, park in a small parking area on the left side of the highway. NOTE: This section of Highway 546 is closed between December 1st and May 15th.

The gable end of this ridge rises enticingly above a section of highway known as Windy Point. Snow free for much of the year, it makes an ideal conditioning hike in spring just after the road opens.

Prior to a widening of the road in the 1930s, motoring around the point in Model-T Fords used to be a hairy business, particularly during winter chinooks when seepages spread ice all over the track. Ruts would be cut in the ice to prevent cars sliding over the edge into the Sheep River. You can't blame the passengers who got out and walked.

To avoid climbing over a barbed-wire fence, walk 250 m west along the highway and cross the Texas gate. To your right, a trail climbs alongside the fence onto the grassy south ridge, which is followed all the way to the summit. In places the going is quite steep above a rising line of cliffs featuring a textbook anticline. Despite the lowly altitude, the view of foothills and mountains is panoramic. While it's not necessary to go farther (the view remains much the same), it's easy enough to gain the higher summit at GR716148.

Climbing the south ridge to the summit at far right.

Looking west to the Sheep River, Highway 546 and Windy Point Ridge.

275 FORAN GRADE RIDGE — map 19

Half-day hike
Official trail with signposts & red
markers
Distance 6 km
Height gain S-N 253 m
Height loss S-N 238 m
High point 1685 m
Map 82 J/10 Mount Rae

Access: Sheep River Trail (Hwy. 546). 1.6 km west of the winter closure gate at Sandy McNabb Recreation Area turn into a small parking area on the right (north) side of the highway. NOTE: This section of Highway 546 is closed between December 1st and May 15th.
Also accessible from Windy Point trail (#273) at the pass and from Sheep trail (#276).

This ridge is a favourite half-day walk for trainee hikers and is usually combined with #273 and #276 to make a 7 km loop.

In the last edition I made an incredibly stupid error by spelling Foran FOREIGN. The ridge and trail are, as Gregg Foran kindly pointed out, named after his grandfather Bill who was a foreman at Lineham's logging camps in the Sheep and the Highwood, ranger at Bighorn Ranger Station and by default, foreman of the road building crew around Windy Point.

The trail crosses a fence and in a large meadow approaches the east side of Foran Grade Ridge. Climb onto the south end of the ridge and follow the crest northwards, clearings at many points allowing stunning views of the Sheep River winding past Nash Meadow into the heart of the mountains. The square block of Gibraltar is instantly recognizable while to its left the big mountain with concertina strata is Mist Mountain (route #204 in profile). This is also a good place to inspect Windy Point Ridge and the normal route that follows the left-hand skyline.

Shortly after the high point is passed, the trail winds down open west slopes to meadows about the pass between Foran Grade and Windy Point ridges and it's here where you join Windy Point trail at the trail sign.

165

276 SHEEP TRAIL — maps 19, 18 & 17

Day hikes, backpack
Official trail with signposts & red
markers, major river crossings
Total distance 41 km

Highway access: Sheep River Trail (Hwy. 546). NOTE: The highway west of Sandy McNabb Recreation Area is closed between December 1st and May 15th.

1. Sandy McNabb Recreation Area. Turn first left into the equestrian parking lot.

2. 1.6 km west of the winter closure gate at Sandy McNabb Recreation Area turn into a small parking area on the right (north) side of the highway.

3. 3.3 km west of the winter closure gate at Sandy McNabb Recreation Area turn left into a small parking area at Windy Point. Via Windy Point trail heading south.

4. Indian Oils day-use area.

5. Bluerock campground. Start from the west end of the campground near site #30 (also the start to Bluerock Creek interpretive trail).

6. Bluerock parking lot and equestrian campground. At the forks turn left into a parking lot.

7. Terminus of highway at Junction Creek day-use area. Use upper parking area.

Also accessible via Death Valley trail (#272), Foran Grade Ridge (#275), Windy Point trail (#273), Price Camp trail (#267), Green Mountain trail (#270), Indian Oils trail (#281), Bluerock Creek trail (#280), Mist Creek trail (#205), and Big Elbow trail (#317).

From its beginning at Sandy McNabb Recreation Area on the eastern fringe of the foothills, Sheep trail follows the Sheep River valley through some spectacular Front Range scenery over a pass to the Elbow River valley. The route is a mixed bag of disused exploration and logging roads, cutlines, fire roads and trails, rarely followed in its entirety, more often used in combination with other trails to make loops. With this in mind I've split it up into logical sections, indicating equestrian trail variations and a number of unofficial alternatives. There are only two bridges across the Sheep River, one at highway access 4 and another upstream of Junction Creek.

The tranquillity of Sheep Lakes at the headwaters of the Sheep River. Mt. Rae to the right. To its left are the north and east peaks of the Rae Creek Hills.

Sandy McNabb to Windy Point

Distance 3.5 km
High point 1433 m
Map 82 J/10 Mount Rae

Highway access: 1, 2 & 3.
Also accessible from Death Valley (#272) and Windy Point trail (#273).

An easy stroll close to the highway.

From highway access 1 Start from the signboard in the parking lot. Turn right and cross Sandy McNabb Recreation Area access road. Keep straight at Death Valley trail junction and enjoy a kilometre-long stretch of aspen meadows. Just after a fence **access 2** comes in from across the highway.

Between here and **access 3** (a T-junction with Windy Point trail 100 m south of Windy Point parking lot), hold on to your kids; a misstep could mean a tumble into the Sheep River canyon.

Windy Point to Indian Oils via Dyson Creek

Distance 13.5 km
Height gain 320 m
Height loss 203 m
High point 1646 m
Map 82 J/10 Mount Rae

Highway access: 3, 4.
Also accessible from Windy Point trail (#273), Price Camp trail (#267) and Green Mountain trail (#270),

The boring nature of the walk improves with the proliferation of meadows and views as you near Dyson Creek. Right off the bat the unbridged crossing of the Sheep River can spell FAILURE during times of high water.

Wind down to the Sheep River and wade at the point where the black shale walls of the canyon break down into trees and meadow. On the west bank the trail climbs to a

terrace, site of John Lineham's lower logging camp, then bears right and crosses a cutline. A few metres farther on turn left up a major NE-SW cutline and climb a hill, but before starting up a second, steeper hill, turn right onto a more moderately-inclined trail that parallels the cutline to the junction with Price Camp trail.

The trail continues running parallel with the cutline, sometimes using the cutline itself, many kilometres of boring plodding under the pines. On cutline ford Dyson Creek and climb to a four-way junction with the Teskey Road.

OPTION Teskey Road

Distance 2.5 km, height gain 97 m. When we first went to Green Mountain and Junction Lookout we took the Teskey Road to Dyson Creek. Though short it has one huge snag: you have to wade the Sheep River.

Pick it up on the Sheep's south bank opposite Gorge Creek bridge on Highway 546. Heading right, it climbs to a hairpin bend with a thrilling view into Sheep River canyon. For eight years trucks from Bighorn Lumber Company rumbled up and down this road without even one incident of brakes failing at Hell's Fire Pass as they called it.

From the canyon top, the road cuts across open country to the four-way junction with the NE-SW cutline. Sheep trail is left and straight.

Turn left and follow the Teskey Road through increasingly open country to an unsigned junction above Dyson Creek meadows. If headed for Green Mountain trail turn left down the bank on what is really Teskey Road continued. Otherwise, stay right and in another half kilometre join a fire road where the official Green Mountain trail turns left and meets the Teskey Road in a V at Dyson Creek crossing. If detouring to Dyson Falls for lunch, why not make use of both these roads?

Turn right on the fire road, keeping right as you climb to a low pass at the head of a Dyson Creek tributary that has been thoroughly logged. In meadows, then, you pass through the gap between Mt. Hoffman (which has never turned me on) and an open hill to the north (GR648098) which I've climbed a couple of times for the view. It was from this top we watched three bears, one pure white, digging around in the cutblocks. Did I mention Dyson Creek is a well-known black bear hot spot?

Keep right as you head down waves of downhills to the Sheep River. At the last bend above the bridge, the next section of Sheep trail turns off to the left through a gate in the fence.

For Indian Oils trailhead **(access 4)** keep right and cross the rebuilt bridge over Tiger Jaw Falls. Follow the fire road up the hill to the parking lot located on the left after the gate. En route, check out the outrageously rough piece of river below the bridge as it squeezes through Devil's Elbow.

Tiger Jaw Falls is crossed when accessing Sheep trail from Indian Oils trailhead.

Indian Oils to Junction Creek via Bluerock Creek

Distance 4 km
Height gain 67 m
High point 1615 m
Map 82 J/10 Mount Rae

Highway access: 4, 5, 6 & 7.
Also accessible from Indian Oils (#281) and Bluerock Creek (#280).

The scenic riverside section with one crossing of the Sheep River.

On the east bank of the Sheep River turn left (or right if joining in from **access 4**) and pass through the gate, following a narrow trail running along a terrace out of sight of the Sheep River unfortunately. (Somewhere between two equestrian cutoffs to Indian Oils trail lies Sheep Falls.) But gradually the trail edges closer to the river, serving up occasional views of Gibraltar as you near the confluence with Bluerock Creek. Just west of Bluerock Creek highway bridge the trail fords the Sheep River at a quiet spot on a gravel bar. On the far bank is a junction.

To access 5, Bluerock campground
Go straight and climb up to Highway 546. Turn right and walk alongside the road to the bridge over Bluerock Creek. At the trail sign on the east bank, climb steps to the far west end of the campground loop road.

To access 6, Bluerock parking lot and equestrian campground
Go straight and climb up to Highway 546. Cross. The trail continues up a steep bank (crossing the old road twice), making a beeline for the equestrian campground loop road. Turn left, cross a four-way intersection and turn right into the parking lot.

To Junction Creek day-use area
Turn left and climb steps to the bank top opposite the equestrian campground access road. Walk a narrow strip of forest between the highway and the Sheep River now closeted in a gorge, rapids and deep pools following one another without variance. Nearing Junction Creek day-use area and loop road you cross a meadow and arrive among picnic tables. Keep left (Junction Creek interpretive trail to right), following the interpretive trail past an interpretive sign about log drives to a T-junction. For the lower parking lots turn right.

Otherwise, turn left, then right (straight on, Junction Creek logging road heads for the river). The trail continues along the bank top above descending trails to a viewpoint above a cliff, then turns away and climbs to the upper loop road near the biffy and upper parking lot.

Junction Creek to Burns Mine

Distance 12.5 km
Height gain 366 m
High point 1798 m
Map 82 J/10 Mount Rae

Highway access: 7.
Also accessible from Mist Creek (#205), and via two shortcuts from Bluerock Creek trail (#280).

Burns Mine is a popular day trip from access 7, particularly if you have a bike and can spend time looking around the mine site. The route is on straightforward old road, the scenery magnificent, dominated by Gibraltar whose menacing presence is useful to measure your progress by.

The ongoing trail (mine road) starts near the biffy at the end of the upper loop road and is really a continuation of the road. Straight off note a trail turning right (shortcut No. 1 to Bluerock Creek trail).

The mine road climbs onto a higher bench offering a more enlightening view into Junction Creek and increasingly dramatic glimpses of Gibraltar up ahead. At a road split officially go left. (If you opt for the grassy right-hand road, keep left.) Below

Shortcut No. 1 to Bluerock Creek trail
Distance 1 km. This well-used trail climbs to a T-junction with a sign indicating "Sheep Horse Trail 1 km". So you keep left and wind about pine forest, over a ridge, into a dip, finally climbing to the *unsigned* T-junction with Bluerock Creek trail (also Sheep horse trail) about 500 m from the trailhead.

Shortcut No. 2 to Bluerock Creek via Whiskey Lake (Sheep horse trail)
Distance 1.3 km. The backpacker's shortcut! Turn right and on official trail with red markers climb to a junction. Turn left, still climbing. Keep right and come to a fair-sized pond backdropped by the mountain known as Shunga-la-she, supposedly meaning "mountain white man shit on". Meadows make this a very pleasant spot in which to linger. Continue on often muddy trail in spruce forest to a four-way junction. Left and right is Bluerock Creek trail (#280).

Shunga-la-she the valley narrows. Here, the right-hand road comes back in and is signed "Sheep horse trail" (shortcut No. 2 to Bluerock Creek trail via Whiskey Lake).

Shortly, a horse trail alternative takes off from the left side of the road at red markers and is well worth taking, the noise of rapids demanding a closer look at the river to see what it's up to. At 4 km you arrive at the bridge over the Sheep River. A bridge nearer the water called Brown's Bridge was superseded by this later edition which, before K Country nailed down more planks, was auditioned for an Indiana Jones movie. There's a danger sign on the far bank for bikers zooming down the hill. So you climb the hill, then make a gradual descent, en route crossing Cliff Creek, back to the Sheep River.

Wade across and climb onto a bench. This is the perfect place to view the north face of Gibraltar—scene of an incredible nine-day climb in 1971 that was the first extended aid climb in the Canadian Rockies. Hardly surprising the first travellers up the valley called it "Sheer Cliff". To

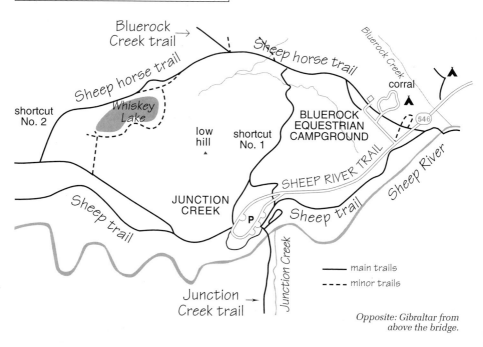

Opposite: Gibraltar from above the bridge.

its right is the more conventionally built Gibraltar Mountain as marked on the topo map. In 1918 four mine workers climbed to the top the easy way and were peering over the drop when the youngest lad—a nephew of Okotoks postmaster George Patterson—slipped and fell down the face. It's sobering to realize his body is still up there somewhere.

As you head west, the valley floor widens and the mountains fall back, letting in the sun. Ahead are new views of Mt. Rae and Storm Ridge. Recross the Sheep River and after one straight kilometre you're in a large meadow, leaning, but not too hard I hope, on a corral fence whose slow disintegration is shown in 30 years-worth of photos. Nearby is a stockpile of coal disguised as a grassy hill, and a signpost. This is where Mist Creek trail takes off up Rickert's Creek. Looking back, you're treated to a magnificent view of Gibraltar showing the northeast face in overhanging profile.

Unknowingly, for the last 3 km you have been travelling through private land, 67 per cent of it owned by the Burns family, the rest held in trust for five charities by the Royal Trust Company. Starting in 1909, Pat Burns bought the mining and surface rights from Julius Rickert, set about obtaining land grants and established the P. Burns Coal Mine Company. (To browse historical trash turn to the sketchmap accompanying route #205.) Today's Highway 546 is actually built on the railbed for the Calgary and Southwestern railway which came to naught when the postwar slump closed the mines in 1923. The mines were reopened briefly in 1945-51 by promoter Mervin Brown of Allied Industries who sent a few truckloads of coal over Brown's bridge to Okotoks.

The town site was located on the sloping meadow up to the left and consisted of bunkhouse, cookhouse, hospital, storage cabins, bathhouse and barns. In 1960 when the Forest Service razed the remaining buildings, they made a pathetic discovery; still lying in the corner of a room in the hospital was a trunk containing all the belongings of the ill-fated Patterson lad.

Burns Mine to Big Elbow trail

Distance 7.5 km
Height gain 314 m
Height loss 131 m
High point 2112 m
Map 82 J/10 Mount Rae

Accessible from Mist Creek (#205), and from Big Elbow trail (#317) west of Tombstone backcountry campground.

Expect flat going on fire road, the only climbing occurring at the end as you climb over the watershed to Big Elbow trail in the Elbow River valley. En route there are many options including a more interesting finish on pack trail. As you will have twigged, the Alberta Forest Service continued the fire road over Tombstone Pass and down the Little Elbow. In the days when you could hike it by car, it was not a road to be taken lightly and, lacking a tank, one came equipped with an axe, chains, hemp ropes and portable logs for *numerous river crossings*. So pack Tevas.

Straight off you cross the Sheep River on collapsed bridge. Between here and the next river crossing 1.2 km farther on, use a horse trail to your left. The next point of interest is Harry Denning's Cabin, a range rider's cabin and barns built in 1947 and used until 1971 when cattle were trailed out of the valley for the last time. Much of it was salvaged from the mine: windows, rough lumber, galvanized iron for the roof, planks for the floor. As the sign reads, "You are welcome to use this cabin. Leave things as you have found them with a little food and dry firewood". Its amenities include a wood stove, table, benches, bunk beds with sagging springs, some covered by plywood, a rhubarb patch and a biffy requiring orienteering skills.

The next creek you wade is Burns Creek. Two more river crossings follow in quick succession. A side road to left is Burns Creek exploration road (#277).

Denning's Cabin.

Recross the river. A long uneventful stretch along the northeast bank between Mt. Burns and the Rae Creek Hills ends with another river crossing. After a rise, pass a wallow to left, then note a couple of game trails heading right. The next trail to right at *a blazed tree* is the alternative finish, the pack trail route to Big Elbow trail at Tombstone backcountry campground.

Shortly cross Rae Creek just upstream of the forks. Strangely, the left-hand fork of the Sheep River which carries 90 per cent of the water is named Rae Creek, the now true head of the Sheep River that has its birthplace below the great east face of Mt. Rae. I say "now", because at one time the true head was the Rae Glacier until the Elbow River, cutting back, captured the headwaters. Here, the river and the road go their separate ways, the fire road angling up onto the watershed ridge. When Dr. George crossed in 1884 the whole ridge had been devastated by fire. It wasn't much different in the 1920s or in the 1960s even, but now it sports an attractive chequerboard look of meadows and young spruce. Look back one last time into the headwaters of Rae Creek and the tantalizing grassy ridges enclosing it to the east. What fine country there is here for further exploration!

Going downhill, easily ignore a trail to right, then, also to right, three prongs of a fork—all routes to Sheep Lakes—just before you cross the creek from Lake Rae (see option). At the bend at GR432148 the Elbow-Sheep cutoff turns off to the left (see Big Elbow trail #317). Cross a side creek and come to the T-junction with Big Elbow trail (left, straight).

DETOUR to Sheep Lakes
Distance 1.2 km to west lake.

Refer to the sketchmap on page 175. At about GR443142 turn east on one of the three prongs, preferably the one nearest to Lake Rae's creek. Continue up the handle, so to speak, cross a dry creekbed and climb onto a bench holding the lakes. Cross an intersecting trail and after trail's end continue crossing meadow to the shallow west lake. Draining west to the Elbow, its greatest asset is Tombstone Mountain as backdrop. Farther to the right, the larger east lake, draining east into the Sheep, offers a reflective view of Mt. Rae and the Rae Creek Hills. In between are two ponds lying smack on the watershed.

SEE ALSO:
PAGE 260 "ELBOW-SHEEP
CUTOFF"
&

OPTION
Lake Rae

Distance 1.3 km from Sheep trail, height gain 128 m, high point 2179 m. This is a popular weekend backpack from Highway 40 via Elbow Lake (#110 vol. 1) and Big Elbow trail (#317) using the Elbow-Sheep cutoff to Sheep trail.

At GR442143 look for an unsigned trail on the west bank of the creek issuing from Lake Rae which is not named Rae Creek, that name unaccountably being reserved for the upper Sheep River. It's a comfortable walk along the bank top through alternating meadows and mixed forest with larches to the lake.

The scene is exquisite, the lake and its surround of larch meadow cradled between the arms of two ridges and backdropped by the fairytale east summit of Mt. Rae.

There is scope here for further wandering. I remember (in the mists of time) parking the car at the pass and clambering over the left-hand arm into the cirque beyond the lake. Much less strenuous, you can follow the trail along the right-hand shoreline to one of those wretched creel survey boxes, then walk up the low ridge to the north at GR433138. I highly recommend this easily gained vantage point for a view of both the lake and the Elbow River valley.

Connection to Elbow-Sheep cutoff

The terrain is pretty well open, so when you lose the trail it doesn't much matter. Start from ridge at GR433138. Find a distinct trail that heads northwest, shortly settling into a traverse across grassy hillside to a prominent triangular-shaped boulder. Beyond the boulder descend a rib that low down curves to the left and eases off. The trail reappears and takes you out to Elbow-Sheep cutoff just east of the gap at about GR427147.

Lake Rae under Mt. Rae. Photo Alf Skrastins.

OPTIONAL FINISH
Via pack trail to Big Elbow trail

Distance 7.5 km from Burns Mine, high point 2088 m. This delightful trail is the direct route for anyone heading to Tombstone backcountry campground or turning east down Big Elbow trail. It starts well but runs into a bewildering number of other trails around the watershed. (As a bonus, you're in position to wander up the lower slopes of Cougar Mountain for the poster view of Sheep Lakes and Mt. Rae.)

As indicated, leave the fire road at GR469105. The blazed trail makes a beeline for Rae Creek and crosses it to a campsite on the far bank. Continue through a buttercup meadow into the valley of the north fork. Cross its tiny creek. The trail heads upstream, then climbs to a bench and levels off. Enter trees and the sketchmap from the right....

Cross a side creek and in open country, keep left as you climb to the day's high point. Aim for meadows north of west

Sheep Lake where you should hit a four-way junction marked by a half-toppled tree. (If you turned left here you would find yourself back on the fire road near to Lake Rae turnoff.) Turn right on the better trail that heads past a corral to a T-junction. To your right is a biffy and farther back a well-hidden Fish & Wildlife cabin where officers lie in wait for poachers.

Turn left here and after the trees end make an abrupt descent to the valley enclosing the creek from Lake Rae and descend its right bank to the Elbow River valley bottom. On reaching Big Elbow horse trail turn left for Tombstone backcountry campground, right for Little Elbow Recreation Area (fords both ways).

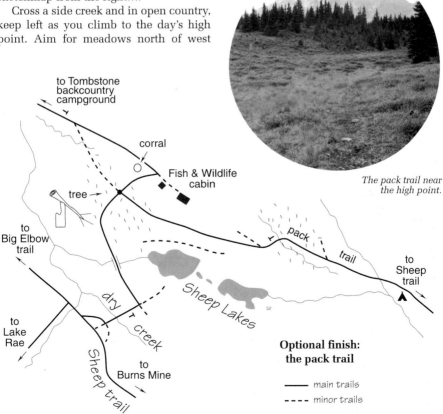

The pack trail near the high point.

Optional finish: the pack trail

——— main trails
- - - - minor trails

Burns Lake. View from the meadow of Storm Mountain.

277 BURNS LAKE — map 17

Backpack
Unofficial trail
Distance 5.5 km to falls, 6 km to lake
Height gain to lake 380 m
High point at lake 2255 m
Map 82 J/10 Mount Rae

Access: Via Sheep trail (#276). An exploration road leaves the southwest side of the fire road at GR489103.

A visit to Burns Creek waterfall, candidate for the highest non-continuous fall in K Country, is a must. Lovers of high alpine lakes should carry on into the cirque above, but be aware a penance must first be exacted in the shape of a stiff 244 vertical-m climb up the headwall. An even more exacting route into the cirque exists from Highway 40. See #201.

To the waterfall Fast time can be made along the road in the spruce-filled valley bottom between Storm Ridge and the Rae Creek Hills. Near the start keep left at the second bend and in mid valley, where the road crosses Burns Creek twice in quick succession, use the bypass trail on the right bank. Near the valley head there is a junction. The upper road to right is the recommended shortcut to the headwall trail. The lower road descends slightly past camping areas to the north fork just above the forks. Below the headwall a side trail leads to the creek below the elegant 150 m-high waterfall; not a single leap like Takkakkaw but a series of high steps connected by ladders of white water.

To Burns Lake via the headwall There is now a trail up the headwall, which does not mean it's any less strenuous. From the lower road keep right near the falls viewpoint and start climbing. The ground levels across the top of cliffs then steepens to a viewpoint where the better trail from the end of the upper road joins in. Continue up tight twisting trail to another viewpoint and a brief levelling. A final climb gains you the grassy ridge overlooking Burns Lake which is pie-shaped, wedged between a boulder field, and a rock wall which makes shoreline navigation difficult. From the crest there is a wonderful view of Storm Mountain showing its best side. The trail continues along the ridge, making a gradual descent through some spruce to the flat meadow of the northwest shore. In the background below Mt. Rae two rivulets from the upper cirques rush feverishly down grassy slopes, sinking underground before reaching the lake.

FURTHER EXPLORATIONS
Connecting with the Rae Creek Hills

A game trail continues along the left side of the ridge on scree, shortly crossing the ridge into a tributary head, then is clearly seen steering northeast just above treeline into the grassy cirque below top GR460094.

The east cirque Continue up the ridge to the right of the deeply incised right-hand creek into meadows below a line of wavy cliffs guarding Rae's spectacular east summit.

The upper tarn

Pick your way up the left side of the left-hand creek (167 m height gain). Another good camping spot a stone's throw away from the route over to Highway 40.

Continuing into the west cirque This is an easy, claustrophobic walk between Mt. Arethusa and King's Ridge on the left and a totty rock ridge on the right. Don't bother with horrible moraines at the end; there is no nice tarn hidden in its folds.

Incredibly, the unattractive slopes rising to King's Ridge were the scene of no less than 10 attempts on Mt. Rae by Don King, the three Blayney brothers and conscripted friends in the 1940s and 1950s. In '49 they struggled to the lower summit in a "furious blizzard" and hurriedly placed a bronze memorial plaque to fellow climber "Cuzzy" Cousins among its rocks. In '51 the plaque had vanished, so scramblers, take a look around as you tackle the pinnacle.

Anyway, on their 11th try in '53 they succeeded *from Highwood Pass* (today's normal route) and learned that Gordon Langille and E. H. J. Smythe had beaten them to it in 1951. That's not the end of the story. While on a recce a few weeks earlier, Langille with Lawrence Grassi had spotted a cairn already on top! So who made the first ascent of Mt. Rae remains a mystery.

Burns Creek waterfall seen from near the top of the headwall.

278 RAE CREEK HILLS — map 17

Backpack
Unofficial trail & route, creek crossing
Distance to highest top 5 km
Height gain to highest top 905 m
High point 2688 m
Map 82 J/10 Mount Rae

Access: Via Sheep trail (#276)

Since K Country closed the fire road (Sheep trail) to traffic, I've been kicking myself for not climbing these delectable grassy hills in the days when you could do your hiking by car. So now they require a backpack and a camp to be made at Sheep Lakes, Rae Creek or Burns Creek. Have fun working out your own routes. The following is just one suggestion from Sheep trail.

Alpine poppies.

From Sheep trail's high point at GR447135 follow a trail down the left (east) bank of a tributary toward Rae Creek valley. Where another trail comes in from the left you cross to the right bank. Close to valley bottom jog right, then cross Rae Creek.

The haul up to **north peak** at GR453117 (2606 m) is not totally straightforward. Above you is a wall of crags requiring a detour to either right or left to gain the north ridge above. We went right, a tortuous climb up steep grass where we stopped often, ostensibly to admire the spectacular east face of Mt. Rae. On the ridge the angle eases past a cairn, then narrows and steepens for the last lap to the summit.

Losing 152 m, walk down the wide grassy south ridge to a col. On game trail head up the ridge to **south peak** at GR460098 (2667 m), encountering a little scree and rock near the top. This summit is marked by a metal post. From this vantage point you look straight down the flat valley floor of upper Rae Creek, the grass a suspiciously bright green colour littered with herds of grazing hippos. To the south there's a new view of Burns Creek, Storm Ridge, and the mountains of Storm and Mist. From this summit's west spur a ridge

branches south to the lovely **south outlier** at GR464090 which rewards with an uninterrupted view of the valley head.

Turn east (left) and descend two easy steps to a col. Start up **east peak** (GR465105). Its broad south ridge, crossed by rock bands, narrows higher up to scree and splintery outcrops—a suitably impressive finish for the highest summit of the day at 2688 m. Not far below the summit on the *north* side we found Woolly fleabanes, which I adore, and its sidekick, Alpine poppy—large bunches of them—growing in the rocks.

Purists should head east on scree ridge to the **east outlier** GR469105 (2636 m) for a view of the Sheep River valley.

DESCENT OPTIONS
From **south peak** you can descend into the cirque to the south and pick up a trail heading southwest to Burns Lake. From **south outlier** follow either the south or east ridges into Burns Creek.

From **east peak** we went north, prolonging the enjoyment of open ridges. Turn the summit crag to the right, and the step to the left. Elk trails lead to a creek crossing at about GR470124 where you're only a few minutes away from the fire road in the Sheep River valley.

#278. Nearing the summit of south peak you get this view of east peak, the highest of the hills. The final ridge is relatively narrow.

#279, Junction Creek. The head of Junction Creek below the Dogtooth Mountains. The main valley trail leads into the cirque to the right.

279 JUNCTION CREEK — map 18

**Long day hikes, backpack
Unofficial trails & routes, one major
river crossing, creek crossings
Map 82 J/10 Mount Rae**

Opposite: The three-tier fall on the main valley trail. Photo Alf Skrastins.

Access: Sheep River Trail (Hwy. 546) at Junction Creek day-use area. Use one of the lower parking lots. NOTE: This section of Highway 546 is closed between December 1st and May 15th. **Also** accessible from Picklejar Lakes (#209).

Junction Creek flows noisily through a dark, spruce and fir-filled valley with numerous side valleys branching off to east and west. It's unusual in that it's completely enclosed by peaks of the Highwood Range barring easy escape to the outside. While the main valley is served by a good trail shared by hunters and equestrians, side valley trails are very rough and best avoided by inexperienced hikers. Of course, everything is dependent on you being able to wade the Sheep River right at the start!

279A Main valley trail

**Distance 11 km
Height gain 549 m
High point 2124 m**

This is the main thoroughfare from which all other trails branch off. The forest trail is more interesting than you might think, particularly where it nears the river and crosses lively tributaries with many rapids and waterfalls to delight in, including the greatest swim hole this side of the Pacific Ocean. Bikeable to the sawmill site.

To Junction Lake junction at 4 km From the middle of the lower parking lots a trail makes a beeline for the Sheep River where it is immediately apparent that attaining the Junction Creek logging road on the south bank is dependent on low water. A better crossing place exists a little upstream at the tumbling dam.

On the south bank follow the logging road which has grassed over nicely, though rock snakes and occasional corduroy require concentration from bikers. At one point you draw close to Junction Creek and view two tumbling dams built to ease the passage of logs over rapids between the sawmill and the Sheep where logs were further jockeyed along the river to the mill in Okotoks. Enter the sawmill site at 3.5 km. As you stand there, slowly sinking in sawdust, look up to the right at a cliff. In 1918 R. B. Spackmann noted a cave "about 12 m in diameter and about 13 m up from the talus". In fact, there are several intriguing holes on the lower slopes of Shunga-la-she.

The old road continues into the trees. A three/four log-high enclosure on the left signals a trail junction on the north bank of the first tributary to the west at GR604044. See #279B, Junction Lake.

To Waterfall Valley junction at 7 km Cross the tributary between waterfalls. The next section of trail follows a high bank (view of the valley head), then drops to crunchy gravel bars. Again you climb high and on the following traverse run into muck where springs puddle below high muddy banks. Or you used to. I'm glad to report that persons unknown—hunters perhaps—have fixed it up into some semblance of a firm trail. Shortly after this, the trail turns right up the second side creek to the west to camping spots. Detour upstream to a lovely three-tier waterfall which must surely be a sight at runoff if you can only figure out a way to cross the Sheep. The trail beyond IS NOT the route up waterfall valley. Return to the main trail and cross the waterfall creek above a waterfall, then climb sharply to a junction with cairn. See #279C Waterfall Valley.

To Junction Mountain cirque junction at 8.5 km Descend to Junction Creek at the swim hole—a magnificent piece of river architecture which starts higher up where a small fall pours into a circular jacuzzi. Separating that pool from the swim hole downstream is a wide, flat underwater *bridge* ideal for lying around on. It even has a ledge for deeper sitting.

If going farther wade Junction Creek and climb steadily up the east slope out of earshot of the river. The trail drops to cross the second side creek to the east (usually dry), then climbs its south bank to a high point and a junction with the trail into Junction Mountain cirque. See #279D.

To valley head at 11 km Keep right at the junction and drop back down to Junction Creek where a side trail crosses the river to a well-used camping spot.

The main trail stays on the east bank a little longer, then crosses above the third side creek to the west. Interestingly, the main creek is often dry above this confluence. Above the trees rises a spectacular cliff which is replaced by a clone as you press on south across the dry creekbed of the fourth side creek to the west. The excitement mounts as you catch a glimpse of the Dogtooth Mountains between the trees.

The valley is curving around to the southeast, but not the trail. Unexpectedly, it turns right and climbs to the lip of the fifth cirque to the west, a grassy flat locked below an impenetrable headwall at the foot of the Dogtooths. Across the valley is Pyriform Mountain whose west slopes offer a steep but straightforward slog up scree to the summit ridge.

279B Junction Lake

Distance from junction 4.5 km
Height gain 506 m from junction
High point 2197 m

On balance, the tarn at the head of this long valley is not worth the long walk in. It's the journey that's so enjoyable; the lush green meadows and the lively stream.

Turn right up the first side stream flowing out of the west. The well-used trail running along the north bank above a little canyon is faster but much less fun than crab-crawling round pools and solving problematical

steps in the creekbed. Sooner or later, though, you have to descend to creek level and rock hop along the right bank past a procession of small waterfalls.

Slow progress ends at the point where the creek turns southwest at GR586038. Here, a deeper rift not apparent from the topo map forces you to climb to a bench high on the north side of the valley. Once you've gained the height, it's fast, easy walking for many kilometres through spruce forest and lush green meadows. As you near the lake the valley unfolds and you leave the trees far behind.

The tarn is not a pretty one despite its dramatic situation in a basin ringed by high nameless mountains. The shore is muddy and after the snowbanks have melted, underground seepage reduces the tarn to two shallow puddles. Earlier in the year water spills over the lip of the basin and tumbles down the rocky creekbed in a waterfall.

Above: The mid section of Waterfall Valley as seen from the sketchy game trail that traverses scree to the first tributary on the left. (Alternatively, you can use the creekbed). After this a trail can be seen following left bank meadows into the lower basin. The low point is the false col.

Opposite: Junction Lake. Photo Alf Skrastins.

279C Waterfall Valley to Picklejar Lakes

Distance from junction 4.2 km
Height gain 606 m from junction
Height loss to Picklejar Lakes 226 m
High point 2405 m at col

This valley leads to the one break in the horseshoe of mountains enclosing Junction Creek. This is not the same as saying the route over to Picklejar Lakes is a doddle. This is a rugged hike with steep scree on the south side of the col. The working name comes from the three-tier waterfall that identifies the valley from Junction Creek.

To col GR579992 At the cairn turn right onto a narrower trail, blazed both sides, that after a few preliminary windings zigs up the steepest slope on the whole ascent. From the top a gently-rising traverse leads to the creek bank near a waterfall step.

A fainter trail rounds the base of a ridge *in trees* (don't on any account attempt the willows higher up the slope), descending slightly *into* the creekbed, likely dry at this point. Either follow the bed to the next tributary joining in from a left-hand cirque (turn rock step on left), or climb a grassy rib up the left bank and traverse scree on

183

#279C. Starting down to Picklejar Lakes from the col. Photo Alf Skrastins.

sketchy game trail to the tributary-creek junction. Either way, pick up/continue on the same trail that follows left-bank meadows beneath a spectacular buttress, crosses another tributary, then climbs a grassy ramp into a basin.

Cross the basin (meadow, larch, spruce), aiming for the "obvious col". But after slogging up scree all you find yourself in is another basin, this one lacking the loveliness of the lower one, just minimal grass and shale. Below a scree glacier sweeping down from Peak GR571002, steer for the lowest gap in the rim, specifically the gap below the rocky knob at GR579992. Down below is a beautiful sight: two of the Picklejar Lakes glittering in the afternoon sun.

To Picklejar Lakes Descend a straightforward scree runnel, worn yellow, for 100 vertical m, then cut across to fourth lake where you can pick up a trail (#209).

279D Junction Mountain cirque

Distance from junction 2 km
Height gain 244 m
High point 2225 m

A trail gets you started into the cirque southwest of Junction Mountain. Carry up water from Junction Creek.

At the junction go straight on a trail that continues climbing up the south bank of the side creek, ultimately petering out in clearings below the mountain wall. Come up here for the view of the Dogtooth Mountains at the head of the valley, their strata revealed more boldly by sun.

Changing direction, head northeast across the two heads of the creek into the cirque. The timberline spruce are particularly beautiful, but the cirque is arid. You were expecting flower meadows? At its head, Junction Mountain is an unappealing mess of steep scree half smothering slabs and cliff bands, not a place for beginner scramblers.

#279D. Junction Mountain cirque, looking toward Junction Mountain.

280 BLUEROCK CREEK — map 18

Day hike
Official trail with signposts, red
markers & cairns
Distance 9 km
Height gain 625 m
Height loss 472 m
High point 2134 m
Map 82 J/10 Mount Rae

*Kiska Mnoga Iyarhe near
the trail's high point.*

Access: Sheep River Trail (Hwy. 546). Follow signs to Bluerock Equestrian campground. At the forks turn left into a parking lot. NOTE: This section of Highway 546 is closed between December 1st and May 15th.
Also accessible from Gorge Creek trail (#283), and from Sheep trail (#276) at three points.

This rather strenuous trail connects the Sheep River valley to the middle section of Gorge Creek. Most people, though, make stunning meadows on the southeast ridge of Bluerock Mountain their destination. With two vehicles, consider a point to point with Gorge Creek (#283) and Indian Oils (#281).

Follow the road around to the corral at the head of the middle fork. The trail, also Sheep horse trail temporarily, starts between the corral and the ramp. Alternatively, use a shortcut that starts to the left of the ramp.

As you follow the logging road disregard every grassy skid road heading right to the sawmill site at Bluerock Creek. An *unsigned* trail to left is shortcut No. 1 to Sheep trail at Junction Creek day-use area. Cross a small creek and come to a signposted junction where Sheep horse trail turns left.

Go straight, continuing on logging road into the confines of Bluerock Creek valley. Just past a clearing with picnic table (available for collapse on the return trip), turn right on a trail and slither down the hill to Bluerock Creek footbridge. You wash the mud off your boots and grumble about losing 100 m of altitude and having to backtrack, both no-no's in the school of advanced trail building. Personally, I'm

waiting for K Country to build a connector from the interpretive trail.

On *terra firma* drag yourself up a steep slope to the left of a side creek. None too soon the trail turns left and makes a long slowly rising traverse, eventually attaining Bluerock's southeast ridge after a two-log side creek crossing. Continue along the broad ridge in the pines. A rise (more zigs) and grassy avenues (cairns) lead to the trail's high point (bench, horse rail) below *Kiska Mnoga Iyarhe* (Ram Mountain)—a beautiful place in meadows that fall gently away into Bluerock Creek. Here's a chance to check out both forks of the rarely visited upper valley, its mysteries revealed from this high vantage point. Forget about climbing Bluerock Mountain from this end; it rebuffs all scramblers' attempts. I refer you to route #283, Gorge Creek.

On-goers should continue along the trail that swings over to the east side of the ridge, revealing an aerial view of Gorge Creek and all its tributaries. Shortly, the trail zigs down into trees, then makes an extremely long descending traverse across the skirts of Bluerock's east face to trail #283 in Gorge Creek. TIP: The tributary crossed at about GR573140 offers a shortcut to Indian Oils trail at GR597133. See #281.

#280. From the high point of Bluerock Creek trail you look into the headwaters of Bluerock Creek.

*#281. Indian Oils trail starting the descent to Gorge Creek.
Bluerock Mountain and Mt. Rose in the background.*

281 INDIAN OILS TRAIL — map 18

Half-day, day hike
Official trail with signposts & red
markers, creek crossings
Distance 7.5 km
Height gain 396 m
Height loss 131 m
High point 1829 m
Map 82 J/10 Mount Rae

Access: Sheep River Trail (Hwy. 546). NOTE:
This section of Highway 546 is closed between
December 1st and May 15th.
1. Longest Indian Oils day-use area.
2. 300 m west of Indian Oils parking lot access
road the trail intersects the highway. Use a small
parking area on the right (north) side.
3. Shortest Sheep River Falls day-use area.
Walk west along the highway for 100 m to where
the trail intersects the highway.
Also accessible from Sheep trail (#276) at two
places: 100 m and 1 km west of the bridge over
the Sheep River at Tiger Jaws Falls. Also from
Gorge Creek (#283), and from the western
terminus of South Gorge Creek trail (#282).

This trail crosses the group of low hills
between the Sheep River and Gorge Creek,
meandering through a typical foothills mix
of meadow, aspen and pine forest. You'll
notice it's carefully routed to include several fine viewpoints.

From access 1 A trail leaves the far end of
Indian Oils day-use area parking lot and in
a few metres arrives at a T-junction. (The
left-hand trail is an equestrian link to Sheep
trail across the Sheep River.) Your trail
turns right and crosses the highway where
it picks up **access 2**.

Begin a gradual climb along a mine access road to a strip mine site where coal
spoil is thinly disguised by new tree
growth. Take time to explore the terrace up-
slope, the site of an Indian Oils well. In
1919, a fire, credited to one of Burns's road
building crew, swept down the valley to the
forest boundary (which accounts for all the
Lodgepoles), in passing burning out Indian

Oils which was luckily not operating at the
time. Later reports indicate a well was
drilled to a depth of 1,130 ft. in 1929.
Around the same time various coal companies were taking an interest in the area
starting with Indian Oils (1929-31), and
ending in 1945-51 with Payne's strip mine.

When you're done poking around, continue along a newer trail to the junction
above a side creek with **access 3**. Turn right.

From access 3 Before setting off, take a 15
minute trip to Sheep Falls. The gravelled
trail starts between the two parking areas
and heads downstream to the overlook.
Interestingly, the bench is in memory of
Bob Iceton, the son of Bill Iceton who decades ago blasted the road around Windy
Point to Bighorn Ranger Station.

Return to the parking lot, then walk west
along the highway for 100 m to where
Indian Oils trail (come in across the Sheep
River from Sheep trail) crosses the highway. Turn right. Shortly, you cross a side
creek and join the trail from **accesses 1 and
2**. Keep left.

The trail follows the north bank of the side
creek for 1.5 km, then zigs over the grassy
ridge to the north (view) into the headwaters of a creek issuing from a small pond—
scenario of the grizzly scare in 1980.
Traverse to a gap between two grassy hills
and descend slightly into the headwaters of
a Gorge Creek tributary.

South Gorge Creek trail (#282) comes in
from the right where the trail bends left,
now aiming for a gap in the hills to the west
where you're treated to a full width view of

Bluerock Mountain. Drop sharply down the west flank to the Gorge Creek drainage. Beyond the drift fence cross a creek that flows through a gap into Gorge Creek. As you'll discover, there are actually *three* gaps separated by small conical hills covered in pines. The trail cuts behind the first hill, then descends to a second side stream where it turns right and passes through gap No. 2. Cross the creek, and a few metres later wade Gorge Creek to the north bank where you pick up Gorge Creek trail (#283).

Westbound hikers can save themselves at least two major fords of Gorge Creek by a bushwhack along the south bank.

Shortcut to Bluerock Creek trail

This unofficial route cuts behind all three gaps and hills, saving you 1 km and four crossings of Gorge Creek.

Leave Indian Oils where it turns into the second gap at GR597133. Cross the side creek and continue in the same direction as previously, following a cattle trail along the right edge of a boggy meadow and through some trees. Cross a tributary and then the stream flowing through gap No. 3. In a large meadow head left (west) on an old track that has come in from Gorge Creek. After the meadow narrows to willowy strips, the trail turns left across the creek onto an alluvial fan falling from Bluerock Mountain. Head upwards, intersecting Bluerock Creek trail on the fan at about GR573140.

---

282 SOUTH GORGE CREEK TRAIL — map 18

Day hike
Official trail, signposts & red markers
Distance 5 km
Height gain NE-SW 213 m
High point 1783 m
Map 82 J/10 Mount Rae

Northeast access: Via Gorge Creek trail (#283), 200 m west of the north fork crossing.
South west access: Via Indian Oils trail (#281) at the head of a Gorge Creek tributary.

This little trail enables the day tripper to make a loop with Gorge Creek and Indian Oils trails. Meadows, pines, aspens and cows just about sums it up.

The meadow.

From Gorge Creek trail Straight off make a beeline for Gorge Creek and cross via three logs wired together. Wind up the bank, then on slightly rising trail through pine forest with alder understorey, head southwest to a big lush meadow. Edge around the meadow to a T-junction with a NW-SE cutline. Turn left and follow the cutline, making one diversion into the meadow to get around a bog. Back in pines, descend slightly to a valley whose creek—NOT named South Gorge Creek—flows into Gorge Creek near Highway 546. Here, turn right onto a trail heading west.

From the junction a gradual ascent is made along the north bank of the creek to the open valley head where you cross the creek on a bridge and join Indian Oils trail at GR 613124, just short of the gap in the hills to the west.

283 GORGE CREEK — maps 18, 17 & 13

Day hike, backpack
Official trail with signposts & red
markers, creek crossings
Distance 14.5 km
Height gain 411 m
High point 1951 m
Map 82 J/10 Mount Rae

Access: Gorge Creek Trail (Hwy.) at Gorge Creek day-use area. NOTE: This highway is closed between December 1st and May 15th. **Also** accessible from the southern terminus of Gorge Link trail (#289), the northeastern terminus of South Gorge Creek trail (#282), the northern terminus of Indian Oils trail (#281), the northern terminus of Bluerock Creek (#280), the western terminus of Volcano Creek (#284) and the southern terminus of Threepoint Mountain trail (#320).

Gorge Creek is a scenic valley of alternating gorges and meadows reaching far back into the Front Range between Mt. Rose and Bluerock Mountain. As you can see by the number of "also accessibles", you can choose from an amazingly large number of connecting trails from which to make circuits and point to points using two vehicles.

It begins beside the biffy. A little way in keep left and downhill and cross a grassy old road. Now on exploration road, dip to a side creek crossing, then gradually descend into meadows above Gorge Creek. Go either way at a split. As you turn right into the north fork listen for the cascade below the trail at the confluence of the two creeks. In spate, water streaming down slabs in a classy lacy effect is worth a scrabble down the bank. Unless heading up the north fork, wade the north fork to the junction with Gorge Link trail at the 1.2 km mark.

Keep left on the old road, passing the northeastern terminus of South Gorge Creek trail a few minutes later. The road follows the undulating bank top, and features three steep climbs which are irritating when you

know the road is descending to valley bottom. Incidentally, the cutline and its access road heading north from near the high point was one of the routes we took pre K Country to Volcano Creek. It's not a bad route up the northwest fork of the north fork.

But back to Gorge Creek trail. At creek level you leave the road and take to a trail heading right. Keep left at a cutline and come to a delightful section of creek where chutes and pools follow one after the other. Not too much farther on watch for where the official trail turns right up a hill and don't blithely carry on into a large meadow. Having paddled my way through the troublesome narrows in the past, this is one ascending trail I welcome. You'll especially appreciate the airy situation of the traverse, the flowers of the shale slope and the view. On your way down again, pass through the drift fence and arrive once more at valley bottom in cow meadows. Framed in the V is Bluerock Mountain. Five km from the trailhead, Indian Oils trail turns off to the left across the creek, passing through the second gap in the hills to the south.

Not far west of the junction people intent on climbing Mt. Ware should note a game trail climbing the right bank of a small gully (see option). Shortly after this you enter a meadow with a lone pine landmark signalling the start of three close-together creek crossings. The third occurs opposite gap No. 3. (Years ago we used to end our Gorge Creek forays by taking the trail through gap No. 3 into the large meadow with range rider's cabin. For some strange reason I never took a photo of that cabin while I now take 10 frames of every questionable ruin

189

even if it's only two logs high! This meadow gave wonderful views of both Bluerock Mountain and Mt. Ware. Nowadays, if you followed the creek far enough you would intersect Bluerock Creek trail. See #281.)

Now on the southwest bank of Gorge Creek, continue to the junction with Bluerock trail heading left. The valley is squeezing in again, forcing a climb up and over a forested side ridge to get around the next bend. Cross the creek for the fourth time and begin climbing the northeast bank in anticipation of the black shale gorge up ahead. The labour of the ascent is well worthwhile for the far-reaching view of the upper valley between Mt. Rose and Bluerock Mountain that is disclosed, the splendour of the scene further enhanced by the dramatic situation of the trail as it follows the lip of the gorge to the big bend where the valley turns west.

Here you part company with Gorge Creek and continue in a northerly direction over the height of land into Volcano Creek. En route you pass the Volcano Creek shortcut and campground trail to right about 300 m before the trail terminates at a T-junction with Threepoint Mountain trail (straight) and Volcano Creek trail (right).

OPTIONS
Bluerock Mountain 2798 m
Distance from big bend 4.5 km, height gain from big bend 863 m. To all you people lusting after the peak from Bluerock Creek trail, Bluerock is an easy scramble from the head of Gorge Creek. But it requires a camp.

At the big bend, leave Gorge Creek trail and head west on a well-used trail that follows the edge of the gorge through alternating forest and small, well-watered allotments of wild onions. In 1.7 km the trail peters out below Mt. Rose.

Now from the topo map it appears you can walk straight up the creek. Not so. A cliff encircles it, requiring a stiff scramble with a heavy pack. I recommend you steer for the obvious gap between Mt. Rose and Bluerock Mountain at GR541168. The going is easy and enjoyable, mainly a wade through great

drifts of valerians, fleabanes and long-stemmed forget-me-nots growing on the damper facets of the hillside. The gap is actually a large meadow sloping into a Cougar Creek tributary (a route into Cougar Creek perhaps?). Pick one of numerous game trails traversing south through trees into Gorge Creek above the cliff. Timberline meadows make good camping places.

The fact that our short evening stroll before turning in evolved into an ascent of Bluerock Mountain explains why I have no photos of the climb, because quite apart from leaving the camera in the tent, the sun was setting. (Please send photos c/o the publisher.) Basically, you walk up the valley, turning the waterfall step on left side scree via the sheep trail. Continue easily toward the notch at GR550154, then grovel up the north face on nice stable rubble to where a breach in the rock band lets you onto the northwest ridge. Turn left and in less than 10 minutes reach the top. The summit is quite sharp, poised above the eastern drop-off. Naturally, there's a view of all the Sheep River trail system. But what makes Bluerock a superior viewpoint is Mt. Assiniboine seen off to the west!

The celebrated view from above the gorge of upper Gorge Creek, Gorge/Cougar Gap, Mt. Rose and a few points of Threepoint Mountain.

Bluerock Mountain. The photo is taken from the upper valley above the cliff band and shows the waterfall step and the easy upper slopes below the northwest ridge.

View from Mt. Ware's summit ridge of Gorge Creek valley, Bluerock Mountain (left) and Mt. Rose.

Mt. Ware 2124 m, GR592155
Distance round trip 4 km, height gain/loss 448 m. Once called Ware Head or John Ware's Head, this shapely little mountain overlooking Gorge Creek is one of my favourites. It has one drawback. It's very attractive to sheep, so, naturally, it's one of the tick summits of the World. On our first trip to the cairn we were targetted by scores of these creepy critters running up our boots in a race to see who could get to our hair first. Uttering "aagh" we dived off the east end as fast as we could slither. Just don't go in spring. OK?

The loop requires off-trail confidence and routefinding ability. Leave Gorge Creek trail just west of Indian Oils junction. As mentioned, a good game trail leads up the right bank of a small gully into pine forest. At the gully top veer left on the better trail that rises gradually to a levelling and appears to peter out. Turn uphill a short way, then wend left below another small gully starting up. A trail climbs up the left side of this second gully (augmented by other trails coming in from the left), higher up dissipating in mule deer meadows just be-

low the broad ridge extending southeast from the mountain.

After gaining the ridge turn left and walk up to "the head". This final slope is steeper and higher than it looks, a mess of gravel, scree, grass and rock. But eventually you pull yourself over the top to the summit cairn. Surrounded by drop-offs, this little summit has a feeling of height remarkable for such a low hill. You'll be delighted by the view of Gorge Creek towered over by Bluerock Mountain, Mt. Rose and Threepoint Mountain. To the north you can trace the route over Surveyor's Ridge should you be heading that way to Volcano Ridge trail.

Walk along the delectable summit ridge to its west end above a cliff. At a weakness on the right side scrabble down easy rocks onto scree, then swing left below outcrops to gain the broad grassy southwest ridge at GR588154. Descend easily in a southeasterly direction to Gorge Creek, aiming to hit the trail between second and third creek crossings. Use the hill at GR594138 as a beacon.

284 VOLCANO CREEK — map 13

Backpack
Official trail, signposts & red markers
Distance 4 km
Height gain 122 m
High point 1951 m
Map 82 J/10 Mount Rae

East access: Via Volcano Ridge trail (#285) at Volcano Creek.
West Access: Junction of Threepoint Mountain (#320) and Gorge Creek (#283) trails.

An improved cow trail along upper Volcano Creek offers an easy link between Volcano Ridge trail and Threepoint Mountain and Gorge Creek trails farther to the west.

EAST TO WEST
The trail leaves Volcano Ridge trail on the north bank of Volcano Creek and follows the north side of the valley the whole way, keeping to dry pasture above a flat valley bottom choked with willow brush. About

halfway along, Bluerock Mountain, framed by forested side slopes, comes into view— a thrilling sight. The trail splits at the valley head, going either side of a low forested hill.

The right-hand trail, still following the north bank of the stream, reaches the Gorge Creek/Threepoint Mountain trail junction in 1 km.

If you're heading down Gorge Creek take the better left-hand trail which crosses the creek and follows an open draw past Threepoint backcountry campground to the four-way junction with Gorge Creek trail (left and right).

Bluerock Mountain from Volcano Creek.

285 VOLCANO RIDGE TRAIL — map 18, 13 & 14

Day hike, backpack
Official trail, signposts & red markers
Distance 12 km
Height gain S-N 290 m
Height loss S-N 268 m
High point 1935 m
Maps 82 J/10 Mount Rae,
82 J/15 Bragg Creek

South access: Via Gorge Link trail (#289).
North access: The junction of Wildhorse (#315) and Threepoint Creek (#295) trails in Quirk Creek.
Also accessible from the eastern terminus of Volcano Creek trail (#284), the eastern terminus of Forgetmenot Mountain (#287) and the western terminus of Link Creek trail (#288).

This Gorge Creek/Threepoint Creek connector takes you over the open ridge at GR609178. It's usually travelled in combination with other trails to make loops, the smallest possible being a 13 km circuit incorporating Gorge Creek, Volcano Ridge, Link Creek and Gorge Link trails. If starting from the south end the watershed is a good objective for a spring conditioning hike that will leave you breathless!

SOUTH TO NORTH

To Link trail The trail branches off Gorge Link trail at GR627161 in the north fork of Gorge Creek. Straightaway it enters a narrow forested valley. You cross a tributary and both forks of the tiny creek, then begin the climb to the watershed, a dusty treadmill up a shaley ridge under the pines. I'd swear the contours on the topo map are not nearly close enough! I'm sorry for mountain bikers who have to push their bikes up this hill, though the downhill run must be a blast. The gradient eases at the traverse preceding the four-way junction with Link Creek trail (right), which is actually a five-way junction with a cutline if you look carefully.

To Threepoint Creek Cross the cutline on old road and curve left onto the watershed ridge at km 3.5, at this point a large shaley meadow with an extraordinary view of foothills and Front Range mountains, Mt. Ware and Bluerock Mountain preeminent among them. The semi-open hill to the northwest is Surveyor's Ridge (see option).

A few metres down the hill on the north slope keep right (Surveyor's Ridge trail to left) and wind down and right into the head of Volcano Creek's south fork. Turn left onto a cutline. In brief, for the next 4 km you follow this N-S cutline and its access road along the west bank of Volcano Creek, en route passing a bewildering number of cutlines and side roads. The main route is always obvious, though.

In more detail. The first major stream you cross is the main fork of Volcano Creek where Volcano Creek trail turns left at a signpost. Next, cross Rock Creek. Farther north the road semicircles to the left to cross an unnamed creek. On its north bank an old road heads upstream to "Black Cow Hill" (see option).

A dip precedes the place where you turn right on a shortcut trail. Regain the cutline/access road (now oriented NE-SW) at a T-junction. Turn right and follow the road downhill and round a bend past coal seams to Threepoint Creek, here idling through a shallow trough. Who would guess that in half a kilometre it would fall over a cliff in a series of spectacular falls quite hidden from any trail.

The road winds uphill to a T-junction with old Forgetmenot Mountain fire road on the north bank where trails #286 and #287 turn left (no signpost). Turn right. Disappointingly, the route has kept well away from the route's most scenic feature, but finally you get your first startling look into the black shale gorge of Threepoint Creek which coupled with Volcano Creek gorge is the grandest of all the gorges in the Sheep. Continue to enjoy the view for another 10 minutes until at Quirk Creek meadow you turn away to the junction with Wildhorse and Threepoint Creek trails.

Descending the hill between Link and Gorge Link trails.

The view from the north end of the trail of Allsmoke Mountain and Threepoint Creek gorge. The watershed you cross is at extreme right.

The loop. The hiker has left Mt. Ware (background) and is hiking up the grassy southeast ridge onto Surveyor's Ridge.

UNOFFICIAL SIDE TRIPS
Surveyor's Ridge (GR592179)

Distance to high point from Volcano Ridge trail 2.5 km, height gain 262 m, high point 2158 m. If you've started early enough from Gorge Creek trailhead and the watershed is under your belt with an hour to go before lunchtime, consider extending the hike to a superior viewpoint: a remote grassy ridge off the beaten track. Getting there entails a little easy bushwhacking so be proficient in off-trail hiking and simple routefinding.

At the unmarked trail division a little way down the north side of the watershed at GR608178 keep left on a cutline access road heading southwest. Within sight of a meadow where the road bends left, transfer to a good trail on the right side that shortcuts across to a NW-SE cutline. Turn right and walk up the cutline between Lodgepoles.

Just *before* you reach the top of the cutline hill turn left into the forest at a spot where the trees are fairly well spaced and steer south-westerly to the gap on the north ridge of your objective at GR594184. Here turn left and clamber up the open right side of the ridge to the summit. It comes as a huge surprise to find this remote foothill decked out with an enormous 2 m-high cairn, a white post and a survey pin to trip over.

The large cairn on Surveyor's Ridge.

From the top you're treated to a full length view of Volcano Creek, all the way down to Threepoint Creek gorge and all the way up to Mt. Rose and Threepoint Mountain. To the south, beyond that delicious little peak of Mt. Ware, lies a diverse landscape of foothills and valleys, and Front Range peaks that you can have fun identifying.

The Loop Experienced off-trail walkers can connect with Mt. Ware and use Gorge Creek trail to close the loop of about 19 km.

Continue along the summit ridge over a second top (grass, shale), and down the other side into pine forest with a shaley floor. At a low point around GR585170, turn left down a southeast ridge, immediately cutting across the ridge to its southwest side which is all grass. Low down, rock steps are turned on the right by a trail that leads straight to the col at GR587159.

A short uphill push through trees gains you the broad northwest ridge of Mt. Ware, the death place of a young moose whose fresh white bones are scattered far and wide about the meadow. Leave this depressing place and head toward the mountain, the ground steepening sequentially to shale scattered with brown rocks, then scree, and finally to cliffs. A weakness on the left side of the buttress gives access to the summit ridge. Now read #283.

"Black Cow Hill" (GR580219)

Distance 5 km from Volcano Creek, height gain 472 m, high point 2270 m. If you hunger for windswept hilltops with 360 degree views, try this side trip on exploration road to the summit at GR580219. The name is unofficial too, named after X's Black Angus (name undisclosed because someone is sure to complain about sloshing through cow patties. This has never been my experience; you are a million times more likely to run afoul on equestrian trails.) Nor is there anything wrong with naming a hill after cows. There are several Bull Creeks about after all, and I'm all for equality among the sexes.

The trail leaves Volcano Ridge trail on the north bank of an unnamed creek at GR605212 and heads west, straight off climbing steeply into scattered meadows. Thereafter the road is gently-angled to the very end. Pass a pond on the right, then opposite a line of crags on the opposite bank, pass a good game trail heading for the creek. Gradually the road and creek curve around to the northwest, the road faint where it crosses three meadows. You would think this a fairly remote place, but this is where we met our Black Angus contentedly munching grass. The final half kilometre of road curls around to the east, ending on the north side of your objective's broad west ridge.

From here it's an easy walk over short grass to two summits. The farther top has a cairn. As I promised, the view is extensive, taking in a large number of Front Range peaks including Bluerock, Banded, Outlaw, Cornwall and Glasgow. Directly north is Forgetmenot Mountain, separated from this ridge by the astoundingly deep canyon of upper Threepoint Creek. When we did it we dropped into the canyon and made a circuit, but it's not something I'd recommend unless you're a scrambler.

Forgetmenot Mountain from "Black Cow Hill".

286 UPPER THREEPOINT CREEK — map 13

Backpack, long day
Unofficial trail, creek crossings
Distance 7 km
Height gain E-W 283 m
Height loss E-W 122 m
High point 1960 m
Map 82 J/10 Mount Rae

East access: Via Volcano Ridge trail (#285) on the north bank of upper Threepoint Creek.
West access: Via Threepoint Mountain trail (#320) at Threepoint Creek crossing.
Also accessible from Big Elbow trail (#317).

Going farther. The flat-topped outlier seen from the trail to the Elbow River.

If you're looking for a direct route from Threepoint Creek to Big Elbow trail it's good to know about this 1920's pack trail through upper Threepoint Creek canyon. It's a beautiful route that, strangely, never became part of K Country's official network of trails. Wrongly marked on the topo map.

EAST TO WEST

Head west on what is Forgetmenot Mountain fire road past two cutlines heading right. Just before the fire road itself bends right, go straight on grassy road along the bank top. Do not turn down the bank too soon. The trail you want starts from the *end* of the road, continuing along the bank top a little way before descending to upper Threepoint Creek. Cross the creek to a camping area, then straightaway recross to the north bank (ignoring a trail continuing along the south bank).

In meadow the trail rises under a line of crags, then enters open pine forest where it's easy to lose the trail in long grass. The trail traverses much higher up than you think to a viewpoint overlooking a side valley. Zigging right, then left on scree, drop into the side valley, then climb out of it below a rising cliff. A traverse high above the canyon leads into a gradual descent over grass and scree back to valley bottom where again you have a problem with the long grass.

To avoid crags lining the riverbed, the trail rises below a small crag, zigs right, then steeply back left into a meadow where it disappears. There are signs the pack trail once carried on in the same line. Nowadays, everyone climbs uphill into the trees where a trail appears and leads to a junction with a very well-defined traversing trail. If you don't find the connecting trail above the meadow you will undoubtedly intersect the traversing trail somewhere along its length.

For Forgetmenot Mountain turn right at the traversing trail junction, then shortly turn left onto an equally good trail heading uphill. (The traversing trail soon ends in a gully.)

For Threepoint Mountain trail go straight (or left if you miss the junction) and circle into a dry side valley, the trail leading unerringly to the start (or end) of a grassy exploration road. All routefinding at an end, simply follow the grassy road out to #320. The valley changes character once again. The floor widens, the hillsides fall back, the river bubbles alongside the track in meadow. At about GR548218 you intersect Threepoint Mountain trail. Turn left for Gorge Creek, right for Big Elbow trail heading east.

GOING FARTHER
To Big Elbow trail
Distance 5.4 km, height gain 67 m, height loss 293 m, high point 2036 m. This is a shortcut to Big Elbow trail (#317) for anyone travelling west.

To viewpoint Turn left onto Threepoint Mountain trail and wade the river. Turn first right on the exploration road continued which crosses a side creek and heads upstream. At this point the valley has opened up into a basin, a soggy catchment area for innumerable small streams seeping off Threepoint Mountain, mixing with oil and trickling in rainbow-hued rivulets through the sedges. At a faint junction turn right across the river and climb through a wooded notch on the basin's west rim to a junction on the Elbow side of the watershed. The trail to the right (pack trail continued) descends to the Elbow River at GR524233. We used it pre K Country—a rather steep forested trail that has seen better days.

I recommend turning left onto a grassy ridge top where you're treated to an unobstructed view looking west of Mts. Cornwall and Glasgow and the rugged outliers of Banded Peak.

To Big Elbow backcountry campground
Continue on old road as it descends to a saddle. (Ahead, a ribbon of grass rises to an alluring flat-topped outlier with an even better view.) The road turns right, heading downhill to a cutline in the trees. Turn left and on cutline make a beeline to the Elbow River at GR513215. Wade across and join Big Elbow horse trail 100 m north of Big Elbow backcountry campground.

OPTION
Forgetmenot Mountain 2338 m
Distance 2 km, height gain 399 m. The lovely south ridge route is better used in ascent, perhaps, because of the difficulty in locating the trail on the way down.

As mentioned, climb up a forested ridge on a really good trail that delivers you to a flat, broad meadow. Continue on grass, noting a small tarn on the right as you aim for a cliff seemingly blocking the way. Scramble up the left side or bypass it altogether on the right through some trees. An open slope above leads to the summit ridge of Forgetmenot Mountain curving around to the left. Traverse all three tops to the high point.

The canyon, looking east.

287 FORGETMENOT MOUNTAIN via the Fire Road — map 13

Long day, backpack
Unofficial trail
Distance 7 km from Volcano Creek
Height gain 597 m
High point 2335 m
Maps 82 J/10 Mount Rae,
82 J/15 Bragg Creek

*Nearing the summit. Note the fire
road to the right of the figure.*

Access: Via upper Threepoint Creek trail (#286), 1 km west of Volcano Ridge trail (#285). **Also** accessible from Forgetmenot Ridge (#316), and from upper Threepoint Creek via the south ridge route (#286).

What is perhaps the highest point and is certainly the sharpest summit of Forget–menot Ridge has been distinguished with the name Mountain. Between 1952 and 1975 it was topped by a fire lookout served by a 25 km-long road from the forest boundary which has since become part of Highway 549, Threepoint Creek and Volcano Ridge trails. With a bike you can make the summit a one day trip via Quirk Creek (#314).

Where upper Threepoint Creek trail goes straight, keep right on the fire road that bends to the right and narrows to trail width. Though the fire road has undergone restoration, it would be hard for anyone to go astray as it sweeps across a steep grassy eastern escarpment, then winds up onto the broad east ridge called Nichi on Wheeler's map of 1895. The gradient eases off and you veer from one side of the ridge to the other through meadows and remnants of old spruce forest. Shortly after passing ruinous rock castles on your right, the trail steepens and zigs up a tapering ridge to the summit ridge which undulates like the Loch Ness monster. On the highest hump a concrete base and steps painted red are all that remains of Forgetmenot Lookout. The horseshoe dangling from a branch in the cairn is ours. Naturally the view is extensive, and includes for those who've wondered about venturing up Cougar Creek a clear look into this secretive valley.

(The trail continues, descending past a metal post, then curving left onto the south face, aiming for a spring at treeline where lookouts supposedly got water. In August we couldn't find any.)

288 LINK CREEK TRAIL — maps 14 & 13

Day hikes, backpack
Official trail with signposts & red
markers, creek crossings
Total distance 10.5 km

Highway access: Gorge Creek Trail (Hwy.).
NOTE: This road is closed between December
1st and May 15th.
1. Ware Creek parking lot 14.8 km north of
Sheep River Trail (Hwy. 546) and 7.1 km south
of McLean Creek Trail (Hwy. 549).
2. Volcano Ridge parking lot 7.9 km north of
Sheep River Trail (Hwy. 546) and 14 km south
of McLean Creek Trail (Hwy. 549).
Also accessible from the western terminus of
Ware Creek (#292), the northern terminus of
Missinglink trail (#290), Volcano Ridge trail
(#285) at the pass, and the northern terminus of
Gorge Link trail (#289).

Named after Link Creek which is followed
by the first section of trail, Link trail is also
a link trail in the sense that is connects trails
in the east Sheep to those lying in the
shadow of the Front Ranges to the west.

Ware Creek to Volcano Ridge parking lot via Link Creek

Distance 6 km
Height gain 198 m
Height loss 60 m
High point 1600 m
Map 82 J/10 Mount Rae

Highway access: 1, 2.
Also accessible from the western terminus of
Ware Creek trail (#292), and the northern termi-
nus of Missinglink trail (#290).

The easy valley section.

Shortly after leaving Ware Creek parking lot
keep straight, the trail passing through a gate
and heading upstream along the west bank
of Link Creek. After about a kilometre, jump

Link Creek and travel to the forks along the
east bank within sight and sound of traffic.
Recross the stream and arrive at the junction
with Missinglink trail within spitting distance of the highway bend at GR677204. Of
course, if transferring to Missinglink don't
bother with the creek crossing.

Keep straight, following the west fork of
Link Creek through lovely meadows usually thronged with cattle. Near the end of
the meadows, jog right, transferring from
improved cow trail to an old road that
climbs through pine forest, making a beeline for the pass at GR657184. Below the
craggy north face of Missinglink Mountain
the road swings south. A little way along
turn sharp right onto a narrow trail (no
marker, branches laid across the old road)
that descends to a branch of Ware Creek.
Jump across and climb up the west bank
onto Gorge Creek Trail the highway, then
slip through a narrow belt of trees into
Volcano Ridge parking lot.

Volcano Ridge parking lot to Volcano Ridge trail

Distance 4.5 km
Height gain 375 m
High point 1914 m
Map 82 J/10 Mount Rae

Highway access: 2.
Also accessible from Volcano Ridge trail (#285)
on the watershed, and the northern terminus of
Gorge Link trail (#289).

A much more strenuous section that climbs
to a couple of watersheds. Combine with
Volcano Ridge and Gorge Link trails to
make a very pleasant 10 km loop which for

us has become a favourite late fall hike in all its variations. One such variation is the side trip to Volcano Ridge summit—a worthy destination by itself.

Descend the bank and ford Ware Creek. The trail—old exploration road throughout—turns left and wanders through alternating pine forest and meadow, one particularly muddy side creek crossing requiring a detour from the trail. At the 1.5 km mark, Gorge Link trail turns left.

Keep right, following the right bank of a side creek. After you cross the creek there's a horribly steep but mercifully short hill to a levelling on a left-hand bend with a view of the boulder-strewn slopes of Volcano Ridge. Continue climbing, first to get out of the valley, then to gain the broad grassy pass at GR619180 between Volcano Ridge summit and a rocky knoll. As you come over the top a view is revealed of Bluerock Mountain and the Front Ranges to the southwest.

The trail continues in the same line, following the rolling height of land between a Gorge Creek tributary on the left and a headwater of Volcano Creek that oozes from the big soggy meadow on the right. A final rise brings you to a four-way junction with Volcano Ridge trail (left and right) in the trees.

OPTIONS
Volcano Ridge summit 2121 m
Distance 2.5 km from Link Creek trail, height gain 244 m. An old exploration road, unmarked on the topo map, leads almost to the summit, and while easy to follow has one steep section that will leave you gasping.

It leaves Link just east of the pass at GR619180 and heads north, following the broad ridge, first on the right side, then on the left some 50 vertical m above a large meadow as flat and as green as a billiard table. The upcoming grass step is tackled head on, making you wish you'd packed a spare pair of legs, but flower and view stops are permissible. The road then resumes its former easy gradient as it contours around to the left onto the west side of the ridge

where I once found Townsendias blooming on the last grey day of October. Where the road starts going downhill, leave it and cut off up and right to the summit. The view has been growing in magnificence and as you reach the cairn you're rewarded by a panorama taking in Calgary and the triad of Mts. Glasgow, Cornwall and Banded Peak.

To the north and 4.5 km away as the crow flies is the northernmost summit of Volcano Ridge which is Allsmoke Mountain, both names dating back to Wheeler's map of 1895. That Volcano Ridge is named for its volcanic formation as is suggested in the current place name book would have geologists holding their sides with laughter. Likely, Volcano derives from Allsmoke's Stoney name *Sudiktebi*, meaning "where bear was smoked to death". On the slopes of the mountain, in the late fall when bears went into hibernation, some Stoneys built a fire at the entrance of a den and smoked a young black bear to death. Not being sure of the outcome, Tom Powderface, being of small stature, was sent in first to see if the bear was dead. Next in was his son Johnny with a rope to slip over the bear's head. Feeling around in the dark young Powderface discovered the bear's head was tucked under his body with one paw draped pathetically above his head. As Powderface moved the head, trapped air in the lungs gushed out in a gurgling noise and scared the hell out of him.

Ridge GR621178, 1935 m
Distance 500 m to top, height gain 30 m. On the south side of the pass there is a sandstone knob whose siren call I can never resist. From its top is a comprehensive view of the pass area as shown in the photo.

A couple of times we've headed south along the ridge above the sandstone escarpment, at one time dropping to Volcano Ridge trail, at another to Gorge Link trail in a raging fall blizzard. Either way, the terrain is mostly meadow or well-spaced pines with a grassy understorey.

Option, Volcano Ridge summit. Near the top, looking west to Banded Peak, Mts. Cornwall and Glasgow.

Looking down from ridge GR621178 to Link trail crossing pass GR619180. You can trace some of the trail leading to Volcano Ridge in the background.

289 GORGE LINK TRAIL — maps 18 & 14

Half-day, day hike
Official trail with signposts, red
markers, creek crossings
Distance 4 km
Height gain S-N 91 m
Height loss S-N 80 m
High point 1661 m
Map 82 J/10 Mount Rae

South access: Via Gorge Creek trail (#283) on the west bank of the north fork crossing.
North access: Via Link Creek trail (#288) 1.5 km west of Volcano Ridge trailhead.
Also accessible from the southern terminus of Volcano Ridge trail (#285).

This useful connector takes you through typical foothill valleys of cow meadows, aspen and pine forests.

SOUTH TO NORTH

First, the meadow section. From the junction on the west bank of Gorge Creek's north fork you head north and in about 100 m cross to the east bank. (Obviously, if you're coming from Gorge Creek trailhead, the two creek crossings can be avoided by staying on the east bank. At high water, though, you may have a problem where the creek washes up against a shale bank.) The next crossing can't be avoided, but because it occurs above the confluence with the northwest fork (arising from Surveyor's Ridge), there is never enough water in the stream to worry about. At meadow's end, recross the creek to a T-junction with the southern terminus of Volcano Ridge trail. Go straight.

Steering northeast, follow a tributary through aspens and the odd meadow. Cross the drift fence. Imperceptibly you cross the watershed into a headwater of Ware Creek evidenced by a change in vegetation to mixed forest and pines. Some tiny side creeks are bridged. After crossing a west fork join Link Creek trail 1.5 km west of Volcano Ridge trailhead.

The meadows of Gorge Creek's north fork.
Looking south to Junction Mountain.

View from the trail's high point of Missinglink Mountain.

290 MISSINGLINK TRAIL — map 19 & 14

Day hike
Official trail with signposts & red
markers, creek crossings
Distance 8 km
Height gain 137 m
Height loss 183 m
High point 1615 m
Map 82 J/10 Mount Rae

Access: Sheep River Trail (Hwy. 546) at Missinglink trailhead. NOTE: This section of Highway 546 is closed between December 1st and May 15th.
Also accessible from Link Creek trail (#288). Fortuitously, the junction lies within metres of Gorge Creek Trail the highway at GR677204.

Almost entirely in Lodgepole pines, Missinglink is a boring old trail for hikers unless you're into plant identification. Winding about a string of cutlines and cutline access roads, it's also extremely complex. Getting lost is a distinct possibility, so pay close attention to the red markers.

To the watershed From the parking lot the trail winds over to what was once called Canyon Creek on account of the small canyon bridged by the highway. En route go straight at a T-junction with a cutline, go either way at a division, then keep left at another trail junction. Down by the creek, actually the west fork of Canyon Creek, turn left at a junction and cross a tributary. An enjoyable half kilometre of riverside meadow overlooked by a rocky bluff across the creek ends when you ford the west fork just upstream of a confluence.

With heart sinking, start up a steepening cutline. Thankfully, long before the top of the hill is reached you turn right onto a trail that descends and crosses a tributary. Angle easing, the trail follows the tributary's right bank (keep left everywhere) to the sign "Leaving Sheep River Wildlife Sanctuary" plonked in the middle of an intersecting NE-SW cutline. Cross the cutline and descend slightly to the watershed, a longitudinal meadow sweeping through the gap from Link Creek on your left into Canyon Creek's north fork which looks very enticing when hiking the trail in reverse direction. When there's snow on the ground this is where you could easily head off down the wrong valley.

To Link Creek Cross the meadow and on cutline access road cross a drift fence en route to the day's high point. This is a viewpoint for Missinglink Mountain. Whereas its south and west slopes present exciting meadows and cliffs dotted with Bighorns, the back side is dark, unappealing forest. As far as I know Richard Leakey hasn't been poking around the Canadian

Rockies looking for another Lucy. I did discover, though, that in the early days it used to be called Missing *Lynx*. Aha!

A steep descent down alder alley brings you to meadows alongside Link (Lynx?) Creek. Just after cattle trails come in from the left, the road turns away from the creek and crosses a major N-S cutline, resuming its northward direction east of the cutline as a trail. Twice it touches on the cutline, before breaking away down left back to creekside meadows. Just in time too. Rearing up ahead is the hill we skied some 20 years ago by kicking steps.

On the following straight cross a NE-SW cutline and go either way at a split—one is as deep as the other. Regain the N-S cutline, turn left and shortly emerge in meadows around Link Creek's confluence with its southwest fork. Posts lead to a crossing of Link Creek and the T-junction with Link trail near the highway.

291 WARE CREEK NORTH BANK TRAIL — map 14

Half-day hike
Unofficial trail, creek crossings
Distance 1.8 km
Height loss W-E 43 m
High point 1405 m
Map 82 J/10 Mount Rae

Access: Gorge Creek Trail (Hwy). Park at the entrance to an old road signed "No Motorized Vehicles" that leaves the southeast side of the road approximately 800 m northeast of Ware Creek parking lot. NOTE: This road is closed between December 1st and May 15th.
Also accessible from 9999 trail (#294) on the north bank of Ware Creek at the crossing.

Though an old road with four creek crossings (avoidable), I much prefer its firm surface to the official black and mucky Ware Creek trail. Use as an alternative to #292 if doing a loop with North Fork, Threepoint Creek and 9999 trails.

The old road straightaway descends to Ware Creek. With temperature hovering around 30 degrees, river crossings are sometimes events to look forward to. You can, however, avoid the first two by searching out a faint trail along the north bank. Back on road, climb over a couple of side ridges to the next pair of river crossings. Again, a bypass trail is available along the north bank. Shortly after, the road enters flat meadows and joins 9999 trail near where it crosses to the south bank.

Opposite: #291. The trail along Ware Creek's north bank is much pleasanter than its official counterpart #292.

292 WARE CREEK — map 14

Half-day, day hikes
Official trail with signposts & red
markers, creek crossings
Distance 2.8 km
Height gain 20 m
Height loss 40 m
High point 1402 m
Map 82 J/10 Mount Rae

Access: Gorge Creek Trail (Hwy.) at Ware Creek parking lot. NOTE: This road is closed between December 1st and May 15th.
Also accessible from the northern terminus of Death Valley trail (#272), the southern terminus of 9999 trail (#294) and the southern terminus of North Fork trail (#293).

This little trail has an importance out of all proportion to its length because it (and the unofficial north bank trail) make possible the popular 18.5 km loop incorporating North Fork, Threepoint Creek and 9999 trails. Additionally, it provides access to the north end of Death Valley trail that in turn connects with ongoing trails south and west of the Sheep River. Creek crossings are avoidable.

Clearly the influence of Death Valley extends to this creek which has also seen its share of strange disappearances. Some of you may remember Lloyd Middleton's cabin "The Retreat" opposite the parking lot. He took over a trapline from an old trapper named Smiley who was found dead in the original cabin on the site. What is it about this place, you wonder, as you leave the parking lot bound for Death Valley.

Turn left before the fence and heading east, ford Link Creek (logs downstream) and cross a meadow to Ware Creek. Officially, you're supposed to cross to the north bank and recross 200 m farther downstream, but there's little point in doing so when there's a nice little connecting trail along the south bank. BUT if you're looping with North Fork trail, then you have to make one crossing because North

Fork trail takes off from the stretch along the north bank.

Between the second crossing of Ware Creek and Death Valley trail the trail alternates between meadows and pine-aspen forest, generally climbing. After a squalid, ever enlarging section of mud, the trail drops to a large meadow where a signpost at GR717221 pinpoints the three-way junction with Death Valley trail to right and 9999 trail to left.

293 NORTH FORK TRAIL — map 14

Day hike
Official trail, signposts & red markers
Distance 5 km
Height gain S-N 229 m
Height loss S-N 198 m
High point 1615 m
Maps 82 J/10 Mount Rae,
82 J/15 Bragg Creek

South access: Via Ware Creek (#292).
North access: Via Threepoint Creek trail (#295).
Also accessible from Gorge Creek Trail (Hwy.). Park in Ware Creek parking lot. Cross the road bridge over Ware Creek and walk northeast along the highway to where the trail crosses the road. NOTE: This road is closed between December 1st and May 15th.

Since the second edition the southern half of this Ware Creek-Threepoint Creek connector has been completely rerouted away from the old telephone trail between Bighorn Ranger Station and North Fork Cabin, and now takes in some lovely meadow country en route to the pass. A big improvement!

From campgrounds on Highway 549, it's possible to make a 18.5 km loop incorporating Threepoint Creek, North Fork, Ware Creek and 9999 trails, the loop best hiked in an anticlockwise direction so you can admire the views without turning around all the time. However, because of ease of access from Ware Creek parking lot and the fact that most people just enjoy a stroll up to the high point and back through the meadows, I am describing the trail from south to north.

SOUTH TO NORTH
From Ware Creek trail on the north bank of Ware Creek, North Fork trail heads north and crosses Gorge Creek Trail the highway about half a kilometre northeast of the highway bridge. Initially it sticks close to the highway within sound of cars changing gear to get up the hill, and it's here where you can pick up the route from Ware Creek north bank trail. No sweat.

Bend left into a large meadow, the first of three. Did I mention that meadows are the real beauty of this trail? From here it's a long steady pull to the high point. A fence must be crossed and a belt of trees before you enter meadow No. 2 which is distinguished by a line of dead trees and an intersecting cutline. The views are all behind you, Front Range peaks poking up above layers of forested foothills. At the high point you're

Near the pass. Looking back to Death's Head.

traversing above the meadow and below a hill named variously Death's Head, Mesa Butte and the Big Hill. To confuse you further, turn to the trail description for Square (Mesa) Butte. Anyway, above the belt of trees you glimpse grass and a belt of gaudy sandstone crags below the summit. It begs to be climbed (see detour).

This high point is not the watershed, obviously. The trail descends an ever-widening mudbath in the trees to a NE-SW cutline. Turn left along the cutline (one small detour), then turn off it to the right, entering meadow No. 3 with a bench and a view down the valley and back to Death's Head. A little downhill of here is the pass at GR683254.

Join with telephone trail for the descent of the steeper north slope, all spruce forest with a damp, mossy understorey. Arrive at a T-junction with Threepoint Creek trail in the valley bottom. Next to the signpost is an old wood sign tacked to a tree indicating 'Threepoint Trail" to the left. Turn right for Highway 549.

DETOUR

Death's Head (Mesa Butte) GR695249. Height gain 110 m, high point 1725 m. In the 1880s surveyors used this hill as a camera station recorded on Wheeler's 1895 map as Death's Head, another strange name to go with Allsmoke, Volcano and Missinglink. Officially it is Mesa Butte but no one ever calls it that. Locals call it the Big Hill, obviously referring to the road on its east flank.

Leave the trail around the high point. All ways up are the same: aspen-pine forest giving way to grassy slopes topped by a line of crags guarding the summit plateau. Find a game trail leading through a weakness, then walk left to a grassy overlook in the angle of the west and north faces. The far-reaching view catches you unaware: Calgary to the northeast, to the west Allsmoke Mountain, Mts. Cornwall and Glasgow, Nihahi Ridge, Moose Mountain, the Highwood Range, and, of course, the pass close in below you.

View from Death's Head of the pass area. Farther away you can distinguish Allsmoke Mountain (left), Forgetmenot Mountain and Nihahi Ridge.

294 9999 TRAIL — map 14

Day hike
Official trail with signposts & red markers, creek crossings
Distance 7 km
Height gain N-S 90 m
High point 1448 m
Maps 82 J/15 Bragg Creek,
82 J/10 Mount Rae

Ware Creek meadows.

North access McLean Creek Trail (Hwy. 549) at Mesa Butte equestrian campground.
South access The junction of Ware Creek and Death Valley trails (#292 & 272) in Ware Creek.
Also accessible from (north to south):
1. The east terminus of Threepoint Creek trail (#295) at Mesa Butte equestrian campground.
2. The north terminus of Curly Sand trail (#297) at Mesa Butte equestrian campground.
3. Gorge Creek Trail (Hwy.). The trail intersects the road 800 m west of McLean Creek Trail (Hwy. 549). Hikers can use this access when Threepoint Creek is in spate.
4. From the southern terminus of Curly Sand trail (#297). The usual starting point for hikers.
5. From the eastern terminus of Ware Creek North bank trail (#291).

If you had been around this area between 1885 and 1902 you would have discovered that cattle grazing the upper reaches of Ware Creek and Threepoint Creek all bore the brand "9999". This was the registered brand of John Ware, the celebrated Negro cowboy renowned for his strength and horsemanship who homesteaded just east of here at the fork of the two rivers.

This trail has one moderate section where it climbs over the hills to Ware Creek where the countryside is at its most beautiful. Muddy equestrian but worth the effort.

NORTH TO SOUTH
After leaving Mesa Butte equestrian campground the trail straightway crosses Threepoint Creek. In another 200 m you join an old road that has arisen from the river and follow it uphill to Gorge Creek Trail the highway **(access 3)**.

Cross the highway onto the powerline right-of-way and turn left. Very shortly, leave the right-of-way at the metal shed and follow the trail into the trees. In 1 km join Curly Sand trail **(access 4)** in a meadow.

Turn right. Initially, the mud is horrible and you suffer, but underfoot conditions improve when you transfer to an old road that has come in from the left. (This road offers an alternative route to/from Curly Sand trail above Threepoint Creek crossing and is marginally less muddy.) Climb to a pass in the hills to the south.

On the sunny downslope, tall, graceful aspens arch over the road. Low down, veer right on a trail, cross a cutline at an angle, then cross the side creek that has accompanied you all the way down the hill. Turn right (white marker) and enter Ware Creek valley at meadows and dried up beaver ponds. In early spring watch Red-winged blackbirds fighting for nesting sites in the willows.

Back on the old road, walk upstream through a string of lovely meadows sweeping up aspen hillsides to the ridge tops. Opposite a side valley south of the creek, the trail turns left (road continuation is **access 5**), and fords Ware Creek to the T-junction with Ware Creek and Death Valley trails in a large meadow.

295 THREEPOINT CREEK TRAIL — map 14

Day hike, backpack
Official trail with signposts & red
markers, creek crossings
Distance 12 km via fire road, 11 km via
the Hogs Back from Mesa Butte
Height gain 375 m via fire road, 420 m
via Hogs Back
High point 1762 m on fire road
Map 82 J/15 Bragg Creek

Below: Nearing the top of
the Hogs Back.

Access: McLean Creek Trail (Hwy. 549) at Mesa Butte equestrian campground, 2.9 km north of Kananaskis Country boundary.

A. Hiker's start 200 m north of Mesa Butte Recreation Area turn west onto a well access road. Cross the bridge over Threepoint Creek and drive 1.7 km to a road junction. Turn left. Park at the end of the road on the verge. Walk along the fence trail toward the river until you intersect Threepoint Creek trail at the northeast corner of the fence.

B. Alternative (unofficial) hiker's start 200 m north of Mesa Butte Recreation Area turn west onto a well access road. Cross the bridge over Threepoint Creek and drive 1.7 km to a road junction. Keep right. Drive another 500 m across Threepoint Creek bridge to Forgetmenot Mountain fire road on the left side of the road.

Also accessible from the northern terminus of North Fork trail (#293), the northern terminus of Volcano Ridge trail (#285) and the southern terminus of Wildhorse trail (#315).

The route (an eclectic mix of trails ranging from fire road to historic pack trail) follows Threepoint Creek, reaching its dramatic conclusion above spectacular Threepoint Creek gorge.

The trail officially starts at Mesa Butte equestrian campground. However, unless you're doing a loop with North Fork trail, you'd be daft not to start from access A, *which cuts out the first 1.9 km*. If the river's high, use access B (two crossings upstream can also be avoided, so don't be put off by spring runoff). Know that Hogs Back option is reserved for hikers.

From Mesa Butte equestrian campground
The start is humdrum. Straightway the trail fords Threepoint Creek alongside the well access road bridge. Alternatively, use the bridge, then head left to a four-way junction with a cutline (right) and powerline right-of-way (left, straight). Go straight on powerline

211

right-of-way, parallelling the access road. Shortly transfer to a trail left of the right-of-way, then cross both the right-of-way and the access road for a stint between the road and the river on meadow. Cross the right-hand branch of the access road. At a division, go either way, then climb to a well site. The spur trail from **access A** comes in at the northeast corner of the chain-link fence.

After rounding the north side of the fence you follow the old telephone trail to the junction with North Fork trail at the 3 km mark. A flat easy walk.

Keep right on old pack trail and shortly wade Threepoint Creek to the north bank. At a T-junction in a meadow join Forget–menot Mountain fire road (**start B**). Turn left and skip the next paragraph!

Start B along the north bank uses the reclaimed Forgetmenot Mountain fire road which can be identified by a rusting gate disguised as deadfall to keep the OHVs away. The first section is sloped grass with a trail a few centimetres wide and three times as deep, a pedal catcher better hiked than biked, eh Pete? It's quite pleasant the way it undulates high above the river. After the drift fence the road descends to a small riverside meadow and the junction with the official trail at a red marker. Keep straight.

Almost flat, the fire road runs alongside the river below flowery banks. Shortly after passing a cutline to right, there is a choice of routes. Unless you're on a bike why continue on boring old fire road when the Hogs Back option is a hundred times more interesting and shorter?

Fire Road

Just in case you have a bike, stay with the fire road which shortly moves away from Threepoint Creek and heads up Muskeg Creek. The basin at its head, co-joined with Quirk Creek used to be called "The Muskeg", and was a grizzly hot-spot before the era of OHVs and gas wells. After the fifth ford, well before the valley head, the fire

road turns west and climbs a gruelling 200 m over a shaley ridge covered in pine forest. On descent the road turns south and you catch your first view of Allsmoke Mountain up ahead. The Hogs Back variation joins in from the left just before the junction with Wildhorse and Volcano Ridge trails in Quirk Creek valley.

Hogs Back option

Turn left onto a trail that wanders up and down the riverbank, at one point traversing a slope of good quality coal! Two river crossings of Threepoint Creek give access to the narrow ridge of land separating Threepoint Creek from Muskeg Creek called the Hogs Back, a name in use since the 1920s when the pack trail between North Fork Ranger Station and the Elbow River came this way. (Both crossings are avoidable by staying on the north bank. Muskeg Creek can be jumped.)

Start up the Hogs Back. After the initial climb the ridge levels and narrows surprisingly, a shale slope on the left falling away to Threepoint Creek. Resume climbing through trees, at the last gasping up a grassy ridge to the top of a hill sliced cleanly down the middle by the eroding action of the river now over 100 m below you. The top is the perfect lunch stop.

A descent kicks off the undulating section that follows the lie of the land through pine and aspen forest. With mounting excitement you climb a final hill to airy meadows high above the fully-fledged gorge. Across the gulf rises Allsmoke Mountain whose alternating rings of cliffs and shale postholed by wandering sheep comes as a huge surprise if you're only familiar with its tamer east side. This is the place to explore a lower terrace overlooking the inner gorge.

Back on the trail, you come to the final, classic viewpoint that looks straight up Volcano Creek Gorge to Surveyor's Ridge. Reluctantly you turn your back on all this drama and descend to the fire road near the junction of Volcano Ridge and Wildhorse trails.

#295, Threepoint Creek, Hogs Back option. Looking up Volcano Creek to Surveyor's Ridge (right).

#296, Square Butte. The Fisher Range from the summit.

296 SQUARE (MESA) BUTTE — map 14

Half-day, short day hikes
Unofficial trails
Shortest distance to top 1.2 km
Height gain by shortest route 198 m
High point 1682 m
Map 82 J/15 Bragg Creek

Accesses: McLean Creek Trail (Hwy. 549).
A. Shortest 4.3 km north of the Kananaskis Country boundary sign turn right onto a gas well access road. Park off-road at the left-hand bend.
B. Alternative start to A 3.9 km north of the Kananaskis Country boundary sign park at the side of the road at three signs warning of fuel gas pipeline. Or park 200 m back in a gateway on the left (west) side of the highway.
C. Ridge route Park 3 km north of the Kananaskis Country boundary sign opposite the Mesa Butte Recreation Area access roads.
D. Longest 600 m north of the Kananaskis Country boundary sign park off-road at a four-way intersection. Or use North Fork campground access road to left.

Signing the summit register.

"The Girls are pretty
The boys are cute
Oh thank Heaven
I made it to Mesa Butte"

There are three main routes to the top of Square Butte. Loops of varying length can be made by using the trails in various permutations in conjunction with Curly Sand (#297), 9999 (#294) and the highway where the greatest danger is speeding pickups spitting gravel. Despite its unofficial status, it is, quite simply, the best half-day hike from the campgrounds.

Is this ever a popular hill! People on foot, on horse, on bike, people sleeping on the top. Then there are the "Moonlight Hikers" from Millarville, Germans and Japanese from Max Gibb's place and Germans and Aussies taking part in Neil MacLaine's Palliser Challenge. On Thanksgiving night another group plods up with food, wine and candles for a little "Beethoven on the Butte". This is all true! You can spend hours reading the summit register put up there by Jim McLuskey whose house can be seen from the summit. *He* comes up every Christmas Day regardless of the weather.

You've spotted the discrepancy in the name? When driving along Highway 762 through Square Butte district I've often puzzled over the name that appears on community hall. I've gone over the topo map with a fine-tooth comb looking for a Square Butte in vain. Turns out Mesa Butte, which has been named as such on generations of topo maps, is officially "Square". The official "Mesa" is across the valley at Death's Head. To complicate matters further, Wheeler's map of 1895 calls it Mesa Hill.

296A Shortest and easiest

Walk up the right side of the chain-link fence. Level with the top a trail turns right into the trees on a slightly rising traverse. Keep right and cross a cutline. Shortly come to the flagged junction with **B**.

Turn left. At the same easy angle the trail curves around to a pass at GR718273 (small meadow) where **C** and **D** join in at a four-way junction.

Turn left (north) and climb the grassy south ridge to the summit plateau. This is a heavenly spot facing south with lush grass to roll around in. One summiter described the view as "so lovely it hurts". It's certainly extensive: above a heaving sea of foothills you can identify the higher peaks of the Highwood and Fisher ranges, while nearer at hand Threepoint Creek leads the eye to Forgetmenot Mountain. And, of course, directly across the valley rises the official if not the original Mesa Butte, alias Death's Head and the Big Hill.

The actual summit lies a little farther on, just inside the forest at a fire circle. En route look for the summit canister under a lone pine on the left side of the trail.

296B, Alternative start to A

Add 400 m, add 55 m height gain. Follow the pipeline right-of-way up the hill to a gas well access road near the well. Cross the road and pick up a well-used trail that heads right alongside the chain-link fence, then back left past a survey marker, ultimately climbing to the flagged junction with A. Keep right....

296C Scenic ridge route

Distance 2 km, height gain 320 m. A grassy cutline access road starts about 100 m north of Curly Sand trail and climbs to the high point of a NE-SW cutline on the tip of Square Butte's south ridge. Continue on trail which crosses the cutline and follows the occasionally steep south ridge to a top. A short descent leads to the pass GR718273 at a four-way junction in a meadow where A comes in from the left. Go straight and follow the regular route to the summit.

To connect with Curly Sand trail
From C, walk northeast along the NE-SW cutline for about 100 m until you see a rather indistinct trail in long grass heading right to join with Curly Sand trail in the gap at GR721264.

296D Longest

Distance 5 km, height gain 320 m. Head north on the exploration road. Keep right on the much older dirt road that crosses a fence and descends slightly to cross Mesa (Square?) Creek. Intersect a NE-SW cutline, then note the pipeline right-of-way to left. Stay on the road as it winds uphill below grassy banks to a second T-junction with the pipeline right-of-way at GR718273.

This is where you leave the road that turns right along the right-of-way. Transfer to a narrow trail straight ahead that slowly gains height to beautiful meadows below the butte's east face. At cow trees the main trail heads uphill, then traverses leftwards through waist-high Timothy to the pass at GR718273. At the four-way junction with A and C turn right for the summit.

Option return for D

With not much in the way of a trail to help you, head northwest along the plateau in the pines, keeping near the east edge. At red flagging cross an intersecting NE-SW cutline infilled with alder. On the far side pick up a trail—rapidly upgrading to cutline access road—running along the east edge. Keep straight at a junction and descend a ridge out of the pines into that sunnier country of aspens and meadows. Where the ridge flattens temporarily the track turns right and drops steeply to the same old road used by D, which is gained at about GR724289.

Turn right and recross the NE-SW cutline. Cross the pipeline right-of-way, still following the old road as it parallels the right-of-way to the east. Lower down, the road crosses the right-of-way and runs along the west side to the junction with the ascent trail at GR718273.

Return the way you came.

297 CURL(E)Y SAND TRAIL — map 14

Half-day hike
Official trail, signposts & red markers
Distance 4 km
Height gain 137 m
Height loss 174 m
High point 1509 m
Maps 82 J/15 Bragg Creek,
82 J/10 Mount Rae

Access: McLean Creek Trail (Hwy. 549).
1. Mesa Butte equestrian campground.
2. Day-use area, North Fork Recreation Area.
Walk up the access road to the highway.
3. K Country boundary. Park on the old road
running alongside the boundary fence. Walk
down the grassy road to Threepoint Creek.
Also accessible from the eastern terminus of
Threepoint Creek trail (#295), from 9999 trail
(#294) in two places, and from Square Butte
trails (#296 C and D).

The ridge viewpoint looking along Highway 549 to John Ware Ridge.

This lovely little trail is named after George William (Curly) Sand of Minnesota who came to the area about 1946, hired by the North Sheep Stock Association to track with his hounds cougars and grizzlies that were killing yearlings up in The Muskeg. "In two years he killed 11 grizzlies and many black bear beside". At his funeral "Curly never let the truth spoil a good story" said the minister, so you hope the numbers are exaggerated.

Officially, it makes possible a loop with 9999 trail for campers with two legs who don't mind sploshing twice across Threepoint Creek. Unofficially, it makes a far better loop with Square Butte trails.

From access 1 The trail starts opposite Mesa Butte equestrian campground entrance and begins by climbing toward a gap in the ridge to the east which is where you can connect with #296C.

Before quite reaching the gap you turn right and climb onto a ridge top. Walk south along the ridge between east slope aspens and west slope meadows to the south end viewpoint. This is the trail's high point,

figuratively speaking, where the meadows sweep down to the highway, sages giving a silvery-blue cast to long, waving grasses.

The trail descends at the edge of the aspens to an exploration road (#296D) which is crossed (gate). (A right turn would bring you out to Highway 549 almost opposite North Fork campground entrance.)

Cross the highway just east of the campground entrance **(access 2)**, then head east between the highway and the campground fence (no access for campers), later passing to the right of a flat meadow, site of North Fork Ranger Station, a home for assistant rangers. Pass through a gate and on the riverbank join an old road that has come in from the highway at the Kananaskis Country boundary **(access 3)** and that is destined to become 9999 trail. But not for a while yet.

Ford Threepoint Creek. On old road climb the bank into a meadow where you forsake the road (seen entering the forest ahead) and wend right to a larger meadow with signpost where you join 9999 trail (left and straight).

298 IRON SPRINGS TRAIL (West Bragg to Highway 66 via Iron Pond) — map 9

Half-day, day hike
Official (ski) trails with signposts
Distance 8 km
Height gain N-S 122 m
Height loss N-S 177 m
High point 1539 m
Map 82 J/15 Bragg Creek

North access: From Bragg Creek village take the road signed "Wintergreen". Cross the bridge over the Elbow River. Turn left and follow West Bragg Creek Road into Kananaskis Country. In 1.3 km the road ends at parking lots for West Bragg Creek cross country ski trails. Use the near parking lot.
South access: Elbow Falls Trail (Hwy. 66) at Allen Bill Pond day-use area. Use the left-hand parking lot. The trail starts amid picnic tables and is signed "Fullerton Loop".

Before the Bragg Creek Hostel burnt down in the spring of 1984, "Elbow trail" (not to be confused with Elbow Valley trail, Big Elbow and Little Elbow trails) was a popular route with hostellers travelling to Highway 66. Nowadays its complex mix of logging roads, cutlines and cutline access roads are ski trails. Rather than follow the original route in its entirety, I'm diverging along the more scenic Iron Springs trail to Iron pond which makes a logical destination from both trailheads if you don't want to go all the way through.

NORTH TO SOUTH

To Iron Pond Retrace your steps along the highway and cross the bridge over Bragg Creek. Turn right and climb the bank at a rehabilitated logging road to a ski trail that has arisen from the right. Keeping a straight line, follow the grassy avenue up the slope. Cross Crystal Line cutline, and on logging road pass a mill site with a view of Moose Mountain. At Sundog ski trail junction turn right past an interpretive sign about tree thinning, harvesting and fertilizing. Keep right past another

sign explaining how the road was 'dozed in 1969 by Spray Lakes Sawmills. At the following junction leave Sundog and go straight on Iron Springs ski trail.

The trail climbs the right edge of a large cutblock to a drift fence at the trail's high point far above the actual watershed. Descend below smaller cutblocks into Iron Creek valley bottom with its string of Guinness-coloured beaver ponds. Cross a cutline. Iron Pond is located where the valley turns sharp left, its surround of flowery meadows making it a favourite halting place for cows and humans.

To Highway 66 To ensure dry feet follow the road down valley en route to Elk Valley Estates. Turn first right and on ski trail cross the creek and double back to the south side of Iron Pond below a cutblock.

Cross the watershed into the Elbow River drainage by turning first left on Iron Springs ski trail (cutblocks, aspen forest) which joins the much less attractive Elbow ski trail (NW-SE cutline/cutline access road) some way down the other side.

Shortly after this junction the road (Elbow ski trail continued) turns right off the cutline. Keep straight twice (cutline access roads to left, then right) and cross a NW-SE cutline. At a sign keep straight down a hill, curving left where Fullerton trail takes off to the right. Near valley bottom turn right on Fullerton/Elbow trail which crosses a drift fence and rejoins the old road for a rebuilt stretch alongside the Elbow River. Nearing the end, the trail bridges Ranger Creek, passes under Highway 66 and enters Allen Bill Pond recreation area.

#298. Iron Pond, looking northwest.

#299. The trail through the well-site meadow.

299 MOOSE MOUNTAIN FROM WEST BRAGG — maps 9

Day, long day hike
Unofficial trail
Distance to route #306, 8.5 km
Height gain 506 m
High point 1905 m
Map 82 J/15 Bragg Creek

Access: From Bragg Creek village take the road signed "Wintergreen". Cross the bridge over the Elbow River. Turn left and follow West Bragg Creek Road into Kananaskis Country. In 1.3 km the road ends at parking lots for West Bragg Creek cross country ski trails. Use the far parking lot.
Also accessible from Moose Mountain normal route (#306), and from Tom Snow trail (#301) in two places.

Before there was Moose Mountain Road the pack train servicing Moose Mountain Lookout from Elbow Ranger Station went up Ranger Creek, then switchbacked up an easterly spur to the main southeast ridge that has become today's normal route up the mountain. All this was built in 1928. Too bad the spur was omitted from the official K Country trail system.

Today, the spur route is most easily accessed via an exploration road to a well site. Biking the road section brings Moose Mountain within range of a one day push. Of course, some bikers with quads like Curt Harnett can pedal all the way to the ridge and most of the way to the summit. Be here in June during Mountain Bike City's annual bike race and prepare to be amazed!

Exploration road section From the parking lot you follow the twice gated exploration road (continuation of West Bragg Creek Road) all the way to a well site. Initially the road runs alongside Bragg Creek which is meandering through meadow. Cross the creek via a bridge, then veer right to a road junction (shortcut to/from Tom Snow trail). Keep left and half way up a hill, cross Moose Connector ski trail.

The winding road passes a trail heading right into a meadow, then a cutline access road turning left before a dip. Beyond the dip, at the top of the hill, Tom Snow trail (#301) comes in from the right.

For the next 2 km Tom Snow trail shares your road as you walk past cutblocks, intersecting cutlines and enticing bits of trail climbing onto open hillsides. Descend and cross Ranger Creek. The following uphill is a real drag, especially if you've got a bike. It was certainly tough in a car! At a right-hand bend with a retrospective view of cutblocks, Tom Snow turns left, heading down the west fork of Ranger Creek.

Keep right on the exploration road and tackle another steep hill. The road ends at well-site meadow at km 6.

Pack trail section The pack trail carries on across the meadow into the pines. There's something satisfying about following historic trails, especially if you have them all to yourself. You can imagine strings of pack horses plodding up the series of beautifully constructed zigs onto the easterly spur where they would stop while the packer checked the loads. The spur is meadow at this point and if you've had enough for one day I recommend the knoll to your left for the view and the flowers.

If carrying on, stay on the trail that crosses the spur, turns left and climbs below the crest into spruce forest, sweeping right across the headwaters of Ranger Creek onto Moose Mountain's southeast ridge. The fire road is gained at GR562437 in a dip. Turn right for the summit, left for the parking lot.

300 WEST BRAGG TO HOMESTEAD ROAD — map 9

Day hike
Official ski trails & unofficial trails
Distance 10 km
Height gain S-N 259 m
Height loss S-N 207 m
High point 1631 m
Maps 82 J/15 Bragg Creek,
82 O/2 Jumpingpound Creek

South access: From Bragg Creek village take the road signed "Wintergreen". Cross the bridge over the Elbow River. Turn left and follow West Bragg Creek Road into Kananaskis Country. In 1.3 km the road ends at parking lots for West Bragg Creek cross country ski trails.

North access: Sibbald Creek Trail (Hwy. 68). At the sign turn south and follow Homestead Road toward the Shooting Range. At 6.1 km turn left and park amid spent cartridge shells before the berm with shot-up wooden post.

The open ridge below North Bragg.

A logging road tour of cutblocks tastefully hidden from highway view between West Bragg and the Jumpingpound doesn't sound too interesting, I admit. In reality, this connector is a good choice for short strolls from either end. From West Bragg, for instance, it takes you to ridge tops *with views*. One time we found fresh wolf tracks at the north end, and sure enough read that researchers, alerted by the radio-collared "cross border shopper", had spotted the Lougheed Park pack hunting in the Sibbald Flats area. The moral? You never know what you are going to see in the most mundane of places.

SOUTH TO NORTH

From West Bragg parking lot head up Telephone ski trail. At the four-way junction on a bench turn left and follow Hostel Loop up the hill to a NE-SW cutline. Cross the cutline (Hostel Loop turns right), and on unsigned track head right alongside the cutline. Cross a NE-SW cutline, then swing left above meadows and up steeper hillside to a viewpoint on a ridge at GR608479. Look east to Logan Ridge which I came to know

intimately during the search for Orval Pall and Ken Wolff. A high point to the south is North Bragg, a triangulation point shown on A. O. Wheeler's map of 1896. I have a vision of him tramping all over the ridge looking for a clearing. A hundred years on there's no problem. The whole ridge is a cutblock logged in 1987.

The logging road crosses the broad ridge (view of Moose Mountain), then on the west flank swings right through a belt of reprieved trees into—another cutblock. At a loop go either way and climb into a higher cutblock folded over both sides of the ridge, the road looping around a very tall tree left standing in a fit of whimsy by the loggers.

At the day's high point (GR598488), cross a few metres of meadow to another logging road and turn left (northwest). This newer road descends into the pines, crosses Telephone trail, then intersects a NE-SW cutline en route to a junction with the road usurping the north leg of Telephone trail (skiers will know what I mean). Keep left.

The final 4 km is a very pleasant walk through a wide, open valley down which trickles a tributary of Jumpingpound Creek. Of interest, a cutline access road heading right just before an intersecting NE-SW cutline offers a route to Pinetop Hill. Stay on the road and raise the white flag as you climb over the berm.

301 TOM SNOW TRAIL — maps 9 & 8

Day hikes, long day hike, backpack
Official trail with signposts & red
markers, creek crossings
Total distance 29.8 km

Highway access:
1. Elbow Falls Trail (Hwy. 66) at Station Flats day-use area.
2. Sibbald Creek Trail (Hwy. 68) at Spruce Woods parking lot on Jumpingpound Demonstration Forest Loop Road. Follow Moose Loop/Pine Woods interpretive trails down the bank. Cross Jumpingpound Creek, then turn right at the T-junction. At the following four-way intersection Tom Snow trail is straight and right.
3. Powderface Trail (Hwy.) at Sibbald Flat. Just 1 km south of Sibbald Creek Trail (Hwy. 68) turn left onto an old road and park at the felled tree. See sketchmap on page 226.
4. Powderface Trail (Hwy.) at Dawson trailhead.
Also accessible from the eastern terminus of Elbow Valley trail (#303), from Moose Mountain from West Bragg (#299) at three places, from the northern terminus of North Ridge of Moose Mountain (#302), and from the northern terminus of Cox Hill (#336).

Named after Chief Tom Snow of the Wesley Band of Stoney Indians, this easy long distance trail connects the Elbow to the Jumpingpound via West Bragg, threading a tortuous route through the forests, cutblocks and natural meadows of the valley bottoms. It would be hard to find a more eclectic route in its use of logging roads, cutlines, new and old exploration roads, new and old trails and interpretive trails, many sections having several aliases. Luckily, it's well marked throughout.

If, like me, you hike low-lying trails like this in early spring and late fall when the more exciting stuff to the west is under snow, you'll find the flowery meadows of summer a revelation.

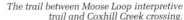

The trail between Moose Loop interpretive trail and Coxhill Creek crossing.

Station Flats to West Bragg via Ranger Creek

Distance 7 km
Height gain 244 m
Height loss 168 m
High point 1570 m
Map 82 J/15 Bragg Creek

Highway access: 1.
Also accessible from the eastern terminus of Elbow Valley trail (#303) at Station Flats, and from Moose Mountain from West Bragg (#299) at three places.

A two-parter: a forest walk up west Ranger Creek followed by a walk on exploration road through cutblocks.

Ranger Creek section A little way in from the trailhead turn right at the junction with Elbow Valley trail. The trail runs between pine hillside and willow muskeg to a small creek that is crossed to the junction with Diamond T Loop.

Go straight. Straight off K Country has a trick up its sleeve for people misguided enough to follow horse trails: a ridge to climb over. What's wrong with going around? It's not as if there's a view. You descend the far side to a NE-SW cutline, turn right and drop straight down the hill, turning left before you reach the bottom. A shorter drop precedes your arrival at Ranger Creek's west fork where a side trail heads downstream to the main fork and Elbow Ranger Station.

Your trail crosses the stream into a small meadow with salt lick. Climb the bank and follow alongside the west fork in the trees, in about 2 km veering right into a side valley with nibbled aspens. Near the valley head cross the side creek and climb steeply out of the valley into a young pine plantation, then grassy cutblock. The trail widens to logging road as you near West Bragg Creek exploration road at GR585442 (signpost). Look east across the main fork of Ranger Creek toward West Bragg.

West Bragg Creek exploration road—the section shared with #299. Keep right, winding downhill to Ranger Creek crossing. Continue along the road for a further 1.5 km, a pleasant enough walk through a chequerboard of pines and cutblocks logged in the mid 1970s. Be alert for a red marker signalling a left turn onto a trail. This occurs before a dip in the road.

To West Bragg ski parking lot
Distance 3 km. If you want to bale out, simply continue along the exploration road (route #299 in reverse), ignoring all side trails and ski trail markers. A final stretch alongside Bragg Creek leads to the parking lot.

West Bragg to Moose Creek via upper Bragg Creek

Distance 11.3 km
Height gain 137 m
Height loss 79 m
High point 1545 m
Map 82 J/15 Bragg Creek

Accessible from Moose Mountain from West Bragg (#299) and from the northern terminus of North Ridge of Moose Mountain (#302).

Ski trails get you started up lovely Bragg Creek valley and over the watershed into Moose Creek. West Bragg ski parking lot is not too far away, available for accessing (or leaving) the trail via #299. It also makes possible (by bike preferably) day trips to the upper valley or to the old Thorne Mine.

To Moose Loop ski trail The trail is cutting across country in a northeasterly direction to Bragg Creek. En route, keep right and cross two cutlines. After slicing through the centre of a six-way junction, the trail runs above a side creek, then corkscrews down the bank to Bragg Creek valley bottom. Turn left and cross the side creek. Come to a four-

The junction of Ranger Creek with West Bragg Creek road, looking east toward West Bragg.

way junction with a cutline and Moose Loop ski trail (straight, right). Go either way.

Moose Loop west leg Keep straight and cross a side creek. The old road undulates to a high point marked by a grassy swath heading up a ridge to the west—Shell Oil's reclaimed exploration road (detour to Thorn Mine). Keep right here and descend to upper Bragg Creek which is crossed. Climb to east leg at a marker in a meadow and turn left. (Shortcutting to #302? Although the logging road heading left before the creek crossing stops short of upper Moose Creek, a string of cutblocks can be used as the connector.)

Moose Loop east leg Turn right on the old road that fords Bragg Creek. The crossing looks innocent, but in a thunderstorm conditions can change in a trice. Who can forget the time we carried our bikes across this ford, the water swirling around our thighs and lightning flashing every few seconds. It was shortly after this we ditched our lightning conductors and went and hid in the forest, making sure the pines were all the same size, naturally.

This road intersects a NW-SE cutline (Moose Connector to right). Turn left, then veer right off the cutline, passing a meadow to right where an unofficial trail leads to West Bragg ski parking lot. A little farther on, the official trail keeps left of Telephone ski trail, turns a corner and descends into meadows above a large beaver pond. Look out across a wide, flat valley floor filled with willows and backdropped by the forested outliers of Moose Mountain sporting their new chequerboard look. You can just make out the tip of Moose. Follow red markers as the trail climbs back into the trees, the trail initially diverging from the ski trail onto the bank top. At the junction in the meadow where Moose Loop descends to cross Bragg Creek, veer right.

223

To West Bragg ski parking lot from Moose Loop east leg

Distance 2.6 km. When coming from the north take the east leg of Moose Loop ski trail. K Country would have you follow Moose Connector ski trail out to West Bragg Creek Road which involves cutline shenanigans and a sure paddle. I just can't do it. Between Telephone trail and the NW-SE cutline, I prefer to turn left on an unsigned trail that crosses meadow to the end of an exploration road at some boulders, then walk down the old road. Since the second edition the bridge has been removed over Bragg Creek, but usually it's jumpable. On gaining West Bragg Creek exploration road turn left and walk out to the parking lot.

Upper Bragg Creek The trail winds along the east bank of upper Bragg Creek through flowery meadows alternating with copses of aspen and pine. Cross a drift fence. Here the trail and the stream squeeze side by side through the narrows, the valley then opening out into a huge waterlogged meadow with some wildly scraggy spruce the Group of Seven would have lusted over. This is the Bragg Creek-Moose Creek watershed.

The trail stays on drier ground in the trees and crosses a NE-SW cutline, becoming cutline access road. Shortly it swings left and you come to the road junction at GR554505. Route #302 goes straight, Tom Snow turns right. (WARNING: Anyone crossing the ridge to the east is likely to be shot at notwithstanding notices riddled with bullet holes all around the perimeter of Homestead shooting range.)

OPTION to old Thorn Mine

10 km return, height gain 396 m, height loss 60 m from Moose Loop west leg. Sadly, a large part of the original wagon road to the mine is either plowed under lumpy cutblocks or infiltrated by impenetrable alder. Incidentally, it was the basis for today's road from Bragg Creek village.

The following is the hassle-free route. So what if there's 30 m of extraneous climbing! From the high point of Moose Loop's west leg turn west on Shell Oil's reclaimed road and follow its wide grassy

swath up a ridge. At the bend GR552472 turn left onto a cutline access road which descends to a west fork of Bragg Creek and crosses it. Turn right at the T-junction on the south bank.

On wagon track cross the creek into spruce forest. Pass the remains of a shack almost completely assimilated by detritus. Look for moose horns, bottles, rusty plates and billy cans. Carry on into the lovely meadow at the forks, remarkable in that it's natural. The mine lies on the east side of the forks, the mound of spoil a dead giveaway. I'm not sure how much coal was extracted but D. D. Cairnes in 1914 states the old Thorn Mine was later worked for disseminated iron pyrites "of no present economic value".

(If you *must* try the valley route turn left at the first intersecting cutline and drop into the side valley. Head upstream on a logging road ending in a string of cutblocks. At the narrows, crossed by a cutline, pick up the wagon road on the right bank. It crosses to the left bank and is assimilated by cutline access road. Farther upstream, keep straight.)

Moose Creek to Spruce Woods trailhead

Distance 6 km
Height gain 58 m
Height loss 195 m
High point 1545 m
Maps 82 J/15 Bragg Creek,
82 O/2 Jumpingpound Creek

Highway access: 2.
Also accessible from North Ridge of Moose Mountain (#302).

The Moose Creek section has changed since the second edition and so has the countryside courtesy of Spray Lakes Sawmills. Ironically, it now offers the best view of the entire route.

At the T-junction GR554505 turn right. Descend to Moose Creek and cross. The trail heads out to a large cutblock. I was dumbfounded the first time I saw what had been done, but have to admit the new view of all three summits of Moose Mountain is superb. The logging road heading left at GR553507 is the west bank route into upper Moose Creek (#302).

Tom Snow turns right and follows the cutblock's right edge until back into trees. Good time can be made down the west bank of Moose Creek. You cross a cutline (likely unnoticed), then the road wends right of a cutline section. Cross Moose Creek twice. Back on the west bank a tributary crossing precedes a beautiful stretch of spruce meadows below a steep bank. In trees, cross meandering former channels and intersect a cutline. Note a cutline access road to left.

The last part of this section has been rerouted to miss out the soggy part of Moose Creek valley where the river regularly overflows into its floodplain, keeping generations of Balsam poplars going. Keep alert for where you turn left onto a new trail that crosses a bridge over a former channel (good spring water) and climbs up the steep bank. Turn right, following the bank top

through a young pine plantation, then swing left through a strip of spruce forest into a 1970 cutblock where you meet up with Moose Loop interpretive trail (straight, right). Just below you on the left Husky Oil's exploration road is about to wind down a draw.

If finishing at highway access 2 there is the option of going right for a floodplain sortie via the interpretive trail's east leg. The Tom Snow trail, however, keeps straight, descending the bank top above the draw to a four-way junction at valley bottom. Tom Snow trail turns left. Straight on leads to **highway access 2**. (To right is the defunct section of old road up Moose Creek.)

To access 2, Spruce Woods trailhead
Distance 500 m. At the four-way junction go straight on Moose Loop interpretive trail. Turn left at the junction with the east leg and cross Jumpingpound Creek bridge. Climb the bank to the trailhead.

Spruce Woods trailhead to Dawson trailhead

Distance 5.5. km
Height gain 105 m
Height loss 21 m
High point 1494 m
Map 82 O/2 Jumpingpound Creek

Highway access: 2, 3, 4.
Also accessible from the northern terminus of Cox Hill (#336).

A very pleasant forest trail with views, shared in part with Pine Woods interpretive trail and assorted snowmobile trails.

At the four-way junction, turn left (or right if coming from Spruce Woods trailhead) on a trail shared with Pine Woods interpretive trail. Head across meadow to Husky Oil's exploration road, which has wound down a draw from the left, and follow it to the bridge over Coxhill Creek. Should the bridge be out, use a footbridge downstream. On the far bank turn left onto Thomas (logging) Road. (Husky's exploration road to right, on the line of the old Thomas Road, crosses Jumpingpound Creek and climbs to Jumpingpound Demonstration Forest Loop Road clockwise of Spruce Woods trailhead. In case you're greedily eyeing the exploration road as bike access to that remote country at the back of Moose Mountain, know that a pipeline is in the works and permission is unlikely to be granted— for now.)

Where Thomas Road turns left across a tributary keep right on a smaller track that climbs the bank below an aspen hillside packed with Paintbrushes. Now follows a long pleasing stretch on grassy banks high above the tributary where you kick up the sand and gaze in all directions at familiar mountains rimming the horizon: Moose, Ole Buck, Deer Ridge and Cox Hill. Pine Woods interpretive trail dives right into a young plantation and emerges some distance later. Keep straight both times.

Around a bend at GR515551 keep right twice where two heads of a cutline/logging road cross the tributary en route to a sawmill site (Sawmill Loop in the second edition). A few metres on, a NW-SE cutline takes off to the right and your route reverts to trail winding pleasantly through forest. This cutline and the next three exits to right (cutline, new logging road, old logging road) are all good ways to highway access 3. I refer you to the sketchmap which saves half a page of tortuous description.

At the third junction with the older logging road, alias snowmobile trail, turn left.

Keep straight where the snowmobile trail (alias Sawmill Loop) turns left. Descend briefly into a natural meadow, then climb back into pine forest where the eye is caught by a vast new cutblock glittering through a fringe of trees. At the T-junction with Coxhill Ridge trail (as signed) turn right down the hill and cross the bridge over Jumpingpound Creek at a NW-SE cutline. Eagle Hill trail joins in from the right just before you reach Dawson trailhead parking lot.

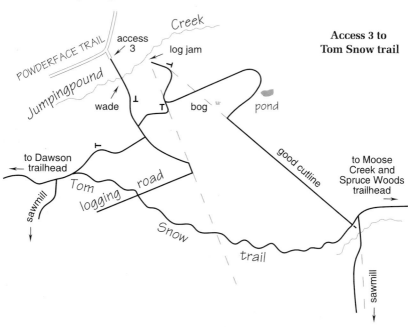

302 NORTH RIDGE OF MOOSE MOUNTAIN — maps 9 & 8

Backpack, long day
Unofficial trail & route, scramble
Distance 10.5 km
Height gain N-S 1085 m
Height loss N-S 152 m
High point 2437 m
Map 82 J/15 Bragg Creek

North peak from the north-north summit.
West peak in the background.

North access: Via Tom Snow trail (#301) in Moose Creek. Two accesses depending on the direction you're travelling the trail.
South access: The summit of Moose Mountain, terminus of routes #306 and #307.
Also accessible from Jumpingpound Mountain east ridge (#334).

This fairly strenuous high-level hike along the delectable north ridge of Moose Mountain is my favourite approach to the summit. On July 28, 1996, it had its first ascent "with bike" by Doug Eastcott and Greg Achten.

Called East Ridge trail in the second edition, it's "the trail that never got built".

However, during the past 10 years, the sheer number of hikers have improved existing game trails without help from a K Country trail crew, leading me to surmise this is the new economical way of trail building. So while there are generally trails below treeline, the ridge above treeline remains largely a route following grassy hogbacks and easy scree ridges with no exposure.

NORTH TO SOUTH
There are now two accesses into upper Moose Creek depending on which direction you're travelling the Tom Snow trail. As follows:

From the south via the east bank At T-junction GR554505 above Moose Creek you'd normally turn right down the hill and cross Moose Creek. Instead, climb straight up an old road following a dry ridge between Moose Creek and the watershed meadow. At a T-junction with the NE-SW cutline (snowmobile sign) turn right and gradually descend to Moose Creek. One small step across lands you in a huge cutblock where the west bank route joins in from the right. Go straight.

From the north via the west bank At the junction GR553507 before the final crossing of Moose Creek turn off right in the big cutblock and on logging road take the direct line across the cutblock into another larger cutblock where you join the east bank access just after it's crossed Moose Creek. Turn right.

Upper Moose Creek and Lucky Valley If you haven't been here within the last few years you're in for a shock. The pines and cutline have vanished, replaced by a huge cutblock and a soft spongy track. In the time it takes to cross this cutblock you can thoroughly appraise the Moose Mountain massif up ahead, the upper part of the north ridge route seen running from right to left along the skyline to the summit.

Suddenly, at the end of the cutblock where the valley pinches in and a snowmobiler's sign announces "trail not maintained beyond this point", there are several things to be alert for. Keep straight and cross a side creek into a meadow and camping area. Disregard a much better road turning left across Moose Creek (it joins Shell Oil's reclaimed road), and similarly dismiss a grassed-over track heading right before the beaver ponds. Down by the creek your road is a mess; it crosses the creek, is the creek, then improving, runs along the left bank. The next crossing is likely the last reliable source of clear sparkling water until you reach the spring on the summit of Moose Mountain.

On the right bank the much improved cutline-road swings away through good camping meadows to a NW-SE cutline winging its way to Coxhill Creek, then returns to the creek which is often dry at this point. Cross back and forth across the creekbed, then settle into a gradual climb along the right bank where you're treated to increasingly exciting close-ups of Moose Mountain's precipitous north face.

Road and cutline, having shared an uneasy alliance thus far, part company at the bottom of a steep hill just after a side creek crossing. Follow the road around to the right. Abandon it at the second bend where the road, having achieved the necessary height gain, is returning to the cutline.

Turn right and push through a belt of trees into Lucky Valley, the heavenly key to the north ridge. There may be a trail by now. Regardless, in the first meadow you come to there's definitely a good trail taking you up the right bank through aspen groves and lush meadows of an amazing bright green colour. Obviously, an underground sprinkler system is in effect with water running everywhere except in the creek which is sluggish. With luck campers may be able to deepen mud holes sufficiently to fill a billy can or two. By the way, this lush valley is a pit stop on the grizzly circuit of Coxhill Creek, which in retrospect probably accounted for the extreme nervousness of the deer when we were camped there, all unknowing. This is where years ago at the dawn of K Country we met Dr. Carl Reich, the well-known advocate of Multivitamin Therapy. He was dismantling his semi-permanent camp, having been discovered by forest rangers, and was talking about heading over the pass into Coxhill Creek. He recently passed over the Great Divide but I did hear he'd found a new heaven in the Livingstone Range.

The trail climbs out of the valley to the small treed pass between Moose and Coxhill creeks at GR515485, then continues onto the north ridge of Moose Mountain, gained at about GR513488.

The north ridge Finally, turn south. A belt of trees precedes the climb up a broad slope of grass, then shale, then scree. From a large cairn a grassy runway leads to a rocky knob that at 2240 m is the first summit of the day, the north- *north* summit for lack of a name. Somebody think of a name quick, and it had better not be Rigel or Husky. One of the delights of this ridge was its remoteness, being several ridges removed from any highway, but down below you to the west are a couple of well pads, a road and a soon-to-be pipeline which takes away any aura of wilderness.

Descend the slabby ridge on the far side to the broad grassy saddle at GR509464 which is within spitting distance of Pad No. 2 on the col between Moose and the east ridge of Jumpingpound Mountain (#334).

It's a long slog up north peak whose billowy grass slopes are pitted with Purple saxifrage. The final few metres narrow to a runner of grass leading to the high point, truly an island in the sky crowned with a cairn and a well-gnawed moose antler that we carried up long ago from the col before the takeover.

At first sight the connecting ridge to the summit of Moose Mountain, all scree and rock, looks intimidating. A few tentative steps should convince you it's nowhere near as narrow as it looks and certainly not exposed; you can just about cross the whole thing with your hands in your pockets. It's the final steep climb, where the ridge abuts against the north face, that's a little tricky, especially if you're carrying a bike. Tackle the first easy rock band direct, then head diagonally right to where talus spills through a gap in a second higher rock band. Above this, move delicately leftwards to the skyline ridge and scramble up 2 m of rock onto boulder slopes lying back at a more comfortable angle. You emerge at the biffy.

On the ridge between north peak and the summit (top left).

303 ELBOW VALLEY TRAIL — maps 9 & 13

Half-day, day hikes
Official trail with signposts & red
markers, creek crossing
Distance 9.5 km
Height gain E-W 347 m
Height loss E-W 265 m
Map 82 J/15 Bragg Creek

Above: The trail starting its wind down to Canyon Creek. In the background is Prairie Mountain.

Opposite: The adit below the trail.

Access: Elbow Falls Trail (Hwy. 66).
1. East access Station Flats trailhead.
2. West access Powderface parking lot. NOTE: This section of Hwy. 66 is closed between December 1st and May 15th.
3. Most popular access Paddy's Flat campground access road. After the road bends right, use the parking lot on the left side. Via River View trail (#305).
4. 300 m up Canyon Creek Road.
Also accessible from the southern terminus of Tom Snow trail (#301), via both ends of River View trail (#305), Moose Mountain Road 1 km from Hwy. 66, and from Powderface and Prairie Creek trails (#311, #309).

The Elbow Valley trail was planned as a long-distance trail between Station Flats and Little Elbow Recreation Area. Now it's been whittled down to end at Powderface Creek. You can, of course, string together Beaver Lodge interpretive trail, Beaver Flat to Cobble Flats (#313), Wildhorse trail (#315) and Big Elbow trail (#317) to reach that destination. However, there's hardly a procession of people doing the east to west trip. Just about everyone uses portions of trail to make loops. The most popular by far is the Elbow Valley/Sulphur Springs loop followed by Elbow Valley/River View loop, both usually accessed from access 3.

EAST TO WEST
Station Flats to Sulphur Springs trail east access At the T-junction a little way beyond the trailhead, turn left along a short section of trail shared with Diamond T Loop. Keep straight where Diamond T turns right and cross the meadow at the mouth of a side valley. It was around here in June of 1996 a grizzly killed a moose in sight of gawking motorists. Naturally, all the trails *east* of Moose Mountain Road were cordoned off. Later that afternoon I was freewheeling down Moose Mountain Road at the exact moment griz was crossing it onto trails *west* of the road, perhaps to meet up with some luckless hiker who felt himself safe. So after late snowy winters be alert for grizzlies driven east in the search for food.

A climb across wooded hillside brings you to Sulphur Springs Creek and a T-junction on the north bank. This is your first meeting with **Sulphur Springs trail** which heads up the creek.

To Sulphur Springs trail west access Cross the bridge and climb onto a low, forested ridge with Calypso orchids in season. In 600 m you reach the **eastern terminus of River View trail** which descends to Highway 66 opposite Paddy's Flat campground access road.

Keep right. The drone of traffic that has never been quite absent fades away as you turn your back on the highway and climb 152 vertical m to the ridge top at GR592389. There are meadows on the ascent but the top is all pines. Some have lopped-off crowns, casualties of 1996 spring winds. From the west end, descend grassy south slopes to a valley where cattle like to congregate. Jump the creek, then climb to Moose Mountain Road crossed 1 km in from Highway 66.

Continue climbing to a terrace below the end slope of Moose Mountain's south-east ridge where you wander through aspen meadows to the four-way junction with **Sulphur Springs trail** to right and **River View trail** to left.

To Canyon Creek Keep straight and begin the winding descent to Canyon Creek, thoroughly enjoying the long grasses, the flowers, the aspens, the view of Prairie Mountain and *Iyarhe ipan* rising above Beaver Flat campground. The trail surface is coal dust where it traverses above a cliff band marking a strip of coal-bearing Kootenay strata. Below you is an adit that can be spotted from Canyon Creek Road. About halfway between the adit and Highway 66, in a shallow gully, is another working, a mess of planks, half-buried metal scrap, coal spoil covered by grass and a loop road—grassy and ditchlike—heading out to the highway above the rockcut. All this is George Ings Mine (also known as Canyon Creek Mines in the plural) that supplied over 1,000 tons of coal to Bragg Creek's Mowbray-Berkeley oil well during the First World War.

The trail zigs back left below the adit, entering Canyon Creek valley. Head downstream on cobbles, cross the creek (easy) and continue down valley to Canyon Creek Road **(access 4).**

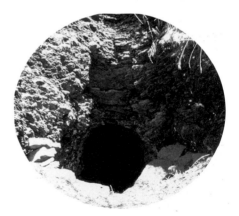

To Powderface Creek The trail resumes on the west side of the road. This final stretch is a rolling forest trail, gradually edging closer to the highway, until finally it edges down the cutbank to Prairie Creek. Cross Prairie Creek alongside the highway and join Prairie Creek trail. Swinging inland, cross Powderface Creek and follow its left bank up to Powderface parking lot.

304 SULPHUR SPRINGS TRAIL — map 9

Day hike
Official trail, signposts & red markers
Distance 4.5 km
Height gain E-W 213 m
Height loss E-W 122 m
High point 1661 m
Map 82 J/15 Bragg Creek

East access: Via Elbow Valley trail (#303) at Sulphur Springs Creek.
West access: The junction of Elbow Valley trail (#303) and the western terminus of River View trail (#305).
Road access: Moose Mountain Road, 2.3 km from Hwy. 66. Park just beyond the trail crossing at a pullout on the left side of the road near interpretive signs.

This is a lovely trail for the Sunday tourist who with very little effort can reach a satisfying viewpoint less than half a kilometre from Moose Mountain Road. Real hikers (and bikers) combine this trail with either Elbow Valley or River View to make loops of varying lengths depending on the starting point. It has become the classic spring tune-up walk.

EAST TO WEST

Head northwest up the east bank of Sulphur Springs Creek to a T-junction with an E-W cutline. Turn left, following the cutline for about 100 m before branching right by the side of a small tributary fed by sulphurous springs pouring out of a 1930s well casing. Shortly the trail climbs out of the valley, levelling off temporarily at an intersection with the same E-W cutline met with earlier, then crosses the head of the creek and climbs some more to a cairn on an intersecting NW-SE cutline. A flat section brings you to Moose Mountain Road.

Cross the road to the well site. This is where anyone parked at **road access** would join the trail. From here you climb rather steeply onto the end buttress of Moose Mountain's southeast ridge which is not of any great height, but a fine viewpoint nevertheless, encompassing all the McLean Creek OHV lands and, of more interest to hikers, waves of ridges—Prairie, Powderface, Forgetmenot and Nihahi (how easily the names roll off the tongue)—receding off to the west. The enjoyment is prolonged as you wind down dry south slopes redolent with sage to a terrace and the four-way junction with Elbow Valley trail (left, right), and River View trail (straight on).

Opposite top: Sulphur Springs trail. Descending grassy slopes off the end buttress of Moose Mountain's southeast ridge.

Opposite bottom: #305, River View trail. Looking down the Elbow River to McLean Hill.

Left: Sulphur Springs.

305 RIVER VIEW TRAIL — maps 9 & 13

Half-day, day hike
Official trail, signposts & red markers
Distance 4.5 km
Height gain E-W 107 m
High point 1539 m
Map 82 J/15 Bragg Creek

Access: Elbow Falls Trail (Hwy. 66) at Paddy's Flat campground. See sketchmap below.
Also accessible from Elbow Valley trail (#303) at two locations.

This trail was built to provide happy campers with a loop longer than the interpretive trail. In fact, two loops are possible: an 8.5 km loop with Elbow Valley trail, and a longer 9.5 km loop with Sulphur Springs trail. Why not add in Paddy's Flat interpretive trail?

Keep right twice at junctions with the interpretive trail and head west along a forested river terrace within earshot of rapids. Shortly after intersecting a NW-SE cutline, note numerous trails descending to a lively section of the Elbow River opposite its confluence with Silvester Creek. The bank is rising in anticipation of the gorge and riffles just east of Canyon Creek, and by the time you've crossed another NW-SE cutline you're a very long way up indeed, travelling on the edge and revelling in the views.

EAST TO WEST

From Elbow Valley trail, east access
Straightaway descend to a red stop sign and a yellow two-way traffic sign possibly aimed at bikers with inner tubes for brains. Cross Highway 66. The trail continues a few metres right of Paddy's Flat campground access road and basically parallels the road on the bank top. Descend to the road opposite access roads to Loops B and C. Inexplicably, the trail sign reads "Elbow Valley trail".

Either get onto the interpretive trail (nearest access is the amphitheatre), or turn right and follow the access road through D Loop into E Loop. Keep left and pick up the trail beside campsite #36.

All too soon the trail turns away and crosses Highway 66 to— another red stop sign. A brief climb up aspen hillsides gains you the four-way junction with Elbow Valley trail (left, right) and Sulphur Springs trail (straight).

Trails through Paddy's Flat Campground

234

306 MOOSE MOUNTAIN normal route — maps 13, 9 & 8

Day hike
Official trail with cairns
Distance 7 km
Height gain 670 m
High point 2437 m
Map 82 J/15 Bragg Creek

Photo taken on July 28, 1996, shows the last stretch of trail rising to the summit (left), and the north ridge extending to north peak (right). Meeting Greg Achten and Doug Eastcott after the first traverse of the north ridge by bike.

Access: Elbow Falls Trail (Hwy. 66). 700 m west of Paddy's Flat campground access road turn north up Moose Mountain Road (unsigned gravel road) and drive for 7.3 km to the trailhead, approximately half a kilometre before a locked gate at GR564425. There is no formal parking lot. NOTE: Moose Mountain Road is closed between December 1st and May 15th. Grades are steep and unsuitable for trailers.
Also accessible from Moose Mountain from West Bragg (#299), the North Ridge of Moose Mountain (#302) and Canyon Creek & options (#307).

This is the mountain you fly over en route to Vancouver. From 13,000 ft. its geological complexity becomes clear. How it is the apex of a major structural feature called the Moose Mountain Dome, an inlay of pale grey Paleozoic limestone surrounded by sandstone rocks of a more recent age covered in trees. And how water eating into the limestone of the dome has carved out such fabulously deep valleys like Canyon and Moose Dome. Although of comparatively low altitude, it has all the characteristics of a Front Range peak: sharp ridges, cirques and talus slopes.

I'm convinced this was the mountain noticed by Thomas Blakiston of the Palliser Expedition when travelling the Stoney trail between the Jumpingpound and Bragg Creek in 1858. He called it "The Family" for obvious reasons.

Fast forwarding, the summit has been topped with a fire lookout since 1929.

Originally, the pack trail left Elbow Ranger Station and went up Ranger Creek and onto the southeast ridge of the mountain via some of routes #301 and 299. Today's normal route follows the fire road which was built in 1950 along the southeast ridge in its entirety. In 1974 the fire road was improved to facilitate the building of the third and latest lookout and again widened in the late 1970s and early 1980s when drilling rigs moved into the area and the first part became Moose Mountain Road.

Top: A lookout.
Bottom: a lookout's best friend.

The gated fire road starts from the right-hand side of Moose Mountain Road and for the first 4 km undulates madly along the southeast ridge below minor tops, occasional west-facing meadows offering views into Moose Dome Creek. Near the beginning there's a particularly tiresome 100 m descent that precedes route #299 coming in from the right at dip GR562437. At GR551454 a side trail climbs a grassy top marking the north end of the southeast ridge, a possible half-day objective for anyone feeling tired.

At the notch at GR546456 the fire road turns west, climbing out of the trees into meadow and making a beeline for the dome-like lower summit (2330 m). Climb its east slope via seven easy-angled zigs or slog up the direct trail bisecting the zigs. Your choice. At the end of the climbing the road passes slightly right of the summit.

Beginner hikers tend to be fearful of the exciting prospect ahead: the final ridge of naked rock rising to the lookout. On closer acquaintance you discover the trail is wide enough for a string of sure-footed pack horses. So stride out confidently, following a line of old 1929 telephone poles down into the gap between the two summits, then climb first on the north side and then on the south side of the ridge above deepening scree slopes falling away into Moose Dome Creek. Five minutes from the lookout there is a choice of route. The pack trail circles around to the west slope and approaches the summit via the helipad. Alternatively, step right onto the ridge crest and pick your way up shattered blocks directly to the lookout building.

The summit commands an unequalled view looking 120 km in every direction. Moose Mountain's most amazing feature, however, is neither the view nor the marmots. Thirsty? Hop down the east ridge for 20 m. Just below where you join the pack trail is a spring of icy cold water and a baling pan thoughtfully provided by the lookout. These days, with the great volume of visitors, lookouts aren't too keen on doling out free coffee. Understandably.

307 CANYON CREEK & OPTIONS — maps 9 & 8

Day hike
Unofficial trail, creek crossings
Distance 15.7 km
Height gain E-W 260 m
High point 1737 m
Map 82 J/15 Bragg Creek

Canyon Creek opposite the Ice Cave (top right). Mountain at top left is the south peak of Moose Mountain.

East access: Elbow Falls Trail (Hwy. 66). Turn north onto Canyon Creek Road and drive 700 m to Ings Mine parking lot at the gate.
West access: Powderface Trail (Hwy.) at Canyon Creek. Park 400 m north of the creek crossing in a parking area on the east side of the highway just south of the memorial cairn.
NOTE: This highway is closed between December 1st and May 15th.
Also accessible from Ford Creek trail (#329), Jumpingpound Ridge trail (#335) and from the summit of Moose Mountain by various routes.

To most people, the words Canyon Creek are synonymous with Canyon Creek ice cave; relatively few hikers bother to go farther up this magnificent valley despite a beckoning trail that goes right through to Powderface Trail the highway. Be prepared

for 19 creek crossings! When George Dawson traversed the "Canon branch" from west to east in 1884 he noted "at high stages of the water the route would be impassible". True. Don't go at runoff.

NOTE: In the fall of '97 Ings Mine parking lot was moved down road "in the name of public safety" to discourage "the unprepared" from visiting the ice cave. Take a bike for the first 5.7 km of road bashing.

EAST TO WEST
From the far end of the parking lot a trail leads back to the road beyond the gate. Turn right and follow the road to a junction at Moose Dome Creek. Keep left to bike racks.

A trail continues toward the Ice Cave. In a few metres turn left and drop down the bank to pick up an old exploration road. Turn right. A long flat precedes a junction. Keep straight on road and cross Canyon Creek for the first time. Clearly visible across the valley is the infamous ice cave, that black slit in the cliff. Discovered in 1905 by Stan Fullerton, its 494 m of passageways beyond the big hall had all been thoroughly explored by the 1970s. For the last 40 years it has been a popular tourist attraction. You could scramble up from down below or take a rough trail, clearly an ordeal for those to whom walking between the parking lot and Market Mall is considered a hike. On average, says Pat Ronald, the mountain rescue had to be called out four times a year. The worst scenario happened three years ago when part of the cliff collapsed and boulders went bouncing down the slope, miraculously missing 48 school kids strung out along the trail and in the woods below.

During the next 2 km the narrow width of the valley floor forces the road to and fro across the stream 11 times. In the dry midsummer, when the heat is reflected tenfold off canyon walls and the water trickles lazily between mounds of riverbed stones, getting through this section isn't a problem. At runoff, or after days of heavy rain, it's another story. Remember, this stream originates in the highest peaks of the Fisher Range. Then, muddy waters raging from bank to bank make it impossible to get through the canyon dry shod, especially in the area of abandoned dry well 16-30 at GR538412. Look for historic trash on both banks: the well casing, a dynamite hut, and the usual mishmash of bricks, buckets, cables, planks and concrete blocks.

The road ends just before the canyon walls converge for the last time. Climb over the drift fence strung across the narrowest part and get onto a five-star cow trail on the north bank—the start of the meadows. There are still numerous creek crossings ahead, some of which can be circumnavigated, though the effort of doing so is hardly worthwhile at this stage in the game as your feet are undoubtedly wet from paddling

through the drift fence narrows from which there was no escape.

At the beaver pond at GR508413, an exploration road starts up and carries on in much the same sort of fashion as before, crossing and recrossing the creek another four times. Half a kilometre to the west of Moose Mountain Creek (passed while you are on the south bank) the road fords Canyon Creek for the last time and arrives at a T-junction on the north bank at GR495418 with a more recent exploration road (see options).

Turn left and follow this new road out to Powderface Trail the highway. Enjoy a very pleasant, undulating walk between Jumpingpound Ridge and an unnamed hill to the south, en route picking up Ford Creek trail from across the river and Jumpingpound Ridge trail at the last side creek to the north. On Canyon Creek/Ford Creek trail/ Jumpingpound Ridge trail walk the last kilometre to west access past two picnic tables.

Moose Mountain Options

Canyon Creek gives the fit adventurous hiker, desperate to get away from the hordes on the tourist route, an alternative access to Moose Mountain and its family of summits. Be familiar with bush, scree, easy scrambling and routefinding. West access from Powderface Trail the highway is the obvious starting/finishing point, but also consider point to points with Ings Mine parking lot and Moose Mountain Road.

West peak (2332 m) GR515442
Distance 7.5 km, height gain 595 m. Walk in from west access. Leave Canyon Creek trail at GR495418 and keep left on the better road that climbs over a rib into Moose Mountain Creek valley. Paddle to the east bank. Leave the road at the right-hand bend (take it from me, there's no ongoing trail from road's end much higher up the hill) and head up valley on a trail. In five minutes turn up the first side valley to the right. Higher up, cross to the left bank, then at about GR502423, on good trail, climb to the dip in west peak's southwest ridge at GR505432.

#307, Moose Mountain options. West peak and the saddle at GR520439 from the ridge rising to the hub.

#307, Moose Mountain options. The north ridge of south peak. Just above the sitting figure is the step.

Climb the moderately-angled ridge to the summit. The going is straightforward between well-spaced trees, then on meadows laced with scree. From the summit a number of options present themselves.

Moose Mountain (2437 m)
Add 900 m, add 150 m height gain. From west peak the sight of Moose Mountain, all slabs and scree, is a real downer to the tired hiker. Worse, before you can even set foot on it you must descend 122 m to the saddle at GR517445. Luckily, on closer acquaintance the slope falls back and the footing is firm. Nevertheless, it is still a labourious climb. At the top consider a loop incorporating Moose's north ridge, the east ridge of Jumpingpound Mountain and Jumpingpound Ridge trail back to Canyon Creek. Alternatively, take the tourist route to Moose Mountain Road.

Descent via Moose Dome (Sulphur) Creek
This is a spectacular canyon, penetrated by Canyon Creek Road climbing to three well sites. Despite rumours of hunters going in picking up the carcasses of animals killed by natural H_2S seepages, there is little to worry about. If the rotten-egg smell bothers you go after rain or during a strong wind. K Country's greatest fear is pipeline breakage; an invisible lethal cloud of gas rolling down the valley, knocking over tourists like ninepins. I wouldn't worry. The overhead powerline operates a sophisticated computer supervisory control system monitored 24 hours a day down at the compressor station in Canyon Creek. But going down this valley is your choice, so don't sue. OK?

From the saddle GR517445 head east down the narrow draw (snow-filled 'til mid June), widening marginally to claustrophobic creekbed between the steep stony slopes of Moose Mountain and centre peak. Tackle the rock band on the left side via a grassy ledge, then follow willowy creekbed to well 16-6 at GR533444. This is where you pick up the road taking you all the way out to Ings Mine parking lot. Because of the new road distance of 11.3 km, a bike 'n' hike from that

access may be preferable. Not far along is the scene from hell where great gobs of sulphurous yellow sludge erupt from the creekbed and flow lava-like around dead black trees.

Centre Peak (2323 m) GR527437
From west peak descend the steepest part of the northeast slope, then traverse right to the saddle at GR520439. Climb to the hub at GR522435. Turn left and on close-cropped grass steer for the summit which is marked by two branches tied together in the shape of a cross.

Descent via the "forever" valley to Canyon Creek at well 16-30.
Start near the hub at GR523435. A steep upper section (keep east of waterfalls), a stony creekbed obstructed by willows and avalanche debris, and a 30 m-high step with a bypass trail on the east side, all conspire to make it twice as long to navigate as the more technical east peak above.

East peak (2262 m) GR539436
Despite what is gleaned from the topo map, the connecting ridge from centre peak has a pesky 7 m-high step below the summit that just as surely brings the non-scrambler to a halt as if it were a 70 m-high precipice. Below the rock bands (three more with ways through) the walk to east peak is easy and from the ridge end a break in rock bands on the west side allows a chossy descent to be made into the "forever" valley.

South peak (2301 m) GR523428
From the hub the rocky north ridge is a delight. Tackle the step below the summit direct (easy scramble) or look for a weakness on the left side.

From the top there are a couple of obvious rib routes into Canyon Creek, one dropping in at GR517415. The other lands you in a side valley at GR508422. At this point a good cow trail conveniently climbs out of the valley and heads south through a string of meadows to the Canyon Creek exploration road, joined at bend GR50342 (faint here). It will have occurred to you this cow trail can be used to make a circuit.

The summit cairn, looking north to the Moose Mountain massif.

308 PRAIRIE MOUNTAIN — map 13

Half-day, day hike
Unofficial trail
Distance 3.8 km to summit
Height gain 716 m
High point 2210 m
Map 82 J/15 Bragg Creek

Access: Elbow Falls Trail (Hwy. 66) at Beaver Lodge parking lot located halfway between Prairie and Powderface creeks. NOTE: This section of Hwy. 66 is closed between December 1st and May 15th. During this time park at the winter gate at Elbow Falls.

A sustained climb on good trail all the way to the top. Prairie has become *the* popular spring conditioner, even before the winter gate opens. In early May of 1996, for instance, the mountain was covered in snow, the wind howling. Not the best day for bagging an ascent, but astonishing to me, I counted 12 parties besides ourselves slithering up and down the trail.

Backtrack to the east bank of Prairie Creek. Cross Elbow Valley trail, and on trail, climb the steep bank overlooking the highway at its left-hand edge. At the top the trail steers left and follows a broad easy-angled ridge in the pines. From one west-facing meadow you look straight up Prairie Creek to the promontory.

Inevitably the climb begins, 350 vertical m of corkscrewing trail up the southeast face of the mountain. At the mid point there's a slight easing on patches of stony ground augmented by cairns (I surmise were built by the Boy Scouts), then comes the final steep push to the summit ridge. Top out onto wind-buffeted meadows at GR545388 (cairn, dead trees).

Turn right and hug the edge of the eastern escarpment around to the summit cairn 1 km distant. The view is extensive to the east, south and west where you'll have a fine old time identifying peaks. Nearer at hand, Moose Mountain totally blocks the view to the north. By walking over to the northern cliffs you can spot the celebrated ice cave above Canyon Creek. Interestingly, Prairie's Stoney name *Iyarhe wida tagichuwaga* translates to "'younger brother of Island mountain", Island being Moose Mountain.

241

309 PRAIRIE CREEK — map 13

Day hike
Official trail, signposts & red markers
Distance 9 km
Height gain 180 m
High point 1692 m
Map 82 J/15 Bragg Creek

East access: Elbow Falls Trail (Hwy. 66) at Powderface parking lot. Via Elbow Valley Trail (#303), also signed "Prairie Creek". NOTE: This section of Hwy. 66 is closed between December 1st and May 15th. During this time park at the winter gate at Elbow Falls.
West access: Powderface Trail (Hwy.). A parking area on the east side of the highway about 100 m north of Prairie Creek crossing. NOTE: This highway is closed between December 1st and May 15th.
Also accessible from Prairie Link trail (#310) and Ford Creek trail (#329).

In Stoney, Prairie Creek is variously named *Sna Wapta* (Prairie Creek), *Chuteja Ozaden Waptan* (Evergreen Point Forks Creek), *Ozade Waptan* (Forks Creek) and *Sna Ozade Waptan* (Prairie Forks Creek). Possi-

bly it was named for the meadows at the west end of the valley. It is rather puzzling that early 20th Century Geological Survey bulletins referred to it as Prairie *Chicken* Creek, perhaps after the Sharp-tailed grouse, but more likely after one of our mountain grouse, named by someone who "didn't know their birds".

Relatively few people follow this trail from highway to highway and so never get to see the prairie. The vast majority start from Highway 66 and either make a loop with Prairie Link and Powderface Creek trails or take a stroll to the 2.5 km mark where the creek is closeted in a most unprairie-like canyon.

Aspen traverse around the big bend. In the background is Iyarhe Ipan.

EAST TO WEST

Prairie Creek trail branches off Elbow Valley trail on the west bank of Prairie Creek and straightaway heads into the valley. The next kilometre of trail has been completely rerouted from the original, the fording of the creek and the slightly hairy traverse above the rock band are gone, replaced by a log bridge and a safe trail through the aspens below the cliff. Back on the original line, the trail traverses around the big bend, climbing all the while above a little canyon to get onto a rocky promontory protruding from the south flank of Prairie Mountain at GR545376. It's a beautiful destination for half-day trippers.

Losing most of the height gained previously, the trail drops to creek level and crosses the drift fence. For the next 2.5 km, it alternates between aspen bank tops and valley bottom cow trails near a string of beaver ponds. Be very careful not to cross the river on a good game trail that was the former route to Powderface Creek; the official **Prairie Link trail** turns left across the creek at a signpost a good half kilometre farther on. At this point the valley floor is wide and grassy, low forested hills on either side framing Compression Ridge where the river has its birth.

Stay on the north bank and cross a side creek. After passing an aspen blowdown area, climb up and over a steep bank above a second set of beaver ponds, then pass through a second narrows. Gradually, the valley fans out into willowy prairie below Compression Ridge.

Close to Powderface Trail the highway you cross a bridge over a side creek and steer for the parking lot located a little south (left) of where Ford Creek trail comes in.

---

310 PRAIRIE LINK TRAIL — map 13

Day hike
Official trail with signposts & red
markers, creek crossing
Distance 2.7 km
Height gain S-N 100 m
height loss S-N 143 m
High point 1762 m
Map 82 J/15 Bragg Creek

South access: Via Powderface Creek & Pass (#311) at 3 km.
North access: Via Prairie Creek trail (#309) at the 5 km mark.

Because the trailheads for Powderface and Prairie Creek trails are only 200 m apart, a circuit using this trail as the connector is a logical and popular 11 km trip, especially with bikers. Amazingly, this is a section of a major pack trail that went up Powderface Creek, along this connector, then west up Prairie Creek and north along the line of today's highway to Sibbald Flat.

SOUTH TO NORTH
Powderface to Prairie—the popular way round This trail crosses the third gap in the hills to the right after you cross Powderface Creek. Starting from a signpost in a meadow the trail follows the east bank of a side creek to the height of land. Contrary to expectation, the trail does not take the most direct line to Prairie Creek, instead choosing to meander in a northwesterly direction through a thick Lodgepole forest strewn with deadfall before starting the descent. Wade the river to Prairie Creek trail at a T-junction on the north bank.

311 POWDERFACE CREEK & PASS — map 13

Day hikes
Official trail with signposts & red
markers, creek crossings
Distance 8 km, 6.5 km to pass from
east access
Height gain 509 m
Height loss 289 m
High point 2027 m at pass
Map 82 J/15 Bragg Creek

East access: Elbow Falls Trail (Hwy. 66) at Powderface parking lot. NOTE: This section of Hwy. 66 is closed between December 1st and May 15th. During this time park at the winter gate at Elbow Falls.
West access: Powderface Trail (Hwy.) at Trail Creek parking area, 7.3 km north of Hwy. 66.
Popular unofficial west access: Powderface Trail (Hwy.) at pass GR492346, 6 km north of Hwy. 66. NOTE: Powderface Trail (Hwy.) is closed between December 1st and May 15th.
Also accessible from Prairie Creek (#309), Prairie Link (#310), and Powderface Ridge (#312).

The name Powderface commemorates Stoney Tom Powderface and his family who lived near the Elbow Ranger Station during the 1920s. Before this time the creek was called Rainy and shown as such on Wheeler's 1896 map, a name resurrected and transposed to the neighbouring valley carrying the highway in 1983.

An exploration road and trail carries you the full length of the creek over a pass to Powderface Trail the highway. Some observations: The fastest way onto Powderface Pass and Powderface Ridge is from the unofficial west access—a mere 1.3 km. Otherwise, this trail works best when combined with either Prairie Link/Prairie Creek trails or with Powderface Ridge which requires two vehicles. Another suggestion is to turn north at the pass for a spot of gentle ridge wandering over Powderface Ridge north.

EAST TO WEST
To Prairie Link junction The climbing starts as soon as you leave the parking lot; waves of uphills on exploration road followed by a long, gentle runout to a crossing of Powderface Creek. Now on the north bank, the road crosses the drift fence and heads through riverside meadows with views up ahead of Powderface Ridge showing its unexciting forest aspect. At the 3 km mark, Prairie Link trail turns off to the right, aiming for the third gap in the hills to the north.

Powderface Creek at Prairie Link junction.

Alternative start

This is NOT the trail that follows the left bank from the parking lot. This trail (the original) starts from Elbow Valley trail some distance above the right bank and traverses hillside through aspens and meadows, joining the normal route just west of the drift fence.

To the pass Keep straight. A creek crossing at 4 km marks the start of a winding climb into the valley head through spruce forest festooned with lichen. One final zig across the infant Powderface Creek and the road ends, abutting against a grassy hillside.

A trail carries on up valley through a more open forest to Powderface Pass (cairn) at the demarcation of forest and meadow. The prevailing west wind is heard from far away as it comes sighing among the long grasses of the west flank, bringing with it the sounds of traffic on the highway only 1 km distant as the crow flies. The view consists mostly of Nihahi Ridge. To your left, route #312 climbs more buffeted hillsides to the top of Powderface Ridge.

To Trail Creek (west access) Follow red markers on solitary trees into the sheltering forest where the trail descends the north bank of a creek. Cross the stream and follow a new section of trail that lower down joins an exploration road for the last few windings to a junction.

For **unofficial west access** keep left on the exploration road which shortly reaches Powderface Trail at the site of a Sacramento rain gauge.

The official trail wends right and re-crosses the creek. Heading north now, it loses another 122 m in elevation as it drops to **Trail Creek parking area**.

GOING FARTHER

Powderface Ridge North 2088 m distance to highest open top 2.5 km, height gain 152 m.

At the pass turn north on a bit of a trail. On short grass meadow and gravelly ground make for top GR498353, then steer northeast over another top to your objective at GR502366 where the view opens up further to include the main backbone of the Fisher Range and Belmore Browne Peak.

Powderface Pass, looking west.

312 POWDERFACE RIDGE — map 13

Day hike
Official trail, signposts & red markers
Distance 8.2 km, 5 km to summit
Height gain 640 m
Height loss 183 m to Powderface Pass
High point 2210 m
Map 82 J/15 Bragg Creek

Access: The junction of Elbow Falls Trail (Hwy. 66) and Powderface Trail (Hwy.) Look for a brand new parking area on the east side of the highway. NOTE: This section of Hwy. 66 is closed between December 1st and May 15th. **Also** accessible from Powderface Creek & Pass (#311) at Powderface Pass.

One of the leftover cairns on the summit ridge. Immediately left of the cairn is Banded Peak.

This is a fairly strenuous walk up a grassy ridge with fantastic views. Unlikely though it may seem, you share the trail with hard-core mountain bikers who, unlike myself who uses a bike to get to the bottom of something, can be seen all along the ridge top, pushing in a north to south direction to take advantage of a challenging downhill. Hikers, too, can combine the ridge with route #311 which, of course, makes it a two vehicle trip. If you're lucky like us you can cadge a lift back along the highway with acquaintances you meet on the summit. Warning: The other "obvious" loop with Ford Creek trail is an arduous undertaking with a height gain of over 1000 m whichever way round you tackle it.

A trail climbs the bank and joins the official route from Forgetmenot Pond just before it delves into the forest. Nearly all the height gain occurs in the next 2 km in a relentless climb to the col at GR523319 between the south end of the ridge and a grassy outlier to the southeast. Anyone ready to call it a day can walk onto the outlying ridge at GR526317 for a breathtaking view of the forks. The Elbow is seen winding between Forgetmenot Ridge and the foursome of Glasgow, Cornwall, Outlaw and Banded Peak, the peaks of Bluerock, Threepoint, Burns and Cougar forming a ragged skyline.

In order to avoid rocky ground at the south end of Powderface Ridge, today's trail traverses in a northerly direction to another grassy col with a cairn. Keep left shortly after and continue traversing across the eastern escarpment, now covered in spruce and damp underfoot. A creek crossing signals a steep zigzag climb through a break in a small rock band to the summit ridge. On topping out you discover this final version of the trail not only misses out the rocks but also a large part of the grassy ridge as well, which was hugely disappointing to me the first time I walked it. If you stroll back south you'll stumble over all kinds of leftover cairns.

The summit is just up to the right. If you're lucky, the day will be calm and you'll be able to enjoy the 360 degree panorama to the full from beds of soft grass. What a place to view Nihahi Ridge!

Often the wind is blasting from the west and after reaching the high point which is totally without shelter, your only thought will be to hurry on down the trail. So you head west down a grassy incline dotted with krummholz between the summit and an outlier, then slip north down steeper slopes to Powderface Pass. There join route #311.

#312, Powderface Ridge summit.

#313. Descending from Highway 66 into Rainy Creek. Route A follows the right bank of the Elbow River through the gap.

247

313 BEAVER FLAT TO COBBLE FLATS — map 13

Half-day, day hikes
Unofficial trails & route
Map 82 J/15 Bragg Creek

Access: Elbow Falls Trail (Hwy. 66). NOTE: this section of Hwy. 66 is closed between December 1st and May 15th.
1. Pullout 300 m west of Beaver Flat campground entrance.
2. Via Cobble Flats day-use area access road. Park at the far end picnic area.

When Elbow Valley trail extended to Little Elbow Recreation Area, there was a glaring gap between Powderface parking lot and Cobble Flats picnic area. Here are two suggestions for people wanting to go right through. To reach access 1 use either Beaver Lodge interpretive trail to Beaver Flat campground entrance, or just walk up the highway. These routes come into their own in May before the winter gate opens and half of Calgary is barbecuing at Elbow Falls. At such times it pains me to see people walking up the highway to Rainy Pass when a pack trail is available. It will also have occurred to you that a loop is possible with A and B.

313A Elbow River route

Distance 5 km, height gain 22 m, high point 1570 m. Expect one easy trail-less section.

From access 1 hop over the guard rail and pick your way down rocks to a metal post. Descend a trail to a T-junction. Turn left. At a junction above cliffs overlooking the Elbow River turn right and drop to river level. Cross Rainy Creek on rocks.

The trail continues, faithfully following the right bank of the Elbow through a scenic narrows once touted for a reservoir, the river racing over a boulder garden below the steep rocky slopes of *Iyarhe Ipan*, meaning "mountain corner" or "mountain point".

The trail shortcuts across a really tight bend and runs below a scree slope to its end at GR559343. The scenery now changes to

alluvial flat, a rather dreary landscape of kinnikinnick, spruce and meandering river channels. Leave the river temporarily and cut straight across to GR555326 alongside the channel heading southwest.

Back at the Elbow River again, turn right. Where the river becomes tight against its bank on an outside bend a trail climbs the grassy bank and can be followed all the way out to picnic tables at Cobble Flats. Emerge on the access road at the turnaround loop. Interestingly, the Stoney call this place *Itusnihan*: "A long time ago one of our forefathers who was named Itusni (the liar) died and was buried at that location".

313B Rainy Creek route

Distance 5 km, height gain 244 m, height loss 183 m, high point 175 m. The forest route on slightly overgrown pack trail.

From access 1 hop over the guard rail and pick your way down rocks to a metal post. Descend a trail to a T-junction. Turn right and on pack trail descend into Rainy Creek valley where the trail is lost in long grass. Make for the creek and cross it.

The much-improved trail rises leftwards then winds about a bit before settling into a slowly rising traverse along the southeast bank of Rainy Creek. Near the beginning endure two short stretches where the tread has been lost on a side slope. After this the going is straightforward and easy. You emerge on the highway cut opposite the road sign "bend". Walk 100 m up grassy ditch to Rainy Pass.

Climb the bank to the start of a grassy road—two highways removed—winding down the hill to Cobble Flats. Shortly keep straight (side road to left takes you *almost* to the open hilltop at GR543336). Lower down the road turn left twice and bottom out at Cobble Flats access road turnaround loop near picnic tables.

314 QUIRK CREEK — maps 13 & 14

Looking across Quirk Creek to Iyarhe Ipan (Quirk Ridge). The trail to the summit can be seen winding up the meadow in the middle of the photo.

Day hike
Unofficial trails, river crossing
Distance 10 km to Wildhorse trail
Height gain 91 m via route No. 2
High point 1646 m via route No. 2
Map 82 J/15 Bragg Creek

Access: Elbow Falls Trail (Hwy. 66) via Cobble Flats day-use area access road. At 1.6 km (before the picnic area) an old road makes a beeline for the Elbow River. This is the Quirk Creek exploration road. NOTE: This section of Hwy. 66 is closed between December 1st and May 15th.
Also accessible from Wildhorse trail (#315).

The valley of Quirk Creek has a pastoral openness that is attractive. Wide and flat throughout, there's hardly any height gain throughout its entire length. You'll have noticed something downright peculiar about Quirk Creek. Half of it is missing! That's because the headwater has been pirated by Threepoint Creek cutting ever deeper and farther back.

Cattle have thronged the valley floor since the 1920s. Naturally, predators found the

yearlings easy pickings so there was a 10-year break in the 1940s while the bears and the cougars were culled. Bear-hunter Curly Sand, brought in by the North Sheep Stock Association, is recorded as having killed *in less than one year* 11 grizzlies and numerous black bear. I'm not sure how many grizzlies there are now, but the cougars are back and according to researchers a wolf pack started denning in the valley in '96.

Interestingly, this valley used to be called "The Muskeg" or *Pterathto Waptan* "Oval-shaped marsh creek". The name Quirk was previously applied to Threepoint Creek that ran past John Quirk's ranch.

Exploration roads make easy but boring walking, so consider taking a bike now that driving is out of the question. The great deterrent is the crossing of the Elbow River right at the start. Bridges come and go with the oil wells. It was thought the latest series of bridges were here to stay, not having been dismantled after the latest foray by the oil companies and I, for one, was dreaming of car trips to the fascinating east side of Forgetmenot Ridge when all the bridges washed out in the spring floods of 1990. Consequently, schedule a trip up Quirk Creek from midsummer on.

With pant legs rolled up as high as they will go and socks stuffed in a pocket, head down the Quirk Creek exploration road to alluvial (cobble) flats where the braided Elbow River changes position between each edition of the topo map. The road ends abruptly above a quiet backwater channel (dry in fall, bridge remains) that anaesthetizes the feet in preparation for two faster, deeper channels to come. No. 3 can be particularly tough. The road resumes slightly downstream.

Straight off a snowmobile trail heads right to join Wildhorse trail on the east bank of Wildhorse Creek—another stretch of the old Elbow Valley trail.

The road steers northeast along the flat gradually rising to a saddle and junction at GR565839 where it turns right (southeast) into Quirk Creek valley. For the next 3 km it undulates through pines just above the meadows, then dekes into grass at Mac Creek crossing. This is where another road to *Iyarhe Ipan* turns left. Keep straight and in another 2 km come to a junction with a sign indicating a right turn. Actually you have a choice:

1. Turn right, staying with the latest edition of the road which climbs to a well site on a ridge. From the clearing descend a cutline to Howard Creek cutline, turn left and join route No. 2 just before Howard Creek crossing. Go right.

2. My choice. Keep left on the older road which takes the valley route through meadows. Re-enter trees and come to the junction with route No. 1 just before Howard Creek crossing. Turn left.

Cross Howard Creek via culvert. Keep straight and cross Quirk Creek by bridge. (Note: If returning via Wildhorse, a trail along the west bank shortcuts to Duke Creek.) On the east bank there is a signposted junction with "Sylvester Loop", a muddy OHV road that heads through a gap into Muskeg Creek.

Turn right here for the last lap along the east bank. The road narrows to trail for a stint through trees, then emerges once again into meadows at the point where Wildhorse trail comes in from the right. No signpost marks this important junction.

OPTION
Iyarhe Ipan (Quirk Ridge) 1996 m
Distance 4.5 km return from Quirk Creek, height gain 396 m. The highest summit of the ridge at GR584328 is well worth climbing for the view, but I can't guarantee you won't be sharing the summit with OHV users. Watch for the wave, as per the K Country brochure, an act meant to appease hikers as gobs of mud spatter your legs.

Leave Quirk Creek exploration road at Mac Creek. Turn left on another exploration road which crosses a substantial bridge over Quirk Creek. This is a good place to view the ridge which presents its aspen aspect. The road wanders about aspen meadows, but does most of its serious climbing through the pine forest of the south and east slopes, approaching the summit ridge from the back. Here it ends.

A good trail carries on along the northwest trending ridge, following meadows above the western escarpment. The summit proper is the jumble of conglomerate rocks on the right which makes fine seats from which to view the western panorama and eat lunch. The trail continues to another viewpoint looking north to Moose Mountain and on over two lower summits before dipping into the forest.

The duck pond between Mac and Howard creeks. One of the buttresses of Forgetmenot Mountain in the background.

315 WILDHORSE TRAIL — maps 13 & 14

Day hike, backpack
Official trail with signposts & red
markers, river crossing
Distance 15 km
Height gain N-S 378 m
Height loss N-S 222 m
High point 1820 m
Map 82 J/15 Bragg Creek

Access: Elbow Falls Trail (Hwy. 66) at Little Elbow Recreation Area. Via Big Elbow trail (#317).
Also accessible from Quirk Creek (#314), the western terminus of Threepoint Creek trail (#295) and the northern terminus of Volcano Ridge trail (#285) in Quirk Creek.

Lovely Wildhorse travels through quintessential foothills country of forest and meadow along the northern and eastern flanks of Forgetmenot Ridge. It's one of those useful trails you can make loops with or long-distance point to points. For instance, the northern leg was once part of Elbow Valley trail.

Mountain bikers have cottoned on to a loop with Quirk Creek trail which means Wildhorse is not as peaceful as it once was and the chance of creeping up on feral horses is almost nil—they're already miles away from the trail. So I count myself lucky that on our first visit we spotted a fine black stallion feeding in a glade and watched entranced from behind some trees for a good 15 minutes until he became aware of us and went crashing off into the trees where further crashing indicated he'd picked up his harem. NOTE: While all small creeks are bridged, the Elbow River is not! However, by fall most of the water at this crossing point has gone underground.

From Little Elbow Recreation Area follow Big Elbow trail as it crosses the suspension bridge over the Little Elbow to the signposted four-way junction. Turn left on Wildhorse (dirt road).

Intersect Big Elbow horse trail and on your way to the Elbow River note a couple of grassy cutlines headed for the Little Elbow. Cross the Elbow River, normally a two-channel, knee-deep paddle and continue below the craggy north end of Forgetmenot Ridge. A large cairn at a side creek crossing signifies route #316 up Forgetmenot Ridge.

After a string of beaver ponds you cross the inlet and turn sharp right on a trail running down the Elbow River valley. The next point of interest is a large meadow liberally sprinkled with impressive heaps of wild horse dung (down one side is a line of well-manured spruce trees). This is the traditional campsite used by the Stoney called *Achohathi snan* "shadow clearing" because it lies in the shadow of Forgetmenot and during the winter receives no sun.

Cross Wildhorse Creek. Unaccountably, a signpost is lacking at the following junction. You turn right. (Going straight brings you to Quirk Creek exploration road—the old Elbow Valley trail continued.)

The middle leg threads a winding route over four pine-covered ridges protruding from the east side of Forgetmenot Ridge whose craggy grey buttresses are a constant backdrop throughout. This is the stretch where bikers have been treed by the resident cougar.

It takes effort to gain the first ridge. The trail is moderately steep, ultimately winding as it draws near the route's high point at a cairn and viewpoint. Descend a grassy draw and cross the twin north forks of Mac Creek in meadows (water). Red markers at the edge of trees signify the resumption of the trail over a low ridge into Mac Creek (often dry). Then it's back into the pines again for the climb over ridge No. 3 into the Howard Creek drainage, erroneously marked on some editions of the topo map as Quirk Creek. Here the trail circles a pond where we once watched open-mouthed as two mallards outsmarted a hawk in hot pursuit. The flying threesome sounded like a nuclear missile headed for us personally. (I was later astounded to learn that mallards can clock 100 km/h in a crisis.) At the last minute the mallards peeled off to left and right into the safety of the reeds while the hawk, like the star performer of the Starbirds Precision Team, zoomed up and over our heads, almost parting our hair with his talons.

I can't guarantee you'll see anything so exciting as you circle the pond, following the rim of a very large meadow to a T-junction with a SW-NE cutline. Turn left. At the point where the cutline starts to rise (shortcut to Quirk Creek), cross Howard Creek and climb over ridge No. 4 into Duke Creek. The trail heads downstream, intersecting a NW-SE cutline on its way to Quirk Creek valley meadows. Just beyond the horse rail a trail turns left; for what it's worth, the west bank shortcut to Quirk Creek trail at Howard Creek. Wildhorse, however, crosses Quirk Creek by bridge to an unsigned junction with Quirk Creek trail (#314). Turn right.

From wide, flat meadow you're treated to a view of Forgetmenot Mountain and of Allsmoke Mountain up ahead with not a hint of the deep gash in between. A signpost points out the side trail to Wildhorse back-country campground which is miles away up a nameless side creek. In some trees there is an unexpected ascent and descent past a cutline (right) to the junction with Threepoint Creek and Volcano Ridge trails.

Having come this far you'd be unusual not to continue to the edge of the drop-off where Quirk Creek valley comes to an abrupt end. With total astonishment you peer into the gorge of Threepoint Creek or *Umsiyathaban Garhe* as the Stoney call it.

The ridge near the summit.
Looking north towards north peak.

316 FORGETMENOT RIDGE — map 13

Day hike, long day hike
Unofficial trail & route with cairns
Distance 7 km to high point
Height gain 740 m
High point 2335 m
Map 82 J/15 Bragg Creek

Access: Elbow Falls Trail (Hwy. 66) at Little Elbow Recreation Area. Via Wildhorse trail (#315).
Also accessible from Upper Threepoint Creek (#286) and Forgetmenot Mountain (#287).

I don't mind telling you this is one of my favourite places; highly recommended to all ex-Brits homesick for the grassy hills of their childhood. But despite Forgetmenot's innocent looking appearance from the west, be warned the approach ridge is rough, steep and strenuous.

The most satisfying way of doing Forgetmenot is a traverse of the whole ridge combined with either Wildhorse and Forgetmenot Mountain, or Big Elbow and Upper Threepoint Creek. On such mammoth one-day expeditions it's essential to check your party beforehand to ensure no one has a dinner date in Calgary at 5 pm.

Leave Wildhorse trail just northeast of the Elbow River crossing, at the point where you cross a side creek. A cairn marks the spot.

The trail kicks off along the left bank of the side creek, then turns up grassy hillside into one of those narrow newfangled cutlines leading straight and steep onto the northwest ridge.

Rough trails continue up the left edge of the rocky ridge, endlessly long in both ascent and descent, all trails petering out before a saddle is reached. A more moderate slope of short-cropped grass gains you the main axis of the ridge at about GR542283. Purists should backtrack to the northernmost top at GR543288 (2240 m) which has a cairn.

As you head south along the broad grassy ridge, you must surely wonder about the Jekyll and Hyde personality of Forgetmenot which appears to be two separate ridges spliced together in the middle. Actually, you're walking on a double fault. This explains why the west flank of Kootenay sandstones/conglomerates is a gentle grassy slope and the east flank of Rundle Formation limestone is cliff.

At GR547271 the ridge jogs to the west, tapering and steepening dramatically as it rises 60 vertical m to a rocky knob entailing a few metres of scrambling. Above, the ridge resumes its former breadth, and shortly its southward march. Pick your way between upheavals of frost-shattered rocks and areas of patterned ground where the rocks are aligned in stripes down the west slope, the ground slowly rising toward the highest summit that 100 years ago was called Old Forgetmenot. As you approach the summit cairn at GR548262 the three-humped outline of Forgetmenot Mountain comes into view.

Throughout the walk you have been treated to a fabulous panorama of Mts. Glasgow, Cornwall, Outlaw and Banded Peak across the shadowy gulf of the Elbow River. It's particularly satisfying in spring when the grass is greening on the ridge, yet the mountains are still mantled with snow, looking the very epitome of Anthony Henday's "Shining Mountains".

GOING FARTHER
Forgetmenot Mountain 2335 m

Distance 3 km, height gain and loss 152 m. The prerequisite to completing a loop with routes #286, #320 & #317.

The disheartening loss of altitude as you head south down a grassy ridge is compensated by a terrific new view looking south past Bluerock Mountain (showing ascent route) to the mountains about Junction Creek. Expect slow going on the long col above Howard Creek which is striped crosswise with patterned ground. Back on grass, regain all the lost height as you climb onto Forgetmenot Mountain's summit ridge, en route picking up a trail that has arisen from a spring.

The golden age of Forgetmenot passed away with the removal of the lookout and the demotion of Forgetmenot Pot as Alberta's deepest pothole. Discovered in 1969, this 85 m-deep rift requires ropes and ladders all the way to the bottom burial ground. Rather than add to the bone count, I'm going to be a spoilsport and not let on the pot's location. However, if you happen to be stumbling around at dusk, bats rising into the sky will give you a clue.

Looking south towards the jog in the ridge. Old Forgetmenot is the high point farthest left.

317 BIG ELBOW TRAIL — maps 13, 12 & 17

Day hikes, backpack
Official trail with signposts & red
markers, creek crossings
Total distance 24.3 km

Highway access: The terminus of Elbow Falls Trail (Hwy. 66) at Little Elbow Recreation Area. Preferably, drive past the campground registration hut to a small parking lot on the right side of the road opposite the suspension bridge. If this is full use the trailhead parking lot and walk the trail alongside the Little Elbow to the bridge. See sketchmap. NOTE: This section of Hwy. 66 is closed between December 1st and May 15th.

Also accessible from the following trails: western terminus of Wildhorse trail (#315), northern terminus of Threepoint Mountain trail (#320), western extension to Upper Threepoint Creek trail (#286), northern terminus of Sheep trail at two places (#276), the western terminus of Little Elbow trail (#322), Piper Creek (#318), the eastern terminus of Elbow Lake trail (#110, vol. 1).

The basis is an old road that follows the Elbow River from its confluence with the Little Elbow to Elbow Lake where route #110 takes over for the last stretch to Highway 40. Here and there the route is complicated by horse trail variations but not to worry, both trails are well marked with signposts and red markers. Though it sounds like a boring old plod up a valley, it's not. The scenery is spectacular as you pass through layers of front ranges to the foot of the Great Divide. There are loops to be made and off-trail explorations up side valleys and mountains to keep you happy for years.

Just about all of it is popular with mountain bikers, particularly the section between the recreation area and Little Elbow trail which is part of the celebrated Elbow Loop. For side trips like Mt. Cornwall and Banded Peak I recommend taking a bike.

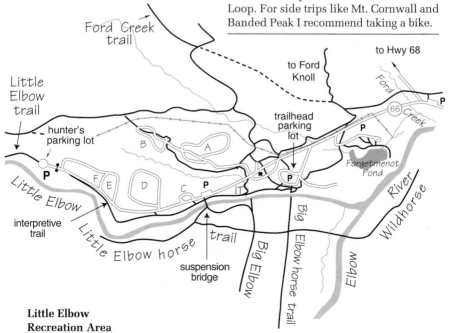

Little Elbow
Recreation Area

The first section of trail just south of Cornwall Creek, looking towards the outliers of Banded Peak. You can see why I advocate biking the hiking trail!

Little Elbow Recreation Area to Big Elbow campground

Distance 8.3 km
Height gain 158 m
High point 1753 m
Maps 82 J/15 Bragg Creek,
82 J/10 Mount Rae

Also accessible from the northern terminus of Threepoint Mountain trail (#320) and the extension of Upper Threepoint Creek (#286).

Mostly, the hiking and horse trails take different routes. Depending on objective I like to bike the old road designated for hikers and hike the horse trail. Your choice.

Cross the suspension bridge over the Little Elbow. The trail winds downhill to the old road and bends right. Shortly you come to a four-way intersection with Little Elbow horse trail (right) and Wildhorse (left).

The road

Go straight. A long uphill past the sign "Are you prepared for your trip?" leads into an undulating traverse below a forested hill, this section ending when the road curves left and drops slightly to cross stony South Glasgow Creek. Ahead is a long straight flat, a tough carpet of Dryas, Creeping juniper and Kinnikinnick where you can spot mountain bikers approaching from far away. At GR522150 a few metres of trail cuts left (red marker) to join the horse trail at a signpost. This is the turnoff for Threepoint Mountain trail.

Detour to Wildhorse Viewpoint
Distance 350 m return, height gain 45 m. The perfect half-day objective. At GR515262 just north of South Glasgow Creek from the west side of the road, a trail climbs a steep grassy ridge. The flat top is a perfect vantage point looking up valley to Threepoint Mountain and the mountains about Cougar Creek.

Continue in a straight line to the crumbling bank of the Elbow River which is intent on taking out the road. Here the road curves to the right and climbs over a low forested ridge into another straight. Cross "Cornwall Creek" amid the cobbles. Shortly the road bends right (keep right), then doubles back left. This left-hand bend is the departure place for "Cornwall Creek waterfall" and "Cornwall Creek" valley.

Another straight leads to a second reclaimed section of road alongside the Elbow River, here rushing noisily past on a pebble bed below the peculiar shape of Threepoint Mountain. Climb over an alluvial fan into a straight in the trees. At GR512210 a side trail to left leads to Big Elbow backcountry campground.

Horse trail

Turn left on Wildhorse. At the following crossroads turn right onto Big Elbow horse trail, a soft dirt trail through pine forest where I've had good luck in finding Morels. Approaching the Elbow River, the trail climbs over a hill you can miss out by sneaking along the bottom. Back in forest, cross a creek (log downstream) and enter the Dryas flat. Beyond the next creek crossing which is South Glasgow Creek (cairns both sides), the trail runs within sight of the road to a signposted T-junction with the connecting trail. Go straight to a signposted junction with Threepoint Mountain trail which heads left toward the river.

Keep right. In another kilometre join the road on the riverbank at GR524242 for a few metres of rock bashing, then turn off left. After a while the trail descends to the flats. Cross "Cornwall Creek", then an older version of the road as you head back to the road at GR513221 for another longer stretch alongside the rushing Elbow.

At the equestrian sign, turn left across a spring channel onto the older road which curves around to Big Elbow backcountry campground. En route at GR513215 the unofficial route to Upper Threepoint Creek (#286) crosses the river. (You can spot the cutline on the opposite bank.)

DETOUR "Cornwall Creek waterfall"
Distance 1 km with creek crossings. Head up the left bank on Dryas flat. Before the start of black shale banks cross to the right bank and pass small drops and pools leading up to a 30 m-high fall shooting over a cliff.

OPTION "Cornwall Creek" valley
Straight off cross the creek on a trail that follows the rapidly rising right bank to a high point above a prominent white shale slope. Head downhill toward the creek above the fall and edge along the bank top to flats with a tremendous view of twin look-alikes Banded Peak and Outlaw. The upper forks are where the real meadows are. I don't advocate scrambling to the Cornwall/Outlaw col from this direction; we were continually pushing back handholds while dodging rocks showering down from above. Nasty!

Big Elbow campground to Little Elbow trail

Distance 11 km
Height gain 350 m
High point 2015 m
Map 82 J/10 Mount Rae

Accessible from the extension to Upper Threepoint Creek (#286), from Sheep trail pack trail finish (#276) and from the west terminus of Little Elbow trail (#322).

A more strenuous leg that leaves the flats and climbs through the narrows into the upper valley. Here and there the horse trail deviates from the hiker's road, not always offering the better option.

Not far from the campground, the road climbs over an alluvial fan with an expansive view of braided river channels backdropped by the entrance to Cougar Creek.

Top: "Cornwall Creek waterfall".
Bottom: Look-alikes Banded Peak and Outlaw from "Cornwall Creek" valley flats.

Back down in forest you round the bend to an entirely different scenario. The mountains on either side are pressing in, and the river is scooting by in great rapids out of a canyon requiring the road to take desperate measures. Actually, the road *splits* at the bridge where hikers/bikers and horses go their separate ways. Both routes are equally hilly, the horse trail requires a river crossing, the hiker's road does not. So faced with a not so tricky decision, follow the road across the bridge and up a hill to about 80 vertical m above the river (views of Mt. Rae, the horse trail and a waterfall), then wind down the other side into the valley above the canyon. A straight leads to bridge No. 2 which is located 1 km west of where it's marked on K Country's map, at GR490183.

Horse trail The first attempt road stays on the northwest bank. A steep start settles into a gradual climb above canyon walls to a high point where the road moves away from the river, gradually descending through dense old spruce forest. A steep drop returns you to the valley bottom. Despite what is shown on the latest edition of the topo map, the reasonable road ends at GR498185. You can imagine the road builders scratching their heads in perplexity. They had it cross the Elbow but so badly is it washed out by high water it barely exists, especially where it joins the hiker's road at GR496184. Here, a side creek pouring out of a culvert has done a thorough demolition job.

Can you get along the bank to bridge No. 2 without crossing the river? Only if you have to.

After crossing the mouth of a cul de sac valley (view of Banded Peak) a stiff climb leads into the roller coaster section. At bend GR477179, preceding the plunge to Outlaw Creek, a cairn on the left side indicates the normal route to Banded Peak.

Climb equally steeply out of the side valley. A little farther on, where the road heads into the river (a section previously shared with the riverbed), a bypass trail is available. This section is merely undulat-ing, a bench at a high point offering a view of Cougar Mountain. On downhills keep right twice as per the signposts. At the second sign the road arises from the river at a camping spot used in 1983 by Boy Scouts at the World Jamboree. There's a lull in the hills to the side creek crossing at GR455163.

Climbing begins again with a vengeance. At the right-angled bend atop the first hill turn left onto a narrow trail that traverses a beautiful grassy bench. The narrows is behind you, perhaps submerged in the deep shade of late afternoon and not too far ahead are the meadows of the upper valley, still in sunshine. It was here we once met a very worried mountain biker who'd got past the "Are you prepared?" sign, asking if the campground was close at hand, meaning Mount Romulus. From what we gathered, his wife had gone off up Little Elbow to the campground with the map and the food and he'd gone up Big Elbow with no map and the tent. We hadn't the heart to tell him there were worse hills ahead.

Rejoin the road which has come in from the right (the horse trail goes left and is described two paragraphs on) and follow it up a long, steep hill, at the top turning sharp left into an even worse set of the roller coasters. These end at the junction with Little Elbow trail (right) which is the better road and one we used to drive. Turn right for Tombstone Pass, Tombstone Lakes and Mount Romulus backcountry campground.

Keep straight for Tombstone backcountry campground which is located on the left side of the road just after you cross the creek from Tombstone Lakes.

Horse trail alternative to Tombstone backcountry campground At the junction keep left on the trail that approaches Tombstone backcountry campground from below. While avoiding the drudgery of unnecessary hills you get to ford the Elbow River twice. Between the two fords the pack trail to the Sheep River (#276) takes off up the left bank of a side creek issuing jointly from Lake Rae and north Sheep Lake.

Little Elbow trail to Elbow Lake

Distance 5 km
Height gain 122 m
High point 2088 m
Maps 82 J/10 Mount Rae,
82 J/11 Kananaskis Lakes

Accessible from the western terminus of Little Elbow (#322), northern terminus of Sheep trail (#276), Piper Creek (#318) and the eastern terminus of Elbow Lake (#110, vol.1).

You'll love this section's meadows and views as you pass between the Opal and Misty ranges on Desolation Flat.

Keep straight, following the road past the turnoff to Tombstone backcountry campground on the left. Cross the Elbow River by bridge. A left-hand bend precedes the junction with Sheep trail (#276) where you turn right onto a much rougher road.

The upper valley is side to side meadow scoured by west winds where trees huddle behind rocks and in sheltered hollows. It's called Desolation Flat from a trip George Edworthy took in 1919 with Dan Webster. Ten years later George and his wife explored the river and to their delight found two waterfalls they named Desolation Falls. In 1986 they were officially renamed Edworthy Falls and like the Edworthys you're going to have to do some searching around to find them.

Gradually you leave Tombstone Mountain behind, pass the mouth of Piper Creek, then draw level with Elpoca Mountain, while to the left your constant companion is the complex mass of Mt. Rae whose diminutive north glacier—the true source of the Elbow River— catches your eye as it shines in the morning sun. As you draw near to Elbow Lake the denuding effect of the wind lessens and the spruce start to take over. A signpost marks the Peter Lougheed Provincial Park boundary near the northeast end of the lake. Here join #110.

Heading east through the open draw.

Elbow-Sheep cutoff

If you're travelling to/from Elbow Lake and the Sheep River, or are hoping to make Lake Rae in one day from Highway 40, there's an unofficial shortcut you should know about.

This narrow trail, used by equestrians, leaves Big Elbow trail downstream of Piper Creek valley at GR420147. Turn east, keep right and climb to a gap between Mt. Rae and a low grassy hill on the left. In an open draw on the other side the trail splits temporarily.

Sheep trail Keep left. The trail crosses meadow past some strange contraption—rain gauge?—to Sheep trail, joined at GR432148.

Cross-country route to Lake Rae Go right at the split, then turn right on a trail starting you up a broad low-angle ridge. Now read #276 (this route works better in reverse direction).

#317. Desolation Flat between Sheep trail junction and Elbow Lake. Elpoca Mountain in the background.

#318. The beautiful valley of Piper Creek from the pass. To the right is Elpoca Moutain, through the gap Mt. Rae and the Rae Glacier.

318 PIPER CREEK — maps 17, 16 (Vol. 1) & 12

Day hike, backpack
Unofficial trail & route, creek crossings
Distance 4 km from Big Elbow trail
Height gain 564 m to pass
High point 2576 m at pass
Maps 82 J/10 Mount Rae,
82 J/11 Kananaskis Lakes

Access: Via Big Elbow trail (#317).

The valley between Elpoca and Tombstone would win hands down a beauty pageant for eastern slope valleys, short length alpine category. For years it was called Elpoca Creek until that name was officially bestowed to another valley on the west side of Elpoca Mountain. In the second edition I named it "Piper" after Norma Piper Pocaterra, George's wife, in her own right an opera singer of international status and well-known singing teacher in Calgary. The name got shot down at the provincial level, but I'm happy to say has been resubmitted by Norma's pianist Dale Jackson with the whole weight of the Kiwanis Music Festival committee behind him (there is, in fact, a scholarship in her and Georgio's name awarded at the festival). This time it will likely become official.

It is said that George called the valley after his wife so that from his mountain top he could look down on his beloved Norma for all eternity.

The trail rises out of obscurity (willow brush). From Big Elbow trail it is clearly seen traversing grassy hillside below the south ridge of Tombstone Mountain south at GR413147, right at the join of two topo maps. So this is where you should aim for. Crossing intervening meadows is not quite as straightforward as it looks. Both the Elbow River and Piper Creek must be crossed.

The trail gains height slowly up the northeast bank of the creek. In mid valley the creek, previously meshed in willow brush, breaks free and falls in cataracts between the icy north face of Elpoca and the

sunbaked slabs of Tombstone Mountain which are arranged in tiers like standing gravestones. Pockets of flower meadows increase until at treeline you're wading through great avenues of fleabanes, trying not to lose trail that leads you out of the trees into the turf of the upper valley before petering out. This is the home of the Alpines, where rivulets interlace across the surface of the grass, sometimes sinking into trenches a metre deep and a few centimetres wide. The main fork, tumbling and leaping over rock steps, issues from a tarn tucked under the highest summit of Tombstone. Across the valley, hidden in a fold of moraine, lies another tarn. Fed by a perpetual snowbank, it lies deep in the shadow of Mt. Schlee, named after Gerry Schlee, a well-known climber who forfeited his own life trying to save two canoeists caught in the Bow River weir in Calgary.

GOING FARTHER
The pass 2576 m
Height gain 137 m. At the valley head to the right of Cats Ears are two passes separated by a ruddy-coloured hump. A white boulder as big as a two-storied house marks the start of a sheep trail heading up easy scree to the lower right-hand pass at GR392175 (cairn). From this high vantage point there is a glorious view back down the valley to Mt. Rae. The view north into the west fork of the Little Elbow is obscured by cliffs and vertiginous scree slopes; only the bright meadows of Paradise Pass can be seen in the distance.

Experienced scree bashers and route-finders can connect up with route #323. On sheep trail descend diagonally left....

319 BANDED PEAK normal route — maps 13 &12

Long day, backpack
Unofficial trails, route & scramble
Distance 5 km from #317
Height gain 1014 m from #317
High point 2934 m
Map 82 J/10 Mount Rae

A useful view of Banded Peak taken from the head of the between ridge. Arrows indicate the good trail to Outlaw/Banded col.

Access: Via Big Elbow trail (#317) at GR477179.

This shapely mountain, mistakenly called "Bandit" by climbers some 25 years ago (hence the name "Outlaw"), is from this direction a simple scree ascent sans band. Getting there requires sure-footedness on steep scree and an eagle eye to search out sketchy trails. By biking up Big Elbow trail it can be done in one exhausting day (37 km return, 1416 m height gain).

To Outlaw/Banded col Don't follow the stream up Outlaw Creek; there are steps. Start at the cairn and head up the hillside on faint trail. Hit a good game trail and turn left downhill. Shortly turn right uphill on a sketchier trail which makes a rising traverse along the east slope of the valley above steepening, deepening scree slopes, the trail adequate until the final skimpy traverse to a grassy bench above the forks. Descend easily to the forks.

Disappointingly, the forested ridge between the forks is miserable (deadfall and small crags), and I advise rock-hopping up the right fork into scraps of meadow and trees beyond the cliff on the left. Either climb onto the by now grassy ridge or continue up the valley, *trending left* away from the main creek. Either way, pick up a useful trail that sweeps left to right across the valley head into the main creek (gained *above* slabby steps), then continues after a break up the grey scree wall to Outlaw/Banded col.

To the summit Follow a sinuous draw to your right. Orange shale steepens to tippy dark grey rubble up which wind strands of "trails" more easily seen on the descent. Strenuous effort ends at the summit cairn (canister) where you can finally relax and enjoy the view shown on the title page.

OPTION
Outlaw 2970 m
A tougher option from the col. Whereas scramblers follow the east ridge and scramble through the rock band, walkers should aim farther to the left where the rock band disintegrates, and grovel up 341 vertical m of south face rubble, a torture when the temperature's hitting 30 and the water bottle's empty. (I have a theory you'd have a better time of it by heading to the col at GR448201, then walking up the southwest ridge.

320 THREEPOINT MOUNTAIN TRAIL — maps 13

Long day hike, backpack
Official trail, signposts, red markers &
cairns, river & creek crossings
Distance 10.5 km
Height gain N-S 467 m
Height loss N-S 162 m
High point 2338 m
Maps 82 J/15 Bragg Creek,
82 J/10 Mount Rae

Below: Entering the meadows of upper Threepoint Creek. Pointy Threepoint Mountain in the background.

North access: Via Big Elbow trail (#317). From the first section horse trail.
South access: Junction of Gorge Creek (#283) and Volcano Creek (#284).
Also accessible via Upper Threepoint Creek (#286).

This scenic trail is an important link between the trails of the Elbow and the Sheep. Crossing the Elbow River is tricky early in the season.

NORTH TO SOUTH
In 100 m wade the Elbow River and to the right of a side creek climb a forested ridge, near the top crossing to the west flank for a lovely stretch on meadows (cairns, survey marker)—perfect vantage points for the mountains to the west. Back in forest, cross the side creek and climb over the watershed. On the downswing the trail follows a grassy draw into the heathy basin of upper Threepoint Creek where it wends left to the unsigned junction with Upper Threepoint Creek trail. Turn right on exploration road and cross Threepoint Creek.

The southern half of the trail undulates through a mosaic of meadow and forest below the dramatic east face of Threepoint Mountain. Straight off keep left where the exploration road resumes its westward direction. Cross a south fork of Threepoint Creek and slip over the height of land into Rock Creek. Cross and climb over another watershed into the headwaters of Volcano Creek. On the north bank is the three-way junction with Gorge Creek trail (straight) and Volcano Creek trail (left).

321 MOUNT CORNWALL, normal route — maps 13 & 12

Long day, backpack
Unofficial trails, route & scramble
Distance 9 km from #317,
12 km from trailhead
Height gain 1338 m from #317,
1399 m from trailhead
High point 2978 m
Maps 82 J/15 Bragg Creek,
82 J/10 Mount Rae,

Mt. Cornwall and snow patch
from the easy slope leading to
Glasgow/Cornwall col.

Access: Via Big Elbow trail (#317). Leave the road before South Glasgow Creek at GR515262.

Mt. Cornwall is the least shapely of the foursome Glasgow, Cornwall, Outlaw and Banded Peak. Glasgow's pyramid, for instance, is instantly recognizable in the engraving of the four peaks by Edward Whymper—Matterhorn conqueror—in the Marquis of Lorne's book *Canadian Pictures Drawn with Pen and Pencil* published in 1885 (contents page).

Cornwall has *other* attributes. Its gloriously long summit ridge of brilliant orange shales is lined both sides with stupendous cliffs of palest grey. And it's famous for its snow patch that lies just below the summit and is visible from Calgary. Rarely missing, it actually disappeared during the hot summer of 1994, but two days of rain (snow at higher altitudes) and it was back by some quirk of topography.

The walker's normal route up South Glasgow Creek follows the first ascent route, a solo ski ascent by Arnold

Choquette in May 1949! It is both easy and safe, with no steep slopes, no scrambling and no exposure to make you feel wobbly. There are even intermittent trails. To climb Cornwall in one day is a dawn to dusk affair despite the help of a bike on Big Elbow trail. If you can work out the logistics, consider doing a traverse to Talus Lake trail (#326) and returning via the Little Elbow, or carrying on over Outlaw and Banded Peak back to Big Elbow trail.

To Glasgow/Cornwall col via South Glasgow Creek Shortcut through trees to South Glasgow Creek. Called Dry Creek in the old days, it is hellishly long and stony, but luckily trails can be followed on pieces of Dryas flat, first on the right side, later on the left some way after the creek bends to the southwest.

Before you reach the foot of the mountains, at about GR503251 on the left side of a tree island, a trail climbs the left bank and faint in places, rounds the next bend above a mini-canyon. If you miss the start climb to the trail before the valley pinches in. This trail is very clear where it crosses to the north bank above the canyon drop-off and starts climbing to get above the V of the upcoming gorge. After the initial climb the trail splinters into several confusing forest trails. Keep left—the angle is always gentle—and likely you'll emerge above the gorge (a savage scene made more dramatic the first time we were there by lightning flashes and cataclysmic thunderclaps), and then, by following a trail along the gorge top you'll be able to figure out where to descend to the creekbed above drop-off No. 2. Or perhaps you'll have found a nice little trail that delivers you to the bank top higher up the valley.

Pick your way up the stony creekbed, accompanied on the left by a long line of cliffs. Eons later, a dramatic narrowing between unstable scree slopes precedes the slabby waterfall at GR467231 (last water). On grass climb above the slab into the grassy upper valley.

Looking along the summit ridge. The route onto the ridge comes up the left-hand slope.

Straightway climb the hillside to the right, above the vegetation veering left up nearly 400 vertical m of comfortably-inclined orange slates to the Glasgow/Cornwall col, an Alpine poppy place. Possibly you'll meet a lone scrambler equipped with two Leki Sport hiking poles doing the Glasgow to Banded traverse.

To the summit From the col Glasgow's south ridge certainly looks a tough proposition for a walker, so head off in the opposite direction along a very broad gently-rising slope. At the steepening in the orange zone a trail of footprints leads to Cornwall's skyline ridge. Turn left and with mounting excitement walk a beautiful scree ridge poised between the snow patch and slopes plummeting to Talus Creek to the summit. The cairn is presently dismantled to foil the flying ants, perhaps.

If you haven't yet been to Talus Lake, this is a fabulous place from which to view not one but two turquoise jewels. The two huge snow peaks in a line with the lakes are Mt. King George and Queen Mary of the Royal Group.

322 LITTLE ELBOW TRAIL — maps 13 & 12

Day hikes, backpack
Official trail with signposts & red
markers, creek crossings
Total distance 21 km

Highway access: Elbow Falls Trail (Hwy. 66) at Little Elbow Recreation Area. Due to a design fault, the parking situation for this trail is aggravating. You'd like to start from the hunter's trailhead, a gated parking lot at the end of the campground loop roads. More often than not, though, you end up in the main trailhead parking lot and have to hike another 1.2 uphill km beyond the campground check-in to reach the trailhead. Dropping off people and packs depends on who's manning the campground check-in. Occasionally you get a real grump (though since privatization the check-in person is more sympathetic to the hiker's plight). Driving slowly through, waving as you go in the hope the check-in person will assume you're returning to a campsite after a hard day's picnicking, results in the ranger chasing after you to give you a ticking off. All this applies to you and me, excepting government researchers and organizations who get a key to the hunter's parking lot. After the Labour Day weekend the gate is unlocked for hunters. See sketchmap on page 255. NOTE: This section of Hwy. 66 is closed between December 1st and May 15th.
Also accessible from the North Fork of the Little Elbow (#325), the West Fork of the Little Elbow (#323) and Big Elbow trail (#317).

The route follows a fire road up the Little Elbow River and its south fork, crossing Tombstone Pass to Big Elbow trail in the Elbow River valley. Serious walkers will look on it as a useful access trail, the jumping-off point to far greater hikes into the alpine. Probably over half the users are mountain bikers cruisin' the celebrated Elbow Loop. Apart from bikes, watch for rangers on quads checking on Tombstone Lakes for illegal campers.

Little Elbow Recreation Area to the Forks

Distance 11 km
Height gain 189 m
High point 1807 m
Map 82 J/15 Bragg Creek

Accessible from North Fork of the Little Elbow (#325) and West Fork of the Little Elbow (#323).

Mount Romulus backcountry campground is located at the forks. The fire road to this point is busy, easy, undulating and rather boring despite the fine scenery. While two sections of horse trail provide softer walking for the feet, river crossings are a deterrent. The horse trail start to the first crossing makes a very pleasant after dinner stroll for campers.

The forks at Talus Creek culvert.
In the background is Mt. Remus.

Horse trail start Via Big Elbow trail (#317). Officially, at the four-way junction with Wildhorse turn right and meander back to the bank top above the Elbow River. Unofficially, at a quarter the distance, turn right after crossing the suspension bridge and follow a trail to the same place.

The trail descends to open flats, a lovely stretch near the river leading to the river crossing at GR492281. The trail joins the fire road a half kilometre farther west.

Hikers start See sketchmap on page 255.

To the hunter's parking lot 1.2 km. From the trailhead parking lot follow the interpretive trail alongside the Little Elbow River. Past the suspension bridge the trail climbs to the campground access road, joining it at F Loop. Turn left. Where F Loop curves right, keep left through a gate and descend to the hunter's parking lot.

From the hunter's parking lot The fire road is mostly flat and sandy with a few downhills which are disconcerting when you're supposed to be going up! On your right, Nihahi Ridge trail turns off at 1.8 km, and at km 2.2 a horse trail comes in from the equestrian campground. Below Nihahi Ridge, the **horse trail start** joins in from across the Little Elbow River.

It's here where the road goes between, which is not, I hasten to add, Pern nonspace, but between meaning *between ridges* into the inner fastness of the Front Range. The gentle grassy slopes of Powderface and Forgetmenot are replaced by a more dramatic scenario of limestone mountains with cliffs. In 3.5 km Nihahi Creek trail turns right just a few metres before Nihahi Creek crossing. Around the next bend is the blue bridge over the Little Elbow—a beautiful spot for a break.

Between the bridge and the forks you can expect flat straights alternating with steeper, longer hills in both directions. I believe the worst is the one up from the bridge. After the following downhill the horse trail turns off to the right.

Accompanying you on the left is a long line of cliffs, those of Mt. Glasgow merging

with the even greater ones of Mt. Cornwall to form an *almost* impenetrable barrier; a stony creekbed at GR443271 is Kane's route up Glasgow. Across the river are a couple of fabulous mountains, Mts. Remus and Romulus, the latter a square black monster topped by the thin line of a cornice that can be seen from Calgary.

After crossing a second stony creekbed the road climbs steadily to the turnoff for Mount Romulus backcountry campground on the right. This access road circles back to the fire road at Talus Creek culvert crossing, the jumping off point for Talus Lake.

Horse trail finish Expect four crossings of the Elbow River. Enough said!

To Big Elbow trail via Tombstone Lakes

Distance 10 km
Height gain 472 m
Height loss 289 m
High point 2271 m at pass
Maps 82 J/15 Bragg Creek, 82 J/10 Mount Rae

Accessible from North Fork of the Little Elbow (#325), West Fork of the Little Elbow (#323) and Big Elbow trail (#317).

The Tombstone Pass section. The highlight is undoubtedly Tombstone Lakes, a favourite weekend objective from Highway 40. Since the second edition camping is not allowed anywhere at the lakes. Use Tombstone on Big Elbow trail.

After the initial pull up the ridge between Talus Creek and the south fork, the road settles into a gentle ascent along the east bank of the south fork, crossing a succession of stony creekbeds channelling from the scree ridge above. At 7 km in an area of willowy meadow you cross the south fork twice and come to a signposted junction offering a choice of route.

The larch forest below Tombstone Mountain.

1. Fire road Continue as before, gradually climbing through a bit of a draw (Mt. Rae poking up ahead) into the longitudinal meadow at Tombstone Pass with an uninterrupted view of Tombstone Mountain.

The initial drop into the Elbow River valley is steep. The surprise here is the thrilling view of Mt. Rae and the Sheep/Elbow watershed which stays with you on the runout to the left-hand bend where route No. 2 comes in from the right. In 100 m reach the junction with Big Elbow trail.

2. Trail The trade-off for all those kilometres of road bashing. Leave the fire road to the bikers and turn right on a dirt track leading to a meteorological station site. Now every step is a joy as you follow a narrow trail that mounts steadily through meadows alongside the bubbly stream toward the watershed. One or two larches multiply into a dazzling forest by the time you reach Tombstone Pass west, one of the premier larch locations in K Country. Above their feathery fronds tower the great cliffs of Tombstone Mountain.

With regret at leaving such a heavenly place you plunge downhill into the spruce forest of Tombstone Creek. Low down in a glade is an unmarked junction with a trail at 2 o-clock heading for upper Tombstone Lake. Here, the official trail turns sharp left and reaches a T-junction with horse rail.

Detour to Tombstone Lakes
Turn right and descend to lower lake, reached at the place shown on page 15. The scene is staggeringly beautiful: silky, dark green water backdropped by the amazing cliffs of Tombstone Mountain. The trail rounds the outlet and continues along the west shore to the upper lake which is distinguished by a rocky islet and a varying water level.

Return to the T-junction. Keep right and descend the east bank of Tombstone Creek to the fire road, gained at the bend GR433159. Finish on road to the junction with Big Elbow trail.

323 WEST FORK OF THE LITTLE ELBOW — map 12

Backpack, day hike from campground
Unofficial trail, route & scramble, creek
crossings
Distance 10 km to tarn
Height gain 655 m to tarn,
823 m to pass
High point at tarn 2393 m, pass 2576 m
Maps 82 J/15 Bragg Creek,
82 J/14 Spray Lakes Reservoir,
82 J/11 Kananaskis Lakes

Access: Via Little Elbow trail (#322) at Mount Romulus backcountry campground.
Also accessible from North Fork of the Little Elbow (#325), Paradise Pass (#324) and Piper Creek at the pass (#318).

The valley at the back of the Opals is a magical place, reserved for people who can hack six major river crossings (five of which can be bypassed at a pinch). Novices should end the trip in mid valley meadows. Getting to the pass is for scrambler/hiker hybrids used to steep scree and uncertain trails. In fact, going over the pass to Piper Creek from this direction is a hell of a drag for anyone: If backpacking, I recommend doing the trip in reverse direction.

To Paradise Pass turnoff The west fork exploration road leaves the campground loop road at the right-angle bend where it returns to Little Elbow trail. Straight off you wade Little Elbow's south fork and are into a kilometre-long undulating straight leading to a viewpoint for peaks GR397225 and 374251 "The Ripsaw". Wind downhill. Just beyond the left-hand bend a narrow trail that is the North Fork of the Little Elbow river route (#325) turns off to the right.

Arrive at the Little Elbow River, here called the west fork. Creek crossings No. 2 and 3 occur in short succession and are a rolled-up pants job. I use the bypass trail on the left bank. Up next is the straight which traverses avalanche slopes below the cliffs of GR397225. After the first side creek crossing a horse trail heads right into valley bottom meadows. The second side creek "the mossy" features a considerable waterfall tucked high up under the cliff. At the end of the straight, the road rises to a bend where both road and river turn southwest, allowing a thrilling view of the Opals, principally of Brock, Blane and The Blade. From both sides of the bend two more horse trails head off to a horse camp on the west bank of the west fork.

Back alongside the river, the road crosses it twice through a bend; use the bypass trail on the left. A short distance along is river crossing No. 6 with horse camps on either side. Luckily, there's always a log available downstream. The road ends not too much farther on at the point where Paradise Pass trail turns off to the right.

To the meadows On a narrower trail you cross Paradise Pass creek, keep left and descend to cross the creek issuing from the cirque between Brock and Blane. For the next 2 km the trail undulates through fairly open forest. It was somewhere along this stretch we shared a drink with some hunters at their camp. They were my kind of hunters. Been coming here for donkey's years and had never shot at anything, being content to scour the hillsides through binoculars. "Did you know you'd just walked right by a sow and two cubs?"

The topo map is remiss in not showing meadows starting at GR378207. Here you jump two side creeks and renew acquaintance with the west fork where it makes a great loop westward, aligning itself up for

The scree slope between the canyon (seen below) and the meadows about the tarn. This photo shows a mere smidgen of the spectacular rock scenery at the back of the Opals.

the canyon ahead. All around is flat meadow carpeted with dwarf willow. What a place to view the back of the Opals! Rock of palest grey goes winging up in great buttresses and airy pinnacles to the highest peaks of the range and in between waterfalls thunder down short steep valleys.

To Tarn not-marked-on-the-topo-map
Wade the west fork. The trail continues through a spruce copse into more meadow and ultimately into trees. You cross a side creek, wind up a draw, then turn sharp right and climb to a ridge top and a junction identified by a mud patch that should be fixed in the mind for the return. Turn left. A little way along it comes as a delicious shock to find yourself overlooking a canyon, the creek below firmly hemmed in by cliffs. Opposite, a waterfall streams down the cliff, and up left are glimpses of ridges impossibly high up, one a dead ringer for the Peuterey Ridge above Chamonix.

Several strands of trail follow the edge of the canyon through alternating tree ribbons and grassy avalanche slopes where Bighorns wander off for a nibble. One last tree ribbon and you emerge on huge scree slopes sweeping down from the left. On our first trip we made the mistake of following ungulates into a scary series of traverses above intermittent canyon walls. So at the last grassy avalanche slope (or at the edge of the scree) I recommend angling uphill to a higher game trail, positively identified on the scree slope by a small crag it passes under. Now you're set. This good trail crosses more moderately-inclined scree to grassy slopes beyond, aiming for a peculiar mud hole where you descend the right bank of its trench to the west fork just above the canyon drop-off—another feature to remember for the return. All that remains is a simple walk up grass to a crescent-shaped tarn tucked under the pass below the spectacular rock scenery of Cats Ears.

To pass GR392175
Above the tarn are two low points in the ridge separated by a reddish-brown hump. The pass is the left-hand gap—worse luck. Clearly a direct approach is impossible, so climb the tongue of brown rubble to the right of the rock band. Some distance above the band choose from numerous sheep trails heading diagonally left toward the gap. You'll be grovelling for about 100 vertical m.

Warning to anyone coming the other way
You've descended safely to the tarn and reached the canyon drop-off. Now is the place to go wrong. A really good sheep trail lures you along the left (west) bank, crossing scree to a bench. Like my friends, you could be on the bench a long, long time trying to figure a way off. So go right and find that mud hole. OK?

The crescent-shaped tarn below the pass which is the left-hand gap. The route follows the tongue of darker-coloured rubble to the right of the rock band, then cuts back left.

The lower meadows. In the background are Mts. Hood and Packenham.

324 PARADISE PASS — map 12

Backpack
Unofficial trail & route, creek crossing
Distance 7.5 km
Height gain S-N 671 m
Height loss S-N 439 m
High point 2576 m
Map 82 J/11 Kananaskis Lakes,
82 J/14 Spray Lakes Reservoir

South access: Via West Fork of the Little Elbow (#323).
North access: Via North Fork of the Little Elbow (#325) just west of the horse camp.

Unlike the pass at the head of the west fork, this is an easy passage between the west and north forks of the Little Elbow River. Who cares if the name "Paradise" is an overused descriptive name. Here, there are fantastic meadows and mountains to drool over, and the chance of spotting large herds of elk and Bighorns. Don't get cross if you're overtaken by a party on horseback. The pass was named and the trail made by the Guinn family who run trips to the Little Elbow from Boundary Ranch.

SOUTH TO NORTH
A narrow trail leaves the west side of West Fork trail just north of the Paradise Pass creek crossing. A short stretch alongside the creek and an equally short climb in forest gains you the meadows. Long grasses and flowers brush against your bare legs (the trail is very narrow) while you lap up a vista of Opal peaks soaring into the sky. Cross two side creeks. A deeper dip than usual into trees marks a third crossing—a sure source of water.

After this the trail zigs right and up, gradually fading as it follows the bank top of the third side creek, initially incised in a mini-canyon, to a huge area of flat meadow. A trail isn't needed. Not too far ahead the pass is obvious, the lowest dip in the long ridge between Mt. Evan-Thomas and "The Ripsaw". Cross the mouth of "Ripsaw's" west cirque and climb an easy slope dotted with krummholz. On the final pull to the pass the trail reappears, climbing up the left side of a shallow, shaley gully. When you top out you never know who or what is coming up the other side. A grizzly? Rick Guinn and his clients? What you don't expect is a near miss with a heli-sightseeing helicopter. I remember windows full of wide-eyed Japanese tourists, their mouths starting to gape as the pilot was forced to take evasive action. This kind of thing certainly ruins your lunch.

From this lofty viewpoint all of the Opal Range is exposed, Blane seen as being the dominant peak. It's satisfying to look all the way up the west fork and catch a glimpse of Mt. Rae and the Rae Glacier rising above the pass. To the north is a new view of the

Coming up to Paradise Pass. In the background is Paradise Creek and farther away the west fork of the Little Elbow with Mt. Rae rising above the pass. The Opal Range is dominated by Mt. Blane.

northern nameless Opals, the tarn at the head of the north fork and the enticing grassy ridges above Camp Creek which make you yearn to carry on.

A clear trail descends the gentle north slope of scree and grass stretching out to a broad grassy ridge. At first trees the trail splits into variations which coalesce at the shallow side creek to your right at about GR357265 and as one trail makes the final drop into the valley of the Little Elbow's north fork. Arrive at a T-junction.

To Evan-Thomas Pass, Mount Romulus backcountry campground The valley floor is flat, wide and wet. Elephantheads and willows give you a clue. Rather than go charging across to the North Fork trail, turn right on the south side trail that crosses the north fork opposite one of Guinn's horse camps. Here, join route #325. For Evan-Thomas Creek turn left, for Mount Romulus backcountry campground and the little Elbow turn right.

325 NORTH FORK OF THE LITTLE ELBOW — map 12

Backpack
Unofficial trails, creek crossings
Distance 6.5 km to Evan-Thomas Pass
Height gain 411 m both routes
High point 2149 m
Maps 82 J/15 Bragg Creek,
82 J/14 Spray Lakes Reservoir

A useful view from the grassy fan at GR394263 showing the junction of the creek route and the high line which crosses the rocky slope on the left.

South access: .
1. Via West Fork of the Little Elbow trail (#323).
2. Via Little Elbow trail (#322) at Mount Romulus backcountry campground.
Also accessible from Evan-Thomas Creek (#55A, vol. 1) in two places, and from the northern terminus of Paradise Pass trail (#324).

This is the connector to Evan-Thomas Pass. There are two starts that join at the mid-point. Which one you use depends on where you're coming from and where you're going. For instance, if starting/ending at Mount Romulus backcountry campground use the high line. The easier valley route used by horse parties starts from the west fork trail and has value if you're approaching from/heading up the west fork of the Little Elbow. Because of an unavoidable river crossing, wait until summer before attempting either route.

SOUTH TO NORTH
1. Creek route (horse trail)
Don't ever ask someone on horseback "How many river crossings?" because the answer will be two and the reality 11 in this case, discounting the Little Elbow. So wear runners and have a good time paddling.

Leave the west fork trail as indicated and follow a rather indistinct trail heading east, then north past a set of rustic camp furniture to the west fork of the Little Elbow. Wade across. If you've failed to find the trail so far, look for it resuming on the north bank where it's much clearer.

You climb the steep bank, then gradually descend into the north fork valley, at this point a claustrophobic V-shape densely clothed in trees with protruding cliffs. Straight off you climb 60 vertical m to avoid a mini-canyon. Back at creek level you're faced with 11 creek crossings, all much the same. After crossing No. 7 the trail is recognizable as a cutline. After No. 9

you're on the right bank below a grassy fan (dry side valley) at GR394263 which is where the high line comes in.

2. The high line

The more strenuous route with views. The great advantage is that it is dry.

At the junction of the west fork trail and the campground access road, follow Little Elbow horse trail between campsites for a few metres, then turn left on another trail leading to the Little Elbow River. Wade. On the north bank the trail heads right to a small meadow, then turns back left.

Initially, the trail gains height gradually as it heads toward the north fork, crossing a meadow and a couple of dry creekbeds. Suddenly you're into a steep climb to gain the traverse line high above the north fork. Look back one last time at the forks and Mt. Cornwall before you slip into trees.

The traverse is rarely level. You cross three gullies, two slithery slopes and one stretch of terrace. After crossing the third gully, the one with water, the trail rises to the edge of a much steeper side slope than normal with slabs. Do NOT head uphill. A thin trail crosses the slope in a downward diagonal using ledges. The angle soon falls back and you pass through a belt of trees into a grassy gully (dry side creek) at a cairn. Walk easily down the fan to the river where you join the river route at GR394263. Turn right.

To Evan-Thomas Pass Upstream of the fan you cross the creek twice in quick succession (alternatively, tiptoe across a mossy curtain on the right bank), then start up the major climb of the day on cutline. Not too far along a rockslide has slid into the trees, resulting in bypass trails to right, then left. Turning northwest, the cutline rises steadily to a meadow below Mt. GR374251, the treat here being the exciting profile of the mountain's jagged northeast ridge. After some trees and a creek crossing enter a long willowy meadow.

Via the cutline Another uphill leads to the high point above Evan-Thomas Pass.

Via the gap At the beginning of the meadow turn left on a trail headed for the river via Guinn's horse camp (entered near the corral). From riverside meadows the entire upper valley is seen to be a wide, flat, soggy meadow extending almost to the foot of Mts. Potts and Evan-Thomas. A side trail crossing the north fork is Paradise Pass trail (#324). A little farther on is another junction with the trail to North Fork Tarn. For Evan-Thomas Creek keep straight and deke through a gap in the forested watershed at GR369283 which is Evan-Thomas Pass. (See #55A, Vol. 1 for ongoing directions.)

GOING FARTHER
North Fork Tarn

Distance 2.5 km, height gain 60 m. At the last mentioned junction turn left on a trail that leads directly to a tarn tucked under Mt. Potts. In greater detail: follow the edge of valley bottom meadow, cross gap No. 2 and climb over a treed hump back to the meadow. Jump the tarn creek a few metres downstream of the outlet and walk along the tarn's east shore to meadow at the south end which features a large rock for jumping off into the deep end. As mountain tarns go, the water is warm, say I, who managed to fall in headfirst while fooling about fully clothed. From the north shore you can discern route #324 crossing grassy slopes to Paradise Pass.

North fork tarn and Paradise Pass (left gap).

Talus Lake. View from the west shore of Mt. Cornwall. Who would guess there are such enormous cliffs below the summit ridge?

326 TALUS LAKE — map 12

Day hike from campground
Unofficial trail with cairns, blazes,
creek crossings
Distance from campground 5 km
Height gain 457 m from campground
High point 2222 m
Maps 82 J/15 Bragg Creek,
82 J/10 Mount Rae

Access: Via Little Elbow Trail (#322) at Mount Romulus backcountry campground (the forks).

Talus Lake is the best short day trip from the campground. With a bike you can reach it in a day from Little Elbow Recreation Area (allow $2^1/_2$ hours total biking time). Mostly, the trail is quite clear and well used with some scree at the end.

Start at Talus Creek culvert crossing at GR420248. On trail, walk up flats on the left (east) side of the creek, being alert for where the trail climbs the steep bank. At about 30 m up it settles into a traverse through lovely open pine forest, sometimes venturing onto the edge of steep banks. Rarely level, it features, in this direction, some mercifully short steep climbs where it dips to cross a succession of dry rocky side creeks. This

section ends in Talus Creek at sunbathing slabs sloping into two tubs, the higher one a shallow bath with built-in jacuzzi, the lower one built more in the Japanese style, for standing in up to the neck. On a hot day you may not get past this point.

The trail crosses above the baths for a short stint on the west bank. Recross after passing a large boulder. Shortly, the trail leaves the valley bottom and after gaining height on grass, loops in and out a shallow scree draw onto a grassy terrace overlooking the boulder-choked main fork. Traverse a shaley bank into a wet tributary which is crossed. Climb the bank and wander through pine forest thinning to a string of interconnected clearings below the huge cliffs of Mt. Cornwall from which scree comes sweeping down almost to your feet. When the clearings end, the trail heads

277

right to the bank top above the main fork. There are *two* parallel trails, both very steep, dropping to the creekbed at a cairn. Cross the creekbed and follow up the right bank to the forks.

Here, the trail veers right into the southwest fork which is just a dry ditch. Cross back and forth three times, then climb onto a bench with grass and boulders in the shadow of a big cliff. Follow the left bank trail to the lower lake where we once watched entranced as a moose came out of the trees and waded about in water the colour of peppermint popsicles.

To reach Talus Lake in the cirque above involves a steeper climb up moderately-angled scree. High up, go either way at a split; both trails join for final stretch alongside outlet pools with stranded water where you may find the odd trout flapping about in a hopeless attempt to get back into the lake. While I do trout rescue with poly

bags, my friends sunbathe on the meadow or visit the rocky north shore to search for Alpines. At midday, when surrounding ridges are in shadow, the rich aquamarine-coloured water is riffled by silver sparkles which join and dart toward you in a silver beam whenever the wind strengthens. Talus Lake is a gem!

SCRAMBLING OPTIONS
Cornwall/Outlaw col (GR450210)
Distance 2 km, height gain 672 m from the forks, high point 2752 m. A rugged route using remnant sheep trails. There are no technical difficulties, just one or two short stretches of arduous scree and a route-finding problem.

At the forks head up the main creekbed or its right bank where necessary. Before the canyon a game trail at GR436213 climbs the right bank where it's open and heads east at the top of grassy banks. At the bend in the canyon, steer south on meadows dug up by a grizzly, near meadow's end descending slightly to cross the creek at the obvious place between rifts.

View from the northwest ridge of Outlaw, looking beyond the Cornwall/Outlaw col to Mt. Cornwall. Farther right, the white summit rocks of Mt. Glasgow gleam in the evening sun.

Continue along the left bank. Where the valley veers left use the sheep trail that climbs above some slabs, or go the rubble route between the slabs and the creek. The going is then easy to where the valley makes another course correction to the left, steepening right across in a perplexing labyrinth of scree, slabs and crags. I'm not sure if a low route is available, but we toiled up dark grey scree as per sheep then headed back to the main creek, en route crossing a left fork below a waterfall leaping over a slanting cliff. Round the bottom of this cliff, then follow hoofprints up and left, passing above the cliff and below another one with yellow streaks. Just before converging on the left fork turn right and grovel up shifting scree to easy-angled ground above.

Head leftish toward the start of a shallow draw in the orange rock zone. Start up the draw, higher up transferring to the uncomplicated slope on the right that delivers you to the col. Flat and wide, it offers not one bit of shelter from the wind.

Why not bag a peak?

Right: the northwest ridge of Outlaw, showing the two steps.

Mt. Cornwall 2978 m

1.8 km from col, height gain 226 m. Cornwall is the easier option, a mere walk along the easy south ridge on deliciously crunchy orange slates. The whole route is displayed in the photo. You can see how it narrows, then steepens just below the summit. If doing the traverse see #321.

Outlaw 2970 m

700 m from col, height gain 218 m. Set off up the northwest ridge. Although scramblers will tackle the first step direct, walkers should follow the trail that traverses right below the crag, then doubles back left beyond the crag to regain the ridge. The second step can be avoided in a similar fashion, but is just as easily taken direct. Watch for one slightly exposed step at the top. Two thirds up, there's an easing before the final rubble slope leading to the summit.

In my opinion Outlaw is the best viewpoint of the foursome. Not only is there a clear view of the routes up Cornwall and Glasgow, but also of Banded Peak, from this direction looking remarkably like a volcano without its trademark band. You can, of course, spot Mt. Assiniboine in an eclectic view that includes Evan-Thomas Pass, Forgetmenot Ridge, Mist Mountain, the pointy Opals, Mt. Rae looking stunning, and the snow mantled peaks of Mt. Abruzzi, the Italian group and Mt. Joffre strung out along the western horizon.

327 NIHAHI CREEK — map 12

The right-hand (north) fork above the canyon is enclosed by the ridges of Nihahi and Compression.

Day hike, backpack
Official trail with red markers & cairns, then route
Distance 4.5 km to forks
Height gain 238 m to forks
High point 1914 m at forks
Map 82 J/15 Bragg Creek

Access: Via Little Elbow trail (#322) a few metres east of Nihahi Creek crossing.

Nihahi, meaning "rocky" in Stoney, is certainly an apt description of this dry, desolate valley reaching far back into the Fisher Range. A trail deposits you in a good position for further exploration. To leave more time for the good part I recommend biking to the start of the trail. Water is hard to find.

Official trail The first 2 km bypasses the canyon altogether. Five zigs up a forested slope brings you to a viewpoint on the brink, then carries on to the creek above the impasse. En route you skirt an impossibly narrow slit in the forest floor that I was incredulous to discover is Nihahi Creek itself. If you want some fun try working your way up the slit without skidding off polished walls into water-filled potholes. Getting in is no problem; getting out involves a tarzan-like manoeuvre up a well-placed tree trunk.

Enter the winding, waterless creekbed where the trail crosses back and forth, cutting off corners, eventually arriving at a red marker in the middle of the creekbed. A little farther on is the final cairn.

GOING FARTHER
The scene ahead is bleak. The valley floor, fully 200 m wide, is wall to wall stones enlivened by clumps of yellow Physaria. On both sides narrow belts of forest are topped off by the cliffs of Mt. Fuller on the left and Nihahi Ridge on the right. Travel is easy. As happens in most seemingly dry valleys, look to the tributaries for water. In this case first water comes off Mt. Fullerton at about GR459318. Of course as soon as it hits the gravel flat it goes underground so you have to listen for it.

At the forks under Mt. Fuller the creek divides into two pincer-like branches converging on Mt. Howard.

The main left-hand (west) fork carries on in much the same way as before. I've only followed it for a couple of kilometres, but it appears to offer scramblers their best chance of climbing Mt. Howard from the west.

The right-hand (north) fork starts off with a little canyon you can walk through, opening out into gravel flats, but lots of meadows too. It's enclosed by the merged ridges of Nihahi and Compression, their slopes offering relatively easy scree flogs to ridge line.

328 NIHAHI RIDGE, South Summit — map 13

Day hike
Official trail with signposts & cairns,
unofficial trail & scramble with a tad of
exposure
Distance 5 km to summit from Little
Elbow Recreation Area
Height gain 753 m
High point 2362 m
Map 82 J/15 Bragg Creek

Access: Via Little Elbow trail (#322).

*Looking down the first scramble step,
the diagonal crack..*

Nihahi Ridge measures 9.5 km from end to end. More remarkable than its length is its character, described by Dr. George back in the 1880s as "remarkably straight and rampart-like", another example of where the McConnell Fault has pushed older limestone over the top of younger sandstones.

An interesting and exceedingly popular scramble that gets you to the southernmost summit of Nihahi at GR482303. Go as far as you feel comfortable.

Official trail After leaving the hunter's parking lot, turn first right onto Nihahi Ridge trail and climb to a T-junction. Turn left. Turn next right on a narrower trail that corkscrews uphill into meadows offering a foreshortened view of your objective. While the meadows are gorgeous, it's a bit discomforting to know this is a grizzly hotspot and that the trail is periodically closed whenever anyone spots a bear.

Traverse across to the south ridge of Nihahi, then climb to a saddle that is the *second* levelling off in the zone of slaty orange rocks. The official trail ends here. What a difference another 50 m of height gain makes. Now you get a bird's-eye view of the Little Elbow River, against the afternoon sun a shining snake winding out of the shadowy recesses of the Opal Range.

To summit Leave 75 per cent of the people behind and head up the scree, turning the first step on the right. The trail hugs the rock base above a large spruce pocket, then zigs to the crest below a second step

where anyone so inclined can walk out to the top of the first one to impress any friends waiting down below at the saddle. The trail continues, traversing below a longer, higher cliff to the scrambling-up place, a 4 m-high diagonal crack easier than the step on Heart Mountain. Above, wend left on scree to the ridge top which is where another percentage drops out. The cliffs ahead certainly look intimidating....

Still the trail continues. Follow it up the scree ridge, circling right below outcrops into the "intimidating" section of ridge that turns left. Amazingly, you never have to look over those cliffs; the trail stays far to the right on an easy rubble slope, climbing directly to a break in the summit cliff band. Most people stop here, either below or above the second scramble step.

The gently rising ridge ahead is a mite exposed, white slabs on the left, an overhanging drop on the right. While the sure-footed will walk the crest with nonchalance, anyone with jelly legs will be glad of a steadying hand on occasions. But shortly you arrive at the south summit which is marked by a little heap of stones. The intervening ridge to the high point of Nihahi, miles away at the other end of the ridge, is not for walkers.

#328. Returning from the south summit of Nihahi Ridge. The route onto the summit ridge follows the left-hand ridge (note tiny figures).

#329, Ford Creek trail. Having a rest partway up the avalanche gully under Nihahi Ridge.

329 FORD CREEK TRAIL — maps 13 & 8

Long day hike, backpack
Official trail with signposts & red
markers, creek crossing
Total distance 19 km

Highway access:
1. South end Elbow Falls Trail (Hwy. 66) at Little Elbow Recreation Area. Just before the campground check-in turn left into trailhead parking lot.
2. Powderface Trail (Hwy.) at a small parking area on the west side of the highway 7.2 km north of Hwy. 66. Via Trail Creek connector.
3. Powderface Trail (Hwy.) at Prairie Creek.
4. North end Powderface Trail (Hwy.) at Canyon Creek trailhead (two parking areas).
NOTE: These sections of Highway 66 and Powderface Trail are closed between December 1st and May 15th.
Also accessible by horse trail from Loop B equestrian campground at Little Elbow Recreation Area, from Ford Knoll trail (see *Canmore & Kananaskis Country*), from Powderface Creek & Pass (#311) at Trail Creek trailhead, from western terminus of Prairie Creek (#309), from Canyon Creek (#307) and from the southern terminus of Jumpingpound Ridge trail (#335).

Basically, this trail runs parallel to Powderface Trail the highway as far as Canyon Creek, connecting Little Elbow Recreation Area to the trails in the Jumpingpound, The name is misleading. For the most part it is NOT the easy valley trail you think it is. It is, in fact, quite strenuous. Clearly, loops can be made, though if you're daft enough to try the obvious one with Powderface Ridge be sure to pack a spare pair of legs for a total height gain exceeding 1000 m.

The geology is interesting. "A line of round green hills" is how geologist D. D. Cairnes described the eight hills below Nihahi Ridge and the two below Compression Ridge in 1905. Apparently, water running off the eastern escarpment cut down through bands of soft shale (valleys), leaving between them hills of erosion resistant cardium sandstones.

Little Elbow Recreation Area to Prairie Creek

Distance 13.5 km
Height gain 555 m
Height loss 402 m
High point 2027 m
Map 82 J/15 Bragg Creek

Highway access: 1, 2, 3.
Also accessible by horse trail from Loop B equestrian campground at Little Elbow Recreation Area, from Ford Knoll trail, from Powderface Creek & Pass (#311) at Trail Creek trailhead and from the western terminus of Prairie Creek (#309).

The trail designers booed on this one. A perfectly logical route exists lower down, passing behind the eight hills of Nihahi, yet this route takes a much higher seesawing line across the eastern escarpment of Nihahi Ridge. Other trails in the area may be clear of snow by late May, but not this one, its numerous gullies are still choked with avalanche debris, a come-on to grizzlies searching out avalanche kill, late sprouting hedysarum shoots and knack–ered hikers.

SOUTH TO NORTH
Leaving Little Elbow Recreation Area See sketchmap on page 255. The trail leaves trailhead parking lot beside the ramp and heads north. Cross the campground access road, keep right and cross the fence to a junction. Turn left. At the next junction turn right and cross a small creek. Climb to the horse trail from Loop B. Turn right and climb to a junction with Ford Knoll trail (straight). Turn left. Throughout this stretch you're treated to fine views looking south to the mountains about the Elbow River.

After crossing a grassy road that 20 years ago we used to follow to Nihahi Ridge, the trail passes between Ford Knoll and hill No. 2, climbing above gap GR504304 on the west side (low trail available). Cross a creek, then head north toward a mini-gap, at the last minute doubling back (oops!) and climbing through the gap to the west of hill No. 3. Thus far the going has been tolerable, but all that is about to change after the next creek crossing. Instead of making for the gap behind hill No. 4 you embark on a gruelling climb up the side creek out of the trees and on up an avalanche gully. Before the summit the trail turns right and still climbing, reaches the top of a forested spur.

The so-called traverse is rarely level. You're either climbing up or down many more of these forested spurs jutting out of the east face of Nihahi Ridge. Numerous in-between avalanche gullies are crossed high in the runout zone where you become intimately acquainted with saplings leaning downhill, small trees with no branches on the uphill side and larger trees with lopped off crowns. Views are dismal, just the forested lower slopes of everything. A longer, steeper descent than usual by the side of Trail Creek signals the end of your misery. Cross the creek and climb uphill (the trail hasn't quite done with you yet) to a trail junction. Go straight. Turn right for Trail Creek trailhead, **access 2**.

Trail Creek connector
Distance 1 km, height loss/gain 80 m.
This rather pleasant trail heads downhill on the north bank of Trail Creek. Slip through the gap between hills No. 6 and 7, cross Trail Creek and in a few minutes reach Powderface Trail the highway.

The trail descends gradually toward the meadows of Prairie Creek, crossing it just north of hill No. 8. Turn right and climb the bank to join a former OHV road that once led to a favourite camp spot. Head right to the highway. The parking area lies a few metres south on the east side of the road.

Prairie Creek to Canyon Creek

Distance 5.5 km
Height gain 152 m
Height loss 131 m
High point 1814 m
Map 82 J/15 Bragg Creek

Highway access: 3, 4.
Also accessible from the western terminus of Prairie Creek (#309), from Canyon Creek (#307) and from the southern terminus of Jumpingpound Ridge trail (#335).

Much better, a pleasant stretch crossing the watershed into Canyon Creek.

Walk north up the highway to the left-hand bend. The trail resumes on the right side.

Head up the east bank of a Prairie Creek tributary under the pines. Below hill No. 9 cross the pass at GR479401 into a tributary of Canyon Creek. At this point you're only half a kilometre from the highway, but after crossing the creek you head off in the opposite direction, crossing it twice more en route to the meadows of Canyon Creek valley. Canyon Creek requires a paddle upstream of the confluence.

On the north bank join an exploration road in a meadow (#307) and turn left, striding out to Powderface Trail the highway. Shortly after passing between Jumpingpound Ridge and hill No. 10 to the south, you join Jumpingpound Ridge trail at the last side creek to the right. Climb a hill, pass two picnic tables and enjoy views of Compression Ridge and the mountains about upper Canyon Creek as you close in on **access 4**.

At the parking lot on the west side of the highway there is a memorial cairn to World War II aircrew, which brings me to the next route—#330, Upper Canyon Creek....

pass

330 UPPER CANYON CREEK — maps 8 & 12

Long day hikes, backpack
Unofficial trails & routes, creek
crossings
Distance to forks 6.5 km
Height gain to forks 213 m
Maps 82 J/15 Bragg Creek,
82 J/14 Spray Lakes Reservoir

The cirque at the head of the west fork.
The gully above the figures is one route to
the secret pass at GR398360.

Access: Powderface Trail (Hwy.) at Canyon Creek. Park south of the bridges at GR461418 where an exploration road signed "No motorized vehicles" takes off up the valley. NOTE: This section of Powderface Trail is closed between December 1st and May 15th.

Lying in the rain shadow of the Fisher Range, upper Canyon Creek and all its tributaries is a pretty arid place of screes, cliffs and unreliable streams, with not much in the way of meadows. A place for the adventurous looking for new valleys to explore and peaks to climb.

To the forks The exploration road, lightly imprinted on stony alluvial flats, can be traced on and off for over 5 km. After the first creek crossing, a large cairn at 1 km acts as a homing beacon on the return trip. In another kilometre you cross the mouth of the north fork. Then comes a most impressive passage between the great red cliffs of Mt. Bryant and the scarcely less impressive crags of Compression Ridge, the ridge framed in the V ahead being the route over to Evan-Thomas Creek. One km after the flats and the road end you reach the forks where three creeks meet at GR412382.

GOING FARTHER
West fork
Distance to cirque 3 km, height gain 341 m, high point 2286 m. The main fork.

The valley narrows quickly. It's probably easiest to walk up the creekbed, the one vertical rock step—sometime waterfall—at the head of a mini-canyon is easily turned on the left side. Where the valley opens out into trees and meadow scraps start looking for pieces of fuselage. Since the second edition more information has come to light about the plane crash that occurred on August 14th, 1941. I'm not sure what an Avro Anson training aircraft from No. 3 Service Flying Training School in Calgary was doing flying up a blind canyon, but likely it was trying to turn when it clipped a tall tree which snapped off the plane's tail. Sadly, flying instructor Ian Sutherland and student pilot Fred Greenfield were killed in the crash. The other student Sandy McGruther suffered a broken leg and was lucky to be found by K Country's first organized search and rescue led by two local outfitters.

At Forgetmenot Pond on a snowy November 10th, 1989, Squadron leader McGruther unveiled a plaque commemorating Sutherland, Greenfield and others lost during the British Commonwealth Air Training Plan of 1939-45. Later the plaque was mounted on a cairn overlooking the scene of the disaster at Canyon Creek parking lot.

But back to the hike. The valley is again narrowing, becoming enclosed by shale walls hard to climb out of. The difficulty can easily be circumvented by walking up the side creek to the right at GR399375. At treeline traverse left and keep a high line as you round the big bend and steer north into the cirque. Easy! All around is an apparently barren landscape of delicately-tinted pinky-coloured shales (a colour repeated on surrounding ridges), but looking more closely you discover the cirque floor is dotted with tiny cushion plants.

South fork

Distance to camping area 2.5 km, height gain 253 m, high point 2194 m. The fork is named Canyon Creek on the topo map.

The creekbed provides easy walking through the narrows into the upper valley. Water is nearly always running in the vicinity of the protruding ridge at GR408360 (at the edge of two maps) below which is a flat meadow with camping spots. This puts backpackers in a perfect position to scramble over the ridge to Evan-Thomas Creek the next day.

South fork camping area.

To Evan-Thomas Creek via pass GR398360

Distance 5.5 km from south fork, height gain 329 m from south fork, 463 m from west fork, height loss 725 m, high point 2524 m. This low point in a ridge has long been known as a route over to Evan-Thomas Creek. Scree slopes on both sides are only moderately steep.

Pass from south fork From the camping area head west up a shallow grassy recess, angling right to reach steeper slopes above an island of trees. Keep moving right and slightly up across a wide slope furrowed with shallow gullies, aiming for the lowest scree shelf. Don't climb the slope above which rears up like a wave about to topple over, but walk along the shelf to a broad scree ridge and follow it more easily to the low point in the ridge line. In early summer a cornice is problematic.

Pass from west fork At GR398374 head south up a side valley turning to scree gully, near the top breaking out left onto the broad scree ridge used by south fork route.

Descent from the pass Endure 240 m of scree to the flat head of an unnamed creek. At the next drop avoid greasy waterfall steps by traversing left through trees to an avalanche chute you can follow down to the creekbed. Straightforward rock-hopping leads to a fork where you turn right. Ten minutes before reaching Evan-Thomas Creek and trail #55A, the placid creek erupts in a short chain of falls and pools.

331 NORTH FORK OF UPPER CANYON CREEK — map 8

Day hikes
Unofficial trails, routes & scrambles
Maps 82 J/14 Spray Lakes Reservoir,
82 J/15 Bragg Creek

Access: Via Upper Canyon Creek (#330) at the 2 km mark (GR447412). Turn right.

I venture into this valley quite a bit. Not only does it harbour the largest lake in the Fisher Range, it has several mountains fit for walkers who can grovel up a bit of scree. Regrettably, lack of space forbids more than a cursory route description of just four.

331A Tarn under Mt. Bryant

Distance 7 km, height gain 381 m from trailhead, high point 2103 m. Intermittent trails and routefinding problems.

After passing through the narrows, occasional trails (starting on the right side) relieve the ache of walking the stony creekbed. Keep left at the forks GR431419 (cairn) and pass the great cirque of Mt. Bryant. Shortly before the upper forks are reached leave the valley bottom at a cairn and flagging.

The tarn below the scree slopes of Mt. Bryant.

On trail climb the steep left bank into the forest. Keep straight and emerge on a scree field. Navigate to a cairn. Above the cairn is a small rock band. Climb the right side of the band by a diagonal break, then continue uphill a bit before turning right on a faint trail in scree where you pick up another cairn. You're now on a bench, travelling from cairn to cairn. Look behind you for a fine view of Mt. GR409435 showing the top half of the route. (Conversely, this summit is a spectacular viewpoint for the tarn.)

At the fifth cairn the trail drops to a meadow (cairn). There are two ways to the tarn from here. I prefer to head for the creekbed, now a grassy draw, and follow it *downhill* to the lake (an anomaly not apparent on the topo map). The aquamarine-coloured tarn occupies a deep hole below the horrendous rubble slopes of Mt. Bryant, and with no outlet, obviously comes equipped with an underwater plug.

View from Mt. GR409435, looking across the north-north fork to Mt. GR427439 (left) and Mt. GR436425 (right). Shows ascent routes.

331B Mt. GR409435

Distance 6 km, height gain 844 m from trailhead, high point 2566 m. A straightforward scree ascent which at the finish calls for willpower and Leki hiking poles.

Continue past A to the upper forks at GR412422 and turn right up the stony creekbed. Shortly, climb to the open bank on the left and follow it to treeline. Turn left into a side valley blocked by cliffs, traversing scree at treeline into an unsuspected stony draw on the right which takes you all the way to the summit. The easy-angled scree of low down steepens high up into a torrent of small stones which are wonderful to descend! Top out a short distance *left* of the summit. Do *not* go right because you run into problems with a slab.

331C Mt. GR427439

Distance 5 km, height gain 634 m from trailhead, high point 2356 m. An easy walk.

Turn right at the forks GR431419 and head up the north-north fork to GR429425. Turning right, plod up a gentle slope (grass, stones) to the summit ridge from where a comfortably wide ridge curves around to the summit at the north end. Connecting with Mt. GR412443 is not for walkers.

Optional return over Mt. GR436425 Extra height gain 131 m, high point 2301 m. Taking in this summit ups the difficulty a notch. From where you first gained the ridge descend to the col at GR434429. If the upcoming scree ridge intimidates, you can still bale out to the right. The ridge steepens alarmingly below the summit, but luckily the higher you get the firmer the footing, and near the cliff edge generations of sheep have trodden out big inundations.

Surprisingly, the ongoing ridge is easy, still the cliffs on the left, but the slopes on the right fall away at a very gradual angle. As you descend, the ridge curves around to the right, becoming rockier and narrower at treeline. Keeping right of outcrops, lose height rapidly down one of those messy mixed slopes to the north fork valley bottom.

331D Mt. GR412443

Distance 6 m, height gain 780 m from trailhead, high point 2502 m. If you pick the right line, a fairly easy ascent.

Continue up the north-north fork past the turnoff for C to the very end of the valley below the "boxing glove". Follow the creek as it turns sharp left, a little way up transferring to a grassy slope on the left *above* a terrace and a line of crags. High up, at the obvious place, traverse right on scree, crossing a left fork and the main fork, continuing on in the same direction, though steeper, to the col between your objective and Mt. GR409435. Turn right and walk up a broad low-angle ridge to the summit (contour lines on the topo map are wildly wrong).

332 BELMORE BROWNE PEAK — map 8

Day scramble
Unofficial trail & routes
Distance 4 km to summit
Height gain 625 m
High point 2332 m
Map 82 J/15 Bragg Creek

Above: Belmore Browne Peak from the highway. The route more or less follows the left-hand ridge. The plaque is located at far right at the demarcation of ridge and forest.

Access: Powderface Trail (Hwy.). Park 14.5 km south of Sibbald Creek Trail (Hwy. 68) at GR440466, opposite what appears to be a side valley but which is actually the headwaters of Jumpingpound Creek. NOTE: This section of Powderface Trail is closed between December 1st and May 15th.

I'd admired this little outlier for years, favourably comparing its triangle of rock to other peaks in the Fisher Range that appeared to be dull heaps of scree. From the highway it certainly didn't look easy for the walker, so I dismissed it from my mind as a possible summit, never for one minute envisaging the momentous events of the early 1990s with which I somehow came to be involved. So I climbed it after all, and it turned out to be a walk-up.

Jumpingpound Creek section Drop down the bank to a logging road that crosses the wee south fork of Jumpingpound Creek. The road heads along the south bank of Jumpingpound Creek into a huge cutblock (nuclear disaster zone), then wends right and crosses Jumpingpound Creek proper into another huge south-facing cutblock growing grass that stretches far up the southeast slopes of your objective—the rocky pyramid poking up above the trees. Far from being a reassuring sight, it makes you wonder how you're going to get up the cliffs without resorting to ladders.

Where the logging road crosses the creek, keep straight on a cutline that regains the creek above all logging. Walk up the stony creekbed, keeping right at a creek junction. Under the scree slopes of Belmore Browne Peak the valley floor narrows.

At GR412459 start the ascent via the mountain's south ridge.

South Ridge Actually, start left of the south ridge, climbing a ribbon of vegetation with trees. When it gives out continue easily to the ridge, gained at the halfway point. Climb the moderately-inclined ridge above, picking your way between small outcroppings of white rock up non-slip scree. By keeping on the edge above the triangular cliff you'll arrive on the east summit, the one with a cairn. There are actually two summits divided by a fissure visible from Rafter Six Ranch Resort.

In the cairn is a canister with a message from Pam Kerr McPhee and Jennifer Noe Mansell of New Hampshire who were the first to climb the peak after the name became official on September 22, 1992 and which contains postcards with Pam's address. Write to her while the supply lasts!

Belmore Browne was one of those people who makes the rest of us look like couch potatoes: an acclaimed American landscape and wildlife artist, director of the Santa Barbara School of Fine Arts (student Ward Kimball went on to create Donald Duck), a climber and explorer (founding member of the American Alpine Club, co-establisher of Mt. McKinley National Park, nearly first ascensionist of McKinley, coming within 40 m of making the first ascent in 1912 and in the process thoroughly debunking Frederick Cook's claim to have reached the summit).

He and his family spent their summers in Banff between 1920-43, later moving to 'Illahee' in the grounds of what is now Rafter Six Ranch Resort. "Aha, so that's the connection". You may find it strange that when he died in 1954 his ashes were not scattered on some snowy Alaskan giant but on this tiny outlier of the Fisher Range. Then you remember that he and his family wandered for 30 years all over the ridges of the Jumpingpound and Elbow and grew to love the place. His death was the start of another grand story covering 40 years (a tale of the first plaque that was lost, then found) that has only just come full circle with the death of Browne's daughter Evelyn. I'll tell you about it sometime when I've got 20 pages to spare.

Descent Retreat to the rift, then either scrabble over the slabby west summit or traverse to the col at GR409465 in the zone of gaudy red rock. Turn left and walk down easy-angled scree into the creekbed/gully you left earlier. It's that simple.

The second plaque on the day it was cemented in, September 3rd, 1993.

OPTION RETURN
Via the plaque at GR415467
This route requires careful navigation and a bushwhack whichever way round you do it. Return down the south ridge to where you first gained the ridge. To your left a sheep trail swoops through the one break in the cliff band to the rocky basin below the triangular slab. Not a place to land a helicopter you would think unless you're a super pilot like Mark Bellamy. Cross the basin below totty pinnacles frozen *in situ* like seracs to GR416465 where you turn the corner and traverse in a northwesterly direction just above treeline to the northeast shoulder. Look up to the left. The plaque is cemented to a boulder, just one of thousands, and faces the ridges of Cox, Jumpingpound and Moose.

Return to GR416465 and drop steeply down grass onto the forested west ridge. At GR422465 turn south, lower down veering left to be sure of hitting the south-facing cutblock that takes you out to the logging road.

GOING FARTHER
A ridge walk

Distance 10 km round trip from the trailhead, high point 2435 m, height gain/loss 838 m. Belmore Browne Peak is well placed for a partial ridge walk around the head of Jumpingpound Creek where you can pick off another three, possibly four summits. Technically, it's all about the same as Belmore Browne with greater routefinding problems and a bushwhack.

From the col west of Belmore Browne, walk onto the backbone of the Fisher Range at hump **GR406466**. If time isn't a factor, it's tempting to take in the big scree heap 800 m to the northwest at **GR403471** (add 200 m height gain)—a spectacular-looking peak from the Porcupine Creek side, usually climbed from route #39.

Otherwise, turn your attention southwards to **Mt. GR406463** (2423 m). For walkers it's a bit worrying that something so simple looking on the topo map turns out to have three steps. Slog up the first step to the left of cliffs, then at the two-tier cliff (unless you're an advanced scrambler), traverse, descending slightly, far out onto the east face to where the band starts to break up and you can regain the ridge. A short third step below the summit is taken on the right.

Stroll down to a col with a splendid view ahead of the tiara peak as I call it, looking totally impregnable from this direction. A third of the way up is a minor bump at **GR406456** (2435 m), the final summit of the day. Tackle the first rock band direct, and avoid the second on the left side.

At the top it becomes apparent why I've sent you up there. And it's not for the splendid view of Belmore Browne Peak. On the east side a convenient ridge descends all the way into Jumpingpound Creek. Easy at first (grass and talus), it narrows at mid section into a rocky promontory, then plunges into forest where you steer between massive cliffs to both left and right. A final bush thrash gains you the creekbed just east of Belmore Browne Peak.

Summit GR406456 overlooked by the tiara peak. The route descends the left-hand ridge.

333 JUMPINGPOUND SUMMIT TRAIL — map 8

Half-day hike
Official trail with signposts
Distance 2.5 km to ridge, 3.5 km to summit
Height gain 326 m to ridge, 417 m to summit
High point 2240 m at summit
Map 82 J/15 Bragg Creek

The summit of Jumpingpound Mountain in November. Looking east to Moose Mountain, west peak and south peak.

Access: Powderface Trail (Hwy.) at the trailhead on the west side of the highway 400 m south of the pass between Jumpingpound Creek and Canyon Creek drainages. NOTE: This section of Powderface Trail is closed between December 1st and May 15th.
Also accessible from Jumpingpound Ridge trail (#335) 1 km south of the summit of Jumpingpound Mountain, and from the western terminus of Jumpingpound Mountain East Ridge (#334).

This is by far the shortest route to the summit of Jumpingpound Mountain, but not as short as the signpost says!

The trail starts opposite the parking lot on the east side of the highway. Shortly it bridges a small creek, follows it upstream a bit, then before reaching cutblocks, seen gleaming palely through the pines, turns away uphill. You follow a thoughtfully engineered series of switchbacks up a subsidiary ridge to an easing at the midway point, then continue in tighter switchback formation through more open forest to the junction with Jumpingpound Ridge trail at a signpost. You've now reached the main north-south ridge.

I've seen people turn around and go back when they reach the ridge, which seems a terrible waste of effort when the summit of Jumpingpound Mountain with its 360 degree panorama is only a kilometre away. So turn left and follow route #335 through more trees to a signpost on open slopes where the summit is in sight. Here turn right and climb past a cairn and a post to a larger cairn where a similar trail descends to the north ridge. Turn right and clamber among a few rocks to the summit.

334 JUMPINGPOUND MOUNTAIN EAST RIDGE — map 8

Long day hike in combination
Unofficial trail & route
Distance 4 km
Height gain E-W 335 m
Height loss E-W 365 m
High point 2240 m
Map 82 J/15 Bragg Creek

West access: Jumpingpound Ridge trail (#335) at the summit of Jumpingpound Mountain. **East access:** North Ridge of Moose Mountain (#302) from the saddle between north/north and north peaks.

Contrary to expectations, K Country never did build the East Ridge trail. It doesn't matter; with or without an official trail, the pleasant east ridge of Jumpingpound Mountain is easy enough *apart* from the drop onto the col between the ridge and Moose Mountain for which an alternative has suddenly become available.

Use it to access Moose Mountain's delectable north ridge. While a number of point to points spring to mind, fit ridge walkers who can hack 1470 m of ascent should consider a 23 km loop starting at Canyon parking lot and incorporating routes #335, 334, 302 and 307.

WEST TO EAST
From the summit of Jumpingpound Mountain head east along the lofty east ridge, a gentle roller-coaster comprising four grassy hilltops where the shooting stars grow thick on the ground and four cols with encroaching forest. The fourth hilltop drops off sharply to a fifth col, the one between the ridge and Moose Mountain's north ridge, or to put it another way, between Moose Mountain Creek and a tributary of Coxhill Creek at GR505462.

If you don't fancy a direct descent to fifth col on talus, just step left from fourth col onto a road that takes you up to the col effortlessly! Since the second edition this once beautiful place has been completely resculptured by a well pad that not so long

ago came equipped with a rig, part of Husky Oil and Rigel Energy corporations' well-publicized oil find on the north slope of Moose Mountain. (The discovery well is just down the road at pad No.1.)

I believe we made the first and last tourist ascent of this road by bike in June of 1994. There's a lot to be said for not wearing Louis Garneau cycling shorts which make your legs look fat, and for looking like middle-aged nuclear physicists, botanists and publishers, because the gatekeeper at Jumpingpound let us in to peddle, as *he* thought, to the camp at Coxhill Creek where we should watch out for the sow grizzly. We, of course, peddled and pushed all the way up the road and did a ridge walk on top of it and returned to the pad to find the harassed gatekeeper in a pickup being given a ticking off by the supervisor who then gave us a ticking off followed by an interesting talk all about what was going on. Of course, Mike Sawyer will say it's the oil companies who deserve a ticking off for messing up the country.

Cross pad No. 2 and find the trail that strikes off uphill in a right to left direction to the grassy saddle at GR509464 between the north peak of Moose Mountain on the right and the north/north peak on the left, regaining all the height lost.

Can you descend via the Husky exploration road to Jumpingpound Forest Demonstration Loop Road? If the pipeline goes ahead the answer is NO. The road is awful boring to walk down anyway.

#334. Looking along the east ridge from Jumpingpound Mountain.

#335, Jumpingpound Ridge trail. A typical view along the north half of the main ridge.

335 JUMPINGPOUND RIDGE TRAIL — map 8

Day hike
Official trail with signposts, red
markers & cairns
Distance 12.5 km
Height gain N-S 610 m
Height loss N-S 549 m
High point 2240 m
Map 82 J/15 Bragg Creek

Access: Powderface Trail (Hwy.). NOTE: This section of Powderface Trail is closed between December 1st and May 15th.
1. **North** at Lusk Pass trailhead.
2. **South** at Canyon Creek parking lot.
Also accessible from the southern terminus of Cox Hill trail (#336), the western terminus of Jumpingpound Mountain East Ridge trail (#334), the terminus of Jumpingpound Summit trail (#333), and the western terminus of Canyon Creek/Ford Creek trails (#307 & #329).

An easy ridge walk along the entire summit ridge of Jumpingpound Mountain takes in some really fine country above treeline that is often in condition right through to December 1st when the highway closes. I recommend hiking the entire ridge and for this you'll need two vehicles because walking back along the highway, like we did once, is the pits.

The grunting you will hear signifies not bears but mountain bikers, while in early September the ridge is the scene of a three-day triathlon for horses.

NORTH TO SOUTH

To Coxhill Ridge junction Straightway after crossing the bridge over Jumpingpound Creek you're into long sweeping zigs up a densely-forested slope rising to Jumpingpound's northwest ridge where the trail straightens, even descends a little. At a second levelling a side trail to right descends to a glade with a spring. Continue climbing to the southern terminus of Coxhill Ridge trail at treeline.

To Jumpingpound Summit trail Turn south and stride along the main ridge, still some 3 km distant from the summit of Jumpingpound Mountain. There are no pretty flower meadows here, only wind-blasted tundra and rocky outcrops providing shelter for trees creeping up lee slopes onto the ridge top. And lots of cairns nearly two metres high. The treat here is the views: Cox Hill and the north ridge of Moose Mountain to the east and to the west a Fisher Range panorama where you can pick out a number of easy scrambling peaks.

The trail passes about 50 vertical m below the summit of Jumpingpound Mountain on the west flank. Barring a thunderstorm or a whiteout, a trip to the top is a must, so on side trail climb past small cairns to the summit rocks where the view to the south—ridge on ridge and range on range receding into the noonday sun—is suddenly disclosed. Return to the trail and turn left. Not long after slipping into the trees you arrive at the junction with #333.

To Canyon Creek Keep left. To avoid a ridge built like a porcupine's back, the trail traverses the west flank in the pines for 2 km, then climbs back onto the ridge, now broad and grassy, bristling on the west side with outcrops made famous by bikers who would have you believe the route travels along a knife-edge ridge. From here you get a fabulous view of 12 km-long Nihahi and Compression ridges.

Back in trees the trail starts its final descent to Canyon Creek, winding about a small creek and squeezing between "The Gates". At valley bottom you intersect an old exploration road (alias Canyon Creek and Ford Creek trails), turn right and follow it out to south access.

Jumpingpound

Banded Peak

Jumpingpound Mtn.

Compression
Ridge   Mt. Howard

Fisher
Peak   Mt. Bryant

GR42743

336 COX HILL — map 8

Day hike
Official trail with signposts, red
markers & cairns
Distance 9 km, 6.5 km to summit
Height gain 872 m
Height loss 314 m
High point 2219 m
Maps 82 O/2 Jumpingpound Creek,
82 J/15 Bragg Creek

*Above: View from Cox Hill summit of
Jumpingpound Mountain (left) and its long
north ridge. Closer at hand is the open
south ridge of Cox Hill. The Fisher Range
makes up most of the backdrop.*

*Opposite: Fooling around on
the summit rocks.*

Access: Powderface Trail (Hwy.) at Dawson
trailhead. Via Tom Snow trail (#301).
Also accessible from Jumpingpound Ridge trail
(#335).

A fairly strenuous climb leads to a superla-
tive viewpoint, superior even to Moose
Mountain because that massif, looking very
unfamiliar from this direction, is also included in the view. Hikers with two vehicles should consider hiking the "Jumpingpound Highline", an amalgamation of
Coxhill Ridge and Jumpingpound Ridge
trails offering 17 km of ridge wandering,
much of it above treeline.

NORTH TO SOUTH
To the summit Start out on Tom Snow trail. A
few minutes from the parking lot keep right
and cross Jumpingpound Creek on a bridge.
Climb to a T-junction with Coxhill Ridge trail.

Turn right, then left onto a NW-SE
cutline. Not far along turn right onto a
narrow trail that starts up the northeast
ridge of Cox Hill.

The hard work is all at the beginning, a
continuously steep slog through pine forest
choked with alder, the slope higher up
becoming open and rocky. The angle eases
as you re-enter forest. Where you pass to the
left of the ridge line a spur trail leads to a
discouraging viewpoint of the summit

GR409435
GR412443
the tiara peak
Mt. Bogart
GR403471
Belmore
Browne Peak
Mt.
Sparrowhawk

which looks as far away as ever. Sighing, you head back to the main trail for another long stint through a forest now bereft of bushes and quite pleasant to walk through.

From grassy bluffs there's a bird's-eye view of Coxhill Creek and Husky's exploration road up the north slope of Moose Mountain. It's just beyond here, below the summit knobbin, where the trail turns right into meadows, then zigs up a steep grass slope to a lower summit with cairn. A short walk along a connecting ridge gains you the

higher summit, the trail, purposely it seems, taking you through a spruce thicket on the brow so the glorious view to the west bursts upon you suddenly. Flat-topped rocks make handy ringside seats where you can spread out the maps. So who was Cox? No one. The hill's proper name is "Cockscomb" after its fringe of summit rocks.

Below you on the west slopes, eight searchers were killed when their Twin Otter went down on June 14th, 1986, during the search for Orval Pall and Ken Wolff. So this hill is forever linked to Memorial Lakes.

To Jumpingpound Ridge trail Coxhill Ridge trail continues along the grassy south ridge. Navigating from cairn to cairn, you make a descending traverse along its west flank back into trees. Descend more steeply into the gap between Cox and Jumpingpound Mountain. For anyone feeling tired, the upcoming climb onto Jumpingpound's north ridge is steeper than one would wish for at this stage, but luckily the trail builders were kind. Two long sweeping zigs gain you a rocky rib at mid height from where the trail contours effortlessly across the north slope to intercept Jumpingpound Ridge trail at GR456388.

337 EAGLE HILL — map 8

Day hike
Official trail with signposts & red markers
Distance 8.5 km from Dawson trailhead, 5 km from Sibbald Lake via A
Height gain 332 m from lake
High point 1722 m
Map 82 JO/2 Jumpingpound Creek

Access:
1. Powderface Trail (Hwy.) at Dawson trailhead.
2. Sibbald Creek Trail (Hwy. 68). Turn off toward Sibbald Lake Campground. At the three-way junction keep left into Sibbald Lake day-use area parking lot.

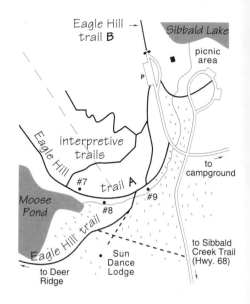

The options from access 2

The trail takes you through typical foothills country of meadows and aspen forests to an amazingly good viewpoint on the northern boundary of Kananaskis Country. I once flushed a cougar from some bushes alongside the trail and other people, within the last couple of years, have been lucky enough to glimpse wolves.

Eagle Hill is a trail writer's nightmare with three different starts—all official. Most hikers will start from access 2.

From access 1. Dawson trailhead to Moose Pond Not far from the parking lot turn left on the narrower trail and cross a NW-SE cutline. The trail runs parallel to the highway, then crosses it and climbs onto the cleared right-of-way for the far-in-the-future highway. Follow the right-of-way below a huge cutblock back to the highway, then veer off left into the forest. Descend in zigzags to Sibbald Flat or *Siktothuthu Eyagubi Tida* (Where-they-castrated-a-grey-stallion clearing). The trail hugs the edge of the trees, then cuts across the huge meadow where buffalo once grazed and where Frank Sibbald ran his cattle at the turn of the century. Cross Sibbald Creek by a bridge just upstream of the road bridge, then cross Powderface Trail the highway close to Sibbald's cabin site. Climb the bank to Highway 68.

The trail crosses the highway and climbs grassy slopes—a hotspot for Scabious—onto the low ridge to the north where Deer Ridge trail turns left. Descend the north slope and circle around the southeast corner of Moose Pond into the big meadow that is crossed left of the Sun Dance Lodge to Sibbald Flat interpretive trail, alias **route A from access 2**.

From access 2. Sibbald Lake to GR488576 A via Moose Pond Take Sibbald Flat interpretive trail if you like, but why climb when you don't have to? I prefer to walk back down the road a few metres and before the outlet stream from Moose Pond turn right on a trail. Soon enough you join the interpretive trail near No. 9 interpretive sign. Keep straight. In a few metres the **trail from access 1** joins in from the left.

Halfway along the northeast shore of Moose Pond beyond sign No. 7 the other leg of the interpretive trail descends from the right. Again, keep straight.

Beyond the lake the trail splits. Forgo the old trail and turn right on the official horse trail that traverses grassy hillside to a NW-SE cutline where you turn left and descend to the original trail. Turn right and circle round the soggy heart of a side creek. At the zenith of the curve, **route B** comes in from the right. Keep left.

B via Camp Adventure Road leads off in the opposite direction from A, continuing along the gated road toward Camp Adventure. Turn first left off the access road onto a cutline access road, then in 300 m make another left turn onto a road that climbs to a ridge top where it joins a NE-SW cutline. Walk left along the cutline for a few metres, watching carefully for where a trail turns left into the trees, losing all height gained previously as it drops to the junction with **route A** in the valley bottom. Turn right.

To Eagle Hill The trail heads back out to the main valley and turns upstream, hugging aspen hillside to avoid the muskeg and willowbrush of the valley floor. Cross a NE-SW cutline. Shortly after the northern access to Deer Ridge turns left at a drift fence, you cross a low pass between two wooded hills. The trail keeps right, taking a high line as it traverses aspen hillside between cutblocks allowing a view of Eagle Hill up ahead. Drop to cross a small creek.

Finally on Eagle Hill, the trail winds up the lower slopes and in a meadow joins a cutline access road that is followed uphill to the NE-SW cutline it serves. Turn left then right to trail's end at a horse rail near the boundary fence between K Country and a block of federal crown land. The summit lies on the other side of the fence, but it doesn't matter because it's closeted in trees and here, on open southwest slopes prickly with wild rose and gooseberry shoots, you can look out across a glorious panorama of the Bow Valley to the familiar outlines of the mountains about Canmore. The view is no less interesting in the southerly direction where Moose Mountain and Cox Hill rise up above Seventy Buck Valley.

View from the summit of Seventy Buck Valley, Moose Mountain (left) and Cox Hill.

338 SEVENTY BUCK VIEWPOINT — map 8

Short day, half-day hike
Unofficial trails, route
Distance 4.5 km loop
Height gain 347 m
High point 1765 m
Map 82 JO/2 Jumpingpound Creek

Access: Sibbald Creek Trail (Hwy. 68) at the unsigned parking lot 4.2 km west of Powderface Trail junction at *Warhpepen tidan.*

A fairly strenuous loop with two steep hills takes you to a favourite viewpoint on a hill top. Expect to do some routefinding in the bush. The logging road start makes a good one-hour leg stretcher.

The unofficial name "Seventy Buck" for the valley does NOT refer to the number of male deer in the area. It goes back many years to a late fall when snow lay on the ground and Percy Copithorne with Len Kumlin were wandering all over the valley looking for six head of cattle. In the process, Copithorne lost his wallet containing—70 bucks. It was never found and is still out there somewhere....

Near the parking lot entrance get onto a grassy cutline/logging road heading northwest along the west flank of Seventy Buck Valley. Where the cutline arches over a side ridge the road detours right and meets the cutline on the other side. Turn right. Shortly come to a junction.

Turn left on the logging road that wanders below a steeply-angled cutblock into another one bisected by a small creek, your waymark for the next section. If you find yourself *descending* a third cutblock back to the cutline you've gone too far.

Follow the right bank of the small creek into the trees where almost straightaway you run into a NE-SW cutline unmarked on any map. Turn left across the creek. Waves of uphills lead directly to the hill top GR450587 under the pines.

Steer ESE, keeping to the right side of the ridge as you descend to a gap and on up to the summit at GR455582. The view catches you unawares, the whole west side of the hill a balcony above a long line of cliffs looking toward Deadman's Gulch and the mountains about the Kananaskis Valley. Someone has even built a rock shelter.

The enjoyment is prolonged as you descend the southeast ridge. A trail along the cliff edge leads to a grassy slope overlooking *Warhpepen tidan*, the sour grass clearing. Entering open forest, drop steeply to the highway west of the drift fence, turn left and walk 400 m to the parking lot.

Deadman's Gulch from GR455582.

Moose Mountain massif from the east summit (Weaver Mountain).

339 DEER RIDGE — map 8

Half-day hike
Official trail with signposts & red markers
Distance 6 km circuit
Height gain S-N 213 m
Height loss S-N 180 m
High point 1698 m
Map 82 O/2 Jumpingpound Creek

Access: Via Eagle Hill (#337) at two locations.

Deer Ridge, the double-headed ridge overlooking Sibbald Flat from the west, is usually climbed in combination with Eagle Hill trail from Sibbald Lake day-use area. Also popular is a quick visit to the east summit viewpoint from the junction of Highway 68 and Powderface Trail, a round trip of 3.5 km.

SOUTH TO NORTH

Leave Eagle Hill trail on the low ridge at GR490564. Heading west, the trail winds up a steepening hillside into the pines of the summit ridge where the angle eases somewhat. Arrive at a junction with horse rail.

Keep left and treading carefully between clumps of Daisy fleabanes, climb the spur trail to the east summit, a rocky overlook above a cliff. According to a weathered sign tacked to a tree, this little summit is really

"Weaver Mountain", a name likely bestowed by the boys and girls of Camp Adventure after the species ploceidae. It has to be said the view of Deadman's Gulch is nowhere near as good as from Seventy Buck, but this nearer vantage point allows you to sort out the different summits of the Moose Mountain massif, and down below your feet Sibbald Creek can be seen tight-meandering into the great meadow of Sibbald Flat.

Return to the junction and turn left. Descend to a gap and climb to the higher west summit that lies in trees. With no incentive to linger you continue on down the northwest ridge to a NE-SW cutline. Turn right and follow it all the way down to the valley bottom. In order to avoid the mid-valley bog, turn left on a grassy old road that heads upstream for 400 m before crossing the valley at the drift fence and rejoining Eagle Hill trail at GR480578.

340 JUMPINGPOUND LOOP — map 9

Day hike
Official trail with signposts & red markers
Distance 9 km loop
Height gain/loss 300 m
High point 1433 m
Map 82 O/2 Jumpingpound Creek

Access: Sibbald Creek Trail (Hwy. 68).
1. **usual start** Pinetop day-use area.
2. Jumpingpound day-use area.
3. Pine Grove group camp.

This delightful trail has two distinct sections, the high line north of the highway and the river route south of the highway. A good choice for early spring and late fall.

On the high line.

Pinetop to Pine Grove via the high line
Walk out to the highway and turn left. The trail starts from the north side of the road and straightway climbs onto aspen hillside with views of Moose Mountain. For the next 2 km it traverses woodlands with Douglas fir and meadows brightened by Buffalo bean, dipping three times into side valleys. In the third is a junction.

Halving the loop
Turn left and descend to the highway. Cross. The trail shortcuts through trees into the Jumpingpound day-use area parking lot and out the other end to the bank of Jumpingpound Creek where it joins the return leg.

Keep straight. After the next meadow you drop into a deeper side valley than usual, cross a reclaimed exploration road and wind steeply up the other side into—another meadow traverse. Descend to a cutline, turn left and follow it a short way before turning off left to Highway 68.

Turn right and walk along the road to Pine Grove group camp access road on the left which is followed for half a kilometre to Pine Grove group campground entrance.

Detour to Pine Grove picnic area
Add 350 m return from the trail. Carry on down the access road to picnic tables, a cooking shelter and a cabin out on the point overlooking the scenic confluence of Bryant Creek with the Jumpingpound. A great place for lunch!

Pine Grove to Pinetop, river route
Just past the campground entrance the trail resumes, heading back east. In a meadow keep right, the grassy road to left being a remnant of "Last Chance Road" which led to Charlie Logan's Last Chance cabin in the large meadow west of the picnic area called *Sawin Ahnibi Sna* "where Blackfoot woman was brought home clearing". Your trail makes a beeline to Jumpingpound Creek, then follows the riverbank to the junction with the shortcut trail.

The trail continues hugging the bank as it rounds the big bend. After an unexpected dip, the trail gradually moves away from the river and climbs to Pinetop.

THE MAPS

Key map

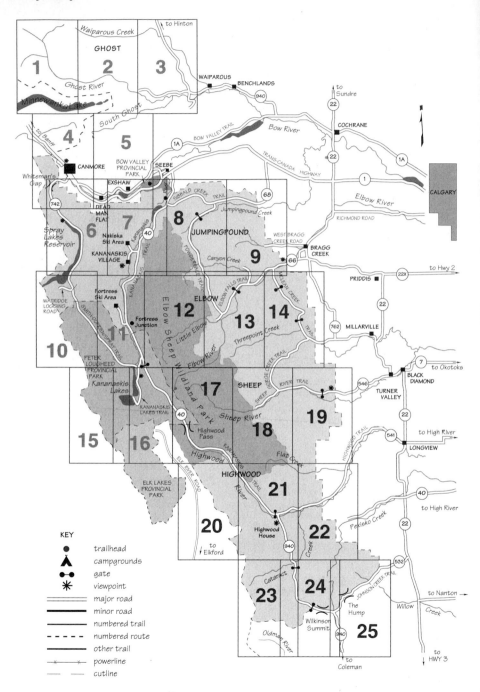

KEY

- ● trailhead
- ▲ campgrounds
- ●—● gate
- ✳ viewpoint
- ——— major road
- ▬▬▬ minor road
- ——— numbered trail
- - - - - numbered route
- ——— other trail
- ✱—✱—✱ powerline
- ——— — cutline

Map 8

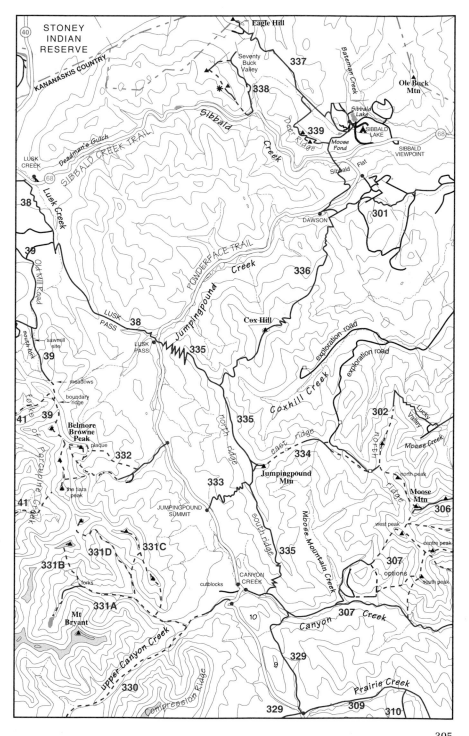

Map 9

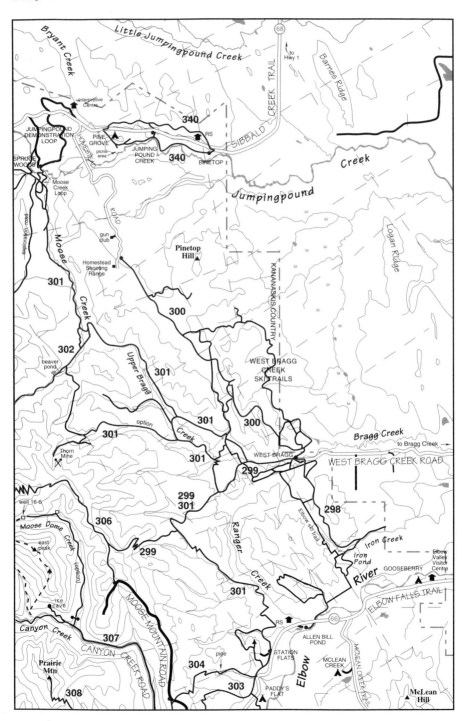

Map 12

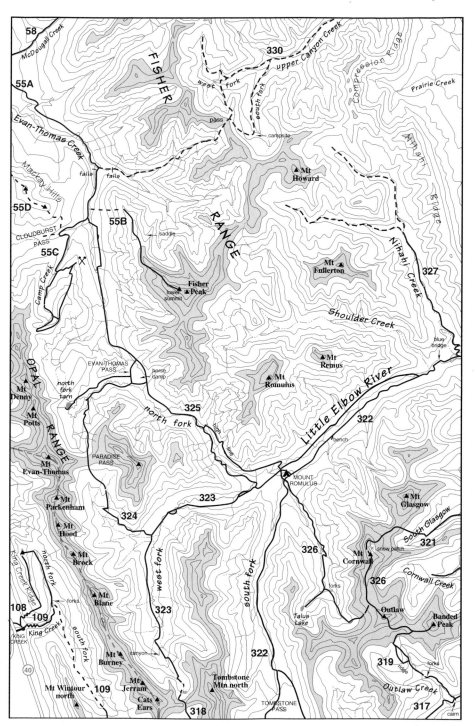

Map 13

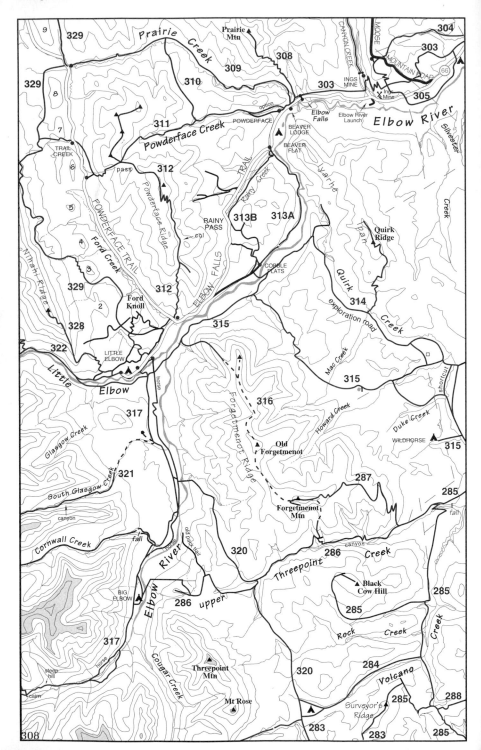

Map 14

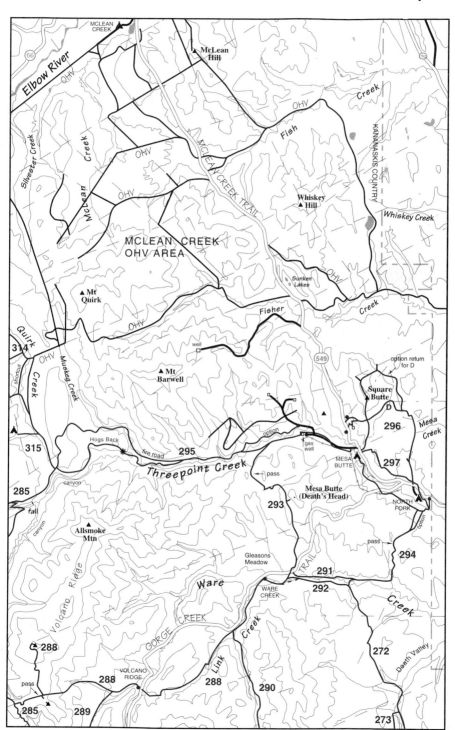

Map 17

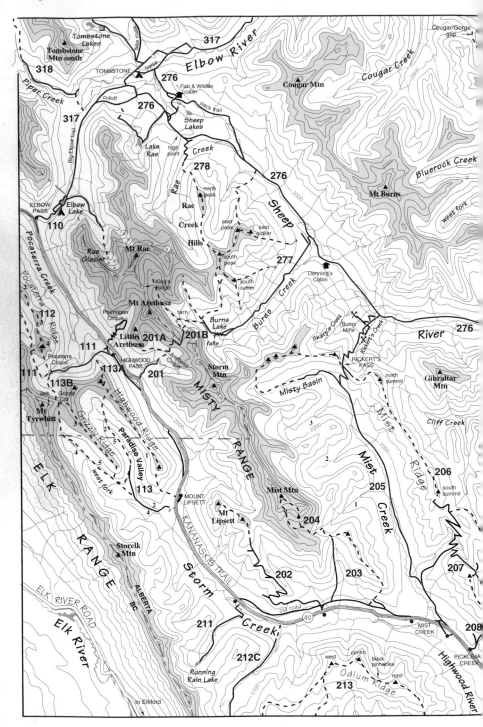

Map 18

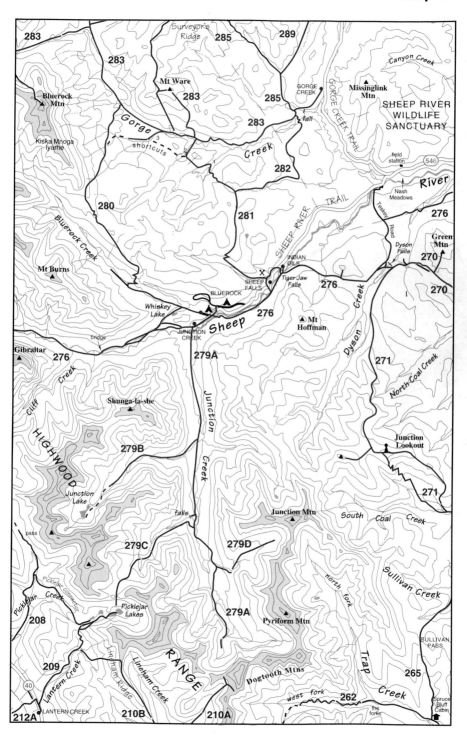

Map 19

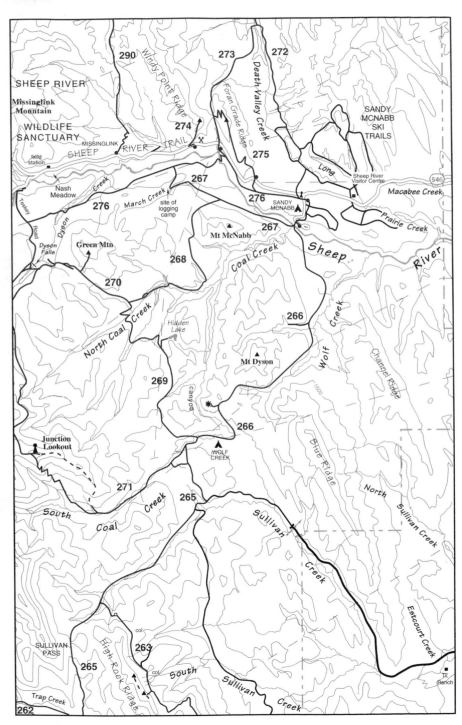

Map 20

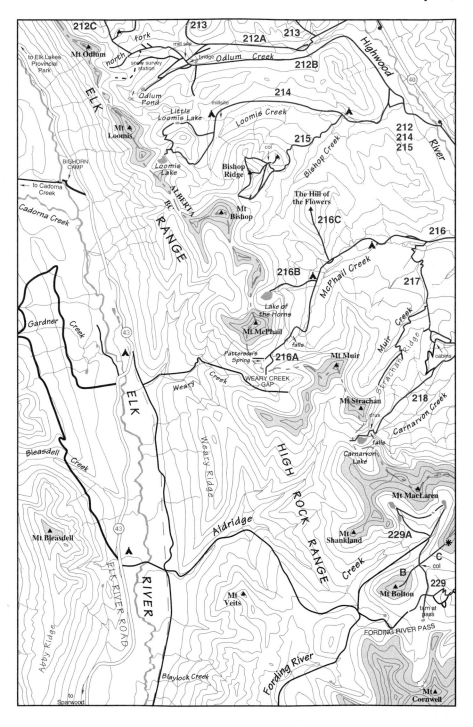

313

Map 21

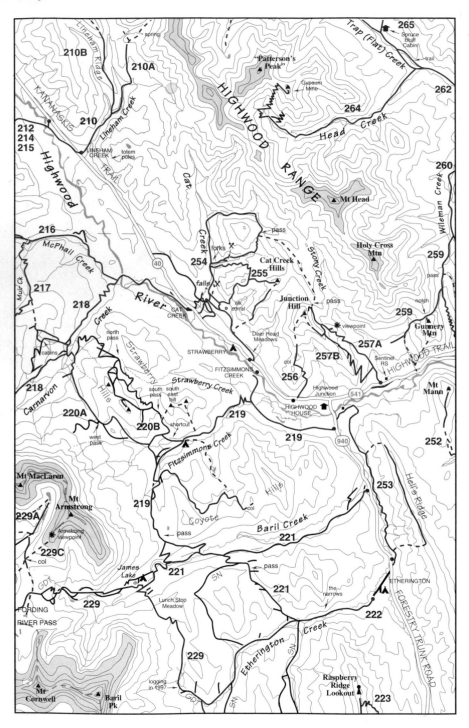

210B

210A

"Patterson's Peak"

265 Spruce Bluff Cabin

trail

HIGHWOOD RANGE

262

Gypsum Mine

264

Head Creek

Lineham Ridge

Lineham Creek

KANANASKIS

210

212
214
215

LINEHAM CREEK

totem poles

TRAIL

Highwood

Cat

Creek

Mt Head

260

Wileman Creek

216

McPhail Creek

Muir Ck

217

218

River

Creek

forks X

254

255

falls X

CAT CREEK

Strawberry

Hills

north pass

cabins

218

Carnarvon

220A

west pass

220B

south east hill

shortcut

south pass

Strawberry Creek

pass

Cat Creek Hills

Story Creek

Junction Hill

elk corral

Deer Head Meadows

STRAWBERRY

FITZSIMMONS CREEK

256

Holy Cross Mtn

259

pass

notch

259

Gunnery Mtn

viewpoint

257A

257B

Sentinel RS

HIGHWOOD TRAIL

Highwood Junction

col

219

219

Fitzsimmons Creek

Hills

HIGHWOOD HOUSE

541

940

Mt Mann

252

253

Hell's Ridge

Mt MacLaren

Mt Armstrong

229A

Armstrong viewpoint

229C

col

GDT

FORDING

RIVER PASS

219

Coyote

pass

col

Baril Creek

221

229

James Lake

221

SN

Lunch Stop Meadow

pass

221

the narrows

ETHERINGTON

222

FORESTRY TRUNK ROAD

Etherington

Creek

SN

GDT

229

logging in 1997

SN

Raspberry Ridge Lookout

223

Mt Cornwell

Baril Pk

Map 22

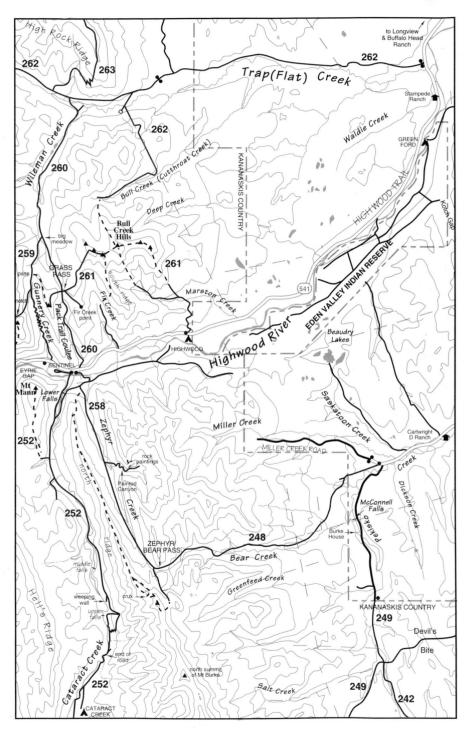

Map 23

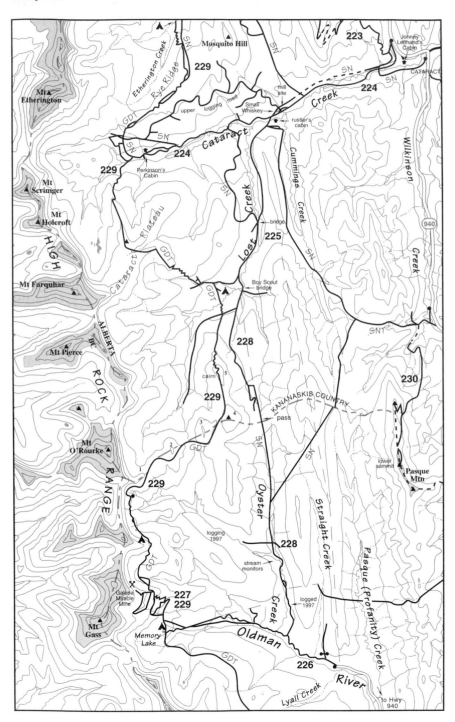

Map 24

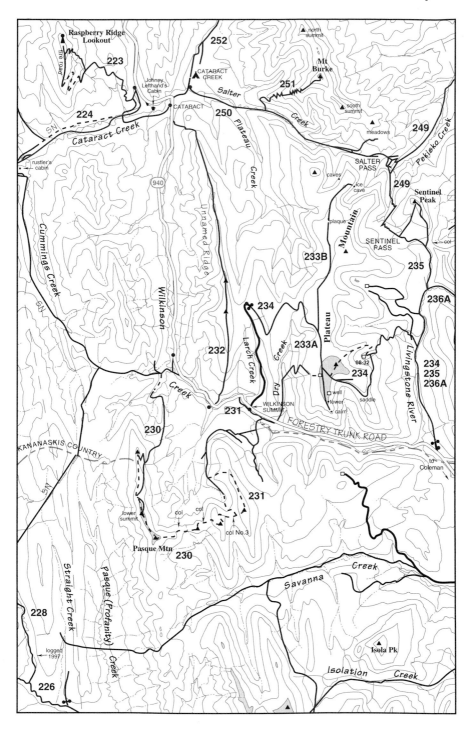

Raspberry Ridge Lookout

223

Tire road

Johnney Lefthand's Cabin

CATARACT CREEK

252

north summit

Mt Burke

251

south summit

CATARACT

224

Cataract Creek

250

Salter

Creek

meadows

249

SALTER PASS

Pekisko Creek

rustler's cabin

940

Plateau Creek

caves

ice cave

249

Sentinel Peak

Cummings Creek

SN

Unnamed Ridge

plaque

Mountain

SENTINEL PASS

col

233B

235

236A

Wilkinson

234

Larch Creek

Dry Creek

233A

Plateau

232

08-32

234

234 235 236A

Livingstone River

Creek

WILKINSON SUMMIT

231

well tower

saddle

cairn

FORESTRY TRUNK ROAD

230

KANANASKIS COUNTRY

SN

lower summit

col col

231

col No.3

to Coleman

Pasque Mtn

230

Straight Creek

Pasque (Profanity) Creek

Savanna Creek

228

logged 1997

Isola Pk

226

Isolation Creek

Map 25

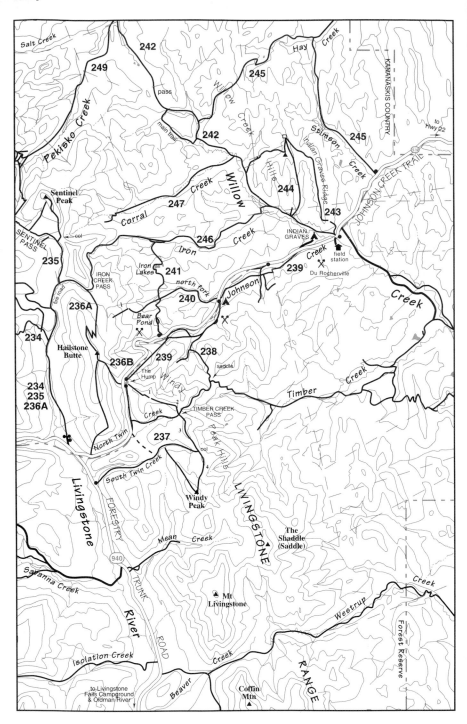